The Transformation of the New England Theology

American University Studies

Series VII
Theology and Religion

Vol. 23

PETER LANG
New York · Bern · Frankfurt am Main · Paris

Robert C. Whittemore

The Transformation of the New England Theology

PETER LANG

New York · Bern · Frankfurt am Main · Paris

Library of Congress Cataloging-in-Publication Data

Whittemore, Robert C. (Robert Clifton)
  The transformation of the New England theology.

  (American university studies. Series VII, Theology
and religion ; vol. 23)
  Includes bibliographies and indexes.
  1. New England theology. I. Title. II. Series:
American university studies. Series VII, Theology and
religion ; v. 23.
  BX7250.W45   1987   230′.044′0974   86-21292
  ISBN 0-8204-0374-1
  ISSN 0740-0446

CIP-Kurztitelaufnahme der Deutschen Bibliothek

Whittemore, Robert C.:
The transformation of the New England theology /
Robert C. Whittemore.—New York ; Bern ; Frankfurt
am Main ; Paris : Lang, 1987.
  (American university studies : Ser. 7, Theology
  and religion ; Vol. 23)

ISBN 0-8204-0374-1
NE: American university studies / 07

Printed by Weihert-Druck GmbH, Darmstadt (West Germany)

This is for Ann,
beloved wife and partner in the making of this book,
whose good sense and wise counsel was indespensable to its completion.

CONTENTS

FOREWORD

My subject is the case for consistent Calvinism as that has been made in the writings of its principal American advocates beginning with Samuel Willard's **Compleat Body of Divinity** (1726), proceeding through the works of Jonathan Edwards and his immediate successors, Joseph Bellamy, Samuel Hopkins, and Nathanael Emmons, given new direction in the writings of Timothy Dwight and Nathaniel William Taylor, and mature expression in the systems of Edwards Amasa Park and Samuel Harris. I argue that it is not only fitting but needful in these times of spiritual renewal and revival that Christians should be reminded of the strength and thrust of that case, since it is by way of being an indispensable prolegomenon to the basic issues of twentieth century Protestant theology as distinguished from denominational dogmatics.

The rubrics of worship and the rules of religious practice and organization must ever bulk large in the view of any devout churchperson, as indeed they did for all of our subjects. Even so, rules and rubrics follow upon doctrine, and it is of differences in the substance and interpretation of justifying doctrine, consistency of systematic Calvinism against the fulminations and exprobations of its cultured despisers that we have here to do.

I believe and argue that neither the current evangelical revival in the nation, nor the transformation of American religious thought from its Calvinist roots to process theology, can be properly understood apart from an appreciation of the role played by the protagonists of the New Divinity. These "New Lights," as they are sometimes called, prize greatly coherence and consistency, which they incline to equate with the rule of reason and with that common sense which, to their way of thinking, is its surrogate. As understood and employed from Willard to Emmons, this common sense signifies hardly more than a Lockean trust in the deliverances of sense experience. However, as the eighteenth century gave way to the nineteenth, and the works of the Scottish school of common sense realism found their place in seminary libraries, common sense took on all the trappings of a technical philosophy, which in the theologies of Dwight, Taylor, and Park, maintains an authority second only to Holy Writ. In the final stages of the quest for a consistent

Calvinism, the measure of the rule of reason becomes the Kantian critique of pure reason, but the presuppositions remain the same and the need for consistency is felt no less by Harris than it had been two centuries earlier by Willard.

PROLOGUE

This Synod having perused, & considered (with much gladness of heart, & thankfulness to God) the confession of faith published of late by the Reverend Assembly in England, doe judge it to be very holy, orthodox, & judicious in all matters of faith: & doe therefore freely & fully consent therunto, for the substance therof.[1]

On June 12th, 1643, the Parliament of England, overriding the objections of King Charles the First, nominated and summoned one hundred and twenty "learned, godly, and judicious divines" and thirty pious laymen representing both Houses to an assembly at Westminster Abbey for the purpose of settling "the government and liturgy of the Church of England and for the vindicating of the doctrine of said church from false aspersions and vituperations." A century had passed since John Calvin's reformation of Geneva, and his doctrine and practice, popularized in England through the preaching of the reformers, Bucer, Bullinger, Martyr,[2] and others, had inspired the rise of Puritanism. Now dominant alike in Lords and Commons, the Puritan party sought to reform the doctrine, discipline, and government of the church in a manner "most agreable to God's Holy Word." The Assembly deliberated for forty-one months and in December 1646 presented to Parliament their **Humble Advice....Concerning a Confession of Faith.** This document, amended in its governmental articles but not in doctrine, was adopted by the General Assembly of Scotland in the following year, and approved by Parliament for England on June 20th, 1648. In August the elders and messengers of the churches of New England, assembled in synod at Cambridge, accepted the Westminster Confession of faith and its cognate Catechisms[3] "for the substance thereof."

The operative term here is 'substance.' In substance all those who called or thought themselves Calvinists, whether liberal or conservative, Old Light or New Divinity, Presbyterian or Independent (Congregationalist), agreed that God is absolutely sovereign, His decrees immutable, His Scripture infallibly authoritative, Mankind tainted by sin and deserving of damnation, some only among them justified and sanctified (these being the regenerate saved by Christ through the agency of the Holy Spirit, "who worketh when, and where, and how he pleaseth"). Their recurrent disagreement, and the continuing internal controversy in American Calvinism as it respects *doctrine,* is in essence one of *means* and *form.* Every faction accepts that God is sovereign and mankind fallen in Adam; all allow the necessity of regeneration and the Atonement antecedent to any such; but how shall we understand the roles of the parties, and what must we believe in consequence of our acceptance of the divine sovereignty? These are the sort of questions which constitute the locus classicus of the disagreement between Old and New. As times changed and new heterodoxies arose to challenge these "orthodox" presuppositions, the controversy expanded from one between schools or factions of Calvinism into one between those who saw themselves as orthodox and those who did not. But throughout, the substance of doctrine, for the orthodox, remained the same.

That this has been overlooked by some historians of the era is, I suspect, owing to their preoccupation with denominational differences in the conception of church discipline and church government. It is not that these are not important. The rubrics of worship and the rules of religious practice and organization must ever bulk large in the view of any devout churchman, as indeed they did for all of our subjects. But when all has been said on this score, these rubrics and rules follow upon doctrine, and it is of differences in the form and interpretation of the doctrine as commonly held, and in the attempts of those who sought to vindicate the truth and consistency of Calvinist teachings against the fulminations and exprobations of its cultured despisers that we have here to do.

II

The vigourous nature of Calvinism, the tough-mindedness inherent in every one of its basic doctrines, and the willingness, even eagerness, of its proponents to accept their harsh implications, tends inevitably to the formation of factions, and thus it is that American Calvinists have divided historically into two parties, each of them prone to further subdivision. The more moderate faction, known to scholarship as Old Lights or Old Side or Conservative Calvinists, tend to accept without question the Confession and its Catechisms.

Their polemics, when they rise to such, are usually directed against those who would deny either the truth or the consequences of the doctrines received from Geneva, Dort[4], Westminster, and the Savoy[5]. For the internal consistency of these doctrines they care little, or not at all. It suffices for them that the Scriptures, known to be the Word of God, have revealed the way and the life, and in this they cheerfully abide. With such as these, in the chapters that follow, we are not concerned, except as their viewpoint bears upon and implies criticism of the other principal party. These latter, the New Lights, or partisans of the New Divinity, contrariwise, care very much for consistency, which they incline to equate with the rule of reason and with that common sense which, to their way of thinking, is its surrogate. As understood and employed from Willard to Emmons, this common sense signified hardly more than a Lockean trusting in the deliverances of sense-experience. However as the eighteenth century wore on and gave way to the nineteenth, and the works of the Scottish School of Common Sense Realism[6] found their place in American private and public libraries, common sense took on all the trappings of a technical philosophy, which in the theologies of Dwight, Taylor, and Park maintains an authority second only to that of Holy Writ. In the latest stages of the quest, the measure of the rule of reason becomes the Kantian critique of pure reason, but the presupposition remains the same and the need for consistency is felt no less by Harris than it had been two centuries earlier by Willard.

Inasmuch as the term 'consistent' in the phrase "Consistent Calvinism" is often understood to refer specifically to those systems of theology produced by the immediate disciples of Edwards, and most particularly to that of Samuel Hopkins, whose Hopkinsianism is taken by some scholars as a synonym for Consistent Calvinism, it behooves us to insist that the phrase as here employed admits of a wider sense and reference. 'Consistent' in our context always signifies in general the Calvinist concern to show forth scripture-doctrine as a spiritually coherent unity of thought, and more particularly to demonstrate that the doctrine in question is true to (consistent with) the received conception of God as absolute sovereign. As the connotations of that conception change from one system to another, or, as Haroutunian has demonstrated, piety becomes moralism, so too must the notion of what makes for a consistent system of scripture-doctrine vary from one thinker to another. Thus to limit the application of the phrase to one particular system or to such few systems as proceed directly form the thought of one master, is to overlook the patent truth that every system seeks consistency, and in cases here expounded professes to have found it.

III

We build upon the past, and the many whose scholarship has provided a base for the present study are acknowledged in the bibliographical essays appended to each chapter. Four chronicles of the quest, and three contemporary surveys, however, merit and require more particular notice, for they have ploughed the field that we might reap the harvest. In 1856 the Rev. David A. Wallace, an Old School Calvinist distressed by what he saw as a falling away on the part of the orthodox from the standards of Westminster as held and taught by the Puritan fathers, resolved to attempt to exhibit the doctrines prevalent in the Congregational churches in his time, and the result was the first overview of The Theology of New England.[7] Wallace was not pleased by what he found. From Edwards to Park he discerned a drifting apart from the great doctrines of the gospel towards a popular liberalism that "smiles complacently on every form of religious belief (except old-fashioned orthodoxy), and insists that one is just about as good as another."[8] Wherefore, he would have all those who take their theology from New Haven, Andover, or Bangor beware of imbibing "spiritual poison."

This first, and vigourously partisan, summary of new Divinity teachings held the field until 1899 when George Nye Boardman, professor emeritus of systematic theology in the Chicago Theological Seminary, published **A History of New England Theology.**[9] Boardman is everything that Wallace was not, sympathetic to Consistent Calvinism, objective in his presentation of its peculiar doctrines, and judicious in his judgments respecting their orthodoxy and truth. The great figures in his account are Edwards and Hopkins, both of whom are, to him, of primary significance as promoters of godliness in and to their own generation. By Boardman's time the New Divinity had become old, and given way to the New Theology with its accomodation to the doctrine of evolution. Thus one might properly have expected from him some notice of the contributions of Park and Harris, but of these he has nothing to tell us, presumably because for him, as for some others more recent, Consistent Calvinism means the systems of the immediate heirs of Edwards. Overshadowed by the better known work of Frank Hugh Foster, Boardman's briefer survey is today largely forgotten, and unjustifiably so, since it retails a wealth of information concisely in a simple servicable prose.

The book that supersedes it, Foster's **Genetic History,**[10] is twice as long and half as readable owing to its author's preoccupation with the dogmatic niceties of the development of the doctrines of the will, original sin, and the atonement, subjects which, given his detailed expositions and analyses, it would be redundant to rehash. Those whose interest centers on the particularities of these subjects can do no better than to consult Foster, and if that concern is specifically with the notion of depravity, I would commend to them Hilrie Shelton Smith's superb study of changing conceptions of original sin from the Great Awakening to recent and contemporary neo-orthodoxy.[11] Both studies are indispensable for a proper understanding of the **dogmatics** of the New England theology.

Radically different in its approach to the issues of the epoch, but of comparable value for the light it throws upon the evolution of Edwardsianism, is Joseph Haroutunian's very readable account of the transformation and passing of the New England movement entitled **Piety versus Moralism**[12] Haroutunain maintains that in its attempt to cope with the Unitarian challenge Calvinism transformed itself into a moralism, and thereby the faith of the fathers was ruined by the faith of the children. Transformed it certainly was, but ruined? The prominence of the moral moment in the later theologians of the quest in undeniable, but so is their piety, and if, as Haroutunian notes, post-Calvinist American Christianity was more concerned with bomfog[13] than with doctrinal consistency, that tells more about the parlous state of recent American religion than it does about "enlightened Calvinism."

Three more recent surveys command the attention of the student seeking to place the quest in the wider context of American religious thought. Each offers brief but perceptive accounts of its major figures. Each is appreciative of the continuing significance of their contribution to the Christian enter-

6

prise. Sydney E. Ahlstrom's monumental but luculent **Religious History of the American People**[14] includes three chapters specifically devoted to Edwards and the New England theology. Alan Heimert's definitive study of the political significance of the religious literature of the decades between the Great Awakening and the Revolution, **Religion and the American Mind**[15] albeit narrower in compass includes a wealth of interpretative material relative to various of the theologies rehearsed below. Unfortunately for the purposes of this study, Bruce Kuklick's synoptic and incisive reappraisal of the course of New England Congregational Calvinism from Edwards to Dewey, **Churchmen and Philosophers. From Jonathan Edwards to John Dewey,**[16] came to hand only after the present work was ready for the publisher. Kuklick maps the terrain; what follows here may serve to fill in the detail. Even so, in light of these, and works previously noted, the reader may well wonder why yet another exposition is needed.

One reason has to do with the transit of time. Fifty-six years have passed since Haroutunian reploughed thee fields; eighty have elapsed since Foster published his **Genetic History.** In the interval much has changed. The pallid orthodoxy of midcentury has given way to a new and vigourous evangelical movement. The rise of process theology has raised anew the question of the nature and role of God. From the perspective of the late twentieth century, the answers provided by consistent Calvinism are no longer dismissable as irrelevant.

Then too, our purpose is not the purpose of Foster, Haroutunian and Company. For we are here concerned not so much with creedal differences, moral options, denominational polity, and the religious foundations of American social and political thought, as with the notion of God, and with what fidelity to that notion entails in respect of doctrine. Our assumption is that the case for orthodoxy is one of perennial interest, if for no other reason than that the generality of Christians are, even today, orthodox. Our thesis is that the case today, as in the eighteenth century, is made or unmade in the sequence of systems from Willard to Harris. Our claim is that the notion of God envisaged by the ministers of the quest, being the same in substance as that still reverenced by the orthodox, is expressed in their thought with a degree of consistency not attained in more recent theologies. It remains to justify the assumption, develop that thesis, and validate this claim.

[1] **A Platform of Church Discipline gathered out of the Word of God and agreed upon by the Elders and Messengers of the Churches Assembled in the Synod at Cambridge in New England. The Preface.** In Williston Walker, **The Creeds and Platforms of Congregationalism** (Boston: Pilgrim Press, 1960), 195.

[2] Martin Bucer (Butzer) 1491-1551, German pastor and catechist, Professor of Theology at Cambridge 1549-1551; Heinrich Bullinger 1504-1575, Swiss pastor and theologian, part-author of the first and second Helvetic Confessions, author of the **Decades,** sermons on various subjects, widely read in England; Peter Martyr (Pietro Vermigli) 1500-1562, Italian theologian and reformer, Regius Professor of Divinity at Oxford 1547-1553, Professor Divinity at Strasbourg 1542-1547 and again 1553-1556. Worked with Cranmer on **The Book of Common Prayer,** Professor at Zurich 1557-62.

[3] See Appendix I.

[4] Dort, meeting place of a Synod called by the States-General of Holland in November 1618 for the purpose of resolving the issues raised by the Arminian Remonstrance of 1610. The Synod condemned the Remonstrance, banished those ministers who had signed it, and reaffirmed the five points of Calvinism, i.e., unconditional election, limited atonement, total depravity, irresistible grace, and the perseverance of the saints.

[5] The Savoy Palace in London, site of the meeting of Elders and Messengers of the Congregational churches of England in October 1658. Its end result was the Savoy Declaration, a revision with additions of the Westminster Confession, to which was appended, as the principal work of the meeting, thirty sections relating to Congregational church-order. The Savoy Declaration, with minor modifications, was adopted for Massachusetts Congregationalism at a Synod in Boston in 1680, and for Connecticut, at Saybrook in 1708. In these forms it became and long remained the standard for American Congregationalism.

[6] A comprehensive and lucid account of the import and purport of this school for American Calvinism is provided by Sydney E. Ahlstrom, 'The Scottish Philosophy and American Theology.' **Church History,** 24 (September, 1955), 257-272.

[7] David A. Wallace, **The Theology of New England** (Boston: Crocker and Brewster, 1856).

[8] Ibid., 105.

[9] George Nye Boardman, **A History of New England Theology** (New York: A.D.F. Randolph Company, 1899).

[10] Frank Hugh Foster, **A Genetic History of the New England Theology** (Chicago: University of Chicago Press, 1907).

[11] H. Shelton Smith, **Changing Conceptions of Original Sin: A Study in American Theology since 1750** (New York: Charles Scribner's Sons, 1955).

[12] Joseph Haroutunian, **Piety versus Moralism, the Passing of the New England Theology** (New York: Henry Holt and Company, 1932).

[13] Brotherhood of man, fatherhood of God. Acronym coined by Nelson Rockefeller. As Haroutunian puts the matter: "Good and intelligent Christians discarded such Calvinism with little remorse. They were busy men, proclaiming the fatherhood of God, the brotherhood of men, and the moral ideal set up by the "gentle Jesus" telling men of the dignity and value of the human soul....They preached these things and expected men to believe and practice them. They were great optimists." Ibid.,282.

[14] Sydney E. Ahlstrom, **A Religious History of the American People** (New Haven: Yale University Press, 1972).

[15] Alan Heimert, **Religion and the American Mind from the Great Awakening to the Revolution** Cambridge: Harvard University Press, 1966).

8

[16]Bruce Kuklick, **Churchmen and Philosophers. From Jonathan Edwards to John Dewey** (New Haven: Yale University Press, 1985). See especially Chapters 4, 7, 14.

The Coherent Calvinsim Of Samuel Willard

"Every truth agrees with the whole, and with every other Truth. The whole body of Divine Truths is Uniform....There is a sweet harmony in the whole Word of God; there are no contradictions to be found there: if any shall judge that there are such, the mistake is not in the Scriptures but in their deceived Understandings."[1]

THE COHERENT CALVINISM OF SAMUEL WILLARD

> The reader will find that these sermons, as to the doctrinal
> part of them, are succinct, solid, and judicious; and that the
> applicatory part, is both powerful and reasonable.[2]

Consistent Calvinists as a class are not noted for their economy with words, and in this respect Samuel Willard is no exception. His "Works"[3] consist of somewhat more than six thousand pages of exegetic sermons, catechetic lectures, hermeneutic discourses, and polemic tracts on various scriptural topics. He published nothing of a purely speculative nature, unless it be held that his constant concern to show forth the coherence of scripture-doctrine is evidence of a leaning to the metaphysical.

For Willard, as for his Puritan predecessors, the original of all Truth is the Bible of the Jews and the Christians. The authority of both Testaments must be acknowledged inasmuch as that Covenant which God made with the Israelites in ancient times is, as Calvin says, the same with that which Christians make through the mediatorship of Jesus Christ. The administration varies, but the Covenant is the same. The reconciliation which the Patriarchs enjoyed and the Prophets preached is the same with that proclaimed by the Apostles. Which being so, it is, Willard thinks, "a grand mistake for any to account nothing Gospel but the New Testament, indeed the greatest part of the Old Testament is Gospel."[4]

'Gospel' because Christ is, according to Willard, the true author of the whole. "Though holy men were the writers of these books, yet his Spirit was the inditer of them."[5] Their very holiness declares his authorship. They breathe nothing but purity. They call upon and direct men to glorify him that is the Author of them. On this fact of divine *authority* our surety of the coherence of Scripture rests, since it is inconceivable to Willard, as indeed it is to all professing consistent Calvinism, that there should be contradictions in the Word of God.

The *style* in truth is diverse, the manner of expression various; there is a great diversity between the language of the Old and New Testaments: but yet the matter is agreeable. One writer does not contradict another, nor do they charge each other with falsehood. One prophet agrees with another, and all of them with Moses. The Evangelists also and the Apostles agree with them. The later written books of the Bible add confirmation to the former. The

Gospel gives assurance of the fulfilling of what was predicted in the law.[6]

The author of these obiter dicta (called Simon in the Concord records), the sixth child and second son of Simon Willard and Mary Sharpe (Willard), natives of Horsemonden in the English county of Kent, was born at Concord, Massachusetts, which town his father had helped to found, on January 31st, 1640. Raised in Concord, he entered Harvard in 1655 and graduated with the Class of 1659. Afterwards he studied for the ministry, and was ordained to the church in 1659. Afterwards he studied for the ministry, and was ordained to the church at Groton in 1663. Complying with the custom of the time, he pledged to serve his congregation for life, but in 1676 Groton was attacked by Indians and its inhabitants scattered. Thus relieved of his obligation, Willard retired to Boston and in 1678 found employment as Teacher of the Old South Meeting. A year later, upon the death of the minister, Rev. Thomas Thacher, he was called to the pulpit.Willard was twice married; first to Abigail Sherman in 1664. She presented him with eight children and died. In 1679 he married Eunice Tyng, sister of the wife of Governor Dudley, by whom he had twelve more children.[7] His connections insured acceptance by the Boston establishment, and he became eventually a pillar of the ruling oligarchy esteemed by his peers and, inevitably, the focus of the antipathy to their rule. As Edward Randolph, the King's Messenger in Boston, noted in a letter home, "we have in Boston one Mr. Willard, a minister, brother (in law) to Major Dudley; he is a moderate man and baptizeth those who are refused by the other churches, for which he is hated."[8] Hated also for his defence of the establishmentarian, Philip English of Salem, and others accused of witchcraft in the dreadful year of 1692, and for his opposition to the efforts of Governor Andros to curb the power of the oligarchs. Willard himself was subsequently accused, but his congregation refused to credit such an absurdity, and the "Salem superstition and sorcery" passed. In 1701, in consequence of President Increase Mather's dispute with the Harvard overseers (Mather did not want to live in the backwater of Cambridge, albeit he very much wanted the salary and authority that went with the presidency) Willard was asked to serve as Vice-President in residence,[9] a duty he faithfully discharged until forced by ill-health to resign the office. He died at Boston on September 12th, 1707, mourned by his congregation and by all those who, like these, realized that Boston had lost a great man. In him Puritanism was, in the pithy phrase of Perry Miller, "if not a rationalism then decidedly a reasonableness."[10] Willard would have wanted no better epitaph.

II

There are no Truths which have more rational confirmations
given to gain men's credit than those of the Word of God![11]

"*Every Truth agrees with the whole, and with every other Truth.* The whole body of Divine Truths is Uniform....There is a sweet harmony in the whole Word of God."[12] That men do not readily perceive it is not owing, Willard insists, to any defect in the Truth itself, but rather to the darkening of human understanding occasioned by the Fall. "The natural man cannot discern spiritual things. We not only want light but eyes too. And though a natural man may understand the *Grammatical* and *Logical* meaning of the Gospel *Theorems,* yet they are foolish things to him, and he cannot see into the mystery of them"[13] until Christ unscales his understanding and causes the divine glory of the Truth to shine in him as it has shone in Calvin, Preston, Ames, and more modestly, in Willard himself.

The great design of Scripture being to discover God to us that we may glorify him forever, the question arises: What is God? The fool hath said in his heart—nothing, but Willard knows better. "The works of *Creation* do undeniably prove the Being of a God....The things that are made, lead us by the hand to him that made them....The subjection of the *Creature* to corruption, proves its generation....Efficiency presupposeth an Existence, which the World had not, when it was not."[14] The harmony of the whole and the admirable suiting of things that are made one to another confirms its, as do the abounding evidences of Providence. God's preservation of his Church through the wrath and fury of seventeen centuries of earth and hell proves it, and so too does the conscience of man. "How justly then doth the Scripture call the atheist a Fool! And how should we all, young and old, labour to get the practical impression of this great truth deeply graven on our hearts, that there is a God!"[15]

But this once gotten, we are at a stop. For as Willard is frank to admit, "though nothing be more knowable than *that* there is a God, yet nothing harder to know than *what* he is,"[16] and that because our knowledge does not extend beyond our power to image or conceptualize the objects of our sense-experience, and God himself is none of these. "There is no Essence or Nature that (in propriety of speech) can be attributed to God: for Nature and Essence bespeak a thing rising out of some foregoing Principles: but there is no Principle of God, for there is nothing before him."[17]

However, God is not completely unknown to us, for if he will not show us his face (which no man can see and live), he does display himself to us in his "backparts," that is to say, in his *sufficiency* and in his *efficiency*. "The final portion of him that may be known by the Creature, may be referred to these two heads; what he *is* and what he *doth:* what he is *able* to do, and what he is *pleased* to do; that he *is* all, and that he *doth* all. These two are the main pillars on which the weight of our faith lies, and by which it is supported."[18]

By his *Sufficiency* (or Alsufficiency) we are to understand his Divine Fulness or perfection, for "there is a *simple* and *absolute* perfection, which comprehends in it the whole and universal fullness of all perfection to the utmost latitude of possibility: and this is the fulness of God."[19] It is a fullness which admits neither of diminution nor addition. In his sufficiency God requires nothing, desires nothing, and is perfectly happy. In truth, "he is not only happy, but *Happiness* in the abstract;[20] he is not merely wise, but Wisdom in the abstract; he is not simply Good, but Goodness in the abstract, and since "abstracts cannot be increased at all,"[21] it follows, Willard argues, that he is, in each of these attributes. Infinite. Since this Infinity is composed of abstracts comprising an abstract absolute Being, no contradiction arises (as would be the case if these attributes and their locus were conceived as concrete), since that which is by us diversely apprehended is, in itself, Pure Act (*actus purus*). That such a notion passes human comprehension, Willard is ever ready to concede. God is Being, so much must we affirm. But "he is not a Being properly, as we conceive of a Being; much less a portion of Being."[22] His Infinity debars our ascribing to him parts of quantity or extension; nor is he, Willard adds, the subject of any mathematical notion.[23]

"These things he is a stranger to because he is not a Being by Participation, but Being in the Abstract. Concrete beings have dimensions, but those that are Abstract exceed all. Sweet things have their degrees, but *Sweetness* itself is above all degrees."[24]

Still, Sweetness, known as such by us, is known from sweet things, and Happiness were a quality unknown, were there no happy people. Experience suggests that it is the concrete which gives meaning and being to the abstract, but, Willard insists, experience errs. The sweetness of sweet things is, to his view, but a similitude of that (abstract) sweetness which is God's alone. The truth is, says our author, that all concrete beings are derived from Abstract Being. He speaks and they are. "His word is the spring of their being....he gives being to his word....he speaks not words but things....All the great and wondrous beings that are in the world, come out of his mouth."[25] It is not clear whether or not Willard intends his hearers to take these statements literally. The authority for them is, of course, biblical ("For he spake, and it came to be; he commanded, and it stood forth." *Psalms* 33:9), and for Willard the Bible is Truth in print. On the other hand, he is not so much the fundamentalist as to deny that God's amanuenses (the term is Willard's) sometimes express their thought in metaphors or allegories. At all events, he makes no attempt to rationalize God's act of creation. With such "fictions of philosophy" as the cosmology of Aristotle and the cosmogony of Plato he will have nothing to do. Like Calvin he would observe the limit which the rule of piety prescribes lest by indulging in an unprofitable degree of speculation, he should lead his reader away from the profundities of the faith once given to the apostles. It suffices, then, to know that in ways surpassing human comprehension, what God has foreordained in his Decree, he brings to pass in his Works. "And if all these Works belong to God, then needs must Alsufficiency belong to him....And it is to be observed, that in all things God keeps his eye fixt upon his Decree: Efficiency is nothing else but His executing of that; it doth neither more, nor less, nor otherwise."[26]

Efficiency is Creation, and that out of Nothing. Heathen philosophy, Willard recognizes, disputes this, arguing that from nothing nothing comes (*ex nihilo nihil fit*), but this principle, he thinks, is not universally true. In the ordinary course of nature things are made of pre-existent matter, which must be, if the world was not created out of Nothing, either identical with God, or in God, or other than God. But it cannot be identical with God, for that would make the world like God, Eternal, and Eternity is, to Willard's way of thinking, an Attribute Incommunicable. Moreover, if the world is God, then God is divisible and capable of corruption and generation, "all of which are *blasphemous Conclusions,* and altogether repugnant to the Nature of God."[27] Nor is it to be said that the matter of the world is in God. True, St. Peter quotes with approval Aratus' "in God we live and move and have our being," and Willard himself sometimes speaks in panentheistic fashion of beings as having their being "in him," or of places as "contained in him," but Willard is no panentheist. He does not intend that his reader should understand him to be saying that these beings and places are *literally* in God. To him, such an interpretation would be no less blasphemous than that pantheism against which he inveighs. But if neither St. Paul nor Willard intend to assert a literal being of all things in God, what do they intend when they speak in such wise? St. Paul offers no clear answer, nor either, so it would seem, does Willard. Lowrie, picking up on Willard's suggestion that the being of God, like the body of the Sun, is comfortably seen only in a reflected light, finds an apt analogy in the world of optics. "God can and in fact does reveal himself to man's finite capacities by *refracting* his inner being through the prism of the world."[28] But Lowrie is quick to admit that this is at best "the approximate truth about that which by definition is singular."[29]

Willard does speak, in another context, of God's Attributes being in the creature by way of analogy of proportion,[30] and implies that the concrete is being is a lesser mode. Like Aquinas, he would have it that God alone *is* Being, all else having being only by participation, and that again not literally but metaphorically.[31] But the position is merely stated, not argued, and the reader is left to wonder what participation can possibly mean in a milieu where to be abstract is to be real. The world, then, being neither identical with God, nor literally in God, must be, if it is literally anything, other than God, which is to say that it must be made by him out of Nothing, and Scripture confirms that it is so.

III

The whole world is a sucking infant depending on the breasts of Divine Providence.[32]

In the beginning God created Time, the constant Natures of Heaven, and the material of the Inconstant Nature of Earth; and this beginning according to Willard, "comes considerably short of Six-Thousand Years."[33] The shortness of the span of days from that first creative act to Willard's day, or even to our own, compels our attention inasmuch as it points up that one difference of outlook between ourselves and all but the more recent of the consistent Calvinists which makes it difficult, if not impossible, to appreciate the coherence of their theology. For we confront a universe of virtually illimitable age and vastness, and nothing is more incredible to us than the thought that all this was Nothing less than six-thousand years ago. We make allowance for the fact that the world that Willard and his posterity knew was somewhat smaller than that which we inhabit, and this helps our understanding of their perspective until we look up and realize that the same immensity of sky and stars that we see, they also saw, and that with greater clarity through cleaner air. Did Willard, could anyone, then or at any other time, really believe that everything was so relatively *new*? We must remember that he had no good reason to doubt it. Nature does not wear its age upon its sleeve, and the chronicle of Man as known from the ancient histories and from Scripture dates back no further than forty centuries before the Christian era. Had we no more than the evidence of these records on which to base our estimate of the oldness of the world, we too must say, "it is unreasonable to think the World should stand so many Thousands of Ages before it had a man in it."[34]

It is unreasonable because of one further assumption which Willard made, and that is that the world was created to be the Tenement of Man, and he its Landlord, and the myriad of creatures were for his comfort and delight. For though "all things were made ultimately for the Glory of God; yet in the Order of their being, there was a Subordination of them, and they were to serve God in serving of Man,"[35] and that, he points out, is proved by the fact that there was no other sort of being created after Man. For the Bible mentions none such, and in the absence of any body of science wherewith to call the biblical witness in doubt, any Christian with a normal complement of common sense would naturally incline to accept the notion of the newness of the world. But concede this and in a trice what before seemed arbitrary and incredible is now coherent and self-evident. For if this immense and complex universe is in fact the very recent product of an omnipotent and omniscient Power who has designed the whole to the end that it shall, through his principal ornament, Man, minister to his ineffable Glory, what is more natural than that he should take a personal interest in his handiwork?

To think that Christ should come to save some part of one small branch of vertebrates on a tree of life evolving for half a billion years is an intolerable assumption; but if the whole is somewhat less than six thousand years of age, and nature much the same today as in its formative period, and Man not just a branch but the Crown of the Tree,—then what is more reasonable than that God should send his only son our Lord to render satisfaction for the shortcomings of those of his Children whom he has foreordained to everlasting blessedness? To believe that the world might end and everyone come to judgment in a time "not far off"[36] is nonsense in the light of current findings in geological and biological science; but if the past is as the Bible has it, then Willard's conviction in that "they are the last days, and the winding up of time that we live in,"[37] is not unreasonable. And the same is true of his doctrine of Man.

The Bible tells us that on the Sixth Day of Creation God made Man; to what purpose we learn thereafter from St. Paul:

> For whom he did foreknow, he also did predestinate *to be* conformed to the image of his son, that he might be the first-born among many brethren. Moreover whom he did predestinate, them he also called: and whom he called, them he also justified: and whom he justified, them he also glorified. What shall we then say to these things? if God *be* for us, who *can be* against us?[38]

No one, the heirs of Calvin would confess, but that for them was not the question.

As Perry Miller has pointed out in his synoptic exposition of the federal marrow of Puritan divinity,[39] by the beginning of the seventeenth century the theological situation in Protestantism had so far changed as to put Calvinism on the defensive. The Calvinist could claim that he was predestined to salvation, but faced with challenges to his complacency from Rome and Canterbury he found himself in need of justifying arguments which the writings of Calvin did not provide. The question of the day was not who, but why and how: How does a man come by the assurance that he is elected to everlasting blessedness? Why should he worry about the doing of his duty if this election has already taken place? Because, said the Dutchman Arminius, his reason tells him that this election is not unconditional; rather is it that it is conditioned upon his exercising his freedom of choice to do his moral duty. But this, William Perkins[40] replied, is to deny the irresistibility of grace and call in question the sovereignty of God, and that is no more Calvinism but devilish heresy! What was needed was an answer leaving this sovereignty and irresistible grace unimpaired even as it justified the Christian's obligation to perform his moral and religious duties, and this answer Perkins and his great successors Ames[41] and Preston[42] thought to find in the various biblical accounts of the covenant of God with his elect.

Perkins had professed to see in the covenant passages evidences of a contract made by God with Man concerning the obtaining of eternal life by the latter upon his fulfillment of his duty to cultivate that seed of grace which God had given him.[43] In the thought of Dr. Ames, the most prominent of the host of English divines influenced by the pulpit oratory of the eminent evangelist, this notion of a contract or covenant is expanded into one of two covenants, the first of these being a covenant of works made with Adam (**Genesis** 2:16), and the second being a covenant of grace made with the entirety of the elect. With Preston, the latter of these covenants is legalized into a formal compact, signed and sealed in the presence of witnesses, and that is now declared to be the basis of a Christian's faith: "you must know it, for it is the ground of all you hope for, it is that every man is built upon, you have no other ground but this, God hath made a Covenant with you, and you are in Covenant with him."[44] This is the compact, described in *Genesis* 17:2-21, made between God and Abraham. As Preston views the transaction:

> these words containe the *Covenant* on both sides, sayth the
> *Lord,* this is the *Covenant* that I will make on my part, I *will
> be thy God*....you shall have all things in me that your hearts
> can desire: The *Covenant* againe, that I require on your part,
> is, that you be *perfect with me* that you be *upright,* that you
> be without *hypocrisie.*[45]

Since man by virtue of the Fall is of himself unable to fulfill these conditions, God requires of him only that he believe on Christ, who, as the mediator
between man and God, is the surety for man's performance of the Covenant.
If he (man) will do this, and faithfully observe his moral duties, then he may
rest assured that he is of those elected to salvation. But he must do this, otherwise the Covenant is void and God no more obliged for his part. Such, in
barest outline, was the answer to their critics devised by the English Calvinists.
In the works of their disciples, Cotton, Hooker, Shepard, and Bulkley, this
answer, elaborated as the doctrine of the Covenant of Grace, was established
as the theological orthodoxy of mid-seventeenth century New England.
Willard imbibed the doctrine at Harvard, preached it for decades, and finally in 1693 published his own improvements on it under the title **The Doctrine
of the Covenant of Redemption.**[46]

IV

> The Unparalleled and Incomprehensible Love of God to sin-
> ful Man, displayed in the wonderful Affair of his Redemp-
> tion and Salvation, is the great thing celebrated in the Scrip-
> tures.[47]

Willard assumes that all Christians will agree. Wherefore, he thinks, it
becomes everyone of us to ponder the provision which God made for our
deliverance in the days of Eternity, "for here we find the first Link of that
chain which fastens all."[48] And if we reflect upon it, "the best and most
suitable notion under which this great Affair may be represented to us for
our Information and Satisfaction, is that of a *Covenant.* Nor is this," he adds,

"a meer notion of man's Invention, but that which hath clear and firm footing in the Word of God, as will in its due place appear."[49]

Now it is certain, declares Willard, "that the whole concern of mans Redemption and Salvation has its determination in God's Eternal Decree," and of these decrees,[50] "those of *Predestination* deserve to be peculiarly remarked by us; because they contain in them the Idea of that special government by which God leads all reasonable creatures to an everlasting state of happiness or misery. And among these, that of *Election* carries in it matters of singular and eminent comfort to all true believers...."[52] Therefore, since the *end* to which men are appointed by Election is life eternal, it follows that we must carefully attend to the *means* by which this Election is secured.

Of these means, that which shines forth most illustriously, according to our author, is "mans deliverance from Sin and Wrath by the *Obedience of Christ*....This way of mans Redemption, had a room in God's Eternal Purpose: Our *Election* therefore was *in him*, and that before the Creation."[53] Before all times the Son of God was appointed to do those things for us which were in time to procure our salvation. It is this appointment or, to use Willard's phrase "Article in the Decree," which "is in the Scripture represented unto us, under the notion of a Covenant between *God the Father*, and *God the Son*, so that by the *Covenant of Redemption*, under our consideration, we are to understand, *An Everlasting Compact clearly made and firmly Ratified, between God the Father, and Men;* and this is a Covenant distinct from that which we call the *Covenant of Works*, which past between God and Man at the first in *Adam* as also from the *New Covenant*, or that of *Grace*, which is Indented between God and Man, in Christ as the Mediator of it."[54] Distinct but not separate, since a subsequent passage informs us that the doctrine of the Covenant of Grace, rightly so-called, comprises this doctrine of Redemption as its first part, and, following from that, the doctrine of Reconciliation, which is called the New Covenant and generally referred to as the Covenant of Grace.

This subsumption of Redemption under Grace is necessary since Willard is forced at the outset to take cognizance of the fact that no Covenant of Redemption is specifically remarked in Scripture. "That the Word of God doth not in Terms mention such a Covenant by such a Title, must be acknowledged; but," he is quick to declare, "that it doth give us the account of a *Covenant,* which cannot be Interpreted of any other, yea which fully amounts to the thing, may safely be affirmed."⁵⁵ Perhaps so, albeit the Jews, as well as those who tend to think that such passages of Scripture as do not *require* a symbolic or allegorical interpretation ought to be taken at face value, must certainly disagree with Willard's interpretation of that particular text which he takes to justify his conclusion. The text in question, quoted by Willard on the title page of his book, and frequently cited thereafter, is **Psalms 89:3.**

> I have made a covenant with my Chosen. I have sworn to
> David my servant.

Does the passage refer to David the King? Is he "my Chosen"? Attention to the purport of the psalm as a whole seems to require an affirmative answer to both questions. Ostensibly, we have here to do with a dialogue between the historical David and his God, in which the latter several times reiterates his intention to adhere to that covenant which, from the servant's point of view, he has by his neglect of David's political interests made void. But if we believe Willard, the ostensible meaning is, in this instance, not the true meaning of the psalm, since David referred to in verses 19, 28, 29 and 36, the David mentioned by name in verses 3, 20, 35 and 49, is not David the King but a Type of Christ! For, as Willard would remind us,

> There are divers texts in Scripture, especially in the Old Testa-
> ment, which have a double reference, partly to the *Type,* part-
> ly to the *Antitype:* or the the *Antitype* under the *Type:* This
> Psalm is one of those portions of Scripture, in which *David*
> is made a notable Type of Christ: Him therefore it mainly
> aims at. The Covenant with him, is here made the founda-
> tion of all consolation to the people of God: Here then we
> have....the Parties in it; God on the one hand; I: God is the
> speaker, Christ on the other hand! expressed in two words:

23

My Chosen. Noting both his *Excellency,* and his *Election; David my Servant;* which must needs ultimately aim at Christ, as many Expressions in the Psalm will undeniably evince, especially those in verse 19, 22, verse 28, 29, 35, 36. Christ is therefore elsewhere called David, see **Jer.** 20:9, **Ezek.** 34:34, 37:24, and if we would know what Covenant this is, the Context clearly indicates it, to be that which concerns the *Redemption* and Salvation of the People of God....[56]

There is, Willard concedes, reference to the covenant of Grace to be found in the psalm, specifically in verses 4, 29, 36 and 37, where God recognizes his contractual obligation to David's Children, but the Covenant plighted with these is, he insists, other than that which "was plighted with David himself, i.e. with Christ."[57]

Should any one remain unconvinced that there are two covenants here involved, Willard would have him consult "that memorable place, **Ezek.** 16:60."

Nevertheless I will remember my covenant with thee in the days of thy youth and I will establish unto thee an everlasting covenant.

There, he points out, "is the *Covenant made with them in the days of their youth,* i.e. in the Wilderness, which was a Covenant of Grace....this God saith he *will Remember....*But how will he do it? He will *establish unto them an Everlasting Covenant,* i.e. the Covenant of Redemption."[58] Grammarians might object that the phrase, 'everlasting covenant' merely repeats and qualifies the covenant of the days of youth, but Willard would deny it, citing **Proverbs** 8:23:

I was set up from everlasting, from the beginning or ever the earth was.

and **Jeremiah** 31:3:

24

> The LORD hath appeared of old unto me *saying,* Yea, I have
> loved thee with an everlasting love: therefore with loving
> kindness have I drawn thee.

in support of his contention. Should the objector persist, arguing that the
context of these passages controverts Willard's interpretation of them, he
would reply, first with a variety of New Testament testimonies to the eternal
Sonship of God, and second with a reminder of the part played by Grace
in our knowledge of these matters.

For further clarification it may be observed:

> That God in discovery of his mind to us is pleased to ac-
> commodate his language to our capacity, clothing divine
> truths with such words as may best suit our understandings.
> When therefore we say, there is such a Covenant, it intends
> that there is that which is *Analogous* unto, and holds a full
> proportion with such a thing; and it best accommodated to
> our understanding and faith by such a resemblance. For
> evidence of this, let us lay together these particulars, and they
> will amount to a demonstration.[59]

From all eternity God has elected a certain number of mankind for glory.
In this decree he has chosen not only the end to which he will bring them,
which is glory, but also the means. Hence by a wise and blameless counsel,
he ordered the permission of man to fall into such a state of misery as to
put him (man) in the need of a Redeemer. Thus among the means, the eternal Son of God was set apart for this purpose. Whereupon the son, answering to his Father's pleasure, engaged himself to do all that was requisite to
the accomplishment of this Redemption. He engaged to assume to his person the nature of man, and to become surety for man by subjecting himself
to the law, and paying the penalty it required. For his part, the Father promised that his Son's performance of this work should have its reward in obtaining the discharge from wrath of those whose guilt he (the Son) had taken
upon himself; that they should be atoned to him and have all spiritual bless-

ings bestowed on them for his sake. The Son having accepted the offer, the Holy Ghost (acting for the Father) undertook and promised that he would see to the application of all the Grace appointed by the Father, and purchased by the son, to those for whom it was designed, and so bring them to Salvation. Wherefore we (the beneficiaries) are assured that in and by this Compact, made and sealed in Heaven in Eternity, the eternal inheritance was purchased and security was given "that *all those for whom it was provided* should be made happy partakers in the benefit of it,"[60] for, asserts Willard, "that Christ became Surety to pay the Price for all, is not to be believed."[61]

Does Christ know then who those are for whom he stands surety in the Covenant of Redemption? Of a certainty, replies Willard: "Those whom he Covenanted for, were a definite Company of particular persons. Not only was the number of them agreed upon in this Transaction, but the individuals also were determined."[62] The Covenant did not run illimitedly, nor did it say that some sorts of persons should be redeemed and others not, "but it took in so many Individual persons, chosen according to the sovereign God."[63] These are they whose names are written in the Lamb's Book of Life:

> **Rev.** 21:27 refers properly to this *Covenant* and they are persons who are written here; they have their names in it. The Son of God *knew* from eternity whom he was to Redeem, and God *knew* them. This is the *Foundation* of which the Apostle speaks, and which hath such a Seal upon it, **2 Tim.** 2:19, *who are his,* this Indigitates the very persons: Our High Priest therefore had their *names written on his breastplate* when he was to offer the Sacrifice for them and make expiation in their behalf in the Holy Place.[64]

But that Sacrifice was yet to come, and they for whom it was to be made were yet unborn. Consequently, there is still something wanting to bring them out into the actual enjoyment of their inheritance, "and for this the Scripture points us to another Covenant distinct from this (Covenant of Redemption), which is by some called the Covenant of Reconciliation; but is more generally known by the name of the Covenant of Grace."[65]

The one is dependent on the other. "The latter hath a manifold dependence on the former: yea, such, as all the Believers solid comfort, and the permanent hope ariseth from it: yea, indeed, all the Grace that there is in this Covenant derives from that, as a stream from a Fountain."[66]

> All the encouragement which an awakened sinner hath to embrace & take hold of the Grace which is exhibited in the gospel covenant, ariseth, or is fetched from the Covenant of redemption. There is a previous Conviction which is wont to be wrought in the heart or conscience of a sinner, in order to the proposal of the Terms of the Gospel to him: and this is requisite, for without this Conviction he cannot be brought to see any need that he stands in of the benefits of the New Covenant.[67]

In short, we cannot enter into the New Covenant except as we recognize that it is the Covenant of Redemption which establishes all the mercies and promises of the Covenant of Grace.

Just so, but Willard would not, for all that, be understood to deny the necessity for a Covenant of Grace.

> When God had made man he placed him near himself, having put his own image upon him, endowing him with such Graces as fitted him for communion with his maker, and to bind him forever to love and obey him, he plighted a precious Covenant with him, engaging his love & favour perpetually to him in case of his being faithful to his duty; but threatening him with his infinite displeasure in case of his disobedience. Matters thus standing, Man, by the instigation of *Satan* was allured and invited, and by the abuse of his own free will led to fall away from his obedience, and become a Covenant-breaker, whereby a wall of separation was set up between him and God; and the Peace thus broken. War was proclaimed between God and man, which controversy can-

> not be composed without a Mediator....This Mediator applies himself both to God and man, making to both a motion of Reconciliation. For this the Son of God made that long journey from heaven to earth, and back again that he might transact this business. Deals with his Father immediately, and with man by the means.[68]

These means are the Articles of Agreement proposed: first, that God's righteous dealing with man in proceeding to condemn him for the apostasy of Adam be acknowledged and justified; second, that man freely and humbly shall confess the indignities his sinfulness has offered to God's glory; third, that due recompense and full satisfaction shall be made to God's justice for every injury and wrong done to his name by the sinner, fourth, that satisfaction being made, God shall forgive and forget all offences; fifth, that from being an enemy, God shall become a father to the sinner, and put on the bowels of a father to him; sixth, that his children shall obediently serve him all the days of their lives; and that seventh, these articles being agreed to, there shall be a new Covenant plighted, signed, sealed, delivered, entered, and enrolled for ever.

Let every sinner then bless God for Christ our Mediator "gone to heaven as our attorney," and let everyone take care neither to neglect nor despise the terms gratuitiously offered; for, Willard would remind us, these may at any time time be withdrawn and man left to the damnation he deserves. But Willard will not pause to dwell upon the horrors consequent upon man's rejection of the terms. "For ministers to preach nothing but terrours, is," he feels, "not the way to promote the work of the Gospel, or conversion of Souls." Unlike his great successor, Edwards, he does not find it seemly to frighten his congregation into heaven, nor would he say with Hopkins that a man ought to be willing to be damned for the glory of God. "There is," he thinks, "a great difference between being willing to be damned and being willing that God should be sovereign."[70] We must of a certainty yield to the latter, but to insist upon the former betrays a lack of confidence in the terms of the Covenant and in that faculty of reason which tells us that acceptance of its terms is the one way to salvation.

V

The true state of the Question is, Whether first the Scriptures doth contain all the Word or Words of God?....I say nay; for the words of God are spiritual, and of an inward nature, as God himself is....[71]

How shall we judge of the Spirit, but by Scripture?[72]

On the 21st of April, 1688, one George Keith[73], a Quaker, posted "in the most publick place in the town of Boston" a call and warning from the Lord to the people of New England to repent of their persecution of the Quakers and abandon the false teachings of their ministers. That they should remain in no doubt concerning the particular doctrines charged as being false, he listed their pernicious errors:

1. That God hath committed his Counsel wholly to Writing.

2. That God hath fore-ordained what-ever cometh to pass.

3. That God hath not afforded, or provided sufficiency of Grace and means of Salvation unto all mankind, whereby they may be saved.

4. That there are reprobate Infants that dye in infancy, and perish eternally, only for Adam's sin imputed unto them.

5. That the Light that is in every man, that convinceth them of their Sins....is only natural, and no ways sufficient to enable any man to do any work acceptable unto God.

6.   That Christ hath not dyed for all men.

7.   That Justification is only by Christ's Righteousness, without us, imputed unto us, and received by Faith alone.

8.   That beginnings of true Sanctification cannot be fallen from totally.

9.   That no man in this life, by any Grace of God given him....can perfectly keep the commandment of God.

10. That no man ever since the Apostles days are assisted by any infallible Spirit to Preach, Pray, or Write.

11. That human and outward learning, without the saving Grace of God, and the holy Spirits inward Revelation and Inspiration, is sufficient to qualifie a man to be a Preacher of the Gospel.

12. That the Scriptures ought to be believed only for their own outward Evidence and Testimony, and not for the inward Evidence and Testimony of the Holy Spirit in mens hearts.[74]

Outraged by this "blasphemous and heretical paper," the ministers, i.e., Samuel Willard, Cotton Mather, Joshua Moodey, and James Allen, took counsel, pondered, and two weeks later gave their collective answer: "If he desires Conference, to instruct us, let him give us his arguments in writing....If he would have a Publick Audience, let him Print."[75] and print he did, a treatise of two hundred pages of exhortation, advice, invective, presumption, and apologetic entitled **The Presbyterian and Independent Visible Churchs of New England brought to the Test, and Examined according to the Doctrine of the Holy Scriptures, in their Doctrine, Ministry, Worship Constitution,**

Government, Sacraments, and Sabbath Day, and found to be No True Church of Christ.

Keith's basic presupposition, proclaimed on page one and presumed throughout, is that "the Scriptures are only sufficiently and savingly believed and understood by the *inward* Illumination and *Revelation* of the holy Spirit, which is the same in kind to that which God gave to the Saints of old." This holy Light of Christ inwardly shining and enlightening the dark hearts and understandings of sinful men alone gives them the ability to rightly understand the Scripture. Without this inward Light "no man is, or can be, a true *Christian*....and therefore without the same, no man can be a Gospel Minister, for that which is absolutely necessary to constitute a true *Christian* or Believer, is absolutely necessary to constitute a true Christian Minister."[67] The inference, as Keith's subsequent exposition makes plain, is that the ministers of Boston are no true ministers of Christ since they lack by their own admission the working in them of that inward light which, according to Keith, gives infallible knowledge. They are, he opines, "like the Harlot which took hold of Joseph's garment, but himself she could not enjoy: so many get the outward form of the *words of Truth,* but the spirit of Truth they have not, and who have it not, cannot minister it."[77]

Greatly disturbed by these gratuitious aspersions and concerned for the effect that Keith's dismissal of the spiritual efficiacy of scripture-words as such might have on their congregations, the Boston ministers shortly produced **The Principles of the Protestant Religion Maintained, and Churches of New England in the Profession and Exercise thereof defended Against all the Calumnies of one George Keith, a Quaker, in a Book lately published at Pennsylvania to undermine them both.** The tone of the treatise is set in the Preface. The authors[78] are horrified and scandalized by the effrontery of "this Quaker heretic....who with Fraud would persuade the people of the Saints of the Most High to unchurch themselves."[79]

> *"But how,"* they ask, *"can you think of parting with an Infinite and Eternal* GOD, *and having a created soul blasphemously placed in His Throne? How can you think of parting with a precious* Bible, *as a Dead Letter, and having*

silent postures *of our own in the Room thereof. How can you think of parting with an Inestimable* REDEEMER, *for a dim light* within *you,* which *may prove Darkness it self....Can you* with any patience behold the glorious Doctrines of *Election, and Justification, and* Perseverance, *depraved with* Opinions *that make* Man *to be,* All, *and* Grace to *have small or no share in the matter of salvation?"*[80]

In Quakerism, they thunder, we see the Vomit cast forth by the Deceivers and Seducers of former days and past ages *"licked up again for a new Digestion, and once more expos'd for the poisoning of mankind....*Indeed Quakerism is *the peculiar plague of this* Age."[81] Which being granted so, they propose to emulate the action of Jesus and, *"taking the brushes of the Sanctuary, to strike down what* Cobwebs *the* Quakers *have been spinning there.*[82]

The argument is operose, and as is commonly the case in such controversies, it too frequently turns upon the exact shade of meaning allowed by the polemicists to terms held in common. Thus 'Revelation', which for Keith embraces the Word and its Truth as envisioned through the spiritual inward light, is, for the ministers of Boston simply a synonym for Scripture. For how, they inquire, shall we Judge of the Spirit except by scripture-word? "That the Spirit of God must open our understandings to discern the spiritual meaning of the Word of God, we never doubted. And that prayer and meditation are helps to it, who questions? But what's this to the purpose?"[83] To confuse the Spirit as Interpreter with the Spirit as Rule is, to their view, "nonsense." "As for his (Keith's) asserting by divine Revelation a Quaker can infallibly know a mans spiritual estate, it is precarious, presumptuous, and false: for tho God knowes all mens hearts, yet He gives infallible Rules to know them by, *ordinarily* or *immediately* cannot be evidenced."[84]

But if we may not Judge of the Spirit except as that is evident to scripture-word then it follows that we must accept the word of scripture as it pertains to those doctrines denigrated by Keith, and must accept as being of equal authority, the silence of scripture with respect to excepting infants from reprobation, for "where there is no Revelation, there is no ground for Faith."[85] This, they quickly add, is not to say that God lacks the power to save infants without outward means, "but to argue meerly from his Power to his will without his own (Scripture) Revelation, is to give laws to the Almighty,"[86] and to profess to know that which no man can know. Keith and his Friends would have it that the light within is the universal salve. "Allow but a Quaker this *Engine* and he will do wonders with it; beat down the foundations of many generations, up-Church all Christendom, make the Scripture intend just contrary to what it speaks; and who shall question him if he tells us he sees all this in the Light, and hath it immediately revealed."[87] Yet question him we must, for nothing is more evident to common sense than that this Light is not, as claimed, natural to all men except perhaps as a light of reason illuminating man's understandings. "That man in his state of integrity had light sufficient to have guided him to felicity, we believe; but all the light of nature in fallen man, will not *objectively* reveal the truths necessary to be known in order to salvation....Besides if this light be connate with men, what needed G.K. to make such a splutter about Immediate Revelations?"[88]

The question was soon answered in a page by page rebuttal entitled **The Pretended Antidote Proved Poison. Or, The True Principles of the Christian and Protestant Religion Defended, And the Four Counterfit Defenders thereof Detected and Discovered** etc.[89] The work shows evidence of hasty composition in considerable heat. Half of the book is devoted to a passionate defense of Quakerism from the onus of heresy, and copious draughts of Scripture are poured to justify the doctrine of the inward light. No new arguments are presented and the character of the work precludes synopsis. The ministers of Boston disdained to reply and thus the disputation ended.

A dozen years passed. Keith returned to England, broke with Quakerism, embraced the Church of England, and in 1702 returned to America as an Anglican missionary. In June of that year he came to Boston, and on July 1st, "being desired by some friends to be present at the Commencement in Cambridge,"[90] accompanied them to Harvard chapel. In those days the graduation exercises included a philosophical disputation conducted by the ranking members of the senior class, moderated, as was customary, by the presiding officer of the college, in this instance, the acting-President, Samuel Willard. The thesis proposed was one in which all present took a lively interest, viz. that the Immutability of Gods Decree doth not take away the Liberty of the

Creature. Keith describes the denouement:

> The matter at last came to this issue, in the Dispute had upon
> that These (Thesis), that the Defender thereof, as likewise
> the President, Mr. Willard, gave their entire assent to the two
> following *Propositions* which the students, who were the Op-
> pugners, did modestly urge were the necessary *Consectaries*
> of that *These.*

first,   *That the Fall of Adam, by virtue of Gods Decree, was
              Necessary.*
secondly, *That every free act of the reasonable Creature is deter-
              mined by God, so that whatever the reasonable Creature
              acteth freely, it acteth the same Necessarily.*[91]

Keith admits that he did not actually hear Willard affirm that all sinful actions of the creature are determined by God, "but their manner of answering and arguing doth clearly enough prove, that it was their Opinion."[92]

Having thus rushed to judgement, he promptly dispatched a letter in Latin
to Willard denouncing and confuting this detestable doctrine which, he confesses, "did some years ago drive me from the society (of those called
Presbyterians) who held it, and taught it, and prepared the way for my turning to Quakerism, whilst by a preposterous zeal I wandered from one extreme to the other."[93] Willard at first ignored the letter, feeling that its
misrepresentations required no answer, but when Keith published an English
version, he was, as he tells us, "prevailed on to give the World a fair account
of the matter which he hath so fouly represented."[94] According to Willard
the two propositions (consectaries) implicit in the thesis debated are:

1. That the Divine Decree is Immutable

2. That the Reasonable Creature enjoys a liberty
   which is not destroyed by this.[95]

Nor is his understanding of the character of the disputation quite that of Keith. "The Question at issue," he notes, "was to be debated *Philosophically,* or according to the Light of Nature, and the principles of *Natural Theology:* in which the *Respondent* was to defend the consistency of these two, by the strength of *Reason,* whereas the *Opponents* province was to attempt the making it to appear that they are inconsistent."[96] For his part, Willard did not doubt but that the two propositions were consistent, "though we cannot fathom it to the bottom, and it is commendable for us, soberly to employ our reason to satisfy us in the *Compossibility* of them, and thereby make it appear that faith doth not contradict right reason."[97] Which he does for fully fifty pages.

The argument, anticipating Edwards, presumes the validity of a distinction between the physical cause of an action and the moral cause of the sinfulness adhering to that action. Keith had contended, as much against his own position as that of Willard, that every second cause (such as every reasonable creature is) is dependent upon the first cause, which is God Almighty, and that this being so, "the Determination of Mans will by God to a sinful action, being the next cause of that sinful action, maketh God to be the Author of that sin."[98] Which argument Willard would evade by drawing his distinction between the physical cause or matter of the action and its moral cause or form.

> Only for a better conception of this, let me observe, that when we say, a sinful action, we consider it in a *Complex* sense, viz. *Physically* as an action, and *Morally* as sinful; and in this Complex sense, Divines do call the former the *substrate matter* of the action, under which they comprehend whatever of *Entity* there is in it, and the other the formality of it, not as an action, but as it is sinful: in which sense it is to be allowed, and what he (Keith) hath said against it, is nothing to the purpose.[99]

Keith, of course, specifically denies the validity of this distinction of material from formal, but this Willard dismisses as a non sequitur, "because the sinfulness of the action, is not from the *Efficiency* of God, but the *deficiency* of the Creature in respect of his *Morals.*"[100]

Yet ultimately it matters little whether the act itself and the sinfulness of it are two in reality, as Willard contends, or a unity inseparable, as Keith insists, for both readily grant that "God is not bound to the same law under which he hath by precept and sovereign authority bound us,"[101] and both will confess that "these things are matters of faith, being fully declared in the things of God."[102]

This mutual willingness to take consistency on faith should have settled the issue, but Keith, ever ready to take offense, found in the **Brief Reply** aspersions sufficient to justify his composing a page by page rebuttal.[103] But in this pamphlet, as in his earlier broadsides, he is more concerned to vindicate his person and his position in the eyes of his reader than he is to advance the argument, and once more Willard found nothing substantial enough to warrant a response. In the event, Keith shortly thereafter retired to England and the tranquillity of a country benefice, while Willard occupied himself with his monthly lectures on the Westminister Shorter Catechism[104] until prevented by his final illness.

In these sermon-lectures he nowhere offers any indication that Keith has had any influence of any sort upon the development of his theology. and yet there is his teaching on regeneration.

> This work of Saving *Illumination* wrought by the Spirit on
> the Soul in passive Conversion, is a secret and mysterious
> work, and better known by the Person who hath received
> it, than capable of being described by words.[105]

Is this an echo of the Quaker inward light? Subconsciously perhaps. It is of a certainty an anticipation of that notion of an immediate and instantaneous working of the Holy Spirit on the sinful heart, which in the preaching of Edwards, Bellamy, and Hopkins will emerge as a cornerstone of the New Divinity.

VI

> There is an order in the World. God sits king and rules over
> all, and therefore let us be quiet....Let reason subject itself
> to faith, and we shall never suspect God's government![106]

In concluding his rather less than rapid survey of the covenant theology, Perry Miller notes the resolute determination of Willard's Puritan predecessors to make Calvinism reasonable. They were, he informs us,

> seeking to understand, to draw up explicable laws, to form
> clear and distinct ideas, to bring order and logic into the
> universe. They could not interpret it as extension and move-
> ment as did Descartes. They could not reduce it to atoms
> as did Hobbes. They could not defy its natural construction
> as did the Newtonians. But oddly enough they could take
> many steps in the same direction once they had seized upon
> their fundamental discovery that God has voluntarily engag-
> ed Himself to regular, ascertainable procedures. The rest
> followed surely and easily from this premise: the validity
> of reason in man, the regularity of secondary causes in
> nature, the harmony of knowledge and faith, the coincidence
> of the arbitrary with inherent goodness, the intimate con-
> nection between grace and the incitements that generate
> grace, the necessity for moral responsibility and activity.
> Everywhere along the line the method of the divine dispen-
> sation, while authorized only by God and remaining under
> His constant control, is actually synchronized with a com-
> pletely scientific account![107]

However, there is, he adds, a caution to be observed by anyone who would rest in this conclusion.

> For reasonable as this system was, coherent and uniform as

> was its cosmology, sequential as was its theory of causation,
> in the final analysis the basis of every contention, the goal
> of every proposition, was still the transcendent, omnipotent
> Divinity![08]

The whole is coherent, but not of itself. God has made it so, and God can as readily annul the rule of reason and unmake the laws of nature. That he has not thus far chosen to do so is no cause for complacency, for God is free to do as he will.

Willard would not deny it, but neither would he dwell overly on the element of unpredictability in the Calvinist conception of God. His message is the good news of God's good faith to those that keep the Covenant, and to his view there is no profit to be had from speculation on the possibilities arising from the need to admit that there is no absolute guarantee that God will perform what he has promised. Scripture teaches us that God is both sovereign and committed to his children, and we cannot but believe that these truths are not contradictory. Nevertheless, he concedes that "there are things which yet though not contradictions, yet surpass our power to see through them, which yet we are to believe, and not reject them because we are nonplusst and ready to say, with *Nicodemus,* how can these things be?"[109] The answer is, the Bible says they are, and for Willard that answer suffices.

That it did not entirely suffice for his sucessors in the quest for a consistent Calvinism, and cannot suffice for us, is no reflection on our author. He could not know how shifting a foundation Scripture really is, nor be expected to foresee the day when men would not accept humility as an answer. In other words, his **Compleat Body of Divinity** is no system for our times. Is this to say, then, that it has for us merely an antiquarian interest? Not at all. To begin with, there is the fact that we have in Willard's system the first truly synoptic body of theology produced in this country, and that is something students of American religious history do ill to overlook in their preoccupation with the writings of the first generation of Puritan theologians, and with those of that member of the third whom Miller has proclaimed "the first consistent and authentic Calvinist in New England."[110] In view of the foregoing, that is perhaps better said of Willard. In any case, one need only look to what

Edwards has to say about the Covenant of Grace in the **Religious Affections** and in the **Freedom of the Will** to see that it is simply not true to say, as Miller does, that "he threw over the whole covenant scheme."[111] Edwards is no less indebted to Willard and the other theologians of the Covenant, for all that his own religious emphasis is placed upon another aspect of Calvinism.

Then too there is the fact, so easily ignored today, that Willard's version of the covenant theology, however fantastic it may seem when seen in the light of the Higher Criticism and the modern world-view, does offer an account consistent at all important points with the Biblical witness. You may, as I do, boggle at the notion of the Persons of the Trinity negotiating covenants with themselves for their dependents, but once allow that this contractual activity is a proper function of divinity, approved as such in Scripture, and the covenants become matters with which all professing Christians perforce must reckon.

Finally, there is the fact, of first importance in the subsequent development of American philosophical theology, of Willard's conception of God as the Abstract. As we have seen, it is, as stated, hardly satisfactory. The conception is not really developed, nor does Willard have any philosophically defensible account to offer of the relation of the Abstract to the concrete. What he does have to offer is a problem which no defender of the orthodox faith can properly avoid. If Edwards is, in truth, the greater thinker, it is only because he has a plausible solution to propose.

Bibliographical Essay

A Compleat Body of Divinity in Two Hundred and Fifty Expository Lectures on the Assembly Shorter Catechism. Wherein the Doctrines of the Christian Religion are unfolded, their Truth confirm'd, their Excellence display'd, their Usefulness improv'd, Errors & Vices refuted and expos'd, Objections answer'd Controversies settled, Cases of Conscience resolv'd; and a great light thereby reflected on the present Age (Boston: B. Green & S. Kneeland, 1726), is methodical, ponderous, and tolerably tedious. A better choice for the reader who would sample Willard is **The Doctrine of the Covenant of Redemption** wherein is laid the Foundation of all our Hopes and Happiness, briefly opened and improved. (Boston: Benj. Harris, 1693. Willard's way with a text is best exhibited in the twenty-eight sermons on **Luke 15:11-32** entitled **Mercy Magnified on a Penitent Prodigal** (Boston: Samuel Green, 1684); in **Heavenly Merchandize,** or the purchasing of truth recommended and the selling of it dissuaded as it was delivered in several sermons upon **Proverbs 23:23** (Boston: Samuel Green, 1686); and in **The Barren Fig Tree's Doom,** being the substance of sixteen sermons preached on Christ's parable of the Fig Tree, **Luke 13:6-9. The Truly Blessed Man,** or the way to be happy here, and for ever, being the substance of diverse sermons preached on Psalm XXXII (Boston: B. Green & J. Allen, 1700), a tome of six-hundred and fifty-two pages, largely given over to the question of original sin and what to do about it, anticipates the issues and solutions later advanced by Willard's posterity. A companion piece to it is **The Fountain Opened,** or the Great Gospel Privilege of having Christ exhibited to Sinful man, etc. (Boston: B. Green & J. Allen, 1700). The volume includes the famous sermon on the conversion of the Jews and the lecture **Evangelical Perfection.** Also worthy of the attention of the serious student are the sermon collections, **The Peril of the Times Displayed** (Boston: B. Green & J. Allen, 1700) and **Spiritual Desertions Discovered and Remedied** Boston: B. Green & J. Allen, 1699). The above, however, by no means exhausts Willard's output. A more extensive, but by no means complete, listing is given in Ernest Benson Lowrie, **The Shape of the Puritan Mind The Thought of Samuel Willard** (New Haven: Yale University Press, 1974). This study, based largely on **A Compleat Body of Divinity,** provides an eminently readable introduction to the major themes of Willard's theology. Those interested in following out in greater detail Keith's controversy with the ministers of Boston should ask for Evans' American Imprints, numbers 472, 502, 515, 1053, 1150, and 1160 (titles as given in text and footnotes above). Seymour Van Dyken, **Samuel Willard, 1640-1707, Preacher of Orthodoxy in an Era of Change** (Grand Rapids: Eerdmans, 1972) is the only full-length biography.

[1] Samuel Willard, **Heavenly Merchandise** (Evans 424), 113. This work, and all others of Willard's writings hereafter cited, have been reproduced on microcards. See **Early American Imprints 1693-1800,** microprint edition keyed to **Evans American Bibliography** edited by Clifford K. Shipton, Readex Microprint Publications, 1950-63. All subsequent references to Willard's works, excepting only those to **A Compleat Body of Divinity** are, like the foregoing, cited by Evans number (in parentheses) and page of the work reproduced.

[2] Increase Mather, To the Reader of Willard's **Covenant-Keeping the Way to Blessedness** (Evans 335).

[3] The principal of these are (in the order of their publication): **Useful Instructions for a Professing People,** several sermons (1673), **Ne Sutor Ultra Crepidam,** anti-Baptist polemic (1681), **Covenant-Keeping the Way to Blessedness,** several sermons (1682), **The Child's Portion,** sermons (1684), **Mercy Magnified on a Penitent Prodigal,** twenty-eight Sunday sermons on Luke 15:ll-32 (1684), **Heavenly Merchandize,** several sermons on **Proverbs 23:23** (1686), **The Barren Fig Tree's Doom,** the substance of sixteen sermons on Luke 13:6-9 (1691), **Rules for the Discerning of the Present Times,** sermons (1692), **The Doctrine of the Covenant of Redemption** (1693), **The Truly Blessed Man,** the substance of divers sermons on Psalm XXXII (1700), **The Fountain Opened,** sermons and lectures (1700), **A Brief Reply to Mr. George Kieth,** polemic (1703), and **A Compleat Body of Divinity** (posthumous, 1726).

[4] **Covenant-Keeping the Way to Blessedness** (Evans 335), 4.

[5] Samuel Willard, **A Compleat Body of Divinity in Two Hundred and Fifty Expository Lectures on the Assembly Shorter Catechism** (Boston: B. Green & S. Kneeland, 1726), Sermon LXXIX, 326/1. Hereafter cited as **Compleat Body,** sermon number in Roman numerals. Inasmuch as each page of the text is divided into two columns, first or second column is indicated by the number after the stroke following the page number.

[6] Ibid.

[7] The Rev. Samuel Willard (1705-1741), minister of the church at Biddeford, Maine with whom Herbert Schneider, in his study of **The Puritan Mind** (98f), seems to have confused our Willard, was, in fact, his grandson.

[8] Thomas Jefferson Wertenbaker, **The Puritan Oligarchy** (New York: Charles Schribner's Sons, 1947), 313.

[9] Apparently to spite Mather, the General Court Granted Vice-President Willard permission to live at his Boston home five days and nights of the week.

[10] Perry Miller, **The New England Mind, The Seventeenth Century** (Cambridge: Harvard University Press, 1954),69.

[11] **Compleat Body,** CXIX, 450/1.

[12] **Heavenly Merchandize** (Evans 424), 113. Willard's italics.

[13] **Compleat Body,** LXXXIX, 326/2.

[14] Ibid., XII, 37/2.

[15] Ibid., XII, 40/2.

[16] Ibid.

[17] Ibid., XIII, 42/1.

[18] Ibid., XV, 46/2.

[19] Ibid.

[20] Ibid., 48/1.

[21]Ibid.

[22]Ibid., XVIII, 56/2.

[23]This caveat would seem to rule out the suggestion that we have in Willard's 'Being Abstract' a notion approximating Whitehead's 'primordial nature of God,' or even Plato's 'Idea of the Good,' both of which embrace the dimensionally mathematic.

[24]**Compleat Body**, XVIII, 56/2.

[25]Ibid., XVI, 50/1.

[26]Ibid., XXXIII, 106/2.

[27]Ibid., XXXIv, 110/1.

[28]Ernest Benson Lowrie, **The Shape of the Puritan Mind, The Thought of Samuel Willard** (New Haven: Yale Unversity Press, 1974), 52. My italics.

[29]Ibid., 53.

[30]**Compleat Body**, XVI, 51/2.

[31]Ibid., XVI, 50/1,2.

[32]Ibid., XLII, 131/1.

[33]Ibid., XXXIV, 108/2. The figure is presumably derived from Calvin himself. See **Institutes** I. xiv. 1.

[34]**Compleat Body**, XXXIV, 108/2.

[35]Ibid., XL, 124/2.

[35]Ibid., XL, 124/2.

[36]**The Child's Portion** (Evans 3980), 96.

[37]**Compleat Body**, CXII, 421/2. The complete passage runs thus: "Only this much in general we may know of it, *viz*, that it will not be long before that day shall come; they are the last days, and the winding up of time that we live in. There are yet some prophecies to be fulfilled, some predictions to be accomplished, some of God's Elect unborn, that are yet to be called, and the world stands in its old posture for the present, on these accounts...meanwhile it is not for us anxiously to inquire into times and seasons, but to use utmost and speedy endeavours, to get ready for the terrible day, that it may not steal upon us unlooked for, or find us unprepared." See also, **The Fountain Opened** (Evans 960), 121.

[38]**Romans** 8:29-31.

[39]Perry Miller, 'The Marrow of Puritan Divinity, originally printed in **The Publications of the Colonial Society of Massachusetts** for February, 1935; reprinted as Chapter III of Miller's **Errand into the Wilderness** (Cambridge: Harvard University Press, 1956). Hereafter cited as **Marrow.**

[40]Perkins (1558-1602) was a famous preacher and Cambridge don, author of numerous works od apologetic and theology in defense of Calvinism. Many of the important figures in seventeenth century English and American Puritanism were his disciples.

[41]William Ames (Amesius), 1576-1633, is considered by some scholars to be the spiritual father of the New England theology. His **Medulla Theologiae** (1623) was for many years the standard text used by aspirants to the Congregational ministry.

[42] John Preston (1587-1628), Puritan preacher and politician, chaplain to the Prince of Wales, was the author of several volumes of sermons, most of them posthumously published.

[43]For the marrow of the argument of this paragraph, I am indebted to Miller. The inferences drawn are, of course, my own.

[44]John Preston, **The New Covenant, or the Saint's Portion** (London, 1629), 351.

[45]Ibid., 38.

[46]**The Doctrine of the Covenant of Redemption Wherein is laid the Foundation of all our Hopes and Happiness. Briefly Opened and Improved** (Boston: Benj. Harris, 1692). Evans 684. Hereafter cited as **Covenant.**

[47]**Covenant**, 1.

[48]Ibid., 3.

[49]Ibid., 4.

[50]The plural is justified, argues Willard, because "although the *Decree* of God, be with respect to him Decreeing, but one simple and undivided act; yet, in reference to the things Decreed, it is various, or hath many parts in it: for which reason the scripture speaks of many *thoughts* and many *purposes* of his." **Covenant**, 6. The philosophical justification of such a position is again our recognition that the abstract may be pluralized without detriment to its unicity qua abstract.

[51]This being acknowledged, it follows, Willard thinks, that the time will come when the Jews will accept Christ as their lord and saviour, "for as God first Chose that Nation to be a peculiar people to himself; so he hath been meet to put their Name upon the Church, even in Gospel times: and there are some places (in Scripture) that cannot bear another interpretation: See **Gal.** 6:15; **Rom.** 2:28, 9:6; Mal.1:11 etc." **The Fountain Opened** (Evans 960), 108.

[52]**Covenant**, 7.

[53]Ibid., 8.

[54]Ibid., 8-9. See Appendix II.

[55]Ibid., 9.

[56]Ibid., 9-10.

[57]Ibid., 107.

[58]Ibid.

[59]Ibid., 11.

[60]Ibid., 93. See Appendix II.

[66]Ibid., 94-95.

[67]Ibid., 100-101.

[68]**Compleat Body**, LXXXIV, 307/2-308/1.

[69]**Mercy Magnified on a Penitent Prodigal** (Evans 379), 205.

[70]Ibid., 254-255.

[71]George Keith, **The Presbyterian and Independent Visible Churches of New England and elsewhere brought to the Test, and Examined according to the Doctrine of the Holy Scriptures, in their Doctrine, Ministry, Worship, Constitution, Government, Sacraments and Sabbath Day, and found to be No True Church of Christ** etc. (Philadelphia: Will. Bradford, 1689), 8, 8. Evans 472. Hereafter cited as **Presbyterian.**

[72]Samuel Willard et al (the Ministers of Boston), **The Principles of the Protestant Religion Maintained, and Churches of New England in the Profession and Exercise thereof defended against all the Calumnies of one George Keith, a Quaker, in a Book lately published at Pennsylvania to undermine them both** (Boston: Richard Pierce, 1690), 39. Evans 502. Hereafter cited as **Protestant.**

[73]A native of Scotland, born near Aberdeen in 1638, Keith was educated at Marischal College, Aberdeen, and designed for the Presbyterian ministry. Converted to Quakerism in 1662, he proselytized in company with George Fox and William Penn, was imprisoned for his pains, and upon his release from an English jail in 1685 emigrated to Pennsylvania. He subsequently traveled throughout New England and the middle states preaching Quaker tenets and engaging in polemics with the representatives of the Standing Order. In 1694 he returned to England, fell out with Penn, was dismissed from meeting, and took Anglican orders. From 1702 till 1704 he traveled in America as a missionary for the SPG. Returned once more to England, he found appointment as rector of the country parish of Edburton, which benefice he held until his death in 1716. The Bishop of Salisbury, a fellow Aberdonian, thought him "the most learned man that ever was in that (Quaker) sect, and well-versed in the oriental tongues, philosophy, and mathematics." He was nothing if not prolific, his published writings exceeding even those of Willard in sheer volume. See Ethyn W. Kirby, **George Keith 1638-1716** (New York: Appleton-Century, 1942), 52-53, 128-129.

[74]**Presbyterian,** 204-205.

[75]Ibid., 205.

[76]Ibid., 37.

[77]Ibid., 51.

[78]Samuel Willard, Cotton Mather, Joshua Moodey, and James Allen. The scholarly consensus is that the writing is not in the style of Willard, and some would argue that this work should not be counted as an expression of his views. Be that as it may, Willard did sign the Preface, and the argument of the treatise, if not the particular words, are as much his as they are Mather's (the probable author), Moodey's or Allen's. At least Keith understood him to be such).

[79]**Protestant,** Preface.

[80]Ibid. Author's italics.

[81]Ibid. Author's italics.

[82]Ibid. Author's italics.

[83]Ibid., 39.

[84]Ibid., 42. Author's italics. In proof thereof the ministers offer the case of Judas, appointed by Christ himself to be an Apostle, and accepted as such by the Eleven who, if anyone should, should have known by the inward light that Judas was an apostate.

[85]**Protestant,** 79.

[86]Ibid., 92.

[87]Ibid., 127.

[88]Ibid., 100.

[89]Philadelphia: Will. Bradford, 1690. Evans 515.

[90]George Keith, **A Refutation of a dangerous and hurtful Opinion maintained by Mr. Samuel Willard, an Independent Minister at Boston, and President at the Commencement in Cambridge in New England, July 1, 1702. Viz. that the Fall of Adam, and all the Sins of Men, necessarily come to pass by virtue of God's Decree, and his determination both of the Will of Adam, and of all other men to sin** (New York: no printer indicated, 1702), 1. Evans 1053. Hereafter cited as **Refutation.**

[91]Ibid., 1-2.

[92]Ibid., 2.

[93]Ibid., 7.

[94]Samuel Willard, **A Brief Reply to Mr. George Keith in Answer to a Script of his, Entituled, A Refutation of a Dangerous and Hurtful Opinion, Maintained by Mr. Samuel Willard** etc. (Boston: Samuel Phillips, 1703), 2. Evans 1150.

[95]Ibid., 7.

[96]Ibid.

[97]Ibid., 8.

[98]**Refutation,** 3.

[99]**Brief Reply,** 21.

[100]Ibid. 22.

[101]Ibid., 35-36.

[102]Ibid., 8.

[103]George Keith, **An Answer to Mr. Samuell Willard** etc. (New York: William Bradford, 1704). Evans 1160.

[104]"This he performed monthly on the (first) Tuesday in the afternoon, in his public congregation; and so continued till April 1, 1707. Soon after which he was prevented from proceeding by a fit of sickness, out of which he was scarce well-recovered before he suddenly died.' **Compleat Body,** Preface.

[105]Ibid., Sermon CXIX, 449/1.

[106]Ibid., Sermon XLVI, 145/1,2.

[107]**Marrow,** 92-93.

[108]Ibid., 93.

[110]**Marrow,** 98.

[111]Ibid.

[112]In this connection it is pertinent to observe that the Rev. Timothy Edwards was a subscriber to the first edition of the **Compleat Body,** which his son must have read in the course of his theological studies.

The Experimental Calvinism Of Jonathan Edwards

"I should not take it at all amiss, to be called a Calvinist, for distinction's sake; though I utterly disclaim a dependence on Calvin, or believing the doctrines which I hold, because he believed and taught them; and cannot justly be charged with believing in everything just as he taught."[1]

THE EXPERIMENTAL CALVINISM OF JONATHAN EDWARDS

> Why should not He that made all things, still have something
> *immediately to do with the Things that He has made?*[2]

In August of 1733 Jonathan Edwards preached to his Northampton congregation a sermon which, according to Perry Miller, "so delighted his people that they persuaded him to publish it." It is, Miller continues, "no exaggeration to say that the whole of Edwards' system is contained in miniature within some ten or twelve of the pages in this work."[3] namely, **A Divine and Supernatural Light Immediately Imparted to the Soul by the Spirit of God, Shown to be both a Scriptural, and Rational Doctrine,** and to the extent that Edwards' system is a system of experimental religion, that is, a religion developed according "to such rules and methods of reasoning, as are universally made use of, and never denied or doubted to be good and sure, in experimental philosophy,"[4] Miller does not exaggerate. From this, the second of his sermons to be published,[5] to the posthumous **Dissertation on the Nature of True Virtue,** Edwards is at pains to promote what Edwards Park a century on will call the theology of the feelings.

At Yale he had read Locke's **Essay Concerning Human Understanding** and been persuaded of the essential truth of the dictum that there is nothing in the mind which was not first in the senses. "'Tis most evident," he thinks, "that nothing is in the mind, or reaches it, or takes any hold of it, any otherwise than as it is perceived or thought of."[6] There are, then, no innate ideas[7], which being so, our knowledge of God, whose existence neither Locke nor Edwards ever for a moment doubts, must be primarily by means of His witness in scripture. The problem is: How to certify this holy testimony? The answer, Edwards believes, in full accord with the Augustinian doctrine of illumination as confirmed by Calvin, is found in attention to the divine and supernatural light. This light, he would have us know, has nothing about it of the nature of conscience or a sense of guilt, nor does it consist in any impression made upon the imagination. It is no new revelation or inspiration such as the apostles had and George Keith claimed. Its nature is entirely different from anything obtained by any natural means. What it is, says Edwards, "is a true sense of the divine Excellency of the things revealed in the Word of God....for here is by this Light only given a due Apprehension of the same Truths that are revealed in the Word of GOD; and therefore it is not given without the Word."[8] "Indeed a Person can't have *spiritual Light* without the Word. But," Edwards reminds us, "that don't argue that the Word properly cause that Light."[9] As the light from the sun makes seeing possible, so does this divine and supernatural light, which is "a Kind of Emanation of GOD's Beauty, and is related to GOD as the light is to the Sun."[10] clarify the Word of God, confirming its authority and his existence.

Edwards came quite naturally by these convictions. As the only son (in a family of ten girls) born to the Rev. Timothy Edwards and Esther Stoddard (Edwards), daughter of the famous "Pope" Solomon Stoddard, minister at Northampton, he was from his earliest years exposed to Calvinist doctrine and had, as he tells us, "a variety of concerns and exercises about my soul from my childhood."[11] His youthful mind was full of objections against the doctrine of God's sovereignty until that happy day when he first experienced "that sort of inward, sweet delight in God and divine things that I have lived much in since" in consequence of reading **I Timothy** 1:17. "Now unto the King eternal, immortal, invisible, the only wise God, be honour and glory for ever and ever, Amen."

> As I read the words there came into my soul, and was as it were diffused through it, a sense of the glory of the Divine Being; a new sense, quite different from any thing I ever experienced before....
>
> From about that time, I began to have a new kind of apprehensions and ideas of Christ, and the work of redemption, and the glorious way of salvation by him. An inward, sweet sense of these things, at times came into my heart; and my soul was led away in pleasant views and contemplations of them.[12]

This sense of divine things, sublimated by the secular studies of his undergraduate years at Yale[13], eventually returned in full force inspiring his

his decision to enter the ministry. In the summer of 1722, following two years of postgraduate study, he received a call to a newly formed Scotch Presbyterian congregation in lower Manhattan and joyfully accepted. Despite the enjoyment of "many sweet and pleasant days," the church did not flourish and he came away a bare eight months later with a sinking heart. He was offered the church at Bolton, Connecticut which he inclined to accept, but before he could take up anew his pastoral duties he was asked to return to Yale as Tutor of the College. A serious illness in September 1725 terminated that employment, albeit "in this sickness, God was pleased to visit me again with the sweet influences of his Spirit."[14] Some months earlier the church at Northampton had begun the search for a colleague pastor to assist the elderly Stoddard. Edwards was invited to apply, and his audition sermon being well received was asked to "settle." He was ordained in February, 1727; married Sarah Pierrepont the following July, and in February of 1729, Solomon Stoddard having passed to his eternal reward, was installed as minister of the church at Northampton.

The story of the Northampton years, the triumphs of the Surprizing Work of God in the Conversion of many Hundred souls and the even greater outpourings of the Spirit in the Great Awakening, the tragedy of his dismissal from the church is better told in total detail elsewhere.[15] In **Some Thoughts Concerning the present Revival of Religion in New England** (1742) and again in his **Treatise Concerning Religious Affections** (1746) Edwards defended at inordinate length the authenticity of the operation of the Holy Spirit in regeneration. His review of the several revivals but confirms his belief in the efficiacy of the supernatural in the granting of true grace. "Upon the whole," he concludes,

> I think it is clearly manifest, that all truly gracious affections
> do arise from special and peculiar influences of the Spirit,
> working that sensible effect or sensation in the souls of the
> saints, which are entirely different from all that it is possible
> a natural man should experience, not only different in degree
> and circumstances, but different in its whole nature....
>   From hence it appears that impressions which some have

50

made on their imagination, or the imaginary ideas which
they have of God....have nothing in them that is spiritual,
or of the nature of true grace![16]

True grace imports a true idea of God, but what is the content of that idea?

II

The being of God is reckoned the first, greatest and most
fundamental of all things that are the objects of knowledge
or belief![17]

This, with Edwards, is established, that mind cannot conceive a state of perfect
nothing. Something, somewhere, there must be; for if we say that there is
absolutely nothing, we talk nonsense, inasmuch as we imply a disjunction
where there is none. "Either being or absolute nothing is no disjunction, no
more than whether a triangle is a triangle or not a triangle. There is no other
way but only for there to be existence. There is no such thing as absolute
nothing!"[18] Some being, therefore, some place necessarily and eternally is. And
if at some place, then in all places, since it is no less meaningless to affirm
that we see this necessary, eternal being must be infinite and omnipresent!"[19]
But if omnipresent then not solid, for solidity is nothing but resistance to
other solidities, all of which we can with ease conceive as not existing, whereas
this omnipresent being "is the very thing that we can never remove and conceive of its not being!"[20] What is this being, then, that no amount of mental
effort can deny? It is, says Edwards, space.

"But I had as good speak plain. I have already said as much as that *space
is God.* And it is indeed clear to me that all the space there is, not proper
to body, all the space there is *without the bounds of the creation,* all the space
There was *before the creation* is God himself. And nobody would in the least
stick at it if it were not because of the gross conceptions we have of space!"[21]
Our imaginations lead us to envision space as an indefinitely large container
of independently existing bodies, and thereby they mislead us; for space "is
a necessary being only as it is a necessary idea—so far as it is a simple idea

that is necessarily connected with other simple exterior ideas and is, as it were, their common substance or subject. It is in the same manner a necessary being as anything external is a being."[22] Which is to say that it is, like all things exterior, utterly dependent for its being on the mind, human or divine, which knows it for the idea that it really is. "Our imagination makes us fancy we see shapes and colors and magnitudes though nobody is there to behold (them). But to help our imagination, let us," Edwards proposes, "thus state the case: also, let us suppose this world deprived of every ray of light....At the same time also, let us suppose the universe to be altogether deprived of motion....Put both these suppositions together, that is, deprive the world of light and motion, and the case would stand thus with the world. There would be neither white nor black, neither blue nor brown, bright nor shaded, pellucid nor opaque, no noise or sound, neither heat nor cold, neither fluid, nor wet nor dry, hard nor soft, nor solidity, nor extension, nor figure, nor magnitude, nor proportion, nor body, nor spirit."[23] Nor, it is proper to add, space. "What then is become of the universe? Certainly," Edwards concludes, "it exists nowhere but in the divine mind."[24] You will say that this makes space to be one of God's ideas rather than God Himself. And so it does, in so far as the space here bespoken is the space that is "proper to body." But, you ask, is any other sort of space even conceivable? This 'space before the creation' of which Edwards speaks, is it not such a conception as anybody must stick at?

Many there are in the history of religious speculation who have not thought so. The conception is implicit in Anaximander's theory of the Boundless (*apeiron*). According to Aetius[25], Anaximenes, in declaring air to be the principle of all things, intends the assertion that air is God! There is a fragment attributed to his disciple Diogenes of Apollonia in which the latter remarks his conviction that "the thing that has intelligence is what men call the Air, and....this is what governs all and has power over all. Just this....is God; and it reaches everywhere, disposes all things, and is in everything, and there is nothing that does not partake of it."[26] So also, Archelaus, the pupil of Anaxagoras, is reported to have held that God is air and intelligence, while Aeschylus proclaims that

Zeus is air, Zeus is earth, Zeus is heaven, Zeus is all things and whatsoever is higher than all things.[27]

"In him we....have our being," sings Aratus, and Vergil echoes the refrain, "in him we move and live." "It is," Plotinus tells us, "inevitably necessary to think of all as contained within one nature; there cannot be as in the realm of sense thing apart from thing, here a sum and elsewhere something else; all must be mutually present within a unity."[28] Eriugena agrees, and after him Cusanus. According to Giordano Bruno, "even as there is in truth one infinite and utterly simple individual entity, so also there is an immense dimensional infinite within that other, and within which is that other, in the same fashion as he is within all things and all things are in him."[29] In our time the notion has been defended at length and in terms not alien to Calvinism by Karl Heim.[30] Situated as he was in a small colonial town lacking in literary resources, Edwards knew little or nothing of these authors or of their works. For him the first encounter with the idea of divine space must have been his reading of it in Newton's **Principia.** Later he would find the notion implicit in Book II of Locke's **Essay** and explicit in John Smith's **Selected Discourses,** a work which his writings reveal him to have studied with some care. Did he, as is commonly believed, read the English translation of Malebranche's **Recherche de la Verité** he must have encountered the idea still once more.

"....a conception to stick at?" Such the identification of infinite space with God may prove to be. But the number and reputation of those who have seriously entertained the idea must give pause to any who would incline to reject it out of hand. For what is here at issue is obviously not merely the question of the intelligibility or meaninglessness of a peculiar conception of space, but also and more so the larger question of the intellectual adequacy of that theological tradition which subscribes to this conception. As Douglas Elwood has truly said, "his (Edwards') great overarching concern was to reconstruct the framework of historic Calvinism along Neoplatonic lines."[31] To this end his identification of infinite space with God is made. Upon the relevance of this reconstruction to the post-Puritan world-view its intelligibility ultimately depends.

Infinite space is God. Is this to say that the Creator is in no wise separate from His creation? The Calvinist in Edwards forbade that he should thus join together what orthodoxy had put asunder, and did it not, his common sense alone would have sufficed to convince him that the way of pantheism was no less beset with difficulties than that classical theism his construction aimed to rechart. The fact was and is, as Elwood has noted[32], that both ways are inadequate and religiously treacherous. The problem is and was to find a way between the two at once preserving the element of truth in each, while yet evading the contradiction consequent upon maintaining one to the exclusion of the other. The solution, the third way taken by Edwards in the course of his reconstruction, comprises, according to Elwood, "a delicate balance of traditional theistic and classical pantheistic elements which can only be called a variety of panentheism or mystical realism."[33]

That it can and should be called something else, what follows purports to make clear. Jonathan Edwards is no panentheist, if one means by that the doctrine of all things literally in God. Nor is he yet even a mystical realist, if the term is taken in its modern sense. On the other hand, it cannot be denied that there are passages scattered throughout Edwards' writings which, taken at face value, lend credence to the Elwood thesis. Thus in number 880 of the Miscellanies it is affirmed that, "God is the sum of all being and there is no being without His being. All things are in Him, and He in all."[34] Which is to say, as Edwards does in number 697, that an infinite being

> must be an all-comprehending being. He must comprehend in himself all being. That there should be another being underived and independent, and so in no way comprehended, will argue him not to be infinite, because then there is something more, there is more entity. There is some entity besides what is in this being, and therefore his entity can't be infinite. Those two beings put together are more than one; for they taken together are a sum total, and one taken alone is but part of that sum total and therefore is finite. For whatsoever is a part is finite. God, as he is infinite and the being whence all are derived and from whom everything is given, does comprehend the entity of all His creatures; and their entity is not to be added to his, as not comprehended in it, for they are but communications from Him.[35]

Such difference as lies between them is, we are told in number 150, "no contrariety, but what naturally results from His greatness and nothing else....So that if we should suppose the faculties of a created spirit to be enlarged infinitely, there would be the deity to all intents and purposes, the same simplicity, immutability, etc."[36] In such a case the shadow would be substance and God All in all. Actually, the supposition is unnecessary, since an identical result follows from our recognition that Locke's "substance" is, properly understood, nothing but the Power of God exercised in that particular manner in those parts of space where He thinks fit. In sum, "speaking most strictly there is no proper substance but God Himself. How truly then," exclaims Edwards, "is it in Him that we live, move, and have our being."[37]

In God we live....a cliche to the orthodox, and to the heterodox—justification, the passage is the hallmark of the panentheist. There is hardly a one in whose writings it does not appear much more than once. In many it is a recurrent refrain, to be invoked where and whenever the writer is concerned to establish or emphasize the Christian character of his cosmology. It is so in Edwards. And yet....

What can a Christian understand by this phrase, "in God"? Does St. Paul intend no more than the assertion that we all live in the sight of God? Is it simply an alternative way of remarking our faith in the continuing efficacy of the Holy Spirit? Or is it to be understood as Aratus presumably intended that be understood, i.e., that in God we (literally) live. Edwards appears to be denying the possibility of this last when he tells us in number 194 that "it is a gross and unprofitable idea we have of God, as being something large and great as bodies are, and infinitely extended throughout the immense space. For God is neither little nor great with that sort of greatness, even as the soul of man—it is not all that extended, no more than an idea, and is not present anywhere as bodies are present.."[38] As for the bodies themselves, we learn in number 45 that "they have no proper being of their own. And as to spirits," Edwards concludes, "they are the communications of the great original Spirit, and doubtless, in metaphysical strictness and propriety, He is and there is nothing else."[39] Doubtless so, since thirty-five years later, in the Dissertation on God's End in Creation, he reaffirms his conviction that "God cannot have his heart enlarged, in such a manner as to take in beings who are originally out of himself, distinct and independent."[40] But if nothing is outside God, and God Himself is, as Edwards teaches, something more and other than His creation, it remains that whatever beings there may be, must be *in* God, and this view is, to Elwood's way of thinking, no less deserving to be called panentheism because the beings in God are spirits and God Himself is Mind.

Were panentheism synonymous with idealism, and the latter self-evidently true, we might, as Elwood does, rest comfortably in this conclusion. Since it is neither, we have no option but to recognize that we are not yet at the heart of the matter. For one thing, there is the problem of the bodies. They have no being of their own says Edwards. But he does not say that they have no being at all, nor could he do so and continue to aspire to write the History of the Work of Redemption. The bodies, then, require to be accounted for; creation requires to be explained and not explained away, and what the explanation is we know already. Creation is God's communication of Himself. "He Himself flows forth, and He Himself is pleased and glorified."[41] Our own "and other minds are made in His image and are emanations from Him."[42] As bodies, we, and all things sentient and insentient, are but images and shadows of the divine, sustained in being at every moment by the power of God, which being withdrawn we must, like the image in the mirror when its cause withdraws, instantly cease to be. God at His pleasure enlarges Himself and the universe appears; at His pleasure He retires into Himself and everything is at an end. The metaphor is that of Christian neo-platonism, and that Edwards is properly classified as such with respect to his ontology is not in question. What is in question, however, is whether or not his being or not his being a neo-Platonist makes Edwards a panentheist.

There are grounds for believing that it does, principal among them the fact that neo-platonism and panentheism alike maintain that there is nothing *outside* God. For Elwood this fact suffices: neo-platonism is panentheism[43]; Edwards is a neo-platonist; ergo, Edwards is a panentheist. If the syllogism is to be sustained, the major premise must be valid. Why then, one wonders, is it a premise so universally overlooked? For the fact is that no one hitherto has seemed to recognize that neo-platonism is panentheism. No history of philosophy records this truth, nor is it to be found in the Plotinus-commentary of Armstrong, Inge, and Brehier. Whittaker and Merlan appear not to have known of it, while Hartshorne and Reese, who, as authors of the only substantial survey of the various philosophies of the panentheistic tradition, must certainly have marked the fact, if fact it is, exclude neo-platonism altogether from their classification of modern panentheistic and quasi-panentheistic positions and surely they are right to do do *if* neo-platonism is the doctrine that God *duplicates* himself." For if there is one tenet in which all panentheisms agree, it is that there is absolutely nothing outside God—*not even God himself!* It makes no difference that what goes forth is no more than an image or shadow of divinity. A shadow or an image is no less external to its source because it is not something in and for itself. An emanation is no less an *outpouring* because what overflows is God. The creation is no less other than the Creator because it is merely a manifestation of his Being. Insofar as neo-platonism intends that 'image', 'shadow', 'emanation', and 'creation', be taken *literally*, or even analogically, if differs in no essential way from classical theism. Which being so, it would appear that if Edwards is a panentheist, he is such in spite of, and not because of, the fact that he is a Christian neo-platonist.

Neo-platonism as it is commonly interpreted is not panentheism. The qualification is necessary because there is an uncommon interpretation which, if allowed, would justify acceptance of Elwood's major premise, and make possible his conclusion. If the fact of the matter is, as P.V. Pistorius has argued in his important but neglected study of Plotinus and Neoplatonism, that

> the three hypostases of the Neo-Platonic Godhead are not
> a gradation of three separate beings, as is generally believed, but a more intimate trinity than that of Christian
> theology, because neither the One, nor the Intellectual-
> Principle, nor the Soul, can conceivably exist as independent
> and separate entities.,[45]

then those who have thought to find in neo-platonism a doctrine of emanation adaptable to the requirements of Christianity have made a fatal mistake. Almost without exception they have understood Plotinus and his school to teach a literal emanation in and out of the Godhead from hyper-essential unity to existential plurality, and this they have no good grounds for doing—if the

Godhead is not a graded triad. For in this latter case, the very nature of the Trinity precludes that its members should have emerged by any process of begetting.

How, then, is the universe related to God? How else, replies Plotinus, save internally.

> Consider our universe. There is none before it and therefore it is not, itself, in a universe or in any place—what place was there before the universe came to be?—its linked members form and occupy the whole. But Soul is not in the universe, on the contrary the universe is in the Soul; bodily substance is not a place to the Soul; Soul is contained in Intellectual-Principle and is the container of body. The Intellectual-Principle in turn is contained in something else; but that prior principle has nothing in which to be: the First is therefore in nothing, and, therefore, nowhere. But all the rest must be somewhere; and where but in the First. This can mean only that the First is neither remote from things nor directly within them; there is nothing containing it; it contains all.[46]

A very similar viewpoint, adapted to the explanation of the Trinity, is expressed by Edwards in number 308 of the **Miscellanies.** "We don't suppose," he writes,

> that the Father and the Son and the Holy Ghost are three distinct beings that have three distinct understandings....We never supposed that (the) Father generated the Son by understanding the Son, but that God generated the Son by understanding His own essence, and therefore the Son is that idea itself or understanding of the essence....The Father understands the idea He has merely in His having that idea, without any other....So that the Son understands the Father, in that the essence of the Son understands the essence of the Father as, in Himself, the understanding of the essence. And so of the Holy Ghost.[47]

The passage is not, to say the least, without its obscurities, but as respects the nature of the relation between the persona of the Trinity it is clear enough. As in Plotinus (as interpreted by Pistorius), so also with Edwards, the hypostases (persons) of the Godhead (Trinity) are not at all to be thought of as a graded triad of three separate (or theoretically separable) beings, but rather as a One containing three in thought. In other words, everything in God and all of it of such sort as to be apprehensible by mind alone. Thus to the extent that the Edwardsian Trinity equates to the Plotinian Godhead the position is plainly—idealistic panentheism in its purest form.

That this conclusion must pose a thundering problem for our comprehension of the reality of the everyday world of sense-experience, no one is better aware than Plotinus himself.

> Body, a non-existence? Matter, on which all this universe rises, a non-existence? Mountain and rock, the wide solid earth, all that resists, all that can be struck and driven, surely all proclaims the real existence of the corporeal? And how, it will be asked, can we, on the contrary, attribute Being, and the only authentic Being, to entities like Soul and Intellect, things having no weight or pressure, yielding to no force, offering no resistance, things not even visible?[48]

The answer, he thinks, rises in our recognition that body is not a synonym for matter. "Matter must be bodiless—for body is a later production, a compound made by Matter in conjunction with some other entity."[49] Of itself, Matter is nothing real:

> the Existence with which it masks itself is no Existence, but a passing trick making trickery of all that seem to be present in it, phantasms within a phantasm, it is like a mirror showing things as in itself when they are really elsewhere, filled in appearance but actually empty, containing nothing, pretending everything.[50]

We know, writes Edwards in his Notes on the Mind, "that the things that are objects of this sense (of Seeing), all that the mind views by Seeing, are merely mental Existences; because all these things, with all their modes, do exist in a looking-glass, where all will acknowledge, they exist only mentally."[51]

What, then, of body? As a compound of form and matter, as sense-object, it participates to some extent in Being. And so it does. But not, Plotinus argues and Edwards asserts, in the sense that the question ordinarily assumes. What gives reality to body, Plotinus holds, is Magnitude.[52] What confirms the material universe in being, adds Edwards, is the omnipresent activity of the Divine Mind. But, he cautions,

> When we say that the World, i.e. the material Universe, ex-
> ists no where but in the mind, we have got to such a degree
> of strictness and abstraction, that we must be exceedingly
> careful, that we do not confound and lose ourselves by misap-
> prehension. That is impossible, that it should be meant, that
> all the world is contained in the narrow compass of a few
> inches of space, in little ideas in the place of the brain; for
> that would be a contradiction; for we are to remember that
> the human body, and the brain itself, exist only mentally,
> in the same sense that other things do; and so that, which
> we call *place,* is an idea too. Therefore things are truly in
> those places; for what we mean, when we say so, is only, that
> this mode of our idea of place appertains to such an idea.[53]

Therefore, he concludes, we would not wish to be understood to deny that things are really what they seem to be. Nor does our view make void all Natural Philosophy. "For to find out the reasons of things, in Natural Philosophy, is only to find out the proportion of God's acting. And the case is the same, as to such proportions, whether we suppose the World, only mental, in our sense, or no.[54]

It is often said of Edwards that he is the most consistent of colonial American thinkers in that his fundamental ideas do not undergo any signifi-cant development, and this is for the most part true. The conception of true virtue as love to Being in general is the same in the Dissertation as in the Notes on the Mind. The doctrine of the Trinity sketched in the Miscellanies is in essence and expression the same with that elaborated in An Essay on the Trinity. However, the idealistic panentheism of the Edwardsian interpretation of the Trinity anterior to creation perforce gives way to a more conventional Christian theism when Edwards, governed by the authority of scripture, is impelled in his later works to an understanding of emanation in a sense compatible with the biblical account of creation.

III

> Therefore to speak more strictly according to truth, we may suppose, *that a disposition in God as an original property of his nature, to an emanation of his own infinite fulness was what excited him to create the world; and so that the emanation itself was aimed at by him as a last end of the creation.*[55]

The Dissertation Concerning the End for which God Created the World makes it clear that the Edwardsian conception of emanation, so far from being metaphorical, is as literal as any biblicist could wish. Thus, he thinks,

> it appears reasonable to suppose that it was what God had respect to as an ultimate end of his creating the world, to communicate of his own infinite fulness of good; or rather it was his last end, that there might be a glorious and abundant emanation of his infinite goodness ad extra or without himself, and the disposition to communicate himself, or diffuse his own FULNESS, which we must conceive of as being originally in God as a perfection of his nature, was what moved him to create the world.[56]

This exercise of God's perfections to produce a proper effect, the manifestation of his internal glory and fulness in a true external expression,[57] the com-

munication of his infinite bounty to the creature, all these, Edwards notes,
at first view may appear to be entirely distinct things; but
if we more closely consider the matter, they will appear to
be one thing, in a variety of views and relations. They are
all but the emanations of God's glory: or the excellent
brightness and fulness of the divinity diffused, overflowing,
and as it were enlarged; or in one word, existing ad extra.[58]

He likens this outpouring of God's glory to a fountain endlessly flowing,[59]
and thinks it "fitly compared to an effulgence or emanation of light from
a luminary."[60] The THING signified by that name, the glory of God,

when spoken of as the supreme and ultimate end of all God's
works, is the emanation and true external expression of
God's internal glory and fulness.... or, in other words, God's
internal glory extant in a true and just exhibition, or external existence of it.[61]

Withal, Edwards would not have us mistake this external existence for
something ontologically equal to, or spiritually separable from, God. As the
beams of the sun are something of the sun, but inferior to the sun itself, so
the creation qua emanation is something of God, but of an inferior order
of being.

Here is both an *emanation* and *remanation.* The refulgence
shines upon and into the creature, and is reflected back to
the luminary. The beams of glory come from God, are
something of God, and are reflected back again to their
original. So that the whole is *of* God, and *in* God, and *to*
God; and he is the beginning and the middle and the end.[62]

This being so makes possible that universal benevolence or love to Being in
general which for Edwards is alone true virtue. The very identification of space
with God is, apart from our human perspective, a reaffirmation of Edwards'

belief that apart from, or without, God, man is literally—nothing.

And here the matter might well be allowed to rest were it not for one fact still demanding explanation, i.e., the fact that Elwood's book clearly evidences its author's complete familiarity with the position just remarked. In view of his awareness of what Edwards has to say about emanation in the Dissertation and elsewhere, how could he have continued to see panentheism in such a view. Certainly his conclusion is not wholly to be accounted for on the assumption, previously noted, that neo-platonism and panentheism are one because they both deny the possibility of there being anything outside God. Nor is it safe to suppose that having made this assumption he was prepared to overlook the repeated references in the Dissertation to the internal glory and external existence. It is, I think, likely that he was influenced somewhat by Luce's misinterpretation of Berkeley, as a panentheist.[63] In the end, however, what does him in is not his misplaced confidence in the efficacy of Luce's argument nor yet his failure to grasp the anti-panentheistic implication of emanation, but rather his assumption that there are no more than three significant possibilities as regards the combination of the conventional two circles symbolic of the relation of God to the Universe. For the fact is that the history of theology evidences at least eight such possibilities, while the logic of the combination of unbroken and broken circles (see below) yields no less than twenty!

Let God be represented by one unbroken circle, and the Universe by another,[64] and we have five possible combinations, thus:

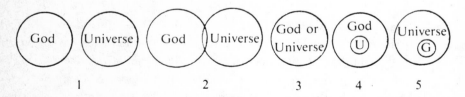

| 1 | 2 | 3 | 4 | 5 |

Having established to his own satisfaction that the Edwardsian conception of the God-Universe relation is not that of traditional theism, i.e., God and the Universe ontologically other (Fig.1), nor yet that of classical pantheism, i.e., God and the Universe mutually inclusive and indistinguishable (*Deus sive Natura*) (Fig. 3), Elwood concludes that the viewpoint of Edwards is that of panentheism, i.e., the Universe (literally) in God (Fig.4). The alternatives presented by Fig. 2 and 5, i.e., that there is something of God in the Universe and vice versa (Fig. 2), or that God is finite and as such inside the Universe (Fig. 5), our author does not pause to consider, presumably because he did not find these latter viewpoints historically relevant.[65]

Given that both God and the Universe are real; granting, that is, that God is not merely a name nor an abstraction, and that the Universe is something of substance for all that it may be the product of a Creator, the five alternatives distinguished above appear to exhaust the possibilities. That they do not really do so, however, becomes apparent in the attempt to determine that figure properly descriptive of Christian neo-platonism. That it cannot be Figure 4 our previous argument establishes. On similar grounds we may rule out Figures 2 and 5, and since Elwood himself has ruled out Figures 1 and 3, this must leave Christian neo-platonism unaccounted for. It remains, then, that our assumption as regards the reality of both God and the Universe is faulty. ("Given that both God and Universe are real...") But what of that theology whose Universe is a *theophany?*

To represent this notion adequately, what we require is not two unbroken circles, each symbolizing a concrete reality, but rather one unbroken circle and its shadow. Heretofore, as regards the circle symbolic of the Universe, provision has been made for the fact that there are two conceptions of the Universe to be accounted for; there is the Universe as Christian common-sense conceives it, the Universe as something real in and of itself, the Creation external to its Creator, and then there is the Universe according to Jonathan Edwards, the Universe as God's image or shadow. Presumably, Elwood would make one circle serve for both conceptions. Since this has neither logic nor tradition to recommend it, I propose a change. Let God, since He is for Edwards the Real as such, be represented as before by an unbroken circle; but let His image (the Edwardsian Universe) now be represented, as it should be, by an image of a circle (pictorialized as a broken line) and the result is five more possible combinations, as follows:

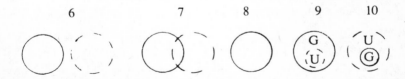

6   7   8   9   10

Here Figure 6 identifies the God-Universe relation as envisaged by Christian neo-Platonism, i.e., the Universe as the image or shadow of a God in no way dependent upon and hence ontologically other than it. That this is, in fact, Edwards' position is, I contend, established by the preceding account and by those several passages in the Miscellanies and in the later published writings wherein he is at pains to emphasize God's immutability and independence of the world.[66] As concerns the relation expressed by Figure 7, i.e., that of a Universe real to the degree that it participates in a God who, as manifest, is mere appearance, it is a position which finds no important advocates in the west,[67] albeit it approximates the Indian Mayavada (allowing that God as here envisaged $=$ Brahman). Nor with the possible exception of Job Durfee, has any American or European thinker ever seriously maintained that the One which, as Universe, is mere appearance, is, qua God, the Real (Figure 8), although the same seems indistinguishable from the viewpoint of the Visistadvaita Vedanta. On the other hand, the relation as pictorialized in Figure 9 is precisely that envisioned by Plotinus as the latter is interpreted by Pistorius (see footnote 44) Lastly, in Figure 10 we have illustrated a relation implicit in some Vedic texts and not unknown in Christian mysticism.[68]

That the foregoing constitutes but the barest sketch of the problem of the God-Universe relation and its various solutions does not, I think, invalidate the conclusion it implies. The illustrations offered of the ten of the twenty alternative possibilities may be in some cases open to question; what cannot be doubted is that the number of historically significant alternatives is such as to render inadmissible by any argument of a sort which suggests that a viewpoint admittedly not theistic or pantheistic is, as it were, by a process of elimination panentheistic. Edwards is a neo-platonist in his conception of the universe as an emanation and in his conviction that "if any creature be of such a nature that it proves evil in its proper place, or in the situation which God has assigned it in the universe, it is of an evil nature."[69] That this does not constitute his position a panentheism analysis of the God-universe relationship envisaged by neo-platonism makes plain and the circles confirm. It remains to consider the meaning and significance of this God-universe relationship as it bears upon the teaching of the major works of the Stockbridge years.

III

> Is it not better, that the good and evil which happens in God's
> world, should be ordered, regulated, bounded and determin-
> ed by the good pleasure of an infinitely wise Being, who
> perfectly comprehends within his understanding and con-
> stant view, the universality of things, in all their extent and
> duration...than to leave these things to fall out by chance,
> and to be determined by those causes which have no
> understanding or aim?[70]

The works of Edwards' later years, **Freedom of the Will, Original Sin,** the
two Dissertations, and the Observations of Faith, The Mysteries of Scripture, and Efficacious Grace, are highly praised and rarely read. Particularly
is this so for the first two books cited. Perry Miller's comment is typical:
"beyond all peradventure," he writes, "the **Freedom of the Will** is the cornerstone of Edward's fame....his most sustained intellectual achievement, the
most powerful piece of sheer forensic argumentation in American literature,"
and lamely confesses that, "actually, most of it is sterile to our reading."[71]
"I more than suspect," he adds, that "the book leads us to the very secret
of Jonathan Edwards,"[72] and coyly forbears to tell us just what the secret
is. Ola Winslow finds it tragic that "a mind capable of fashioning such an
architecture of defensive proof (could) fail to turn its own incisive powers
against the premise on which the argument (against Arminianism) rested,"[73]
while Alfred Owen Aldridge concludes that "in the realm of theology he (Edwards) was not a dynamic force."[74] To these, and other Edwards scholars inclined to the liberal side in matters religious, it is incomprehensible that a
thinker of Edwards' stature and "incisive powers" should fail to share their
progressive and emancipated views, and rather than involve themselves in the
question as to *why* he would actually *choose* to defend such doctrines as inherent depravity and moral necessity they prefer to decry these perverse positions as polemic, and never pause to recollect that no one was more sensitive to the condescension of the educated elite or more acutely aware of
the contempt in which evangelical religion was then held than Edwards himself.

> From this secret delusion (of their intellectual superiority)
> and prejudice they have almost all their advantages: 'tis the
> strength of their bulwarks and the edge of their weapons.
> And this is the main ground of all the right they have to treat
> their neighbors in so assuming a manner, and to insult others,
> perhaps as wise and good as themselves, as weak bigots, men
> that dwell in the dark caves of superstition, perversely set,
> obstinately shutting their eyes against the noonday light,
> enemies to common sense, maintaining the first born of ab-
> surdities, etc.[75]

For such as these, there is, Edwards believes, but one palliative. An impartial
consideration of the purpose of the **Freedom of the Will** and the rest "may
enable the lovers of truth better to judge, whose doctrine is indeed absurd,
abstruse, self-contradictory, and inconsistent with common sense, and many
ways repugnant to the universal dictates of the reason of mankind."[76] He is
serenely confident it will not prove to be experimental Calvinism.

Among the more recent interpreters of Edwards' thinking, only James Carse
sees clearly that beyond the anti-Arminian and contra-Pelagian polemic there
lies a deeper intention, and even he seems to think it to be nothing more than
a delineation of the fundamental propositions respecting our knowledge of
man.[77] It appears not to have occurred to any one save Clyde Holbrook, and
he only in part, that the Stockbridge writings are all of a piece; that the Observations are subsequently incorporated in substantial numbers into **Freedom
of the Will** and **Original Sin;** that these two are in content and intent not
two separate and distinct treatises but rather the two aspects of the subject
of one great volume whose pervading purpose is the squaring of the scriptural teaching with the conception of God as absolute sovereign. They seem
not to have appreciated the significance of the fact that the argument in each
and all of these works, excepting only the **The Nature of True Virtue,** is sustained and justified by copious draughts of scripture, and if this is lacking
in the second dissertation it is only because Edwards sees no pressing need
to remind his reader of the duty demanded in the first and great
commandment.

We have postulated that the **Freedom of the Will, Original Sin,** the two Dissertations and the Observations, particularly those respecting Efficacious Grace, all are parts of one great whole whose implicit purpose is the demonstration of the consistency of the doctrine maintained by Edwards and his school with the conception of God as absolute sovereign. If this is the case, then the proper question to be asked concerning these works is not whether Edwards or his antagonists have the better of the argument according to our modern perspective, but rather which of the two camps, the Arminian or the Calvinist, is in its teaching the more consistent with that conception of God which, as Edwards delights to point out,[79] both accept! The question is, whether Edwards correctly states the fact of the matter when he declares, "that 'tis the Arminian scheme, and not the scheme of the Calvinists, that is utterly inconsistent with moral government, and with all use of laws, precepts, prohibitions, promises, or threatenings," and adds, "neither is there any way whatsoever to make their principles consist with these things."[80]

The Arminians and their libertarian descendants affirm the freedom of the will and deny original sin. thereby, Edwards insists, they impugn the absolute sovereignty of God. For they say, that will only is free which is self determined, contingent and, prior to its act of willing, in a state of perfect indifference. But perfect indifference and absolute sovereignty are logically and ontologically incommensurable![81] Consequently, we must, Edwards argues, deny freedom of the will and affirm original sin.

If God is sovereign, that is, if he is and has "supreme, universal, and infinite *power,* whereby he is able to do what he pleases, without control, without any confinement of that power, without any subjection in the least measure to any other power; and so without any hindrance or restraint, that it should be either impossible, or at all difficult, for him to accomplish his will; and without any dependence of his power on any other power, from whence it should be derived, or which it should stand in any need of; so far from this, that all other power is derived from him, and is absolutely dependent on him,"[82] then it cannot be that man's will is free, at least in the sense in which Arminians and those like-minded envisage freedom. Liberty of indifference must and does give way to the determination of the will by the strongest motive;[83] self-determination of the will may be and is refuted by our recognition that every act of willing is excited by a motive which is the cause of that act of willing, and that (qua effect) by an antecedent cause, and so forth back to the eternal cause which is God. But if nothing can come to pass without a cause or reason why it exists in one manner rather than another, then "it will demonstrably follow that the acts of the will are never contingent, or without necessity....inasmuch as those things which have a cause, or reason of their existence, must (necessarily) be connected with their cause."[84]

Do we, then, by this assertion deny freedom of moral choice? By no means, answers Edwards, for "that necessity which has been explained, consisting in an infallible connection of the things signified by the subject and predicate of a proposition, as intelligent beings are the subjects of it, is distinguished into moral and natural necessity."[85] By the latter we are to understand what the term signifies in common speech, viz. that which must be avoided, is completed, inevitable, or unpreventable. But this is not the sense of the term as employed in the phrase 'moral necessity.' Here,

> It must be observed, that in what has been explained, as signified by the name of "moral necessity," the word "necessity" is not used according to the original design and meaning of the word; for....such terms....in common speech, and their most proper sense, are always relative; having reference to some supposable voluntary opposition or endeavor, that is insufficient. But no such oppositon, or contrary will and endeavor, is supposable in the case of moral necessity; which is a certainty of the inclination and will itself: which does not admit of the supposition of a will to oppose and resist it.[86]

That competent authorities can and have disagreed with respect to the cogency of Edward's distinction is not to the point. What matters most to Edwards is that what is said of the difference between moral and natural necessity, as well as what might be said of the cognate difference between natural and moral inability,[87] is what must be said if the sovereignty of God is to be rendered consistent with moral freedom of man.

A similar concern informs his defense of the doctrine of original sin. However, in this instance, the argument is not so much directed to the demonstration of the consistency of sin with sovereignty, as it is to showing the inconsistency of sovereignty with self-determination. That God could have created a sinless universe had he been so inclined, Edwards is not disposed to deny. That he was not so inclined, scripture bears witness, and Edwards is sufficiently impressed by this testimony to devote fully forty percent of his treatise on **Original Sin** to its exposition and exegesis. Of itself, he is inclined to think this witness sufficient. "'Tis fit, we should all know, that it don't become us to tell the Most High, how often he shall particularly explain and give the reason of any doctrine which he teaches, in order to our believing what he says. If he has at all given us evidence that it is a doctrine agreeable to his mind, it becomes us to receive it with full credit and submission; and not sullenly to reject it, because our notions and humors are not suited in the manner, and number of times, of his particularly explaining it to us."[88] "I cannot doubt," he adds in a passage subsequent to his scriptural exposition,

> but that a proper consideration of what is apparent and undeniable in fact, with respect to the dependence of the state and course of things in this universe on the sovereign constitutions of the supreme Author and Lord of all, "who gives none account of any of his matters, and whose ways are past finding out," will be sufficient, with persons of common modesty and sobriety, to stop their mouths from making peremptory decisions against the justice of God, respecting what is so plainly and fully taught in his Holy Word, concerning the derivation of a depravity and guilt from Adam to his posterity; a thing so abundantly confirmed by what is found in the experience of all mankind in all ages.[89]

Having thus laid the foundation and established the ultimate line of defense for the Great Christian Doctrine of Original Sin, Edwards is prepared to meet the attack of its most prominent critic, the English liberal theologian, John Taylor.[90]

70

While still minister at Northampton, Edwards had borrowed, read, and been much disturbed by, Taylor's **Scripture-Doctrine of Original Sin,** [91] and particularly by the argument "that if we come into the world infected with sinful and depraved dispositions, then sin must be *natural* to us; and if natural, then *necessary;* and if necessary, then *no* sin...."[92] That sin is necessary,Edwards agrees. Mankind, he is convinced, "are all naturally in such a state, as is attended, without fail, with this consequence or issue; that they universally run themselves into that which is, in effect, their own utter eternal perdition, as being finally accursed of God, and the subjects of his remedy-less wrath, through sin."[93] "Men are naturally so prone to sin that none ever fail of *immediately* transgressing God's law....as soon as they are capable ot it. In short, Taylor is, so far, correct; sin is natural to us, and as natural, necessary. But, Edwards insists, it does not follow from this that, if necessary, then no sin. For the necessity at issue is not natural necessity but moral necessity, and this latter does not absolve the sinner form the responsibility for his sin.

Moral necessity or no, the Arminian rejoins, the denial of self-determination to the will coupled with the affirmation of a necessary connection of the eternal cause to the created effects makes God the author of sin. I don't deny it, cries Edwards, if by the phrase 'the author of sin' "is meant the permitter....of sin....I say, if this be all that is meant, by being the author of sin, I don't deny that God is the author of sin (though I dislike and reject the phrase, as that which by use and custom is apt to carry another sense)....This is not to be the *actor* of sin, but on the contrary, of *holiness*....And I don't deny, that God's being thus the author of sin follows from what I have laid down."[95] But this, he contends, is no advantage to the generality of Arminians who acknowledge the absolute foreknowledge of God, For if God knows this much, in the utmost certainty and perfection,

> the way by which he comes by this knowledge makes no difference. If he knows it by the necessity which he sees in things, or by some other means; it alters not the case. But it is in effect allowed by Arminians themselves, that God's inviting and persuading men to do things, which he at the same time certainly knows will not be done, is no evidence

of insincerity: because they allow, that God has a certain
foreknowledge of all men's sinful actions and omissions. And
as this is implicitly allowed by most Arminians, so all that
pretend to own the Scriptures to be the Word of God, must
be constrained to allow it.[97]

If the Arminians, or those like-minded, would have it otherwise, they must
modify the conception of God as absolute sovereign to something less and
other than that, and they must demonstrate that this other and lesser Being
is the same with that self-revealed in scripture. Or, alternatively, they must
abandon scripture altogether and rely upon unaided reason to establish their
case. Failing either, Edwards triumphs.

For Edwards himself, however, the triumph would be meaningless without
the additional blessing of God's efficacious grace in that circumcision of the
heart which is called regeneration. For, he observes, "everything in the Christian scheme argues, that man's title to, and fitness for, heaven depends on some
great divine influence, at once causing a vast change, and not any such gradual
change as is supposed to be brought to pass by men themselves in the exercise of their own power."[98] This divine influence is, we are told, something
immediate and physical,[99] an infusion of the heart by God as the doer of
it;[100] the result of which is the attainment of the habits of true virtue and
holiness.[101] In the popular phrase, it is "a being born again,"[102] the same with
that spiritual resurrection spoken of in scripture as a dying unto sin and a
living unto righteousness.[103] In Edwards himself implicitly, and in his disciples
Bellamy and Hopkins explicitly, this cataclysmic change of heart, or being
born again, is the one thing essential, that which opens our eyes and hearts
to the truth of scripture and establishes our title to the name of Christian.

IV

With all his defects and the limitations of his techniques,
Edwards is a great modern in his refusal to confess that the
eternal world is an utter mystery....The apologist for emotion is no fundamentalist or anti-intellectual, and he could
criticize the Enlightenment because he was enlightened![104]

So says Perry Miller, and his scholarly reputation is such as to command our respect for his judgement. Not lightly, then, do I submit that in this particular conclusion he is mistaken. Edwards is no modern, great or lesser, if by that term one signifies a theologian free to frame his conception of God in accordance with the findings of contemporary science and psychology. Conversely, if to take every passage in the Bible at its face value be fundamentalism, then he is self-evidently a fundamentalist; if perpetually to champion revelation at the expense of reason be anti-intellectualism, then he is patently an anti-intellectual. Nor are these conclusions to be evaded by supposing, as Miller does, that there is in Edwards' public preaching and published writings "a gift held back, some esoteric divination that the listener (and reader) must make for himself."[105] If Edwards writings really are, as Miller suggests, "an immense cryptogram....an occult secret....almost a hoax, not to be read but to be seen through,"[106] then all is in the wind and we may as well make of the sermons, treatises, and dissertations anything—or nothing at all. If, on the other hand, they are, as seems likely, intended by their author to be received as arguments in defense of a consistent Calvinist Christianity, then Vincent Thomas' devastating criticism of Miller's view of Edwards is very much to the point. So far, in this case, is Edwards from being "a great modern," that it is more accurate to call him, as Tomas does, "a medieval philosopher."[107]

Everything here, of course, turns upon the question as to what constitutes a philosophy "medieval" rather than "modern." Tomas, following H.A. Wolfson, thinks that "a philosopher living in the eighteenth, or even the twentieth, century would be a "medieval" philosopher if his philosophy placed itself at the service of Scripture and was willing to take orders from it."[108] Is Edwards' philosophy at the service of Scripture? The case for an affirmative answer is, as Tomas makes it, exceptionally strong. "There are," he reminds us, "numerous places where he arrives at conclusions unacceptable to the modern mind, by arguments not entirely cogent to the modern mind. Yet these conclusions were credible, and these arguments were cogent, to Edwards. The reason is that he accepted Scripture as revealed truth, and the modern mind does not. In this sense, Edwards "took orders" from Scripture, just as an empiricist will not "take orders" from Scripture, but only from experience."[109] In this sense, then, his philosophy is "medieval." Is this to say it lacks contemporary relevance? On this question, Tomas hedges. Unlike Miller, he will not categorize medieval philosophy as "scholastic rubbish." But neither has he anything to say on its or on Edwards' behalf. We are left with the impression that a philosophy in the service of Scripture is no philosophy for our times.

Edwards' editor and biographer, Sereno Dwight, testifies that "he took his religious principles from the Bible and not from Treatises, or systems of Theology, or any work of man....he adhered to the main articles of the Reformed Religion, with an unshaken firmness and with a fervent zeal....As a theologian, he is distinguished for his *scriptural views* of divine truth."[110] Inspection of the Stockbridge writings confirms it. Excepting only the Dissertation on the Nature of True Virtue, and that only in part, all are shot through with scripture quoted, explained, and cited as authority. The enquiry into the Freedom of the Will, which Miller calls the cornerstone of Edwards' fame, has no other purpose than to justify the sovereignty of God to men of reason. The defence of the Great Christian Doctrine of Original Sin which, according to Miller, "is a strictly empirical investigation, an induction, in the manner of Boyle and Newton, of a law for phenomena," is actually nothing of the sort. Miller justifies his characterization by calling attention the methodological difference between **Original Sin** and the earlier **Freedom of the Will:** "this time the Arminian position is refuted as an inadequate hypothesis to account, scientifically or historically for the facts."[12] However, as Tomas points out, and Miller himself concedes, the word 'fact' as Edwards nearly always employs it, means statements in scripture taken as facts. When Edwards declares that his intention in **Original Sin** is "to proceed according to such rules and methods of reasoning, as are universally made use of, and never denied, or doubted to be good and sure, in *experimental philosophy,*"[113] his presupposition is not Cartesian but Biblical. Thus if service to scripture of itself suffices to constitute a philosophy medieval, then Edwards is without doubt a medieval philosopher.

Is this to say that Miller's characterization of Edwards as a "great modern" is wholly false? Not necessarily, and this because the respective criteria here offered for determining whether a philosophy is modern or medieval are logically independent of each other. To Miller, medievalism means scholastic logic-chopping[114] and service to scripture has nothing to do with the matter. Tomas conversely, is content to ring the changes on the theme of service to scripture, all the while refusing to commit himself on the question of the modernity of the Edwardsian ontology. Neither commentator, unfortunately, has anything specific to offer concerning the Edwardsian notion most relevant to the resolution of the question: modern or medieval?

I refer, of course, to Edwards' conception of Being. For in the final analysis, what constitutes a philosophy medieval or modern is not, as Miller seems to think, its cognizance of the conative process and its employment of reason (both are features of medieval scholasticism), nor yet as Tomas appears to believe, its espousal of scripture (for not every modernist disdains the Biblical witness), but rather its ontological orientation towards the categories of Being or Becoming. To the degree that an ontology stresses Being to the exclusion of Becoming, to that extent, all other factors being equal, it approximates medievalism; whereas to the degree that it emphasizes process and views permanence in terms of endurance rather than identity, to that extent it approaches the modernist perspective of Reality. By these standards it is evident that Edwards is much more the medievalist than the modern. His **Freedom of the Will** supposes that "there is a great absurdity in the nature of things simply considered....in denying being in general.[115] "Nothing," he adds afterwards, is more impossible than that the immutable God should be changed, by the succession of time; who comprehends all things, from eternity to eternity, in one, most perfect, and unalterable view; so that his whole eternal duration is *vitae interminabilis, tota simul,* and *perfecta possessio.* [116] That this "being in general" on which everything depends, and apart from which nothing exists, is God we learn from the Dissertation on the Nature of True Virtue, and God, as we know, changes not nor is changeable. Were it needful, it would be possible to multiply citations from the Stockbridge works testifying to Edwards' complete commitment to the category of Being. As for Becoming, that category has no part whatsoever in the Edwardsian ontology. In the treatises on Will, Sin, and Virtue the notion is nowhere even mentioned. In these, as in the Observations, there is nothing ontologically out of step with Scholasticism. In these, as in all of his writings, Edwards is at the service of, and taking his assumptions from, classical Christian dogma.

That Edwards was throughout inhibited by dogma Miller himself concedes in **Errand into the Wilderness**. There was, he notes in the essay 'From Edwards to Emerson', nothing to prevent the transcendentalists, "as there had been everything to prevent Edwards, from identifying their intuitions with the voice of God, or from fusing God and nature into the one substance of the transcendental imagination." Where Emerson could, and in Miller's view did, give himself over unrestrainedly to becoming a transparent eyeball of the Divine, Edwards "forced into his system every safeguard against identifying the inward experience of the saint with the Deity Himself, or of God with nature."[118] He was, as Miller says, "much too skilled in the historic problems of theology to lose sight of the distinction between God and the world or....to blur the all-important doctrine of the divine transcendence."[119] No more than Calvin himself was he prepared to compromise the divine perfection by proclaiming nature the garment of God. For him no less than for St. Thomas Aquinas[120]

> it is evident, by both scripture and reason, that God is infinitely, eternally, unchangeably, and independently glorious and happy: that he cannot be profited by, or receive anything from, the creature; or be the subject of any suffering, or diminution of his glory and felicity from any other being. The notion of God creating the world, in order to receive anything properly from the creature, is not only contrary to the nature of God, but inconsistent with the notion of creation; which implies a being receiving its existence, and all that belongs to it out of nothing.[121]

He too believes that "the first Being is self-existent, independent, of perfect and absolute simplicity and immutability, and the first cause of all things."[122] "The pure and perfect act of God is God, because," for Edwards as much as for the Doctor Angelicus, "God is a pure act."[123]

Of course, it may be, as Elwood appears to imply when he takes A.O. Lovejoy to task for associating Edwards with the theology of Aristotle, that the

Edwardsian "pure act" is not synonymous with the 'actus purus' of Scholasticism, since the former, so he seems to think, presupposes, as the latter does not, a creative power-to-be.[24] However, if the respective conceptions do differ,. it is surely incumbent on Edwards to explain, if he can, how God can be at once creative *and* immutable. In brief, it makes no real difference that his conception of "pure act" is as neoplatonic as it is aristotelian. The same questions arise in either case or in both cases taken in conjunction. How God can be once immutable and, as the hell-fire preacher says, so "dreadfully provoked" by sinners as to consider them "worthy of nothing else, but to be cast into the fire,"[125] baffles the post-Puritan imagination. The question that tormented St. Anselm: "how art thou compassionate, and, at the same time, passionless?....How, then, art thou compassionate and not compassionate, O Lord?"[126] is answered in the **Miscellanies,** as it was in the **Proslogium,** by an affirmation of both sides of the contradiction. The problem of St. Thomas respecting the unchangeability of the unchangeable will of God is resolved in the **Freedom of the Will,** as it had been in the **Summa Theologica,**[127] by a play on words.

In view of these similarities (and the list is indefinitely extendable) between the Scholastic ontology and that foreshadowed in the Miscellanies and developed in the Dissertations, the answer to the question 'medieval or modern?' is plain to see. Indeed, I submit that Perry Miller himself has supplied it in the foregoing passages cited. Nor is this answer to be impugned by recalling, as Miller is wont to do, the influence of Locke, and Smith, and Newton upon the Puritan sage. Edwards' modernism, such as it is, derives from his acceptance of the Lockean canons of empiricism and from his Humean conception of causality (with the factor of necessary connection added). He is classical in his conception of God and medieval in his belief in the existence of the devil, his assumption of the historicity of Adam, his expectations respecting the millenium, and in his firm conviction that the universe is somewhat less than six-thousand years of age.[128] By their cosmologies and ontologies shall ye know them, and the fact of the matter is that the cosmology and ontology of Jonathan Edwards departs in no important respect from that which Anselm adumbrated and Aquinas made the measure of Christian theological orthodoxy. If any further proof of it were needed, it is available in Edwards' expression of the doctrine of creation.

Committed by his faith to **Genesis** and **Malachi**,[129] Edwards can no more evade the insoluble problem implicit in the scriptural account of creation than could his medieval prodecessors. If God is perfect, why should he have troubled himself to create a world at all? The question, says St. Thomas, is impertinent. The matter is a mystery; the fact is a datum of the faith.[130] The answer, Edwards replies, is apparent in our conception of God. He is Good, and it is the nature of Goodness to communicate itself. To communicate himself, therefore, is God's motive in creation. But to communicate himself to whom? To the creature? For Edwards the communication *is the creation* of the creature! A strange conclusion, surely, and one not made much less so by our realization that the creature Edwards presumably has in mind is the spiritual Adam, the same who in **Original Sin** is conceived of as one with all humanity, which latter are many because God thinks of them as individuals.[131] How do we justify these assertions? By revelation, answers Edwards. The fact is a datum of the faith.

The same conviction sustains his notion of the physical creation. In number 1263 of the Miscellanies we read: "the creation of the matter of the material world out of nothing, the creation even of every individual atom or primary particle was by an operation perfectly arbitrary....it was by arbitrary act divine that the primary particles of matter were put into motion."[132] Subsequently, by a secondary operation, God employs the laws of nature antecedently established to bring to pass the world as it discloses itself to our experience. "So that the creation of particular natural bodies...was," Edwards concludes, "by a mixed operation partly arbitrary and partly by stated laws."[133] To this mixture of arbitrary with natural operations there is, however, one exception: the highest order of creatures viz., intelligent minds, are, he maintains, "wholly created, complete in their kind, by an absolutely arbitrary operation."[134] That there might be an inconsistency between this paraphrase of **Genesis** and the neoplatonism earlier noted seems not to have occurred to Edwards. As the remainder of number 1263 makes clear, for him the Six Days of Creation and the neoplatonic ladder of descent from the One are but slightly differing versions of the same event. Were it, however, to be brought to his attention that these cosmologies conflict in rather more than the matter of detail, there is no doubt but that he would opt for the cosmology of the Six Days. His every book and sermon witnesses his devotion to the scriptures. Where the Bible is inconsistent he will be inconsistent too. The inconsistency of his philosophy is, for the most part, no more than the consequence of this consistent biblicism. With St. Thomas he will have it that "the argument from authority based on divine revelation is the strongest."[135] What Aquinas is to neo-Thomism, Edwards ought to be to neo-orthodoxy. Indeed, it Elwood is to be believed,[136] that he already is.

V

> ...if every intelligent Being is some way related to Being in general, and is a part of the universal system of existence, and so stands in connection with the whole; what can its general and true beauty be, but its union and consent with the great whole?[127]

The two dissertations were not published in Edwards' lifetime. Written in 1755, towards the close of Edwards' Stockbridge sojourn, they remained with the mass of manuscript materials transferred by Sarah Edwards to her husband's sometime student, lifelong friend, and literary executor, the Rev. Samuel Hopkins. In 1765, seven years after Edwards' untimely death in consequence of an aberrant smallpox inoculation, he saw them through the press. For Hopkins the task was something more than a duty owed to a beloved mentor, more even than a labor of love, because for him these two short works, most particularly the second on the Nature of True Virtue, are the last and most important word of specification and justification of that true holiness which is the heart and soul of the new divinity.[138] For Perry Miller they are all this and then some: "These fragments," he rhapsodizes, are Edwards at his very greatest. The man for whom such studies as weary ordinary minds were "a natural play of genius" here let his mind play freely and spontaneously. He was prevented from completing the monumental system, but the heart of it is in these two extracts, albeit in miniature."[139] One may disagree with

Miller's hyperbole, indeed in this wise Miller disagrees with Miller, and yet concede the core of truth in his effusion, namely, that these are Edwards' most important contributions to the metaphysics of consistent Calvinism.

As with all seminal notions, so also here, the conception is at once sweeping and simple. The first and great commandment abjures us to love and glorify God and honor mankind even as we honor Him. In the language of philosophy this is to say that anything less than this, such as love of self, of others, of country, or of life itself, is not that love commanded. "Therefore," our author concludes,

> there is room left for no other conclusion, than that the primary object of virtuous love is Being, simply considered, or that true virtue primarily consists, not in love to any particular Being, because of their virtue or beauty, nor in gratitude, because they love us; but in a propensity and union of heart to Being simply considered; exciting *absolute* benevolence, (if I may so call it), to Being in general. I say true virtue *primarily* consists in this. For I am far from asserting, that there is no true virtue in any other love than this absolute benevolence.[141]

This other, "second object" of virtuous love recognized by Edwards is "virtuous benevolence itself in its object,"[142] by which he understands those other intelligent beings exhibiting a similar obedience to the great commandment. In the end, of course, benevolence excited in us by the benevolent propensities of other beings, comes to the same thing as pure benevolence to being in general. "For he that has a simple and pure good will to general existence, must love that temper in others, that agrees and conspires with itself. A spirit of consent to Being must agree with consent to Being."[143]

Simple enough, but Edwards will have it that this temper or frame of mind whereby such benevolence is excited is not something such as arises by the agency of any moral sense or sentiment, but rather comes to those thus blessed in the guise of a spiritual sense given by God, "whereby they *immediately* receive pleasure in the presence of the idea of true virtue in their mind."[144] "I observe," says Edwards,

> that God in giving to the creature such a temper of mind, gives that which is agreeable to what is by absolute necessity his own temper and nature. For, as has often been observed, God himself is in effect Being in general; and without all doubt it is in itself necessary, that God should agree with himself, be united with himself, or love himself....[145]

"He Himself flows forth, and He Himself is pleased and glorified."[146] To this conception everything that Edwards wrote converges. On it his arguments anent necessity and depravity depend. Failing to see this, much of the criticism and most of the compliment addressed to Edwards and his works is besides the point.

"I believe in order that I may understand." As it was with Anselm, so it is with Edwards, except that the object of the latter's belief is more particularly the witness of scripture and the assurance of a regeneration effected by God's efficacious grace. Grant that this belief is well-founded, and the value of his teaching, for those who, like himself, are servants of "the sovereign God," is unquestionable. Thus Bellamy will faithfully delineate his argument for necessity, and Hopkins apply his conception of spiritual rebirth to a later generation. Emmons will ground his system in the Edwardsian notion of divine sovereignty, while Park emphasizes the role of the religious affections. Dwight and Taylor will wrestle with the freedom of the will, and Woods and Ware agree to disagree about original sin and other serious matters. In sum, wherever in Nineteenth Century America the theological issues are debated, one finds Edwardsian ideas, defended, criticized, sometimes ridiculed, but never, or scarcely ever, ignored.

If the really seminal thinker is he who defines the problem rather than they who work away at solutions, then Edwards is a thinker of the first rank. By any other criterion, his philosophy is an anachronism. There are today no neoplatonists as such. Nor is the Sixth Way a live option in contemporary Western theology. The modern mind does not rest easy in a view which makes of man and nature shadows of a substance unimaginable. He was by his own lights a consistent Calvinist, nor did he ever aspire to any higher dignity than that phrase implies. What he required of those ministerial candidates who

came before him for examination, namely, to be sound in the faith and of
a disposition to be faithful, he ever, in life, strove to be.

> And there is reason to hope that though dead, he will yet
> speak for ages to come, to the great advantage of the church
> of Christ, and immortal welfare of many souls--and that his
> publications will produce a yet greater harvest of happiness
> to man and glory to God in the day of the Lord![47]

82

Bibliographical Essay

An excellent and comprehensive introduction to the Edwards literature published up to 1970 is provided by Everett H. Emerson, 'Jonathan Edwards', in **Fifteen American Authors before 1900: Bibliographic Essays and Criticism,** edited by Robert A. Rees and Earl N. Harbert (Madison: University of Wisconsin Press, 1971). Since the publication of this bibliography, three more volumes of the definitive Yale Edition of the **Works of Jonathan Edwards** have been issued: **Original Sin** (1970), edited by Clyde A. Holbrook; **The Great Awakening** (1972), edited by C.C. Goen; and **Apocalyptic Writings** (1977), edited by Stephen J. Stein. Yale has also issued in paperback **Freedom of the Will** (1957), edited by Paul Ramsey, and to complete the series published to date, **Religious Affections** (1959), edited by John E. Smith. The important Dissertation on **The Nature of True Virtue** is available in a paperback edition (1960) published by the University of Michigan Press (Ann Arbor paperback #AA37). The long promised volumes of the Miscellanies, to be edited by Thomas Schafer, are still awaited as of this writing. In the meantime, the available selection remains that of H.G. Townsend, **The Philosophy of Jonathan Edwards from His Private Notebooks** (Eugene: University of Oregon Press, 1955). For the reader new to Edwards there are two anthologies: Clarence Faust and Thomas Johnson, **Jonathan Edwards, Representative Selections** with Introduction, Bibliography, and Notes (New York: Hill & Wang, 1962) and Ola Elizabeth Winslow, **Jonathan Edwards, Basic Writings** (New York: New American Library, Signet Classics, paperback, 1966). Of the two, Faust and Johnson is the most substantial (434 pages to Winslow's 253). Both, however, offer carefully abridged versions of the major sermons and treatises plus a variety of biographical materials and excerpts from the philosophically important early notes and essays. A more recent selection of much the same material is Harold P. Simonson, **Selected Writings of Jonathan Edwards** (New York: Ungar, 1970).

Ola Elizabeth Winslow, **Jonathan Edwards 1703-1758** (New York: Macmillan, 1940) is still the standard biography. Winslow endorses the received view, i.e., that the greatness of Edwards as a thinker is seriously qualified by his decision to defend in detail "an outworn dogmatic system instead of

letting the new truth find more appropriate forms of its own." (326) She gives
short shrift to the quest and none at all to the neo-platonic conception of
God. In these respects, Perry Miller, **Jonathan Edwards** (New York: William
Sloane Associates, 1949) is much to be preferred. The organization of the
book, juxtaposing chapters of doctrinal expositon with chapters of external
biography, works very well. Miller's judgements are always interesting, frequently provocative, and, in the opinion of this reader, occasionally wrong.
But all in all this is a brilliant book. The distaff side of Edwards' life is engag-
ingly delineated by Elizabeth D. Dodds, **Marriage to a Difficult Man, The
"Uncommon Union" of Jonathan and Sarah Edwards** (Philadelphia:
Westminster Press, 1971).

The student of Edwards is fortunate in the number and quality of recent
critical and expository studies devoted to the various facets of his thought.
Since Emerson is a sufficient guide to the pre-1970 literature, it were
superfluous here to echo his remarks in re: John H. Gerstner, **Steps to Salvation: The Evangelistic Message of Jonathan Edwards** (Philadelphia, 1960);
James Carse, **Jonathan Edwards & the Visibility of God** (New York, Scribner's,
1967); Alfred Owen Aldridge, **Jonathan Edwards** The Theology of Jonathan
Edwards, A Reappraisal (New York: Doubleday Anchor, 1966); Edward H.
Davidson, **Jonathan Edwards: The Narrative of a Puritan Mind** (Cambridge:
Harvard University Press, 1968); and Roland Andre Delattre, **Beauty and Sensibility in the Thought of Jonathan Edwards** (New Haven: Yale University
Press, 1968) With the exception of this last, which I find rather more significant than does Emerson, I would not disagree in substance with any of his
judgements, with one exception. I do think he is overly harsh in his estimate
of Elwood when he says that "the book lacks both seriousness and conviction." For all that I disagree with Elwood's thesis in re Edwards' alleged panentheism, I find Elwood's insight into the Edwardsian conception of God
superior to that of any of the aforementioned. As for works published subsequent to Emerson, perhaps the most useful is Clyde A. Holbrook, **The Ethics
of Jonathan Edwards: morality and aesthetics** (Ann Arbor: University of
Michigan Press, 1973), albeit the book would be the better for the author's
having the courage of his convictions. Tending to the opposite extreme as
regards sectarian advocacy is Harold P. Simonson, **Jonathan Edwards,**

Theologian of the Heart (Grand Rapids: Eerdmans, 1974). The author, a professor of English, approaches his subject from the standpoint of a literary critic, which is perfectly justifiable particularly if he were more objectively critical. A similar reluctance to come to terms with basic principles diminishes the usefulness of William J. Scheick, **The Writings of Jonathan Edwards Theme, Motif, and Style** (College Station: Texas A & M University Press, 1975). This is largely a rehearsal of the themes of the major works. Nothing new is advanced, but the beginning student may find Scheick's summaries helpful. Then there is **Jonathan Edwards, His Life and Influence,** papers and discussion by Conrad Cherry, Wilson H. Kimnach, Charles Wetzel, Donald Jones, and Edward Cook, moderated and edited by Charles Angoff (Cranbury: Associated University Presses, 1975. This is a transcript of an afternoon of Edwards-talk, most of it generalities. Lastly, a book I have not seen, but look forward to reading, Miriam Luisi, **The Community of Consent in the Thought of Jonathan Edwards** (New York: Fordham University Press, 1976).

The periodical literature on Edwards is extensive, and again, for articles published before 1974, I would refer the reader to Emerson and to the substantial bibliographies supplied in Faust & Johnson, Delattre, Cherry, and Scheick. Of the studies published since 1974, two by the general editor of the Yale edition, John E. Smith, are noteworthy: 'Jonathan Edwards: Piety and Practice in the American Character,' **Journal of Religion,** 54 (1974), 166-180, attempts to clarify the meaning of Edwards' appeal to religious experience and to explain the experimentally empirical character of his theology; with this should be read Smith's, 'Jonathan Edwards as Philosophical Theologian,' **Review of Metaphysics,** 30 (1976), 306-324, which emphasizes the Edwardsian conception of God as self-communicating being. William J. Scheick, 'The Grand Design: Jonathan Edwards' History of the Work of Redemption,' **Eighteenth Century Studies,** 8 (1975), 300-314, reviews and analyzes the 1739 series of discourses on the continuity of Divine Providence. At the other end of the Edwardsian philosophical spectrum is J.D. Stamey, 'Newton's Time, Locke's Ideas, and Jonathan's Spiders,' **Proceedings of the New Mexico and West Texas Philosophical Society** (April, 1974), 79-87. The consequences of the life of true virtue are explored by Robert B. Westbrook, 'Social Criticism and the Heavenly City of Jonathan Edwards,' **Soundings,** 59 (1976), 396-412. A number of recent estimates of Edwards' thought are reviewed by Roy R. Thomas, 'The Relevance of Jonathan Edwards' Thought to the Problems of Twentieth Century America,' **Journal of International and Comparative Studies,** 5 (Spring, 1972), 68-69. Unfortunately, the reviewer does not come to any specific conclusion with respect to the question implicit in his title.

Some of the books noted above began as dissertations. The following dissertations, relevant to our subject, may well end up as books: Patricia Anne Wilson, **The Theology of Grace in Jonathan Edwards,** Ph.D dissertation, University of Iowa (Department of Religion), 1973; Richard C. DeProspo. **Nature and Spirit in the Writings of Jonathan Edwards,** Ph.D dissertation, University of Virginia, 1977; Donald Louis Weber, **The Image of Jonathan Edwards in American Culture,** Ph.D dissertation, Columbia University, 1978; Margaret S. Batschelet, **Jonathan Edwards' use of Typology: A Historical and Theological Approach,** Ph.D dissertation, University of Washington, 1977; and Marcus D. Bryant, **History and Eschatology in Jonathan Edwards: A Critique of the Heimert Thesis,** Ph.D dissertation, St. Michael's College (Canada), 1976.

[1] Jonathan Edwards, **Freedom of the Will,** Volume 1 of **The Works of Jonathan Edwards** edited by Paul Ramsey (New Haven: Yale University Press, 1957), 131. Hereafter cited as **FoW.**

[2] Jonathan Edwards, **A Divine and Supernatural Light Immediately imparted to the Soul by the Spirit of God, Shown to be both a Scriptural, and Rational Doctrine** (Boston: S. Kneeland, 1734), 25. Evans 3768. Hereafter cited as **Light.**

[3] Perry Miller, **Jonathan Edwards** (New York: William Sloane Associates, 1949), 44.

[4] Jonathan Edwards, **Original Sin,** Volume 3 of **The Works of Jonathan Edwards** edited by Clyde A. Holbrook (New Haven: Yale University Press, 1970), 167. Hereafter cited as **OS.**

[5] The first being **God Glorified in the Work of Redemption, by the Greatness of Man's Dependence upon him, in the Whole of it** (Boston: Kneeland & Green for Henchman, 1731). Evans 3415.

[6] **FoW,** 142.

[7] This is not, however, to say that, for Edwards, there are no *innate dispositions!* See **OS** 224, 228, 229, 389-412.

[8] **Light,** 10, 16.

[9] Ibid., 17.

[10] Ibid., 26.

[11] Jonathan Edwards, **Works** (Worcester: Isaiah Thomas, 1808), I. 31.

[12] Ibid., 34.

[13] Three of these were actually spent at Wethersfield. Only in his senior and postgraduate years was Edwards resident in New Haven.

[14] **Works** 1. 41.

[15] Memoir in **Works** 1, iv, 62-81. See also, C.C. Goen, Editor's Introduction, **The Great Awakening,** Vol. 4 of the Yale Edition of **The Works of Jonathan Edwards,** and Ola Elizabeth Winslow, **Jonathan Edwards,** Book Two.

[16] Jonathan Edwards, **Religious Affections** (New Haven: Yale University Press, 1959), 210.

[17] Jonathan Edwards, Preface to Joseph Bellamy's **True Religion Delineated** etc. in **The Great Awakening** (New Haven: Yale Univesity Press, 1972). 569.

[18] Jonathan Edwards, 'Of Being', in **The Philosophy of Jonathan Edwards from His Private Notebooks,** edited by Harvey G. Townsend (Eugene: University of Oregon Press, 1955), 9. Hereafter cited as **Notebooks.**

[19] **Notebook,** 1.

[20] Ibid.

[21] Ibid., 2. My italics.

[22] Ibid., 30.

[23] Ibid., 7, 8.

[24] Ibid., 8. Or, as Willard might say, in the Abstract.

[25] Francis MacDonald Cornford, **Greek Religious Thought** (Boston Press, 1950), 42.

[26] Ibid., 128.

[27] **Heliades,** Fragment 7.

[28] **Enneads** (McKenna translation), 2nd edition, revised by B.S. Page (London: Faber and Faber, 1956), VI. vi. 7.

[29]**On the Infinite Universe and Worlds** translated by Dorothea Waley Singer in **Giordano Bruno, His Life and Thought** (New York: Henry Schuman, 1950), 270.

[30]Most specifically and particularly in **Christian Faith and Natural Science** (New York: Harper and Brothers, 1953). See R.C. Whittemore, 'Karl Heim: Panentheism and the Space of God', **Concordia Theological Monthly**, 30 (1959), 824-837.

[31]**The Philosophical Theology of Jonathan Edwards** (New York: Columbia University Press, 1960), 6. Hereafter cited as Elwood.

[32]Ibid., 21.

[33]Ibid., 57.

[34]**Notebooks**, 87.

[35]Ibid., 262.

[36]Ibid., 183.

[37]Ibid., 17, 18.

[38]Ibid., 183.

[39]Ibid., 48.

[40]**The Works of President Edwards** in ten volumes, edited by Sereno Edwards Dwight (New York: G. & C. & H. Carvill, 1830), III 38. Hereafter cited as **Works (Dwight edition).**

[41]**Notebooks**, 152.

[42]Ibid., 47.

[43]In fairness to Elwood it should be noted that he nowhere specifically says as much. On the other hand, the whole tenor of his book implies his acceptance of the proposition, and, indeed, were it not presupposed his argument must dissolve.

[44]Everything here turns upon the meaning attached to 'duplicated'. The religious assumptions of a later (Christian) age have invariably operated to equate emanation with duplication and the latter with creation. Unable to put off the presuppositions of their Christian environment, the generality of commentators have tended to perpetuate the conviction that duplication is creation. A detailed account of the difficulties and inconsistencies attached to this Christianized neo-platonism, particularly as that is expressed in the interpretations of Plotinus offered by Edward Caird and Dean Inge, is provided by Philippus Villiers Pistorius, **Plotinus and Neoplatonism.** (London: Bowes and Bowes, 1952).

[45]Pistorius, 20. For a detailed analysis and evaluation of the Pistorius interpretation see, Robert C. Whittemore, 'Panentheism in Neoplatonism', **Tulane Studies in Philosophy,** XV (1966), 47-70.

[46]Plotinus, **The Enneads.** Translated by Stephen McKenna. Second edition revised by B.S. Page (London: Faber & Faber, 1956), V. 5, 9. All subsequent references are to this edition.

[47]**Notebooks**, 260.

[48]**Enneads,** III. 6, 6.

[49]Ibid., III. 6, 7.

[50]Ibid.

[51]**Notebooks**, 36.

[52]Magnitude, as Plotinus understands it, "is not, like Matter, a receptacle' it is an Ideal-Principle; it is a thing standing apart to itself, not some definite mass." **Enneads,** III. 6, 17.

[53]**Notebooks**, 39.

[54]Ibid.

88

[55]Jonathan Edwards, **Dissertation Concerning the End for which God Created the World,** in **Works** (Worcester: Isaiah Thomas, 1808), 6. 34. All future references are to this edition. This work, as Hornberger notes, is widely regarded by competent authorities as Edward's most important work, containing his most mature opinion respecting ontology. Consequently, what it has to tell us about the meaning of 'emanation' must be taken as definitive. See Theodore Hornberger, 'The Effect of the New Science on the Thought of Jonathan Edwards', **American Literature,** 9 (1937), 204.

[56]**The End for which God Created the World, Works** 6. 33.

[57]Ibid., 6. 116.

[58]Ibid., 6. 117.

[59]Ibid., 6. 32.

[60]Ibid., 6. 119.

[61]Ibid., 6. 117.

[62]Ibid., 6. 120-121. Those who have heeded the distinction earlier noted between panentheism and neoplatonism will not, I hope, be tempted to read panentheism into Edwards' employment of this phrase 'in God', etc.

[63]A.A. Luce, **Berkeley's Immaterialism** (London: Nelson, 1945), 69-77. 'Misinterpretation' because Luce falls into the same trap as ensnares Elwood; he too takes the fact of immaterialism's implying nothing outside God to mean that immaterialism is panentheism. See Elwood, 40, 169-170.

[64]A similar symbolism (a dot inside a circle) is used by Edwards himself. See **Original Sin** (Yale edition), 87 322n.

[65]In fact, Figure, 2, God and the Universe in partial interaction and both real, is the position of the German philosopher, Christian Ehrenfels and the American theologian, Edgar Sheffield Brightman, while Figure 5 approximates the view point of John Dewey as expressed in **A Common Faith** (God there standing for men's real values and ideals).

[66]See **Notebooks,** 146-149; also **FoW,** 182, 377, 383; also **True Virtue** (Ann Arbor paperback edition), 17-18, 30, 40-41.

[67]Herein is exemplified one basic difference between oriental and occidental philosophical theologies. For the relation signified by Figure 7 is precisely that envisaged by Sankara.

[68]I omit consideration of the remaining ten logical possibilities, the first five of which reverse the relation pictorialized in Figures 6-10; the final five comprising the possible combinations of two broken-line circles.

[69]**OS,** 125.

[70]**FoW,** 405.

[71]**Jonathan Edwards,** 251.

[72]Ibid., 276.

[73]**Jonathan Edwards 1703-1758,** 303. My italics.

[74]**Jonathan Edwards** (New York: Washington Square Press, 1964), 163. According to Aldridge, "he led the resistance to change for a time, but established no major school and imposed no new direction." Ibid. It is basic to the thesis of the present work that Aldridge is, at least as far as this particular conclusion is concerned, egregiously mistaken.

[75]**FoW,** 363-364. See also **FoW** 430n-431n and **OS** 423f.

[76]Ibid., 364.

[77]James Carse, **Jonathan Edwards and the Visibility of God** (New York: Scribner's, 1967), 53.

[78]In his Introduction to the Yale edition of **Original Sin,** Holbrook notes that Edwards "apparently....contemplated producing one major treatise which would have included what we now know as **Original Sin, The Nature of True Virtue,** and the **End for Which God Created the World."** **OS** 22. See also **OS** 433.

[79]**FoW** 416. See also **FoW** 257-269, 277-280, 286, 328-333, 349, 435.

[80]Ibid., 304.

[81]Ibid., 194, 198, 207, 212, 238, 259, 419, 424, 433.

[82]Ibid., 378-380.

[83]Ibid., 141-142, 148, 225, 394.

[84]Ibid., 213. See also **FoW** and for a different perspective, **OS** 194-195.

[85]Ibid., 156.

[86]Ibid., 159.

[87]See **FoW** 305, 307, 311.

[88]**OS** 272.

[89]Ibid., 409.

[90]A Lancashireman, born at Scotford in 1694, and educated at the non-conformist academy at Whitehaven, Taylor was ordained to the charge of a chapel at Kirkstead, in Lincolnshire in 1716. In 1733 he was called to the Church at Norwich, which parish he served first as junior and later as senior pastor for twenty-five years. Here were written the works which disturbed Edwards, i.e., **The Scripture-Doctrine of Original Sin** and its companion volume, **A Key to the Apostolic Writings and a Paraphrase with Notes on the Epistle to the Romans.** In 1757 he left Norwich for a divinity tutorship at Warrington Academy. He died in 1761.

[91]John Taylor, **The Scripture-Doctrine of Original Sin, Proposed to Free and Candid Examination** (London, 1740).

[92]**OS** 375.

[93]Ibid., 113.

[94]Ibid., 134.

[95]**FoW** 399.

[96]Ibid., 416.

[97]Ibid.

[98]Jonathan Edwards, **Observations Concerning Efficacious Grace,** in **Works** (Worcester edition), 5. 472.

[99]Ibid., 454.

[100]Ibid., 453.

[101]**OS** 363.

[102]Ibid., 361-369.

[103]Ibid., 364.

[104]Perry Miller, **Jonathan Edwards,** 237-238.

[105]Ibid., 50-51.

[106]Ibid., 51.

[107]Vincent Tomas 'The Modernity of Jonathan Edwards', **The New England Quarterly**, XXV (1952), 71.

[108]Ibid., 70.

[109]Ibid., 77.

[110]Memoir, in **Works** (Dwight edition), I. 609. Dwight's italics.

[111]**Jonathan Edwards**, 267.

[112]Ibid.

[113]**OS** 167.

[114]Unfortunately for his thesis, he appears to have overlooked a perfectly splendid piece of Edwardsian scholastic logic-chopping in re God's will respecting sin. Note **OS** 409 and compare with St. Thomas Aquinas, **Summa Theologica** I. Q. 19, article 9, reply objection 3.

[115]**FoW** 182.

[116]Ibid., 268.

[117]Perry Miller, **Errand into the Wilderness** (Cambridge: Belknap Press, 1956), 203.

[118]Ibid., 195.

[119]Ibid.

[120]It will be rejoined that Edwards himself was so far from being aware of the affinity of his ontology with that of Aquinas, that he ridicules the writings of the latter as being so much scholastic rubbish. And so, by implication at least, he does (see **FoW** 228). On the other hand, there is nothing in Edwards' works, published or unpublished, to suggest that he enjoyed anything more than a hearsay knowledge of the Summas.

[121]**Works** (Dwight edition), III, 13.

[122]**FoW** 377.

[123] **Notebooks**, 256.

[124]Elwood, 28.

[125] Jonathan Edwards, **Sinners in the Hands of an Angry God** in **Works** (Dwight edition), VII, 170.

[126]St. Anselm, **Proslogium** (Chicago: Open Court, 1948), 13.

[127]St. Thomas Aquinas, **Summa Theologica I**, Question 19, article 7.

[128]These convictions are expressed in various of Edwards' sermons and most dramatically in his unfinished **History of Redemption.**

[129]Specifically, **Malachi** 3:6 and those related passages in scripture which Edwards takes as his authority for asserting the immutability of God (see **FoW** 254).

[130]**Summa Theologica I,** question 46, article 2.

[131]**OS** 260, 389-391, 410, 422.

[132]**Notebooks**, 187, 188.

[133]Ibid., 188.

[134]Ibid., 189.

[135]**Summa Theologica I,** question 1, article 8, reply objection 2. For Edwards' views on the subject, see **Observation on the Scriptures;—their Authority and Necessity**, in **Works** (Dwight edition), VII, 244-261; a;nd also **The Insufficiency of Reason as a Substitute for Revelation**, Ibid., 261-277; and also **Notes on the Bible, Works** (Dwight edition), IX, 115-158.

[136]Elwood, 3, 7, 9-11, 155.

[137]Jonathan Edwards, **Two Dissertations,** II, **The Nature of True Virtue** (Boston: S. Kneeland, 1765), 117. Evans 9962. For readability the edition of this work edited by William K. Frankena (Ann Arbor: University of Michigan, Ann Arbor paperbacks, 1960) is much to be preferred. For reference, however, I have preferred to use the original edition despite, and because of, its author's penchant for italics and capitalization of key words. These do, I submit, make for a definite affective tone which it was Edwards' intention to emphasize, and that, I think; ought to be preserved. Then too, the Frankena edition is itself a modernization of a later edition in which a number of words and phrases in the original have been deleted for reasons known only to the editor.

[138]See Chapter IV, Section II of the present work.

[139]**Jonathan Edwards,** 285.

[140]Recalling Miller's similar claim with respect to **A Divine and Supernatural Light** (see above) and keeping in mind his fulsome praise of the **Freedom of the Will** (see above beginning Section III).

[141]**True Virtue,** 121.

[142]Ibid.

[143]Ibid.

[144]Ibid., 185. My italics.

[145]Ibid., 186.

[146]**Notebooks,** 152.

[147]Samuel Hopkins, **Memoir of the Rev. Jonathan Edwards** (London: James Black, 1815), vii-ix.

The Commandment Calvinism
Of Joseph Bellamy

"He wrote extensively; he thought deeply: he opposed his critics vigourously. But all of it, as he saw it, was in defense of the soverign God."[1]

THE COMMANDMENT CALVINISM OF JOSEPH BELLAMY

> Thou shalt love the Lord thy God with all thy heart, and
> with all thy soul, and with all thy mind.
> This is the first and great commandment. And the second
> is like unto it. Thou shalt love thy neighbor as thyself.

On August 4th, 1750, five years before he would finish his dissertation on the Nature of True Virtue, Jonathan Edwards signed his Preface to Joseph Bellamy's **True Religion Delineated**. The chronology is of interest because it suggests the possibility that it was Edwards who was indebted to Bellamy for the root idea of what Joseph Haroutunian has felicitously named 'The Theology of the Great Commandment,'[2] and not, as is usually assumed, Bellamy, who, unoriginally, echoes Edwards. Withal, there is no hard evidence, apart from this fact, that Bellamy published prior to Edwards, to confirm any such indebtedness, and it is probable that Commandment Calvinism, so-called from its assumption of **Matthew** 22:37-39 as the theological norm, owes as much to the one as to the other.

They were very good friends, had been so, indeed, since young Bellamy, aged seventeen, recently graduated from Yale,[4] and determined to a career in the ministry, had arrived at Edwards' door bent upon obtaining the tutelage of the brightest of the New Lights. Despite his tender years Bellamy was no tyro in theology. He had had the usual dosage of divinity in college, and afterwards read the standard authors with his pastor, the Rev. Samuel Hall of Cheshire. Sometime shortly before his application to Edwards, he had undergone a conversion experience,[5] and following his departure from Northampton in the spring of 1737, he obtained his license to preach. For several months thereafter he supplied various pulpits in Massachusetts and Connecticut and western Massachusetts, principally at Worcester, and subsequently at North Purchase (Bethlem), Connecticut, at which place he remained for fifteen months in 1738-39. The following year, their petition to the General Assembly having been successful, the Bethlehem[6] congregation was formally incorporated, and Bellamy's preaching and person having proven eminently satisfactory to them, he was invited to settle. He was called in February 1740, accepted the call in March, was ordained to the church as their pastor in April, and remained with them until his death on March 6th, 1790.

Like Willard before him and Emmons after, Bellamy's medium was the sermon, and even by the severe standards of the day, his product was prodigious. Tryon Edwards tells us that in the years 1741-43 he preached some 458 sermons in 213 pulpits in addition to the lectures and sermons regularly delivered to his Bethlehem congregation. By far the greatest portion of his published work is sermonic in source and structure. **True Religion Delineated,**[7] the most widely read of his various writings, is itself the reworked substance of some two score and more sermons on the major themes of Calvinism as these are understood and justified by Edwards and his circle. Neither aspiring to the dignity of a system of doctrines nor condescending to the simplicities of a popular exposition, the book aims to vindicate the new divinity to the educated laity, and in this it was successful to a degree beyond anything achieved by Edwards himself.

II

The grand question before us is, What is true religion? And this is the general answer: It consists in a real conformity to the law, and in a genuine compliance with the gospel.[8]

What is the precise measure of the duty which God requires of us in his law? Just that, replies Bellamy, which is expressed by our blessed Saviour in his answer to the question: "Master, which is the great commandment in the law? To which he answers: Thou shalt love the Lord thy God with all thy heart, etc."[9] To thoroughly understand this commandment, and the second like unto it, is, Bellamy believes, to know at once every duty enjoined in the law and inculcated by the prophets.

We are commanded to love, which presupposes knowledge of the object of that love, that is, that we see God to be just such a one as justifies the love demanded. "For," declares Bellamy, "if our apprehensions of God are not right, it is not God we love, but only a false image of him framed in our own fancy."[10] He is thinking here of the notion of God as framed by philosophical speculation and employed in natural theology. Such a notion, he is sure, must be false,

> For such a knowledge of God as consists merely in specula-
> tion, let it rise ever so high, and be ever so clear, will never
> move us to love him. Mere speculation, where there is no
> sense of beauty, will no sooner fill the heart with love, than
> a looking-glass will be filled with love by the image of a
> beautiful countenance....And a mere speculative knowledge
> of God, will not, cannot, beget a sense of his beauty in be-
> ing what he is![1]

Indeed, the more such knowledge one possesses, the likelier their dislike, or even hatred, of all things divine. The clearer sight and sense the sinner has of God, the more plain his perception of the contrariety between the divine and the depraved.

> From all of which it is exceedingly manifest that the clearest
> speculative knowledge of God is so far from bringing an
> unholy heart to love God, that it will only stir up the more
> aversion; and therefore that knowledge of God which lays
> the foundation of love, must imply not only right apprehen-
> sions of what God is, but a sense of his glory and beauty
> in being such![2]

Now it is manifest, thinks Bellamy, that rational creatures, acting as such, are always influenced by motives. The principal motive to an action is, he argues, always the ultimate end of that action; hence, if God appears to us as the supreme and most worthy good,

> then God, his honor and interest, will be principal motive
> and ultimate end of all we do. If we love God supremely,
> we shall live to him ultimately; if we love him with all our
> hearts, we shall serve him with all our souls', just as, on the

other hand, if we love ourselves above all, then self-love will absolutely govern us in all things; if self-interest will be the last end.[13]

But to love God so as to serve him, is precisely what the law requires; consequently, to love self, so as to serve self, is rebellion against the majesty of heaven.

Consequently, the first and chief motive bearing upon our adherence to the great commandment is "his infinite dignity and greatness, glory and excellency; or, in one word, *his infinite amiableness.* We are to love him with all our hearts, because he is the Lord; because he is what he is, and just such a being as he is."[14] Bellamy can never quite bring himself to speak with Edwards of God as Being-in-general. For the disciple, God is always "a being," albeit a being necessarily infinite in power, understanding, wisdom, and goodness: eternal, unchangeable, independent, self-sufficient and all-sufficient.

He takes state; sets up himself as a God; bids all the world adore him, love and obey him, with all their hearts; and that upon pain of eternal damnation, in case of the least defect; and promises eternal life and glory, in case of perfect obedience.[15]

Such, according to our author, is the right representation and apprehension of the object of that love which is required in the first and great commandment. No more than Edwards, will he allow that even the least degree of self-love is compatible with the disinterested benevolence all men owe to deity. The perfect love which both require precludes the slightest self-esteem. Before God the only proper creaturely conduct is complete submission and unflagging obedience. Only that love to God is of the right sort which effectually influences the creature to obey God's every command. "If we loved him only from self-love, from the fear of hell, or from the hope of heaven, we might," Bellamy opines, "at the same time, hate his law; but if we love him for being what he is, we cannot but love to be like him, which is what his law requires."[16]

What he is is perfection itself, and such is the goodness of his nature that he needs no motive to excite him to do good. "Thus unmoved and unexcited by anything from without himself, of his own mere goodness, he did, in the days of eternity, determine to do all that good, which ever will by him be done, to all eternity, when there was nothing existing but himself, and so nothing to move him but his own good pleasure." [17] Why, then, did he decree that misery and sin should be mankind's lot? It was not because he lacked power or failed to consider the consequences, for, Bellamy insists, it is certain that, in affair of such a nature, and of such consequence, he could not stand by as an idle, unconcerned spectator, that cares not which things go. [18]

> When he first designed to create the world, and first laid
> out his whole scheme of government, as it was easy for him
> to have determined that neither angels nor men should ever
> sin, and that misery should never be heard of in all his domi-
> nions, so he could easily have prevented both sin and misery.

Why did he choose not to do so? Because, says Bellamy, he did not think it best on the whole that the world should be without sin. Not best because his grand end in creation is not so much the happiness of his creatures, although that is most dear to him, as it is that his creation shall glory in the display of his infinite perfections. "Why look," cries Bellamy, what end he is at last like to obtain when the whole scheme is finished, and the day of judgement past, and heaven and hell filled with their proper inhabitants. And what will be the final result? What will he get by all?" [19] And answers,

> Why, all in all he will exert and display every one of his
> perfections to the life, and so by all will exhibit a most perfect
> and exact image of himself. And now, as he is infinitely and
> glorious in being what he is, therefore that scheme of con-
> duct which is perfectly suited to exhibit the most lively and
> exact image of him, must be infinitely glorious too; and,
> therefore, this is the greatest and best thing he can aim at
> in all his works: and this, therefore, ought to be his last end. [20]

98

The holiness and justice, goodness, mercy, and grace of God will shine the more brightly for sin and misery having been permitted to enter God's world. Surely God thought it was so, else he could not have done as he did. And, Bellamy concludes, if we view things as God did, with a temper and frame of heart like unto his, we shall think so too. Therefore, let us cease our questioning of God's motives, recognizing that it is "infinite impudence" for such worms of dust as we "to dislike his conduct, and find fault with his dispensations."[21]

God in his work acts out his perfections, and, in his Word, lays the whole before our eyes in writing. And from these words (**Genesis** 1:27), we have reason to believe that Adam was created in the moral, as that he was in the natural image of God. "In this his image was his creature, man, created; not in part of his image, for there is no such intimation in all of the Bible; but in his image, comprising his moral, as well, and as much, as his natural perfections."[22]

Now the moral image of God consists, according to Bellamy, "in a temper of mind or frame of heart perfectly answerable to the moral law, being as it were, a transcript of the moral perfections of God."[23] Such was the moral image of Adam before the Fall. He saw plainly what God was, and his infinite glory in being such, and loved him with all his heart. And he saw also that if he in any thing should disobey his sovereign Lord and rightful Governor, "it would be right, infinitely right, that he should be miserable forever."[24] Wherefore, our author thinks, "it is plain and evident, from facts, that Adam was considered and dealt with under the capacity of a public head, and that death, natural, spiritual, and eternal, were included in threatening; for all his posterity are evidently dealt with just as if that had been the case."[25] But Adam fell, and consequently we are born into the world entirely destitute of the moral image of God. "We are, in fact, born like the wild ass's colt, as senseless of God, and as void and destitute of grace....We have an appetite for happiness, but no appetite for holiness....We have a heart to love ourselves, but no heart to love God."[26] In all that we would do, we are moved by no higher principle than that self-love which is sin.

But, it is objected, God decreed that Adam should fall, and therefore we are blameless. Not so, replies Bellamy. "He did not decree that Adam should fall, any more than he did that the seed of Adam should turn out such a stiff-necked, rebellious race. He decreed to *permit both* to do as they did: but this neither lessens his goodness, nor their sin; for God is not obliged to put his creatures under such circumstances as that they shall never be tempted nor tried."[27] Arminians and Pelagians would have us believe that God aims only at the happiness of his creatures, and were it so, then every man must love him. But the God they invoke and the human character they conjure, is none such as Scripture reveals, and Scripture, as Bellamy never tires of telling, offers our only safe way home.

The law requires us to love God perfectly and absolutely, but the native bent of our heart is to a supreme love of self. "And this is the case with every graceless man living, whatever his attainments may otherwise be....For, ever since our first parents aspired to be gods, it has been the nature of all mankind to love themselves supremely, and to be blind to the infinite beauty of the divine nature; and it remains so to be with all, until renewed by divine grace."[28] Herein, Bellamy thinks to find the spring of all false religion, "for all,, however different in other things, yet all agree that they take their rise from a principle of self-love. Not only the idolatrous religions of the heathen world, but every denomination of christianity that harbors graceless men rests on this princple of self-love. So that we may say with the apostle Paul, "All seek their own and not the things which are Jesus Christ's."

In this self-love is found the root of all sin, for, argues Bellamy, in preferring our personal interests to those of God we act directly contrary to not only the first and great commandment, but also to the second like unto it. "From this same root, this disposition to love ourselves supremely....and delight in that which is not God wholly, proceeds all our evil carriage towards our neighbor."[29] We do that which we ought not to do, and that because the disposition to self-love is natural to us. We are born into the world not only destitute of a conformity to the law of God, but diametrically opposed to it in the native bent of our hearts to be inordinately selfish.

Is this to say that our disposition to selfishness is innate? And if so, is it a disposition concreated in us by God? Inasmuch as any affirmative answer to these questions must serve to mitigate our bent to selfishness and thereby reduce the stain of our original sin, whereas a negative to both gives away too much to the Arminians and Pelagians, Bellamy takes refuge in a verbal distinction. Our disposition to selfishness, he would have us believe, is not *concreated* but *con-natural*.

> These propensities (dispositions) perhaps, in some sense, may be said to be contracted, in opposition to their being strictly and philosophically natural, because they are not created by God with the essence of the soul, but result from its native choice. But most certainly these propensities are not contracted in the sense that many vicious habits are, namely, by long use and custom. In opposition to such vicious habits, they may be called connatural.[30]

Even so, says Bellamy, we have been brought to this state in consequence of Adam's fall, are wholly to blame for our sins of selfishness, and every one of us is without excuse and guilty before God.

Why and how this may be is evident in the realization that our inability to perfectly conform to God's law is a moral, and not a natural, inability, Borrowing from Edwards, Bellamy will have it that our impotency of heart is not natural but moral, and therefore instead of extenuating, it does magnify and enhance our fault.

> The more unable to love God we are, the more we are to blame. Even as it was with the Jews, the greater contrariety there was in their hearts to their prophets, to Christ and his apostles, the more vile and blameworthy were they. And in this light do the Scriptures constantly view the case. There is not one title in the Old Testament or in the New, in the law or in the gospel, that gives the least intimation of any deficiency in our natural faculties. The law requires no more than all our hearts, and never blames us for not having larger natural capacities. The gospel aims to recover us to love God only with all our hearts, but makes no provision for our hav-

ing any new natural capacity: as to our natural capacities,
all is well.[31]

Which being so, it is, Bellamy contends, most evident that the supreme governor of the world has not the least ground or reason to abate his holy law
or recant his condemnation of our disposition to disobey.

Nor will Bellamy allow that there is any substance to the claim that God's
sovereignty implies his authorship of, and responsibility for, our sins.

> God only creates the naked essence of our souls; our natural
> faculties; a power to think and will, and to love and hate;
> and this evil bent of our hearts is not of his making, but
> is the spontaneous propensity of our own wills; for we, be-
> ing born devoid of the divine image, ignorant of God, and
> insensible of his glory, do, of our own accord, turn to
> ourselves, and the things of time and sense, and to anything
> that suits a graceless heart.... so that the positive corruption
> of our nature is not anything created by God, but arises mere-
> ly from a privative cause.[32]

Before God, and under God's holy law, we are totally responsible for our
acts, for God requires of us no more than we are naturally and morally able
to perform. Our natural powers being thus sufficient to God's purposes, he
is under no obligation to grant to any of mankind any supernatural advantages. "The truth is, that God's sending his Son into the world to die for the
redemption of sinners, instead of freeing us from our original natural obligations to keep the law, binds us more strongly to do so."[33] Nor are we due any
special thanks for our obedience to God's commandment. If we love God with
all our hearts, we but do our bounden duty and deserve no praise. "The divine
law makes no allowances, no abatements, but insists upon the same—the very
same it ever did: "Thou shalt love the Lord thy God with all thy heart."[34]

To suppose that the Son of God came into the world and Christ died that
the law in its threatenings might be repealed is to suppose Christ become an
enemy to God's justice. Which is not only impossible, but unnecessary. "For

if, in justice, it (the law) ought to have been repealed, there was no need of his dying to procure this; or if, in justice, it ought not to be repealed, then his dying could not procure it, and so would do no good."[35] If the righteous God in his omniscience had perceived the law to be unjust, he must have repealed it of his own accord, but this, Bellamy reminds us, he did not do, and thus the law stands in all its threatenings. Why, then, did the Father send his only begotten Son into the world if it was not to save sinners from the burden of the law? "The truth is," answers Bellamy, that "Christ came into the world, and died to answer all the demands of the law; that so, although the sinner be saved, yet the law might never be repealed, but be firmly establish-ed....And indeed it was nothing but God's infinite aversion to repeal the law, as a thing in itself infinitely unfit and wrong, that was the thing which made the death of Christ needful."[36] For if the law were of no effect, every sinner might be saved; but as it is not, its demands must be satisfied or every sinner is damned.

Christ must die that the ends of moral government and the honor of the moral governor might be secured and a way opened for God to honorably declare himself reconcilable to a guilty world.[37] "And now Christ stepped in and did this, and so secured the honor of God's holiness and justice, law and government, and opened a way for the sinner's salvation."[38] Wherefore, the apostle says, "Do we make void the law through faith? God forbid! yea we establish the law."

Inasmuch as some have sought to see in this "governmental" theory of the atonement a departure from the position of Edwards, it is needful to note that Bellamy's account follows directly upon the teaching of Edwards in the latter's extended sermon on Justification by Faith Alone.[39] For Edwards too will have it that the Saviour "spilled his blood out of respect for the honor of God's majesty and in submission to his authority,"[40] thereby vindicating by his obedience "the honor of God's legislative authority."[41] Both also are as one in their concern to rebut the Arminian contention that Christ died that our imperfect obedience might be made acceptable to God. "For," notes Edwards, (as I have observed elsewhere),[42] "They (the Arminians) hold that God in mercy to mankind has abolished that rigourous constitution or law, that they were under originally; and instead of it, has introduced a more mild constitution, and put us under a new law, which requires no more than imperfect sincere obedience, in compliance with our poor infirm impotent circumstances since the fall."[43] Now, he asks, how can these things be made consistent? And answers, in no way. Bellamy echoes his thought. "As for this (Arminian) opinion (that God purposed to offer salvation to all, and use means with all, and save those who, of their own accord, will become good men), I think," he opines, "that they never learnt it from the Bible....Or rather, I may say, convince them, first of all, what God is, and what the law is....and what it means to be a good man, and there will be no difficulty then to convince them of the depravity of mankind."[44]

Where they differ, and I would emphasize that the difference is more apparent than real, is not in their understanding of Christ's motive in the atonement (for both follow Grotius), nor yet in their appreciation of its consequences, but simply and solely in their view of the elect. For Edwards the elect are the chosen of God, by his universal and absolute decree,[45] and since that decree ostensibly includes the career of Christ, it is for these that atonement is made. For Bellamy, conversely, the elect are not those whom God has chosen but, as Anderson has noted,[46] those who choose God. And inasmuch as this choice is open to all, he is rightly held to teach a general atonement. However, when due attention is paid to the outcome, this distinction (of limited and general atonement) is, as between Edwards and Bellamy, seen to be no real distinction:. Thus, following scripture, Bellamy proclaims that Christ dies for all men, but recognizing that what God foreknew, he did by his eternal decree predestine, he concludes that "God never designed to bring the non-elect to glory....He designed to declare himself reconcilable to them through Christ, to offer mercy....but they being obstinate, he designed to leave them to themselves, to take their own course, and, in the end, to deal with them according to their deserts."

The same view, in somewhat different context, is expressed in **Freedom of the Will.** "From these things (God's foreknowledge and decree)," argues Edwards, "it will inevitably follow, that however Christ in some sense may be said to *die for all,* and to redeem all visible Christians, yea, the whole world by his death; yet there must be something particular in the design of his death, with respect to such as he intended should actually be saved thereby."[48] In sum, both will allow that the door of mercy is open wide enough for all the world to enter in, even as both confess, which as scripturalists they must, that some are damned as God's design dictates. And neither will concede that this tells against such freedom as those who are not elected have, since their refusal to obey God's command arises not out of any natural inability, but solely and wholly from their moral inability.[49] Finally, to dispel any lingering impression that general atonement is synonymous with universal election, Bellamy vigourously and explicitly disavows the Arminian assertion that God designed salvation for all men.[50]

To the Arminian objection that it is not consistent with the divine perfection to create mankind with such dismal prospects, Bellamy's answer is God's answer to Job: "But who art thou, O Man, that repliest against God? Shall the thing formed say unto him that formed it, why has thou formed me thus? That we are born into the world devoid of the moral image and disposed to love ourselves supremely, is, he reiterates, an undeniable fact. By comparing ourselves with the holy law of God, as it has been already explained, we may also learn that we are born into the world not only destitute of a conformity to the law but that we are natively diametrically opposed to it in the temper of our hearts. Consequently, the clearest revelation of God cannot bring sinners to love him as his commandment requires. "And therefore, besides the external revelation which God has made of himself by his works and in his word, there is an absolute necessity that he should internally reveal himself in his glory to the heart of a sinner in order to beget divine love there."[50]

Bellamy would not have us think that this internal revelation is in any way supplementary to that which is objectively unfolded in scripture. "We do not need the Holy Spirit to reveal any new truths concerning God, not already revealed....We do not need to have the holy Spirit immediately reveal all these truths concerning God over again to us, by way of objective revelation, or immediate inspiration."[52] We are not called to be prophets or apostles but to regeneration. "We only need to be effectually awakened to attend to those manifestations which he has made of himself in his works and word that we may see what he is....and have a spiritual taste imparted to us by the immediate influence of the Holy Ghost, that we may have a sense of his infinite glory in being such."[53] We must be recovered from our present sinfulness, from what we are by nature, to the image of God, to what we may be with grace. We must be subjectively awakened to the sight and sense of the eternal dignity and moral excellency of the divine sovereign objectively revealed in his word and work. Only thus, Bellamy believes, does our fulfillment of the great commandment in all its severity become a real possibility. "It is divine light, imparted by the Spirit of God to the soul, which lays the foundation of all."[54]

Herein lies the essential and irreconcilable difference between the orthodox Calvinism of the Old Lights and the new divinity made manifest by Edwards in his essay on the nature of true virtue. This insistence upon the operation of the Holy Spirit in the affair of regeneration, which operation alone, according to Bellamy, makes possible the human expression of that total love demanded in the great commandment, defines and differentiates "true religion" from its pious counterfeits. He but articulates the common opinion of all new divinity men when he claims that

> this is specifically different from every kind of false religion
> in the world; for all kinds of false religion, however different
> in other things, yet all agree in this, to result merely from
> a principle of self-love....All the idolatrous religion of the
> heathen world....arises from this principle....so does all the
> religion of formalists and legal hypocrites, in the reformed
> nations. It is a slavish fear of hell, and mercenary hope of
> heaven, which, from a principle of self-love, sets all a-going....
> And this is the case with every graceless man living, of
> whatever denomination....whether Churchman, Presbyterian,
> Congregationalist, or Separatist; whether a Pelagian, Armi-
> nian, Calvinist, Antinomian, Baptist or Quaker.[55]

In sum, it is, Bellamy thinks, no certain evidence that a man is a good man because of his good works and church membership, for "a man cannot know that he is a good man by the degree of his religion but only from the special nature of it."[56]

How may one know that he or she is the beneficiary of grace, blessed with this "special nature," illumined by the "divine light"? Bellamy finds the question gratuitous, and that because to his view true grace is always perceptible! For, he argues, a man cannot but perceive his own thoughts and know intuitively his own design. Much less then is it possible that there should be so great a change of heart and life as is evident in regeneration and conversion and yet the beneficiary know nothing of it. "From the nature of things, it is evident that grace is perceptible: yea, in its own nature, it must be as perceptible as corruption....But if true grace be, by its own nature, perceptible, and if it be also specifically different from all counterfeits, it is self-evident that a good man may know that he has true grace."[56]

To the objection that this helps us not at all to distinguish the possessor of true grace from those whose claims to such are counterfeit, Bellamy suggests self-interest as the litmus test. We have but to determine whether the slightest tincture of self-interest or self-love is present in the makeup of the claimant to know the counterfeit, for

> this is the case with every graceless man living, whatever his attainments may otherwise be; though he hath all knowledge to understand all mysteries, and can speak with the tongues of men and angels, and has faith to move mountains, and zeal enough to give all his goods to feed the poor, and his body to be burned, yet he has no charity: he is perfectly destitute of this genuine love to God and his neighbor, and has no higher principle in his heart, from which all his religion proceeds, but a supreme love to himself.[58]

Such a one, to Bellamy, is as the Israelites who sang God's praise at the Red Sea. "They loved themselves, and therefore they rejoiced at their wonderful deliverance....But the love of God was not in them, and....after a while, they return to folly, as the dog to his vomit, and as the sow that was washed to her wallowing in the mire."[58]

Even by the modest standards of mid-eighteenth century publishers, Bellamy's **True Religion Delineated** was far from being a theological bestseller. It was warmly welcomed by Edwards and the partisans of the new divinity, found an honored place in their parsonage libraries and in those of their more affluent parishioners. But there is nothing in the religious literature of the period to support the belief that the work enjoyed a wider circulation. It did bring Bellamy to the immediate notice of his ministerial peers, made him a smallish profit, and led to the offer of a Manhattan pulpit. After much soul-searching (in those days ministers did not lightly change congregations), Bellamy elected to remain in Bethlem.[59]

If he was disappointed at the failure of the orthodox to recognize the significance of his contribution to Calvinist theology, he kept it to himself. For the fact is that neither then, nor, with one main exception even now,[61] has the Reformed community properly appreciated Bellamy's improvement of Edwards' theory of true virtue. Where the latter had been content to provide a principle, and a sketch of its ethical implications, the former articulates a comprehensive system of doctrines. In lieu of love directed to the metaphysical abstraction 'Being-in-General', we have here love offered to the infinitely lovable moral governor of all creation. Bellamy's repudiation of the moral value of sentiment and self-interest is sharper and more vigorously argued. Edwards' tendency to compromise the requirement of the great commandment (vide his chapters on secondary beauty, natural conscience, and the moral sense)[62] has no place in Bellamy's system. Nor has Edwards as plainly perceived the theological implications of the great commandment for the conception of God. Ahlstrom concludes that "the most conspicuous of Bellamy's theological innovations was his conception of God as Moral Governor," and insofar as that conception is understood to indicate the subject of the disinterested benevolence commanded, the conclusion is justified. Even so, the point to remember, as Bellamy's spiritual heir, Nathaniel William Taylor is at pains to make clear in his **Lectures on the Moral Government of God**, is that only a God so conceived is inherently worthy of the unqualified love that Bellamy, and Edwards before him, requires.

III

The grand point of difference is precisely this: I believe, that the infinitely holy and wise God, in every part of his conduct relative to the intellectual system, does that which is

really wisest and best for him to do; most for his glory, and
the good of the system, in the whole; and, therefore, that
God's present plan is, of all possible plans, the best; most
for his glory, and the good of the system.[64]

Having decided that it never was, "or ever will be, my duty to remove and
settle at New York,"[65] Bellamy gave himself over for several years to the duties
of his parish, the care of his growing family,[66] and the oversight of the several
students[67] who, attracted by his rising reputation, now sought to prepare for
the ministry under his guidance. His only publications during these years were
two sermons, **The Great Evil of Sin, as it is committed against God** (1753
and the famous sermon-discourse, **The Law our School-Master** (1756).[68] A
year later the theological waters were violently disturbed by the appearance
of a tract for the times entitled, **A Winter Evening's Conversation upon the
Doctrine of Original Sin between a Minister and three of his Neighbors** etc.[69]
It was a blow to the heart of commandment Calvinism, and it provoked, as
the author, the Reverend Samuel Webster[70] intended that it should, a war of
pamphlets pro and con.

The opening of the **Conversation** is all sweetness and light. The first
neighbor expresses his concern respecting the differences dividing the clergy
on questions of doctrine, and is reassured by the minister that these are much
fewer and smaller than "the many great and fundamental matters wherein
they are agreed."[71] Among these matters is the conception of God, which for
Webster, no less than for Bellamy, is the "One God, infinite in wisdom, power,
holiness, justice, goodness and truth, the same from everlasting; the maker,
governor, and judge of the world."[72] Webster concedes also an identity of
belief as respects Jesus Christ, "the glorious Redeemer and Saviour of Men,
appointed by God, and therefore able to save unto the uttermost all who come
unto God by him."[73] He avows the Holy Ghost, the final authority of scripture, and the moral law. All of which would appear to call in question the
validity of Haroutunian's contention "that the conflict between Calvinism
(Bellamy et al) and the sentiments of the new age (as expressed in the **Conversation**) can be epitomized as a conflict between the conceptions "Almighty
God" and "our compassionate heavenly father,"[74] this last being Webster's

phrase. Far from being a process of substituting new dogmas for old, as Haroutunian suggests,[75] Webster's position in at one with that of command-ment Calvinism on all major doctrinal points excepting only natural depravity and original sin.

To be sure, these are large exceptions, and a change of viewpoint with respect to either must, it would seem, call in question the propriety and relevance of that particular conception of God maintained by Webster and Bellamy alike. In other words, the question is: Given the conception of God as in-finite in wisdom, power, holiness, etc., which view of original sin, the Calvinist or the Arminian,[76] logically follows? This is not, of course, the question as Webster poses it. For him,

> the question is, whether we, and all Adam's posterity, are charged by God with this first sin of his, so as that men, women, and children, are exposed *by this alone,* to the eter-nal damnation of hell?[77]

The first neighbor, confessing that this is precisely what he has always been taught, and taken for granted as plainly proven by scripture, doubts not but that the answer must be—yes! The minister is shocked. "What," he replies, "and do you think that in consequence of this there are many infants now weltering in the lake of fire....and that they deserve that damnation?"[78] I don't doubt it at all, answers the neighbor. The minister is appalled. How, he cries,

> can you reconcile it to the goodness, holiness, or justice of God, to make them heirs of hell, and send them into the world only to breathe and die....What! make them first to open their eyes in torments; and all this for a sin which they certainly had no hand in....a sin, which, if it comes upon them at all, certainly is without any fault or blame on their parts; for they had no hand in receiving it; nor ever approv-ed, or so much as heard it, til they came to hell and heard it from their tormentors—and all this from the holiest justest and kindest Being in 'heaven and earth May'nt we venture to say 'tis impossible?[79]

The first neighbor agrees, but the second is not so easily put off, and suggests that the harshness of the docrine is ameliorated by the saving act of Christ. But this won't do, rejoins the minister , for Calvinists agree that without repentance there is no remission of sins, without repentance sinners perish, and such is the case of infants unless they are forgiven by an absolute act of grace without their knowledge. And why should they not be so forgiven, asks the second neighbor. Because, says the minister, there is no hint of any such thing given in the gospel. And besides, "what an unaccountable thing must it be for an allwise God, first to put on, and then to take off this sin, both without so much as their knowledge."[80]

The third neighbor is convinced, but the second again demurs. Well, then, says the minister, why must they be sinners at all, before they are moral agents, before they are capable of good or evil, or know anything of either? After all, there are, he avers, but two ways in which we become sinners, first by natural generation from Adam, and the other is as he is our federal head and representative. But the first is impossible, unless we are willing to believe that not only the first sin, but all the sins of our parents from Adam downwards are imputed to us, and this no one believes. As for the other way, he asks, does it appear in the Bible that there was any such covenant made with Adam that he should stand as our federal head and representative for all posterity? I assure you," he tells his neighbors, "I have searched the scriptures diligently, and can find no such thing. And," he adds, "let any man in the world find it that can: and till this is plainly shown, men ought to be silent about our answering for Adam's sin; for without this, it is plain it must be a mere castle in the air."[81]

Moreover, why should we, granting that Adam is our representative, be charged with his sins? "Are we charged with the sins of our representatives, even those of our own choosing? For if we are not chargeable with their sin, whom we have voluntarily chosen to represent us, then surely not with his, who was not chosen by us. so that even supposing that, which cannot be proved, that Adam was our federal head or representative, according to all the maxims of equity in the world, we only suffer the ill consequences of his folly; but are not, nor can be (in any proper sense) chargeable with his sin."[82]

The fact of the matter is that sin and guilt are personal, hence not transferable from one person to another, or from Adam to each of us. "No imputation, in either case, can make the thing to be mine which is not mine, any more than one person may be made, in the like way, another person."[83] Nor is this all that may be said of the impossibility of the thing, for we may ask: Is Adam the father of our spirits, or of our flesh only as the scriptures teach? Of our flesh only, answers the neighbor. Well, then, is the body of itself capable of sin? In no way, by itself and apart from the soul can the body be said to sin. But if the body is not itself a sinner before the soul is added to it, the soul so added cannot make it to a sinner, insists the minister. But, the neighbor objects, does not the Bible specifically teach this doctrine? Not at all, replies the minster, and warming to his topic, as ministers are wont to do, he proceeds to lecture his neighbors as to the correct interpretation of the scriptural proof-texts alleged to support the doctrine of original sin.

The word of God, rightly understood, is absolute truth. On this, all parties are agreed. The question is: What are the criteria for the correct understanding of scripture? For Webster, the answer is obvious. God has given us reason that we may discern truth and common sense that we may recognize absurdity when we encounter it. Applied to scripture, this means that "you can argue nothing here from the weakness of your reason in favor of receiving *absurdities* from scripture."[84] Thus when God in **Genesis** warns Adam that he shall not eat the fruit of the tree of knowledge lest he die, and afterwards tells Eve that he will multiply her sorrows because of her transgression, reason and common sense tell us that he is not, as the proponents of original sin would have it, decreeing the damnation of their posterity, but only their physical death and temporal suffering. When Paul remarks in **Romans** that by one man sin entered into the world, and death by sin, the common sense of his words is that we are subject to physical sufferings and temporal death. "For strictly and properly speaking we can no more be made sinners by the sin of Adam, than Christ can be made sin (**2 Cor.** 5:21; **1 Peter** 2:24; **Isaiah** 53:6) for our sins. According to the letter, both are absurdities, and equally and glaringly so."[85]

And, Webster contends, the case is similar with respect to every proof-text commonly cited: **Genesis** 6:5-12, 8:21, 20:9; **Exodus** 20:5; **Job** 14:4, 15:14; **Psalms** 51:5; **Romans** 5:12; **1 Corinthians** 15:21-22; and **Ephesians** 2:3, one and all not only admit of, but reasonably require, a naturalistic interpretation. "Upon the whole, therefore," the minister concludes,

> when it is said that we all sinned, or were made sinners by Adam's sin, I conclude is mean't neither more nor less than that God so far laid upon us his iniquity, or treated us as sinners, as to sentence us all to death, or to return to the dust. And considering the extreme absurdity, if not utter impossibility, of our being, strictly and literally speaking, chargeable with the fault and blame of his sin, and the dreadful consequences of such an opinion, I will venture to leave it, with every unprejudic'd mind, whether this in not most probably the true sense of the words.[86]

How, then, the neighbor inquires, do you account for the rise of the doctrine of original sin, if not from scripture? It is, the minister replies, an invention of the fourth century, ascribable to Augustine,[87] and before him unknown to Christianity.

With this doctrine, therefore, the minister concludes, true Christians will have nothing to do. It is heretic, redolent of Catharism in that it tends to discourage those who believe it from having children. "For if every child that is born is a monster leadin' with sin, and adds one more rebel against God, and one more heir of hell: What friend to God or man would chuse to be an instrument in the production of such wicked and exposed creatures?"[88] By making him thus to be the author of sin the doctrine of total depravity impeaches God's holiness and dishonors his goodness. "For how shall they strive to be holy, who believe not that God is holy; or how imitate his goodness, who apprehend that, at best, cruelty is predominant in his character? Will man, can man," the minister asks, "love him who made them objects of his hatred, and brought them into being under a sentence of damnation? Is there, in such a representation, any proper foundation for love? And does it naturally lead men to love God with all their hearts and souls? Who can say it?[89] Surely not the proponents of commandment Calvinism. God forbid, then, cries the minister, that we should ever receive such a doctrine as this, which tends to sap the foundation of all religion by making us rue the day that we were born.

The uncommon vigor and common sense of Webster's arguments hit the

Calvinist clerisy where they lived, and none more so than Bellamy and his ultra-orthodox colleaague, the Rev. Peter Clark,[90] minister of the church at Salem Village (Danvers), Massachusetts, who, beating Bellamy to the punch, rushed to publication a wordy (132 pages) apologia entitled, **The Scripture-Doctrine of Original Sin, stated and defended. In a Summer-Morning's Conversation, between a minister and a neighbor.** The neighbor is Webster's first neighbor, now portrayed as having second thoughts, which Clark's minister loses no time in correcting. Original sin and native depravity, the neighbor is assured, are facts of experience, received as such by sinners in all ages, and there is no disputing against fact and experience.

Nor yet from scripture, since original sin, according to Clark, is clearly laid down in **Romans** 5:12 and other texts. As for our native depravity, that he roundly asserts, is propagated by natural generation from Adam, whose sin is consequently imputed to all mankind, not excluding infants, albeit few, he thinks, will go so far as to maintain that these latter suffer the torments of the damned. Certainly Clark himself does not wish to do so. He is more than willing to leave the fate of infants to the secret counsel of the Almightly, it being, he informs the neighbor, "safest to leave unrevealed things to God alone."[92] As for the balance of Webster's "pelagian" and "socinian" heresies, he will have it, following St. Paul (**Romans** 9:20), that "it much more becomes us to be silent and submissive."[93] Bellamy, assuming the persona of the second neighbor, is inclined to agree. In **A Letter to the Reverend Author of the Winter-Evening's Conversation on Original Sin,** from one of his candid Neighbors etc.,[94] he reiterates his conviction of the absolute righteousness of the divine law damning disobedience (for either the curse of the law was righteous or Christ's death was needless), and suggests that the Reverend Author would be well advised to study Edwards' sermons on Justification and the Judgment of God in the Damnation of Sinners, for these, together with his **Great Christian Doctrine of Original Sin Defended,** contain all that is necessary by way of response to Webster's calumnies.

Clark's and Bellamy's efforts to dampen down the controversy ignited by Webster's argument from the innocence of infants was doomed to failure. Edmund March,[95] a minister of the church at Amesbury, rushed to publish **Fair Play! A Needful Word, to Temper the Tract, entitled, A Summer-**

Morning's Conversation.[96] March was much put out by Clark's "misrepresentations" and "injudicious distortions" of Webster's argument, and he wanted the five ministers who had lent their authority to Clark's tract to know that his Salisbury colleague spoke nothing more or less than the plain truth respecting Calvinist preaching of infant damnation. Samuel Hopkins was moved by this to defend Clark in an anonymous letter to the author of Fair Play!, entitled **A Bold Push,**[97] and was shortly followed into print by Charles Chauncy,[98] who, expressing **The Opinion of One that has perused the Summer-Morning's Conversation,**[99] proceeds to lay bare the incongruity between the Calvinist doctrine of original sin and Clark's attempt to mitigate that doctrine as it applies to infants. Clark, he argues, in hedging on the issue of infant damnation has, in effect, abandoned Calvinism to its enemies. Not so, rejoins Clark, in his **Remarks on a late Pamphlet entitled the Opinion,**[100] etc. A man may well favour the Calvinist doctrine in general and yet not espouse every point of Calvinism. Renewing his attempt to find a middle ground, he grants to his critic, "that all the posterity of Adam, as his children, even Infants, are *mediately* or *remotely* liable to the Pains of Hell; being, as they grow up to the age of discretion, or a Capacity for moral Actions, prompted by a corrupt, depraved nature, derived from him, to those actual sins, which, the Scripture teaches, will expose them to eternal Torments."[101] This revised view of the matter he defends as "scripture-doctrine," as distinguished from the "Calvinistical doctrine." "For," he declares, "I take the holy scriptures alone for the Rule of my faith, and not the Doctrine of Calvin, or of those who are his followers."[102]

Even so do I, rejoins Webster in **The Winter-Evening's Conversation Vindicated,**[103] and is at pains to spell out the positions on which he and Clark are agreed. He indignantly rejects the description of his view as pelagian: "I despise Pelagius (if he is truly represented by his enemies) as much as he, and as much more different from him, than Mr. Clark is from me."[104] "I am, " he adds, "further still from doubting of the actual Degeneracy and Apostasy of Mankind, whatever be the cause....the Fact—the melancholy Fact, is too plain to be doubted."[105]

Who denies the real apostasy of human nature, the fall of

Adam, or a real original corruption? I have not....Who denies
the necessity of supernatural grace, redemption by the blood
of Christ, regeneration by the Spirit, or Justification by Faith
in the Scripture sense? I have not done it in one single article.[106]

Wherein, therefore, do we differ? Only in this one part, that I deny what Clark
affirms, namely that there is sin before sinning. "I suppose this Corruption
of Nature we bring into the World with us—whatever it is—to be our Affliction....He—that it is our real Sin in the strict, proper sense; and imputed
therefore by God as such, so as to justly merit or deserve the Wrath of God." [107]
Why this should be so, he (Clark) is willing to leave to God's secret counsel,
whereas I contend that whatever in scripture appears repugnant to reason cannot be God's true word.

For the truth of Holy Scripture can not otherwise be proved
to any Man that doubts of it; but by reducing him so some
Absurdity, or the denial of some avow'd Principle of
Reason....The moment therefore which your Reason tells you,
that there are absurdities and impossibilities in Scripture,
your Evidence of their Truth or Divinity....must be weaken-
ed or wholly fail....Tis therefore in vain to think of
establishing Absurdities and Impossibilities, by the Bible.[108]

It was a point shrewdly taken, which Clark,[109] as a professed proponent of
reasonable religion, could hardly deny. And, as matters turned out, neither
could later generations of consistent Calvinists, as we shall see when we come
to consider the systems of Hopkins and Emmons. Impelled by this same principle (of sufficient reason), they too will echo Webster's conviction that there
is no sin before sinning.

IV

That God permits sin, is plain fact, cannot admit of dispute,
and needs no proof....And this fact, that God permits sin,

> gives rise to this question, namely,—Is it wisest and best that
> God should conduct as he does in this affair?[110]

In the same year (1757-58) as the foregoing Conversations, Bellamy preached four sermons on The Wisdom of God in the Permission of Sin![111] Ostensibly, they have nothing specific to do with the issue of the innocence of infants. Bellamy is here concerned with principles, but the principles are precisely those which, if granted, will justify the generalities of his Letter in response to Webster.

In the days of eternity, long before the foundation of the world, this system, now in existence, and this plan, which now takes place, and all other possible systems, and all other possible plans, lay open to the all-encompassing view of the Almighty. His wisdom was infinite, his nature the same from everlasting to everlasting, and he had none to please but himself. Of the myriad possibilities "open and naked before him; he knew which was the best; and he chose this; and therefore this, to him, appeared preferable to any other, and therefore it was really the best."[112] But if all God's works are uniform, and this with Bellamy is a self-evident principle, "we may," he argues, "venture to affirm, that of necessity it must be the case, that the nature of the parts will certainly show the nature of the whole."[113] Moreover, "we may not only argue from the wisdom of particular parts to the wisdom of the whole, but also from the special nature of particular parts to the special nature of the whole; and so, from a right idea of particular parts, which we are able to comprehend, we may have some right conceptions of the whole, although the whole is too great for our conception."[114] To these principles we need only add the authority of Holy Scripture, and the foundations of the case are complete. "So let us but attend to the divine conduct, as recorded in that book, which may justly be denominated the history of the Deity, and enter into his views and designs, in particular instances of his conduct, and we may," Bellamy believes, "with sufficient certainty, determine his moral character, and the general nature and design of his whole plan."[115]

What then shall we understand by the wisdom of God in the permission of sin? Surely not that he (God) loves sin, or that there is anything in the nature of sin of which he approves. Nor are we, Bellamy adds, to imagine that God in permitting sin, deprives the sinner of his freedom of will. The truth of the matter is that "God's permitting sin consists merely in not hindering of it."[116] That is to say, God never permits sin, but only when, all things considered, he judges it best not to interpose to prevent its commission. The affair of Joseph, as narrated in **Genesis,** and of Moses, as told in **Exodus,** are prime examples. The evil done by Joseph's brothers, the cruel tyranny of Pharaoh, the idolatry of the Israelites in Sinai, seen in context as particular parts of the system of the whole, are, Bellamy argues, manifestly contributory to God's grand design. That some have failed to see just how these, and countless other affairs instanced in scripture and world-history, work for the best, is no argument against their so doing. "Since we are but just emerged out of nonexistence; have so very small an acquaintance with God's world, and so feeble and weak a taste; so poor a discernment of what is beautiful and best, it must not seem strange to us if we can see but a little way into the glories of the divine plan."[117] Better that we remember that God in his capacity as Creator has done well by us his creatures, than that we continue to occupy our minds with fruitless questioning of the divine design.

We tend to forget, says Bellamy, the excellence of God's provision for mankind in erecting "a grand and noble theatre....completely furnished out, as a place of habitation."[118] We tend to forget that man was made capable of knowing, loving, obeying, and enjoying God; "as also of seeing the beauty, and tasting the sweetness, of the fruits of paradise."[119] We tend to forget that man was made for society and given an "agreeable companion" to share his days, "and he had open to his view all the glories of the visible creation to inspire him with sublime and exalted thoughts of God."[120]

And having made such provision, "God, according to Bellamy, took it for granted that he had done enough and said enough; and might, as becoming his character, not only demand, but reasonably expect, obedience, and justly suspend his everlasting welfare on this condition."[121] He did not think himself obliged to be man's keeper, undertaking to preserve him from sin by continuing interposition, but judged that he might now leave man to his duty. "And, accordingly, "God did leave him to his choice."[122]

In view of the belief, fostered by Haroutunian and asserted by Ahlstrom and others, that Bellamy's characterization of God as "Moral Governor" represents an innovative improvement upon the traditional Calvinist notion of God as Absolute Sovereign, it is important to realize that, for Bellamy, God's moral government extends no further, as far as his interposition in human affairs is concerned, than the fall of man. The nineteenth century identification of God's moral government as a continuing compassion finds no place in commandment Calvinism.

> When the great Omniscient saw that rebellion would break out in heaven, and the infection reach down to his lower world, and spread over all the earth, he practically said, "After all I have done for them as their Creator, and said to them as their moral Governor, I and my throne are guiltless; to themselves I leave them." [123]

Man is required to love God, and that with all his heart, but after the fall, God is under no obligation to cherish man. To Bellamy's way of thinking, "God had done so much for all intelligences in their first creation, that he was under no obligation to do any more....To have concerned himself only for his creature's good, unsolicitous for the rights of the Godhead....had been to counteract his own nature, and his chief maxims of government." [124] The moral government of God, then, stops just before that point at which the liberal Christian conceives it to begin. This latter position, that the welfare of creatures is the only thing of worth, and the only thing to be regarded by the moral governor of the universe, is, to Bellamy's mind, "one of the most groundless, irrational, unscriptural, positions, that ever was laid down." [125] And he will have no part of it.

Given, therefore, that God's plan for mankind is in the best manner suited to honor and glorify God himself, then is his wisdom in the permission of sin vindicated, "for wisdom consists in proposing the best ends, and in choosing the best means for their accomplishment." [126] It will be said that condemning sinners to eternal damnation is hardly the "best means," and, says Bellamy, "if vindictive wrath were nothing but groundless arbitrary vengeance, it would be quite another thing; but as it is, in the Governor of the world, nothing but love to God, to virtue, to the best good of the system, bearing down, in a wise and righteous manner the enemies of God, of virtue, and of the system, it cannot but appear infinitely amiable in the eyes of the inhabitants of heaven."[127] Vindictive wrath, in the Governor of the world, nothing but love to God? Just so, answers Bellamy: "Vindictive justice, if I mistake not, arises wholly from love, and is always under the direction of divine wisdom, And if so, it is an amiable perfection in the Deity. Love is the sum of the moral law, which is a transcript of the moral perfections of God; therefore love is the sum of God's moral perfections. Love to God, to virtue, and to the system, will naturally induce the Governor of the world to punish those who are obstinate enemies to God, to virtue, and to the system, according to their deserts."[128] There is no room for confidence. "Hell is our proper due; and free grace through Jesus Christ our only hope."[129] Wherefore, counsels Bellamy, let us watch and pray that we enter not into temptation.

Comes now one Samuel Moody.[130] He has read Bellamy's Sermons, been offended as much by their tone as by their "fatal and pernicious consequences," but what really bothers him is Bellamy's Calvinist arrogance. "Mr. Bellamy," he fumes "has no right to be so violently confident....Great dishonour is done to God, and infinite Prejudice to Religion, by being over curious and positive in Doctrines and Demonstrations abstruse and mysterious."[131] For his part, Moody will not presume in his **Attempt** to offer any such demonstration. Conceding that he cannot prove that Bellamy's account of God's scheme for mankind is not in fact the best possible, most for God's glory, and the good of the system, he proposes to limit himself to pointing out "some false Principles" laid down to support Bellamy's position.

To begin with, does it follow, he asks, that because God overruled the perfidiousness of Joseph's brothers, and thereby brought good out of evil, that evil is essential part of God's plan? "I confess," he writes, that it is "above me to conceive,"[132] and having thus absolved his conscience, proceeds to note a "second fallacy,"namely, Bellamy's belief that happiness arises from privative (i.e. sinful) causes. "Is the Cause adequate to the Effect? Does he not suppose such an Increase of Happiness, as is shocking to common sense? What unworthy apprehensions of the citizens of heaven must he have who imagines that they are made more happy than before by the misery of the damned."[133]

Surely, says Moody, "God could with infinite Ease have conveyed a proper Conception (of his Truth, Holiness, and Justice) without this tremendous scene?"[134]

> What new Perfection, I pray, is discovered, by all this Woe, *essential* to their Holiness and Happiness, which God could not without this have revealed.... And how did the Inhabitants of heaven do for Happiness before this Apostasy and Misery? Why upon Mr. Bellamy's scheme they were very poorly off.[135]

However, remarks Moody, I believe he will persuade none who will properly exercise their reason, that God has not better ways to raise the happiness of his creatures to heavenly levels with this "awful Expedient."

The third fallacy in Bellamy's account, according to our critic, is his claim that the present scheme is most for the glory of God because he is obliged to will and to do that which is most for his declarative glory. But, Moody objects, given that God is infinite in power and extension, there must be room for an endless display of God's glories. "And therefore may we not with utmost Safety affirm, that there is not *now* such a Display? And may we not be naturally led from this is to doubt, whether God has so much Glory from the Things which now exist, as he might have had? Especially when we consider the obvious Defects and Blemishes there are; and can easily imagine how these may be corrected by infinite Wisdom?"[136]

Which question leads him to inquire whether there may not be a fourth fallacy here, namely, the supposition that the present scheme is God's. Scripture, Moody points out, nowhere testifies that moral evil is an "essential, express part" of God's scheme. "No; this seems to be a novel discovery."[137] Nowhere, he contends, is it so much as suggested that sin is most for the honour of the divine perfections and in the best interest of the Creator. "To God therefore and his Agency is ascribed all the Order, Good, and Happiness of this system, and all the Sin, Confusion, and Misery to Satan and wicked Men."[138] These matters being beyond our understanding, Moody bids us repress too busy a curiosity and be satisfied with the teaching of scripture.

But he is as yet far from done with this "perfidious" scheme. Bellamy's denials notwithstanding, Moody will have it that his doctrine makes God the author of sin and Satan the occasion of good; makes Adam's "vile act of Rebellion" an advantage, and the greatest sinners the highest instruments of the glory of God. Which things, he thinks, tend to the increase of Deism and Infidelity. How much better were it, he speculates, if we recognized that it had been really most for God's glory that all rational beings continued holy and perfect, thereby promoting order and Harmony throughout the universe. "If Obedience, Loyalty, and Order had not been more for the Honour of the supreme Law-Giver, and the Good of his subjects; than the Reverse; why were they made and plac'd in such Circumstances? And if it were best that they (Adam and Eve) should be loyal, obedient, and happy, I cannot see," says Moody, "that they should rebel and be miserable." [139]

If obedience to God's command was not for the best, why should he have enjoined it? And if it was for the best, how could it be best for our first parents not to persevere in their obedience?'

> To be best to stand, and best to fall; best to obey, and best
> to rebel; best to be happy, and best to be miserable, sound,
> at least, like Contradictions. [140]

We are forced by logic to choose but one of the alternatives, and Moody has no doubts whatsoever as to the choice we should make in light of the scriptural evidence of God's displeasure at the apostasy of Adam, and his indignation at all that which followed from that original sin. With this in view, we must need to be persuaded that the scheme of universal happiness and universal holiness is more for God's glory than that which willy-nilly postulates the permission of sin. Nor, adds Moody, is this conclusion to be avoided by calling attention to the fact of the matter. If the fact of sin conduces to the glory of God, then it must be that the more sin there is, the greater the glory. "Will not this Doctrine," he asks, "supply the Wicked with unanswerable Objections to all that can be urged from Scripture and Reason to dissuade them from their vicious Courses?" [141] "Will not our libertine young Gentlemen be extremely oblig'd to this pious zealous Divine, for a Scheme

122

so favorable to their Indulgencies?"¹⁴² "Nay, will not this Doctrine have worse Consequences still? Will it not prove, that Men cannot possibly do any Thing which will not be for the best?"¹⁴³ "If I mistake not," concludes Moody, "on these principles, should every vicious Man, upon the face of the Earth....commit the most atrocious Crimes....all will be best, most for God's glory." ¹⁴⁴

Posterity, in the persons of Foster and Haroutunian,¹⁴⁴ has found Moody's arguments "solid," "formidable," "epoch-making," and of such a cogency as "could not but have made his orthodox opponents writhe with pain."¹⁴⁵ And posterity would be right *if* Moody's insights had extended to include a consideration of the principles presupposed in Bellamy's case, and to a critique of the conception of God which Bellamy and all consistent Calvinists assume. Unfortunately for posterity, Moody does neither. He fails even to recognize, let alone appreciate, the importance of the holistic principle to Bellamy's argument, and his concession to the authority of scripture, conjoined with his confession of inability to demonstrate the falsity of Bellamy's assumption that the present scheme is most for God's glory, leaves him wide open to Bellamy's pious claim in the Preface to his **The Wisdom of God in the Permission of Sin Vindicated**¹⁴⁶ that his design in "the following pages is not to vindicate myself but to vindicate God."¹⁴⁷

It is Bellamy's clever and devastating conceit to pretend that Moody writes against his Maker, "for he does not deny the fact that God permits sin; but endeavors to prove, that God in this, as well as in some other things, has not done what is most for his own glory."¹⁴⁸ Given Moody's fatal admission that he cannot prove the negative to a demonstration, Bellamy has no difficulty showing that, in accordance with the principle that the part mirrors the whole, God does that which he knows to be best. For who can deny it, he asks, unless he is willing to set himself in his imaginings in opposition to God. "If I can imagine in my own fancy a better natural world, and a better moral system, yet, as I do not imagine that my own imaginings are right, I have not the least reason to call in question the wisdom of the divine conduct, unless I put more confidence in my imaginations than in "supreme wisdom, which cannot err.'"¹⁴⁹ Moody's modesty forbids that he should dispute the point, and with his failure to do so the case against commandment Calvinism collapses.

What is remarkable about this exchange of pamphlets is not, as Haroutunian asserts, "how incapable he (Bellamy) was of grasping the temper and the import of Moody's convictions,"[150]; but rather how oblivious Moody and his admirers are to the different conception of God those convictions presuppose. For Bellamy, in **Wisdom Vindicated** grasps only too well what Haroutunian and Foster grasp not at all, namely, that the only way to sustain such progressive convictions as those espoused by Moody is to conform one's conception of God to that which these convictions purport. In Bellamy's day this meant replacing the God of Calvin with that of English Deism, in our's it entails substituting panentheism for classical theism. In this respect, Moody is perhaps more advanced than his admirers, inasmuch as he realizes, as they apparently do not, that Bellamy's scheme suggests a very unworthy conception of God.[151] For Moody, however, whose distaste for Deism is no less than Bellamy's, such a substitution is simply not to be thought of. Consequently, he is left with a notion of God, which he can neither admire nor bring himself to repudiate, and a set of progressive principles, which do not square with that notion. And the rest you know.

V

> The persons in question either have, in the judgment of charity, a justifying faith, or not. If not, they, and consequently their children, are not baptizable.[152]

In the twenty years preceding the outbreak of the American Revolution, the Calvinist clergy of Old and New England were agitated by two other controversies far removed from the political arena. In England in 1755 a country minister, the Rev. James Hervey,[153] published a series of dialogues and letters on the doctrine of Christ's satisfaction under the title **Theron and Aspasio**,[154] to which the methodist, John Wesley, replied in a carping letter[155] calling attention to what he considered to be antinomian implications in Hervey's definition of "Justification,"[156] and was shortly answered by the latter in eleven letters titled **Aspasio Vindicated.** To enter into the details of this controversy, and the pamphlet war to which it gave rise, were to embark upon an endless recitation of obscure differences and ambiguous agreements, most of them so subtle and recondite as merely to compound the confusion created by the original dispute. Suffice it to say, then, that Bellamy was among those who, following Wesley, were disturbed and distressed by Hervey's failure to stress the essential difference between Justification in the sight of God: and the persuasion in our own minds that we are Justified.

> One is the act of God, our Judge; the other is the act of our
> own minds. God's act must be necessity be, in order of
> nature, at least before our act. We must be justified before
> we can know that we are Justified.[57]

In other words, "I must actually understand the gospel, believe it with all my heart, and in the belief of it actually receive Christ....before I am justified."[58]

In his major contribution to the Justification controversy,[59] a series of three dialogues and five letters entitled Theron, Paulinus, and Aspasio,[60] he defines his position through a specification of twelve differences between 'true faith' and that faith maintained by Hervey and his defenders,[61] the sum of which is Bellamy's contention that true faith presupposes regeneration,

> wrought in the heart by the Holy Spirit, imparting divine
> life to the dead soul, opening the eyes to behold divine truths
> in their glory and reality; in consequence of which, the gospel
> is understood, believed, and embraced with all the heart.[62]

This same requirement, that regeneration is the prius of true faith, supports Bellamy's position in the second great controversy of the pre-Revolutionary decades, the revival of the dispute concerning the theological propriety of the Half-Way covenant.

In the Synod of 1662, the ministerial establishment of New England, perturbed by the falling birth-rate and the rising number of church-goers who remained unwilling or unable to make full or formal profession of a saving faith, drew up a report recommending that children of such technically unregenerate parents as had owned their baptismal vows, be baptized, but that neither the children nor their parents be permitted to participate in the Lord's supper. Members they could be, but unless and until they publicly confessed to being justified, not communicants. Now in 1769, similar conditions prevailing, the issue was raised anew with the publication of a pamphlet by the Rev. Moses Mather,[163] minister of the Church in Middlesex parish (Darien), Connecticut, entitled, **The Visible Church in Covenant with God: or an Inquiry into the Constitution of the Visible Church of Christ Wherein the Divine Right of Infant Baptism is Defended, and the Admission of Adults to compleat standing in the Visible Church though destitute of a saving faith, is shown to be agreeable to the Revealed Will of God.**"[164]

Mather was convinced that the churches of New England were in danger of perishing for a lack of members owing to the steadily increasing numbers of sober and righteous persons who could not in all honesty lay claim to having been born again. Faced with this dismal prospect, he boldly affirms that God has been pleased to appoint a Visible Church by an External Covenant for the purposes of mercy in the Covenant of Grace, to which persons in an unregenerate state may be joined, thereby becoming the real members of the visible church of Christ.[165] Not so, replies Bellamy there is but one covenant, the covenant of grace, and that requires public profession of real holiness and godliness as a prerequisite of admission to the company of the visible church. "Those who comply with this Covenant have, in the sight of God, an equal right to baptism for their children, and to the Lord's Supper for themselves."[166] As for Mather's distinguishing of an external covenant, it is, insofar as additional to the covenant of grace, graceless, and hence no true covenant.

In another pamphlet on the same subject, published in that same year, Bellamy specifies the particular words of the covenant to which he himself was sealed by his minister, the same as he now requires of applicants for membership in the Bethlehem congregation:

> You do now, in the presence of the dread Majesty of heaven and earth, and before angels and men, in the sincerity of your soul, avouch the Lord Jehovah to be your sovereign

> Lord and supreme Good, through Jesus Christ; and solemnly
> devote and give yourself up to his fear and service, to walk
> in all his ways, and keep all his commands, seeking his
> glory.[167]

He who does not willingly own the covenant by such a public profession before his pastor and the assembled church-membership, remains unregenerate. It matters not at all, argues Bellamy, that he should believe everything that the Holy Scriptures say concerning God and Christ. If he does not consent with all his heart and mind and soul that this God shall be his God, and this Christ his Savior, he and his children have no right to baptism in the sight of God.

Now ensued another war of pamphlets, Mather replying to Bellamy,[168] Bellamy responding anew to Mather,[169] and entering the lists on behalf of the Half-Way practice, the Rev. Ebenezer Devotion,[170] minister of the Church at Scotland, Connecticut, "I am," he writes,

> fully persuaded and confirmed in this opinion, (viz) that all
> persons who believe the scriptures of the old and new
> testaments, to be the word of God, live morally honest lives,
> or, who sufficently engage that their children shall be train-
> ed up, and educated in the Christian religion, have a right
> to have their children baptized![171]

Do you, then, Bellamy retorts, set yourself in opposition to the standards of orthodoxy proclaimed by the assembly of divines at Westminster? "If I understand you right, and you are in earnest in this declaration, then you believe that the unconverted are, in a measure, really holy....And if this be so, then you are not sound in the faith....Indeed, you may think our confession of faith not agreeable to the word of God, and you may think the same of the articles of the Church of England. If, therefore, you would act a consistent part, you should join, neither with us, nor them; but rather form a new church, on a new plan, with those who think as you do."[172] This was precisely the point, although Devotion professed in a **Second Letter**[173] not to having seen it, and reiterates his own version of the point at issue, namely, "whether a man who knows he has no grace, can be an honest man and own the covenant."[174]

Devotion finds nothing in the Westminster Confession to debar it, and refuses to be read out of the ranks of "calvinistick divines." Nor in his time (he died in 1771) was he or, indeed, any of the liberal faction denied the name of Calvinist. A generation later, a new church, on a new plan, was formed in Boston, and Bellamy was proved a prophet. But by then he too had been decades dead.

In November 1786 Bellamy suffered a massive stroke which left his side paralyzed, his speech impeded, and his intellect "greatly impaired." In this condition he survived, confined to bed and chair, for more than three years. On March 6th, 1790, in the fiftieth year of his ministry and the seventy-second of his age, he died and was laid to rest in the churchyard at Bethlem. Neither as gifted intellectually as his mentor Edwards, nor as great a theological influence as his contemporary, Hopkins, his theology of the great commandment clarifies and justifies the one, and in many of its positions anticipates and validates the other. He was, as he would probably be the first to admit, a man of essentially one root idea. But that idea is basic, and in his manifold works is expressed as clearly and perceptively as has ever been done by any preacher of the new or old divinity. After Bellamy, there can be no doubt as to the nature of true virtue or the meaning of the great commandment.

Bibliographical Essay

There are two separate but largely similar collections of works, **The Works of Rev. Joseph Bellamy, D.D.**, late of Bethlehem, Connecticut, in three volumes, edited by Stephen Dodge (New York: J. Seymour, 1811-1812), and **The Works of Joseph Bellamy, D.D.**, first pastor of the church in Bethlem, Conn. with a Memoir of his Life and Character by Rev. Tryon Edwards (great-grandson of Jonathan Edwards), in two volumes (Boston: Doctrinal Tract and Book Society, 1850, reprinted 1853). The following works of Bellamy, not included in the above are available on microcards, Evans American Imprints series: **A Letter to the Reverend Author of the Winter-Evening Conversation on Original Sin** Evans 8080), and **Remarks of Rev. Mr. Croswell's Letter to Rev. Mr. Cumming** (Evans 9340).

There is no full-length biography of Bellamy. The man as his parishioners knew him is profiled by Newell Meeker Calhoun, **Litchfield County Sketches** (Norfolk, Conn, Litchfield County University Club, 1906), and Arthur Goodenough, **The Clergy of Litchfield County** (New York; DeVinne Press, 1909).

The periodical literature specifically devoted to Bellamy or to aspects of his thought is skimpy in the extreme, consisting of two unsigned review articles published eighty and seventy years after the publications they review, i.e., 'Review of True Religion Delineated,' **Quarterly Christian Spectator, II** (1830), 397-424, and 'Review of Bellamy on the Permission of Sin,' **Quarterly Christian Spectator, II** (1830), 529-540; a written-to-order account of Bellamy as a schoolmaster, Percy Coe Eggleston, **A Man of Bethlehem,** Joseph Bellamy, D.D., and his Divinity School (New London: printed for the Bethlehem tercentenary, 1908), and two cursory notices, Elizabeth deWitt Root, 'Joseph Bellamy and Theological Education,' **Hartford Seminary Bulletin** (Winter 1955-56), 33-37, and Joseph B. Stephens, **Rev. Joseph Bellamy, Bethlehem's Famed Preacher,'** Sunday Republican Magazine (The Waterbury Republican), July 26th, 1964. 8-10.

A compact and comprehensive exposition of Bellamy's theology is provided by Frank Hugh Foster, **A Genetic History of the New England Theology,** Chapter V. Foster finds special significance in Bellamy's view of atonement.

"Upon this topic," he thinks, "Bellamy's services were epoch-making, for he introduced to New England thinking an entirely new theory of the atonement." (113) On the other hand, Foster has but little to say about Bellamy's theory of the great commandment.

There are two unpublished dissertations: Glenn Paul Anderson, **Joseph Bellamy 1719-1790: The Man and His Work,** Ph.D dissertation, Boston University Graduate School, 1971, in a mine of information. The comprehensive bibliography appended to this work includes letters, manuscripts, public records, genealogies, and much more. The other dissertation is by Michael P. Anderson, **The Pope of Litchfield County: an Intellectual Biography of Joseph Bellamy, 1719-1790,** Ph.D dissertation, Claremont Graduate School, 1980. This I have not myself seen. For further biographical information, see Franklin Bowditch Dexter, **Biographical Sketches of the Graduates of Yale College** (New York: Henry Holt, 1885), I, 523-529.A brief account of what she takes to be the central themes of **True Religion Delineated** is interpolated in Chapter XXIX of Harriet Beecher Stowe's novel, **Oldtown Folks** (Boston: Fields, Osgood & Co., 1869), 370-376.

[1] Glenn Paul Anderson, **Joseph Bellamy 1719-1790: The Man and His Work,** unpublished Ph.D. dissertation, Boston University, 1971. 662. The author is a minister, professor of church history, and dean of the North Park (Chicago) Theological Seminary.

[2] Joseph G. Haroutunian, 'Jonathan Edwards: Theologian of the Great Commandment', **Theology Today,** I (October, 1944), 361-377.

[3] Joseph Bellamy, the fourth son and fifth of the six children of Matthew Bellamy, farmer and merchant of Cheshire (Wallingford), Connecticut and Sarah Wood (Bellamy) was born February 20th, 1719 at the family farm in the township of Cheshire. Of his early years nothing definite is known. His mother died when he was but two, and he was brought up by his stepmother. She must have been about her business, for at the tender age of twelve Joseph qualified to enter Yale, from which he graduated at sixteen with the Class of 1735.

[4] His class rank, based on social standing rather than on academic merit was 23rd in a class of 24.

[5] No specific testimony to this event survives. Tryon Edwards tells us only that "he became the subject of those serious impressions which, there is every reason to believe, issued in his saving conversion." **Works** I viii. Writing some twenty-two years after the event, Bellamy himself, in his **Theron, Paulinus, and Aspasio (Works** II. 251-252) has Theron describe his own conversion experience, but whether the mature Bellamy is recalling his own youthful conversion or merely inventing one such for Theron is impossible to determine. Against the view that it is Bellamy's own conversion experience that is here recollected in tranquillity is the fact that he identifies his own viewpoint in these letters and dialogues with that of Paulinus. But perhaps this is a designed misdirection.

[6] Although the town is and was called Bethlem, for reasons unfathomed the church society was then, and is now, called Bethlehem.

[7] **The Works of Rev. Joseph Bellamy, D.D.** New York: J. Seymour, 1811-1812, vol. 1.

[8] **True Religion Delineated, Works** (Edwards) I. 217. Hereafter cited as **TRD** with page number in **Works** (Edwards), I.

[9] Ibid., 14.

[10] Ibid., 15.

[11] Ibid., 16.

[12] Ibid., 17.

[13] Ibid., 22-23.

[14] Ibid., 25.

[15] Ibid., 34.

[16] Ibid., 24.

[17] Ibid., 41-42.

[18] Ibid., 43.

[19] Ibid., 44.

[20] Ibid.

[21] Ibid., 43.

[22] Ibid., 135.

[23] Ibid.

[24] Ibid., 136.

[25]Ibid 233. "To explain myself," he adds, "I may just observe that the original constitution with Adam as public head (**Genesis** 2:17) was a positive appointment. After he was turned out of the garden, he ceased to sustain the character or capacity of a public person; nor are his posterity accountable for any but his first trangression." Ibid 242.

[26]Ibid., 137.

[27]Ibid., 230. My italics.

[28]Ibid., 133.

[29]Ibid., 150.

[30]Ibid., 139.

[31]Ibid., 100-101.

[32]Ibid., 253.

[33]Ibid., 65.

[34]Ibid., 56.

[35]Ibid., 71.

[36]Ibid.

[37]Ibid., 302.

[38]Ibid., 71.

[39]Edwards **Works** (Worcester edition), VII, 9-130. Hereafter cited as JFA with page number.

[40]Ibid., 74.

[41]Ibid., 71.

[42]Ibid., 33.

[43]**FoW** (Yale) 300.

[44]Ibid., 308.

[45]**FoW** (Yale) 434-345.

[46]dissertation, 749.

[47]Ibid., 307.

[48]**FoW** (Yale) 434-435.

[49]Ibid., 304n.

[50]Ibid., 73, 307-308.

[51]Ibid., 48.

[52]Ibid., 49.

[53]Ibid. Bellamy is well aware of the unexpressed assumption here made, the assumption, that is, of the orthodox conception of the Holy Trinity, and doubts not but that it is justified by the authority of scripture. "That there are three persons in the Godhead....and that these three are one God, the Scriptures must believe, or we cannot understand the gospel. How they are three, and how are one, is not revealed, nor is it necessary for us to know; but that there are three persons in the Godhead, and yet but one God, we must believe; and what characters they sustain, and what parts they act in the affair of our salvation, we must understand." (Ibid 218-219).

[54]Ibid., 331.

[55]Ibid., 132-133.

132

⁵⁶Ibid., 179.

⁵⁷Ibid., 178.

⁵⁸Ibid., 133.

⁵⁹Ibid., 87.

⁶⁰For the details of this episode see, **Works** (Edwards), I xvi-xxiv.

⁶¹The exception is Frank Hugh Foster who concludes: "Above all, a new air breathes through Bellamy's writing—the air of freedom; and a new intellectual disposition is everywhere manifest—the disposition to discuss, not merely in order to refute, but also to learn, and to meet new difficulties by new propositions suited to the day." **Genetic History**, 128.

⁶²**The Nature of True Virtue**, Chapters III-V.

⁶³Sydney E. Ahlstrom, **A Religious History of the American People** (New Haven: Yale University Press, 1972), 407.

⁶⁴Joseph Bellamy, **The Wisdom of God in the Permission of Sin Vindicated, Works** II. 104.

⁶⁵Bellamy, **Works** (Memoir), I. xxiv.

⁶⁶On April 27th, 1844, his ministerial tenure secure, Bellamy married Frances Sherman of New Haven, by whom he had five sons and three daughters. Mrs. Bellamy died in 1785, and a year later the widower married the widow of a clerical colleague, Mrs. Abiah Storrs. Of this marriage there was no issue. She survived him.

⁶⁷In the course of his fifty-year ministry at Bethlem, Bellamy is said to have prepared more than sixty young men for clerical careers, a number exceeded only by the redoubtable Nathanael Emmons.

⁶⁸**Works** I. 363-416., 463-490.

⁶⁹complete title: **A Winter Evening's Conversation upon the Doctrine of Original Sin between a Minister and three of his Neighbor accidentally met together, Wherein the notion of our having sinned in Adam: and being on that account only liable to Eternal Damnation, is proved to be unscriptural, irrational, and of a dangerous tendency** (Boston: Green and Russell, 1757). Evans 8060. Hereafter cited as **Conversation**.

⁷⁰Albeit neither the **Conversation** nor its sequel **The Winter Evening's Conversation Vindicated** carried its author's name on the title page, there was no mystery as to his identity. Born in 1718, ordained to the second church at Salisbury, Massachusetts in 1741, Webster served his congregation for fifty-five years until his death in 1796. Virtually forgotten today, he was arguably the ablest liberal theologian of the pre-revolutionary period, surpassing his younger and more famous colleague Jonathan Mayhew. See Thomas Cary, **A Funeral sermon**. Evans 30170. See also **Sibley's Harvard Graduates**, X. 250-259.

⁷¹**Conversation**, 3.

⁷²Ibid., 4.

⁷³Ibid.

⁷⁴**Piety versus Moralism**, 24.

⁷⁵Ibid.

⁷⁶For Bellamy and those like minded, 'Arminian' is synonymous with what a later generation will call 'liberal'. In both usages the sense is prejorative.

⁷⁷**Conversation**, 6. My italics.

⁷⁸Ibid.

[79] Ibid.

[80] Ibid, 7.

[81] Ibid., 8.

[82] Ibid.

[83] Ibid., 9.

[84] Ibid., 11. author's italics.

[85] Ibid., 15.

[86] Ibid., 16.

[87] "The plain truth is, this and the doctrines connected with it, have been bones of contention ever since they were vented by Austin." Ibid., 24.

[88] Ibid., 26.

[89] Ibid., 29.

[90] Peter Clark, seventh child of Uriah Clark, farmer and landowner, was born March 12th, 1694 at Watertown. He attended Harvard, graduating with the Class of 1712. Ordained in 1717 to the church at Salem Village, he served his congregation until his death in 1768. See **Sibley's Harvard Graduates**, V. 616-623.

[91] Published at Boston by S. Kneeland, 1758. Hereafter cited as **Summer-Morning**.

[92] **Summer-Morning**, 11.

[93] Ibid., 49.

[94] Published at Boston by S. Kneeland, 1758. Evans 8080.

[95] The second son of Lieutenant John March, saddler and innkeeper of Newbury, was born at Newbury in 1704. He prepared for the ministry at Harvard, graduating with the Class of 1722. He was ordained to the church at Amesbury in 1728. In 1742, irreconcilable differences having arisen between March and his congregation, he resigned his pastorate and went to live with his wealthy uncle, Rev. Christopher Tappan, at the latter's parsonage in Newbury. There he spent the remainder of his long life, for several years as an aide to Tappan, and afterwards to his successor. He died at Newbury in 1791, long since forgotten by Old and New Lights alike. See **Sibley's Harvard Graduates**, VII. 91-93.

[96] Published at Portsmouth by Daniel Fowle in 1758. Evans 8166.

[97] I have been unable to come by a copy of this letter (pamphlet). It is not included in Hopkins' Collected Works, nor is it to be found in **Evan's American Imprints.**

[98] Charles Chauncy, the third of the name, was born on January 1st, 1705. His father, a merchant died when Charles was six and he was left to the care of relatives who paid for his education. His academic achievements at Harvard (Class of 1721) led to his post-graduate appointment to a series of scholarships, which he held until called by the First Church in Boston in 1727. As minister of perhaps the most prestigitous of the Boston churches, Chauncy played a leading role in the intellectual life of the community and the academic affairs of Harvard (as ex officio member of the Board of Overseers). His theology was Arminian, his politics liberal to radical (he was a firm supporter of the patriot cause), and his preaching "notoriously involved and awkward in grammar and dully simple in thought." Withal, his books and sermons marked him, after Edwards, for the most prominent clerical scholar of his times. Chauncy died on February 10th, 1787, honoured as much for his exemplary patriotism as for his writings. See **Sibley's Harvard Graduates**, VI 439-467.

[99] Published at Boston by Green and Russell, 1758, Evans 8100.

134

[100]Published at Boston by Edes and Gill, 1758. Evans 8102. Hereafter cited as **Remarks.**

[101]**Remarks,** 31. My italics.

[102]Ibid., 8.

[103]Full title, **The Winter-Evening's Conversation Vindicated; against the Remarks of the Rev. Mr. Peter Clark of Danvers** (Boston: Edes and Gill, 1759). Evans 8283. Hereafter cited as **Conversation Vindicated.**

[104]**Conversation Vindicated,** 15.

[105]Ibid., 14.

[106]Ibid., 113.

[107]Ibid., 22.

[108]Ibid., 61.

[109]In his **Defence of the Principles of the Summer-Morning's Conversation concerning the Doctrines of Original Sin against the exceptions of the author of the Winter-Evening's Conversation Vindicted,** etc. (Boston: Edes and Gill, 1760), a 160 page point by point reply to Webster's **Conversation Vindicated,** he rests his case on Holy Scripture as the infallible rule of judgement.

[110]Joseph Bellamy, **The Wisdom of God in the Permission of Sin Vindicated** etc. **Works** (Edwards), II. 3-96.

[111] See **Works** (Edwards), II. 3-96.

[112]**The Wisdom of God in the Permission of Sin,** Sermon II, **Works** (Edwards), II. 35. Hereafter cited by Sermon number and page.

[113]Sermon II. 29.

[114]Ibid., 28.

[115]Ibid., 30.

[116]Sermon I. 9.

[117]Sermon III, 42-43.

[118]Ibid., 43.

[119]Ibid., 44.

[120]Sermon III. 44.

[121]Ibid., 45.

[122]Ibid.

[123]Ibid., 46.

[124]Sermon III. 51.

[125]Sermon IV. 89-90.

[126]Sermon III. 60.

[127]Sermon IV. 84.

[128]Ibid., 84n.

[129]Ibid., 96.

[130]Samuel Moody, son of the Rev. Joseph ("Handkerchief") Moody, the eccentric minister of York in Maine, and grandson of the better known revivalist minister, Samuel Moody (1698-1747), was born at York in 1726 and educated at Harvard (Class of 1746). He thought himself a Calvinist and sought a career in the ministry, but after several unsuccessful efforts to secure a permanent

pulpit ("he had a low opinion of his abilities and was discouraged by the fact that whenever he became excited he began to shake") he abandoned the quest, turned to teaching, and "soon made a name for himself." In 1763 he was chosen to be the first master of the newly extablished Dummer Academy, which office he held until "the family weakness of mind" forced his retirement in 1790. Earlier, Dartmouth had honored his services to education by awarding him in 1779 the M.A. degree *honoris causa*. Moody died in 1795 and was buried in the York meetinghouse graveyard. He never married, and his sole publication of note was his reply to Bellamy. See Cliffor K. Shipton, **New England Life in the 18th Century,** Representative Biographies from **Sibley's Harvard Graduates** (Cambridge: Belknap Press of Harvard University Press, 1963), 546-552.

[131]Samuel Moody, **An Attempt to point out the fatal and pernicious consequences of the Rev. Mr. Joseph Bellamy's doctrines respecting Moral Evil** (Boston: Eades and Gill, 1759), 6. Evans 8418. Hereafter cited as **Attempt.**

[132]**Attempt,** 8.

[133]Ibid., 10-11.

[134]Ibid., 11.

[135]**Attempt, 11.**

[136]Ibid., 13.

[137]Ibid., 14.

[138]Ibid., 15.

[139]**Attempt,** 20.

[140]Ibid.

[141]**Attempt,** 28.

[142]Ibid., 28n.

[143]Ibid., 29.

[144]Ibid., 29-30.

[145]Foster, **Genetic History,** 124-126; Haroutunian, **Piety vs Moralism,** 36-38.

[146]Haroutunian, 36.

[147]Complete title, **The Wisdom of God in the Permission of Sin vindicated; in Answer to a late Pamphlet intitled** (sic), **An Attempt** (Boston: S. Kneeland, 1760), Evans 8541. **Works** II. 97-155. Works version hereafter cited as **Wisdom Vindicated.**

[148]**Wisdom Vindicated,** 100.

[149]Ibid.

[150]Ibid., 114.

[151]**Piety versus Moralism,** 38.

[152]**Attempt,** 18.

[153]Increase Mather, **A Discourse concerning the subject of Baptism** (1662). Quoted by Bellamy, **Works** II. 669.

[154]Born at Hardingstone near Northampton in 1714; educated at Northampton Grammer School and Lincoln College, Oxford, where he encountered Wesley and methodism, only to reject the latter in favor of Calvinism. Hervey took Anglican orders in 1737, serving as curate in various parishes for fifteen years. In 1752 he succeeded to his father's living at Weston Favell. His **Meditations** and **Contemplations** were devotional best-sellers, going through fourteen editions in as many years. He died in 1758.

[155] James Hervey, **Theron and Aspasio or, a series of Dialogues and Letters upon the most interesting and important subjects.** To which is added **Aspasio Vindicated,** in Eleven Letters from Mr. Hervey to the Rev. John Wesley (London: Thomas Tegg and Son, 1837).

[156] Wesley's letter is included in the edition cited.

[157] According to Aspasio (Hervey), "Justification is an act of God Almighty's grace; whereby he acquits his people from guilt, and accounts them righteous for the sake of Christ's righteousnes, which was wrought out for them, and is imputed to them: **Theron and Aspasio,** 20.

[158] Bellamy, **A Blow at the Root of the Refined Antinomianism of the Present Age, Works** I. 492.

[159] Ibid., 493.

[160] Bellamy's other important works bearing upon the question of Justification are, **An Essay on the Nature and Glory of the gospel of Jesus Christ,** etc. (1762), **Works** II. 271-452; **A Blow at the Root of the Refined Antinomianism of the Present Age** (1763), **Works** I. 492-525; and his reply to the Rev. Andrew Croswell's **A Letter to the Reverend Alexander Cumming** (1762), Evans 9099, entitled **Remarks on the Rev'd Mr. Croswell's Letter to Mr. Cumming** (1763), Evans 9340.

[161] Published at Boston by S. Kneeland, 1759.

[162] The chief among whom are the Rev. William Cudworth, author of **A Defence of Mr. Hervey's Dialogues against Mr. Bellamy's Theron, Paulinus, and Aspasio** (1762), Evans 9100; David Wilson, an English scholar, author of **Palaemon's Creed Revived and Examined** (1762). Bellamy's **Blow at the Roots** is, in the main, a response to Wilson's thesis and to the Rev. Andrew Croswell, author of the aforementioned **Letter.**

[163] **Works** II. 222-223.

[164] Born at Lyme, Connecticut in 1739, and educated at Yale (Class of 1739), Mather was ordained to the Church in Middlesex Parish in 1744, remaining with them for the entire sixty-four years of his active ministry until his death in 1806. See Dexter, I. 626-628.

[165] Published at New York by H. Gain, 1769. Evans 8415.

[166] **The Visible Church in Covenant, 4.**

[167] Bellamy, **There is but one Covenant** (New Haven: T. and S. Green, 1769), ii. Evans 11174.

[168] **Works** II. 672.

[169] Mather, **The Visible Church in Covenant with God Further Illustrated** (New Haven: T. and S. Green, 1770).

[170] Bellamy, **A Careful and Strict Examination of the External Covenant** (New Haven: T. and S. Green, 1770). Evans 11565.

[171] The most aptly named of all the New England clergy was born in 1714. Educated at Yale (Class of 1732), he was ordained to the Church of Scotland, Connecticut in 1735, which congregation he faithfully served until his death in 1771. See Dexter I. 451-453.

[172] Devotion, **The Parishioner having studied the Point,** etc. (Hartford, 1769), 5. Evans 11237.

[173] Bellamy, **The Sacramental Controversy brought to a Point** (New Haven: T. and S. Green, 1770). Evans 11631.

[174] Devotion, A Second Letter to the Reverend Joseph Bellamy occasioned by his Fourth Dialogue, whcih he calls, The Sacramental Controversy Brought to a Point (New Haven: T. and S. Green, 1770). **Evans 11631.**

[175] Devotion, **Second Letter,** 8.

The Consistent Calvinism
Of Samuel Hopkins

"Every Christian is at heart a Hopkinsian or a consistent Calvinist. Theologians ought to be Hopkinsians in their brains, if they have any."[1]

THE CONSISTENT CALVINISM OF SAMUEL HOPKINS

And there is reason to hope that though dead, he will yet
speak for ages to come.

The hope that Hopkins here expresses is very much more than a pious platitude. No man in America, with the possible exception of Joseph Bellamy, was better qualified to judge of the value to posterity of the thought of Jonathan Edwards. He had come to Northampton in December of 1741 as a raw and diffident young ministerial apprentice newly graduated from Yale, and the elegant and accomplished Sarah Edwards took him in (her husband was away on a preaching tour), made him one of the family, and encouraged his religious exercises. If Edwards Park's conjecture is on the mark, she also provided the seed for what was to grow into the most notorious notion of Hopkinsianism, namely, the belief that we ought to be willing to be damned forever, if such is necessary to the greater glory of God.[2] The relationship thus happily begun ripened into a firm and enduring friendship based, one suspects, as much upon Hopkins' admiration of and devotion to Sarah Edwards as on his respect for and dedication to the character and principles of her husband. Nine years later, the apprentice, now established as the minister of the Congregational church at Great Barrington, would be instrumental in securing the churchless Edwards his appointment as missionary to the indians at Stockbridge, and eight years after that his would be a strong voice on the council recommending that Edwards accept the proffered presidency of the College of New Jersey. Following the President's untimely death, barely a month after his assumption of the office, the widow confided to Hopkins all of Edward's unpublished manuscripts and sermons. In 1765 he would see through the press two of the most important of these, the dissertations **Concerning the End for which God Created the World** and **The Nature of True Virtue.** In this last, Hopkin's own theology will find its spirit and its principle, and in defending the Edwardsian position transcend it.

He came from solid Puritan stock, pridefully descended from the first settlers of Massachusetts Bay. Timothy Hopkins, his father, was a pious farmer, a sometime justice of the peace, and from 1727 until his death in 1749 a frequent representative to the colonial legislature. Timothy's wife, Mary Judd Hopkins, was as devout as her husband, and raised their nine children to obey their parents and respect the sabbath. Samuel, "the first child of my parents that lived," was born at the farm, in the township of Waterbury, on the Lord's Day, September 17, 1721. As a youth he worked as a farmhand and aspired to no greater station in life until in the winter after I was fourteen years old, I retired much to a chamber in my father's house, and spent considerable time in reading, especially in reading the Bible." His father, finding this evidence of a godly disposition, shortly sent him to board with a distant neighbor, the Rev. John Graham. Here, with a number of others like-minded, he fitted for college, was examined, passed, and admitted to Yale in September, 1737. His inclination to the ministry was strengthened by the visit to New Haven in October, 1740 of the celebrated English evangelist George Whitefield. He approved mightily of Whitefield's powerful preaching, and even more so of that of another visitor, Gilbert Tennent, "the greatest and best man, and the best preacher that I had even seen or heard." He now resolved to take instruction from Tennent, but his enthusiasm was dashed by his classmate, the saintly but eccentric David Brainerd, who convinced him that he was not a true Christian inasmuch as he was, to Brainerd's view, deficient in his religious affections and exercises. For years afterward Hopkins would worry about this. His later intense concern during the regeneration controversy with the facticity of the immediate operation of the Spirit of God in quickening the sense of the heart, has its source in Brainerd's careless verdict.

In September of 1741, shortly before commencement, Jonathan Edwards preached in New Haven. Hopkins heard him and conceived such an esteem for his person and his preaching that he resolved to apply to study with him at the earliest opportunity. To that end he rode to Northampton in December, with what result we have seen. He would spend a total of eight months at various times during the next two years under the tutelage of Edwards, after which, having been examined and licensed he accepted the call to Great Barrington. He would serve them for twenty-five years and twenty-one days" until, like his mentor Edwards, and for much the same reasons, he came to grief and was dismissed. Given his pulpit performance (W.E. Channing, who knew him well, noted that he had the worst speaking voice of any preacher he had ever heard); given his austere personality, and given the harshness of his theology, it is surprising that he lasted so long, Crushed in spirit, he contemplated abandoning the ministry and retiring to his farm. His controversial views, aggressively maintained, had alienated most of those who might have been inclined to recommend him to other churches. Moreover, he had by now a wife and eight children requiring his support. He had ceased to hope for a call when he was invited to preach, with a view to settling by the first church at Newport, Rhode Island. After hearing him, the congregation decided not to extend a call, However he was asked to deliver a farewell sermon, which so moved them that they reversed the decision, and in April, 1770 he was installed as minister. Here he would remain (except for the war years 1776-1780) until his death on December 20th, 1803.

II

Then said one unto Him, Lord, are there few that be saved?
And he said unto them, strive to enter in at the strait gate:
for many, I say unto you, will seek to enter in, and shall not
be able.

Is man justified by faith alone, or are works also necessary to salvation? In mid-eighteenth century New England this was a primary question, dividing, on the one hand, the New Divinitymen, who, following their leader Edwards, tended to rely on faith quickened by the active operation of the Spirit of God, and on the other, the Arminians,[4] who were, in the eyes of their Calvinist critics soft on original sin, weak with respect to the divinity of Christ, and strong on the efficacy of works. Chief among those thus characterized was the Rev. Jonathan Mayhew, the urbane and erudite pastor of the fashionably liberal West Church in Boston. Certain it was that he profoundly distrusted the endemic emotionalism of the New Divinity, but what disturbed him most about the followers of Edwards was their tendency to ignore the role of scripture in the awakening of faith. Thus it was that in 1761 he preached and published two sermons on Striving to Enter in at the Strait Gate in which he vigourously contended for that interpretation of the role of scripture which gave encouragement to the strivings of the unregenerate.

In light of the ensuing controversy, which was to see much arguing at cross purposes owing to the habit of each disputant of investing the term with his own particular bias, it is important to be clear about Mayhew's usage. The unregenerate of whom he speaks are not those who deliberately deny God, nor yet those absolutely impenitent. He is not referring to atheists, pagans, or heretics. Rather is it that the term as he employs it is an exact synonym for the phrase 'awakened sinner', the eight characteristics of which are, according to Mayhew: a speculative belief in the gospel; consciousness of sin, guilt, and misery; an earnest desire for the salvation offered through Christ; taking care to be rightly informed; praying earnestly to God for illumination; watchfulness against temptation; endeavouring to abstain from that which God has forbidden; and perseverance.[5] Since scripture is strewn with passages exhorting awakened sinners to strive to exhibit each and all of these characteristics, Mayhew thinks to have established his basic point, that is, that salvation is offered to the unregenerate on the condition of their striving. Unlike the partisans of the New Divinity, who had no difficulty in separating the saved sheep from the damned goats, Mayhew found it inordinately difficult to draw a clear and certain distinction between the regenerate and the unregenerate mass of mankind, including presumably, most of the members of his own congregation, who shied away from public profession of their redemption. The true question is, he thinks, not whether any special act of grace is necessary to regeneration, but whether there are in the words of God in gospel promises made respecting the unregenerate from whence it may be inferred that if they strive they shall obtain. For himself, Mayhew was convinced that there are such promises given, for otherwise where would be the incentive for anyone to strive to be saved? "How unreasonable, how unscriptural," he tells them, "were it to suppose, that, by those who hunger and thirst after righteousness, our Lord intends only the regenerate."[6] How contrary to reason and good sense to deny that salvation is also offered to those who seek it. His congregation agreed, but those Calvinists who remained convinced that God has eternally elected some (the regenerate) to salvation, even as he has condemned others (the unregenerate) to perpetual punishment, were dismayed. To Hopkins the notion that salvation is offered to every repentant reader of scriptures undercut the very foundations of Calvinism and he undertook to set Mayhew straight in his **Enquiry Concerning the Promises of the Gospel** published in 1765.

Where Mayhew has gone wrong, he thinks, is in ascribing to the unregenerate expressions and exercises which are applicable only to the endeavours of the regenerate. "The doctor has thro' his whole performance exalted the unregenerate and their doings too high; and in order to support what he contends for, has represented them as having those exercises which indeed they never have, but are peculiar to the regenerate."[7] Hopkins concedes that the unregenerate, while they continue as such, may in some sense desire salvation. "They may desire deliverance from natural evil ....and they may desire safety and happiness, under a conviction of conscience that it is to be had in no other way but by sharing in the salvation which is by Jesus Christ."[8] But that this is a striving or desire for salvation such as scripture mandates cannot be admitted since, according to our author, "there is not one instance in scripture of any persons being spoken of as desiring salvation, who was not readily willing to accept it as it is offered....But such desires as these are holy desires; and therefore are found nowhere but in a regenerate heart."[9]

Had Hopkins been content to say no more than that, the controversy might have faded to a minor disagreement respecting usage. But he was never one to let well enough alone, and having corrected, to his own satisfaction, Mayhew's blurring of the distinction between regenerate and unregenerate, he seized the opportunity to spell out the absolute difference separating the one (regenerate) from the other (unregenerate). The plain short view of the case is, he declares, that "man is not only by sin plunged into a state of infinite guilt; from which he cannot be delivered....unless he is interested in, or united to, the Mediator; but he has also by his apostasy lost the moral image of God, or all true holiness: and consequently is wholly corrupt....This corruption or viciousness of heart being so great and universal, the sinner will not repent, or have any right exercises towards God and his law, until his heart is in some degree renewed and set right."[10] His condition, in scriptural terms, is "emnity against God," and he will continue to be an enemy to God until his heart is changed. "This change, therefore, called regenera-

144

tion, by which a new heart is given....(is) wrought by the Spirit of God immediately and instantaneously, and altogether imperceptibly to the person who is the subject of it; it being impossible that he should know what God has done for him, but by a consciousness of his own views and exercises, which are the fruit and consequence of the divine operation." these views and exercises adds Hopkins, are what men mean when they speak of being born again, "and this is sometimes called by divines *active conversion* to distinguish it from regeneration, or that change in which men are passive."[12]

Since holy scripture, as Hopkins reads it, reserves to the converted antecedently regenerated the promise of pardon and eternal life, it follows logically that "there are no promises of regenerating grace made to the exercises and doings of the unregenerate,"[13] and that consequently Mayhew and his followers are refuted by the word of God himself. Anticipating the objection, that if this is so, that if there are no promises made to the endeavours and doings of the unregenerate in seeking the salvation of their souls then there can be no encouragement to their striving to enter in at the strait gate, Hopkins desires us to observe and bear in mind, that when the unregenerate sinner is spoken of as seeking salvation, the expression is "to be understood in a sense consistent with his really at heart opposing, hating and rejecting the salvation which the gospel offers,"[14] and this because the true desire of the unregenerate is something else, namely, deliverance from eternal misery, or hope of everlasting happiness, and these are consistent with "the greatest love to sin and the most perfect opposition of heart to holiness. The unregenerate sinner, therefore, who truly understands his situation must inevitably be drawn to despair. Knowing in his heart that he has no true desire for salvation, and that there is no foundation for him until his heart is changed, "he will therefore despair of ever attaining to this in an unregenerate state: and consequently, if he is made to believe that none can obtain a new heart but those that have these good desires, he will of course despair of ever obtaining it." The argument is reminiscent of that of Soren Kierkegaard in his **Sickness unto Death,** and the remedy is the same—regeneration through repentance.

Even so, Hopkins cannot, consistent with his reliance on the authority of scripture, discount the Bible as a means to salvation. "Therefore," he concedes, if repentance and faith in Christ are necessary in order to salvation, a knowledge of things contained in divine revelation, without which there can be no such exercise, is equally necessary. But this knowledge can be obtained only in the use of means."[16] That the unregenerate are capable of great degrees of this "speculative or doctrinal" knowledge he freely admits: "they may have a clear view and affecting sense (which is indeed, strictly speaking, something more than mere speculation) of the truths of Christianity, and particularly of their own state as sinners."[17] Unfortunately, such knowledge, Hopkins believes, does the unregenerate no good at all! For, he maintains, "it is certain that the unregenerate do not exercise any true virtue in their attendance on the means of grace , however engaged and diligent they are, and whatever pains they take....And there is no connection between the instruction or knowledge they obtain hereby, and holiness."[18]

Here, then, the difference between the viewpoints of Hopkins and Mayhew is made plain, and it is the difference between mere attendance to the gospel and attendance preceded by repentance. Without this last, Hopkins contends, attendance is more vice than virtue. "Yea," he cries, "the impenitent sinner who continues obstinately to reject and oppose the salvation offered in the gospel, does in some respects, yea, on the whole, become not less, but more vicious and guilty in God's sight, the more inclination and knowledge he gets in attendance on the means of grace....The awakened, convinced sinner, who has taken a great deal of pains in the use of means....and yet continues impenitent, is in this respect much more guilty and vile, and a greater criminal in God's sight, than if he had never attained to this....knowledge....Yea, his impenitence, and all his sins are so aggravated by the light and conviction he obtains, that whatever particular ways of known sin he has forsaken, and how many soever external duties he attends upon; yet, on the whole, he is undoubtedly a greater sinner, than he was when he lived in security and the neglect of the means of grace."[19]

The statement is extreme, and designedly so, albeit Hopkins did not intend that it should be interpreted as a slap at Mayhew's and other liberally inclined congregations. They, on their part, liked to think of themselves as awakened sinners in the road to regeneration; he, for his, wishes to shock them into that state of repentance without which no salvation is possible. As if realizing that he has perhaps put the matter too strongly, and being very aware that his statements have laid him open to the animus of antinomianism, he subsequently allows that those who attend to the report of the gospel are "in a more likely way to be saved than....he who either does not live under the gospel, or if he does, never attends to it, and uses no proper means to understand it."[20] The allowance, however, went unnoticed. The recognized successor to Mr. Edwards had spoken, and the liberal clergy, the same whose spiritual predecessors in the previous century had rallied in defense of the half-way covenant, took to their studies to compose denunciations and refutations of this denigrating New Divinity, which seemed to them to be in a fair way to destroy the churches of New England by rejecting as unregenerate and thereby damned that large majority of sober and righteous citizens and churchgoers who neither would, nor in conscience could, lay claim to a particular possession of a special gift of God's good grace.

The first to tilt a lance at Hopkins was the elderly and highly respected minister of the church at Stratford, the Rev. Jedidiah Mills, a Connecticut yankee with a large disdain for "subtle metaphysical reasoning." He finds Hopkins's arguments absurd and, what is worse, lacking in common sense. "What," he exclaims, "is there no possibility that the drunkard, the thief, the liar, etc....should become on the whole, less vicious in God's sight while unregenerate, by reforming all this atrocious wickedness tho' on no higher principle than that of natural conscience, awakened by the common influences of the spirit—Strange absurdity this."[21] "It is," he thinks, "needless to observe here that these things never did agree to the common sense of mankind; or of the Christian world; and to my weak understanding, I must say they sound too strange to be true."[22] Like Mayhew, he takes it to be a self-evident fact that men under the gospel do exhibit degrees of internal light and sensibility of conscience. "A sensibility of divine things awakened in natural conscience by a greater degree of internal light surely cannot be more sinful than ignorance and stupidity."[23] That Hopkins can believe such a thing, according to Mills, is owing to his failure to distinguish between the external light of the evidence of the truth of the gospel, and the internal light of an awakened conscience; arguing indifferently from the one to the other, as tho' they were the same in nature, kind, effects and properties; and in all respects would bear the same predications, reasonings, and conclusions."[24] He has confused the self-revulsion felt by an awakening conscience with growing actually worse. As Mills sees it, "to be sensible of sin and to realize and feel their own badness is one thing, and to grow steadily more hardened and stupid is another very different from the former, so that the one may be without the other."[25] With Mayhew again, he sees the unregenerate evincing degrees of goodness and vileness, whereas Hopkins sees only a difference in kind. And he fails entirely to take the latter's point respecting the entire opposition between conscience and benevolence to being in general.

What Mills does see clearly, however, is that Hopkins's division of sinners into sheep and goats, redeemed and damned, presupposes the high Calvinist conception of God as infinitely perfect and its converse, mankind, as totally depraved. For himself Mills will not have it so: "whatever be the state to which mankind is reduced by the fall: yet there is found in him some remains of natural principles and affections...."[26] Mayhew would agree, as would the generality of Americans conversant with the French and English Enlightenment. But neither Mills nor Mayhew, nor any of their enlightened colleagues in the Massachusetts ministry, saw the need to face up to the previous question: between the infinite perfection of God, and man infinitely vile, can there be any theologically defensible middle ground? Hopkins says no. Mills allows that "altho' it should be utterly beyond the power of the creature, to explicate and shew the manner of this consistency, between the infinite purity of God's nature and...the unregenerate, infinitely vile; this....would be no argument against the truth, that the weak intellect of the creature, should not be able to understand the matter how 'tis reconciled; since the fact is certain."[27]

Perhaps. But not to Hopkins, who two years later replied in detail and at interminable length with **The True State and Character of the Unregenerate Stripped of all Misrepresentation and Disguise.** Mills, he insists, has misrepresented his position, which is concerned with the case of the awakened sinner, that is, the Pharisee, who is fully aware of the gospel and yet remains impenitent. "Mr. M. makes the reformation of the convinced sinner to keep pace with his light and conviction of conscience....he makes him to be one who....comes up to *all known duties.*By this he grossly misrepresents me, and the whole matter in dispute....The sinner I speak of is supposed not to comply with the light and conviction he has, but to rebel against it....and in this I placed his greater sinfulness."[28] This is he who is more vile precisely because he is—impenitent. Whatever his amendment of life, sober, righteous, churchgoing, his continuing refusal to display the overt evidences of regeneration constitutes his greater guilt. In brief, Hopkins and Mills are in basic disagreement as to the character to be ascribed to the unregenerate sinner. The former sees him as an odious and abominable enemy to God, while the latter, in common with the Christian liberalism of every age, views the unregenerate once-born as morally weak, but awakened to his faults and striving, and therefore the less guilty for making that effort. But the Bible, protests Hopkins, knows no such creature as Mills and the liberals describe! "Such a character is the invention of Mr. M. and a thousand others in direct contradiction to the whole of divine revelation."[29] And on this point he proposes to rest his case.

But his opponents will not have done with the matter. A fresh and angry partisan of Mayhew's gospel of striving, the Rev. William Hart, pastor of the First Church at Saybrook, surfaces to inquire in his **Brief Remarks on a Number of False Propositions and Dangerous Errors** etc., how it can be held more wicked to act righteously in part, than not to act at all. For himself, Hart holds it cannot, that Hopkins's view is indeed utter nonsense. "This new scheme of divinity," he rails, "is....heresy...for it contains a monstrous medly (sic) of great truths and great errors, utterly inconsistent with them....This new system, or rather chaos of divinity, is a hard-hearted, arbitrary, cruel tyrant, a tormentor of souls; it scandalously misrepresents the character and conduct of God, and implicitly blasphemes the dispensation of his grace to a sinful world."[30] Stung by this gratuitous insult, Hopkins rushed into print his **Animadversions on Mr. Hart's late Dialogue,** etc. "The teaching of mine that he opposes," writes Hopkins, namely, "regeneration by the immediate influence of the Spirit of God, in opposition to his own view of regeneration by moral suasion, he calls new, and thereby frights people and seeks to raise their prejudices against it. But what evidence is this? It is at least *possible* that there is some truth contained in the Bible, which has not been commonly taught, yea, has never been mentioned by any writer since the apostles: and whenever that shall be discovered and brought out it will be *new*. And who knows but that such *new* discoveries may be made one day?[31] Indeed, have been made by Edwards in his dissertation on True Virtue, and earlier yet in his Religious Affections. In truth, says Hopkins, "the doctrines which have of late been called by many *new* divinity are really a revival and improvement of sound Calvinism, being founded on scriptures, and the doctrine of total depravity."[32] To deny either is Arminianism and infidelity, and, he opines, Hart and Mills are guilty of both.

Provoked to an indignant rejection of these aspersions on his orthodoxy, and realizing, as Hopkins had tartly reminded him, that the new divinity as here conceived was but an extension and development of basic principles derived from Edward's dissertations, Hart returned to the fray with **Remarks on President Edwards's Dissertations concerning the Nature of True Virtue: shewing that he has given a Wrong Idea and Definition of Virtue, and is inconsistent with himself.** The wrong idea is Edwards's notion that true virtue, properly understood, lies not in, nor arises from, any moral sense common to mankind which there is in natural conscience, but rather finds its source and meaning in benevolence to being in general. Or, as Edwards adds, "to speak more accurately, it is that consent, propensity and union of heart to being in general, which is immediately exercised in a general good will."[33] For, he asks, given that "every intelligent being is in some way related to being in general, and is a part of the universal system of existence....what can its general and true beauty be, but its union and consent with the great whole?"[34] Hart does not presume to know, but he is clear in his own mind that as between benevolence to being in general and love to God there is a difference in kind. The point is, that "being in general, or simply considered, is not God: it has none of the peculiar distinguishing characters of the Godhead," it is, in fact, "a mere abstract idea, a creature of the mind."[35]

> Mr. Edwards presents us with three grand objects of virtue's primary and most essential regard, viz. Being in general, considered simply, as intelligent, uncloathed (sic) with any personal, moral or relative characters; the universal system of intelligent beings, and God the author of being, and head of the system; and says that these are in effect one....But each

150

of these objects has peculiar characters, which give ground
for distinguishing them from each other, and they ought
never to be confounded. There can't be three *first* and
supreme objects of virtuous love.[36]

Moreover, to represent benevolence to being simply considered as the essence
and root of all true virtue, is to put the cart before the horse, since on this
view the Bible loses all efficacy as a *means* to regeneration. Rather is it, Hart
believes, that our hearts are put in motion towards Him, and attract or tend
towards him, by our awakening to the word of God in scripture. "Tis in vain
to expect a miraculous exertion of properly creating power, to form their hearts
anew, or regenerate them, without....the word of gospel truth."[37] This
miraculous change Edwards suggests and Hopkins defends is, as it were, "wro't
(sic) in the dark, and without *means*." 'Means', that is to say, the teaching
of the Bible, is for Hart, as for Mayhew and Mills before him, the only proper way to being born again. What all of them really fear the most about
the new divinity is that its insistence on an immediate operation of the Spirit
of God as the fruit of regeneration must tend to the neglect and disregard
of the Bible. Thus Hart challenges Hopkins to speak out plainly that people
might understand whether this is really what the new divinity portends.

Excepting only Edwards on True Virtue, the most important contribution
to the regeneration controversy is Hopkins's **Inquiry into the Nature of True
Holiness.** In essence it is a restatement of the Edwardsian thesis expanded
and clarified to embrace true virtue's synonym, true holiness, which Hopkins,
following Edwards, defines as love to being in general. "This is the whole
of true holiness; it consists in this love, and in nothing else."[39] "This universal benevolence or love to being in general," he adds, "must have God, who
is infinitely the greatest and most excellent, and the sum of all being and
perfection, for its object."[40] "He who exercises true benevolence towards any
particular being does it," he maintains, "as a friend to the whole; so that
his love to him is really love to being in general, as he belongs to the whole
and is included in it."[41] Only that self love which is part and parcel of our
disinterested benevolence to the whole which includes ourselves is permitted
in the sight of God. That self love which is contracted to particular affection

is in every way sinful. "Therefore," Hopkins concludes, "we are left at no loss about the nature of true holiness in God and in the creature. It consists in disinterested benevolence, and all that affection which is included in this, in opposition to self love."[42]

To Hart's objection that being in general is an abstract idea and, as such, no proper object of benevolence, Hopkins replies, "if being in general was something distinct from God and the creature, and more than these and not included in them, the objection would....have some foundation."[43] But that is not the case, for these, qua whole, are being in general, so that the love commanded by God is exercised towards them not in any limited confined sense, but as parts of the whole. Had Hopkins been gifted with a truly holistic imagination, the conception of God here implied would be a panentheism. That it is not such is owing to the fact that the sense of the terms 'whole' and 'being in general', as here understood, is not *ontological* but *scriptural.* When Hopkins declares that "love to being in general is obedience to the law of God, since God and our fellow-creatures are being in general and comprehend the whole of being,"[44] he is thinking only of **Matthew** 22:37-40. It seems never to have occurred to him that being in general must comprehend and include— Nature. Of course, he was not alone in this oversight. It did not occur to Hart, or to his other critics, Moses Hemmenway[45] and Samuel Langdon.[46] As things turned out, Hopkins did not find in their polemics anything new to controvert, and so the controversy died away.

III

For I could wish that myself were accursed from Christ, for my brethren, my kinsmen according to the flesh. **Romans** 9:3.

Hopkins's answer to Hart was published in 1773, but by then the regenerate and unregenerate alike were swept up in the approaching storm of the Revolution. In August of 1769 the patriots of Newport had struck the first blow by scuttling the British armed sloop; Liberty, and add a second with their destruction of the armed schooner Gaspee in June 1772. Subsequently

Newport was blockaded, and in December 1776 British troops occupied the town. Anticipating the event, Hopkins many months earlier had sent his family to the safety of their farm at Great Barrington, and now in December as the British drew near he hurried to join them. In October 1779 the British withdrew and the following spring Hopkins returned to find his meeting-house a shell (the British had used it for a barracks) and his parishioners scattered. He was sixty years old, impoverished in spirit, health, and pocket, and barely up to the task of rebuilding his church and revitalizing his congregation. In the twenty years remaining of his ministry he would make but little progress to these ends. The meeting-house was repaired (thanks to generous donations from some Boston churches) and some saved souls were gathered in, but the pre-war prosperity was never regained. As Edwards Park succinctly remarks, "They remained poor. He lived and died poor."[47]

His precarious health and penury notwithstanding, Hopkins continued to engage in polemics. Newport in the decades before and after the Revolution was recognized as "the great slave market of New England," and Hopkins was a witness at first hand to the inhuman consequences of this despicable traffic. "It is said," writes Park, "that Hopkins often looked upon the cargoes of Africans who were landed at the wharves near his meeting-house and parsonage. His church members, his best friends, his nearest neighbors, nearly all the respectable families of the town, were owners, and many of the most accomplished merchants on the island were importers of slaves."[48] In such an environment, to speak out against the slave traffic was to risk mortally offending those very people who as parishioners supported, however niggardly, his ministry. Even so he could not bring himself to keep silent, and from 1770 to the end of his life he preached and pamphletized for abolition. His courage was recognized and appreciated, yet even as he was honoured for his contributions to the abolitionist cause, his theology was under bitter attack, much of it directed against his notion that Christians ought to be willing to be damned for the greater glory of God.

Believing that this criticism had its source in a general failure of his critics to attend to the plain truth of scripture, Hopkins undertook to vindicate his position in **A Dialogue between a Calvinist and a semi-Calvinist.**[49] He begins by clarifying the notion to be defended. If by being willing to be damned is meant choosing damnation for its own sake, then this is, he concedes, an impossibility, which no one has ever believed or asserted. "But if by being willing to be cast off by God forever be meant, that however great and dreadful this evil is, yet a Christian may and ought to be willing to suffer it, if it be necessary in order to avoid a greater evil, or to obtain an overbalancing good, if such a case can be supposed; this," says the Calvinist (Hopkins), "is true, and ought to be maintained as essential to the character of a Christian....For it is essential to true benevolence to prefer a greater good to a less, and a less evil to a greater, and that whether it be private or public good or evil."[50]

The Calvinist, unlike his opponent who can conceive of no greater evil than the eternal damnation of a soul, is here thinking quantitatively. Thus he has no difficulty in establishing his point, i.e., that the eternal misery of one must yield to the eternal happiness of the many, should the glory of God require it. "Supposing," he asks, "it were necessary for one individual to be miserable forever in order to save a million from this misery....ought he not be willing to perish in such a case and on this supposition?[51] St. Paul makes the same supposition when he says, "I would wish that myself were accursed from Christ, for my brethren, my kinsmen, according to the flesh," 'You misunderstand St. Paul' retorts the semi-Calvinist. By being accursed from Christ he intends no more than suffrance of a temporary evil. 'It makes no difference,' replies Hopkins, for if you concede that benevolence will lead a man to suffer even one degree of evil in order to save others from a hundred degrees, then to be consistent you must admit the reasonableness of requiring that he suffer a hundred degree in order to save his neighbor ten thousand degrees of evil, and where will you call a halt? "It here appears that the apostle Paul spoke the language of true benevolence, and declared he felt, as he ought to feel, when he said he could wish himself accursed from Christ, if by this means his brethren might be saved, if we understand him as meaning that he was willing to be lost forever for their sake, that they might be saved. And why should he not be understood to say what he ought to say, and to speak the language of true benevolence, since this is the natural import of his words, and to be accursed from Christ cannot mean less than eternal damnation, without putting an unnatural, forced meaning upon them."[52]

Secure in the conviction that his is the only consistent ("natural") interpretation of the passage in question, Hopkins now shifts his ground, suggesting to his adversary that they attend more particularly to the matter of
the glory of God. "You will grant," he argues, "that the glory of God....is
of the highest importance, and that it is reasonable, and our duty, to make
this our highest and superior end?" I grant it, replies the semi-Calvinist, "but
this will be so far from making me willing to be damned, that it will lead
us to desire and pursue our salvation that he may be glorified in that forever."[53]
Hardly, thinks Hopkins, for scripture itself teaches us that "it is not for the
glory of God that all should be saved, but most for his glory that a number
should be damned; otherwise all would be saved. We will, therefore, now make
a supposition, which is not an impossible one, viz., that it is most for God's
glory, and for the universal good, that you should be damned, ought you
not to be willing to be damned, on this supposition, that God could not be
glorified by you in any other way?"[54] To reject the proposal, Hopkins argues,
is to place your personal interest and happiness above all things, it is so far
from being impossible to be willing to be damned....that he could not will
or choose anything else. He must say, 'let God by glorified, let what will
become of me.'"[55]

To the religious temper of our times, the argument may appear completely
repellent, for all that it is *consistent* with the notion of true benevolence as
that is defined by Edwards and Hopkins. But repellent or not, if scripture
is the revealed Word of God, and if God, as Hopkins affirms, "has revealed
it to be his will to punish some of mankind forever,"[56] if these assumptions
be true, then the conclusion that the Calvinist has drawn perforce must be
granted by every *real* Christian who accepts the *whole* of the Bible as God's
truth. If scripture is the standard, no other position is possible since, as
Hopkins reminds us, we cannot know whether we are one of the damned or
among the saved. "Whether you shall be saved or damned depends entirely
upon his will. And supposing he sees it most for his glory and the general
good that you should be damned, it is certainly his will that you should be
damned. On this supposition, then, you ought to be willing to be damned;
for not willing to be damned in this case, is opposing God's will, instead of
saying, 'Thy will be done.'"[57]

For the moment the semi-Calvinist is silenced, but then it occurs to him, as perhaps to you, that it cannot be right to be willing to be abandoned to sin and enmity against God. "Therefore," he thinks, "no man ought to be willing to be damned, unless he ought to be willing to be God's enemy....to assert which would be shocking, and no man, surely, can believe it."[58] The objection, Hopkins allows, is plausible, but no more than that, since given the truth of the previous supposition, it would imply a contradiction, which cannot be allowed. Hence there is no contradiction.

> You have granted, and all must grant, that we ought to be willing that some of our fellow-men be abandoned to sin and ruin, and be continued enemies to God forever....And not to be willing, in this case, and to refuse cordially to consent to it, would be rebellion against God. So that there is no other way for us, not to turn enemies to God ourselves, but to be willing that some of our fellow-men should be enemies to him forever. And why must not this be just as true in our own case? ....Not to consent to it on this supposition would be an act of enmity against God, and to be an enemy to him. But to consent to it, and be willing that God's will should be done for his own glory and the general good, would be so far from being friends to sin, that it would be an exercise of love and friendship to God, and benevolence to being in general.[59]

Unless one is willing to be an enemy to God, which willingness makes one a friend, one is an enemy to God. The New Testament theology offers no finer example of consistency carried through to its logical conclusion. That it is a conclusion which many then, and most now, find utterly unpalatable does not lessen its force. The fact is, says Hopkins, that "a denial of this truth, and most of the arguments to support such denial, do misrepresent the nature of disinterested benevolence."[60] Consequently, he who would deny this truth must deny at once the teaching of the dissertation on True Virtue respecting the object of that benevolence, and, inasmuch as the conception of that object is the scriptural conception of God, he must end by denying God and scripture alike! To the pious mind of Samuel Hopkins this is a prospect beyond belief, although situated as he was in a place and time of rampant infidelity, he was only too well aware that it was a prospect relished by the advocates of Enlightenment. Thus it is that at the age of seventy he sets himself anew to the task of setting the Doctrines of Christianity in a clear light, and of vindicating yet once more the ways of God to his fellow-men.

IV

Is not a System of Divinity as proper and important, as a
System of Jurisprudence, Physic, or natural Philosophy?[61]

Most studies of Hopkins[62] have tended to slight the **System of Doctrines,** justifying their dismissal of it with the implicit excuse that the System adds nothing new to the case for consistent Calvinism made in the earlier works. In this, rather cavalier, assumption the commentators and critics are at once right—and wrong. Right, in that no radical departures from, or additions to, the positions taken in the regeneration controversy and in the **Dialogue** are here to be found;[63] wrong, insofar as they conclude from this that the case is closed. In the twenty years intervening since the publication of **True Holiness,** Hopkins had rethought his arguments, and now in the **System** he presents them anew, clarified, and freed from their earlier polemic environment.

He begins by reminding his reader that his system is most particularly a system of *biblical doctrines,* albeit he does not pretend to include therein every doctrine of Christianity. It is enough, he feels, "that the most important and essential truths are brought into view: And of these some are treated more concisely; and others are more particularly examined and vindicted. Nor, he adds, "was it thought necessary, or expedient, to mention all the objections which have been made to the doctrines here advanced, as they are sufficiently obviated, by establishing the truth, from scripture and reason."[64] As this latter testifies to the existence of a God who is the efficient cause of our own existence and the things we behold around us, so also does scripture.

"Not by being there abundantly asserted (although for Hopkins himself that suffices); but by the existence of such a book as the Bible." For, he argues, "it is as much impossible that there should be such a book were there no God, as that there should be such a world as we see without an invisible cause."[65] As the Bible serves to reinforce the classical arguments from efficient causation and design, so do these in turn confirm "the inference....that the Bible is a revelation from heaven,"[66] and justify our conviction that "there is one chain, or consistent scheme of truth, which runs through the whole (of it)."[67]

The chain is God, represented in scripture as "an *infinite* being....without limits or bounds," "unchangeable in all respects," "perfect and infinite in understanding and knowledge," "omnipresent," "almighty," "invisible," and "incomprehensible."[68] This last is of the first importance, "for," writes Hopkins, "if we will not believe anything respecting God, which we cannot comprehend....we shall not believe there is a God."[69] We shall not believe that all created existence is nothing when compared with him; and indeed is comprehended in him, and is really no addition to existence, it being only an emanation from him, the fountain and sum of all existence."[70] Nor shall we believe that God exists in a Trinity of persons if we will not believe what God has revealed of himself in scripture. That God is three in one, and as such incomprehensible, scripture affirms, and this, Hopkins believes, obviates the need to "shew the particular manner of the distinct subsistence of the three persons in the divine Trinity." "Therefore," he adds, "nothing of this kind will be attempted here."[71]

Fair enough, given that God is—incomprehensible. But the same cannot be said in support of Hopkins's failure to justify his assertion, four times repeated,[72] that created existence is an *emanation* from God. The repetition debars dismissal of the assertion as an aberration, and it is certain that Hopkins did not find either the word or the notion revealed in any canonical scripture. The idea is, as we have seen, foundational to the Edwardsian conception of God, and it is obvious that Hopkins is here echoing his mentor. But not, be it added, to the extent of accepting the Edwardsian metaphysics of the sixth way. His common sense, no less than his basic biblicism, precluded any lapse, however temporary, into neoplatonism. His system is still no system of Berkeleian idealism. The Hopkinsian doctrine of emanation is to be justified, if at all, only in the context of the Hopkinsian Christology.

In his conception of the Christ, Hopkins hews closely to the formula of Chalcedon. Jesus Christ is one person in two natures: "The human nature of Jesus Christ is not a distinct person, separate from the divine nature, or his Godhead. The human nature exists, and began to exist, in union with the sacred person in the Trinity, the Word; so that both natures are but one person....This same person is God, and he is man. This person was in heaven, and was visible on earth at the same time."[73] In this last, if anywhere in the System, lies Hopkins's understanding of emanation. To him the word is, so it would seem, nothing more than a synonym for the visibility of the Logos. "The Word assumed the *human nature,* not a *human person,* into a personal union with himself, by which this complex person exists, God-man."[74] Unless this be granted, Hopkins thinks, the Old Testament cannot be reconciled with the New, or the New Testament with itself. The conception is, he concedes, incomprehensible from the standpoint of *uncommitted* reason. The divinity of Christ, and the manner of his existence, and of his subsisting, is, as much as that of the Father, a wholly unaccountable mystery.Even so, we should not, he feels, "be forward to pronounce it inconsistent with reason, and absurd; but be convinced, that to do thus, is very bold and assuming; and that it may be consistent and true, notwithstanding anything we may know; though it be mysterious and incomprehensible."[75]

Having thus, to his own, satisfaction, accounted for any possible objection to the truth of Trinity, Hopkins proceeds to the specification of its undertakings. The principal of these, antecedent to creation, is for him, as it had been for Willard, the covenant between the Father and the son respecting the redemption of man, by which the distinct part which each person in the Trinity was to play was fixed. "This is an eternal covenant, without beginning, as is the existence of the triune God, and as are all the divine purposes and decrees. The second person was engaged to become incarnate, to do and suffer all that was necessary for the salvation of men. The Father promised that on his consenting to take upon him the character and work of a Mediator and Redeemer, he should be in every way furnished and assisted to go through with the work; that he should have power to save an elect number of mankind, and form a church and kingdom, most perfect and glorious. In order to accomplish this, all things, all power in heaven and earth should be given to him, until Redemption was completed: And then he should reign in the exercise of all his offices, as Mediator, church and kingdom forever."[76] In all of this, "the third person in the Trinity, the Holy Spirit, is not expressly mentioned as covenanting, or engaging to perform any part of this work; yet he is necessarily understood as concerned and included in this covenant....and therefore must be considered as taking that particular part by consent and agreement."[77] This particular part is that immediate operation of the Spirit of God previously mentioned whereby the unregenerate are become regenerate and redeemed.

The position remains, in essence, the same as that previously remarked in Section II above, but the passage of twenty years has worked to effect a large improvement in the manner of its expression. The polemic mood is not entirely absent, but it is much diminished. The tone throughout is temperate. The basic assumption, however, remains unchanged: "Man is naturally, and while unrenewed, in a state of total moral depravity. His mind, his heart, is enmity against God, and his law."[78] "Therefore," writes Hopkins, with Mayhew and Hart still presumably in mind, "no man has a right to direct sinners to any thing as duty....or to flatter him that he may do some duty, while he continues wholly impenitent and wicked,"[79] and that because "impenitent sinners do no duty."[80]

As before, 'impenitence' is that which characterizes all those who lack the heart for love to being in general; these then "are the unregenerate, who have no disinterested affection; but are wholly selfish in their religious exercises," and, our author continues to insist, "their religion, whatever appearance it may put on, is false and destructive."[81] If the will be not renewed, or a new heart not be given, by an immediate operation of the Spirit of God, nothing else can or will avail. "Men are not regenerated in the sense in which we are now considering regeneration, by light or the word of God."[82] Nor yet, be it added, by good works, sound morals, or church attendance. But when the imperceptibly instantaneous and immediate energy of the holy Spirit suffuses his heart, then, and then only, is the sinner turned about, renovated, illuminated, and formed for the exercise of universal disinterested benevolence.

160

Then only is the unregenerate become regenerate.

Thus far nothing new. But now in the closing pages of part I, the theological part of the System of Doctrines,[83] Hopkins finds it proper to observe,

> that though the heart or will be the seat of this illumina-
> tion, and moral light and darkness are as the disposition of
> the heart is, yet the whole mind, in all the faculties of it,
> is concerned, and in some way included and affected in this
> affair. Intellectual light and conviction, considered as distinct
> from the heart, is included in this illumination. Ideas are con-
> veyed to the heart by this medium. Where there are no
> speculative ideas, which are in some measure agreeable to
> the truth, and no right judgment and conviction respecting
> intellectual objects; the benevolent heart will not be proper-
> ly illustrated, or be under advantage to exercise itself pro-
> perly toward external objects. When the single eye is form-
> ed, it will receive light and view the objects of moral sight,
> by the medium of the intellect. Therefore there appears to
> be a propriety, that there should be some degree of
> speculative light and conviction in the minds of the adult,
> before a new heart or single eye is given, in order to prepare
> them to discern the truth properly, and to have exercises
> agreeable to it.[84]

We are called not to a blind faith, but to a true discerning founded on a rational revelation.

V

> He lacked the intellectual grasp of his master, and therefore
> could not but modify his teaching at every turn. His dialec-
> tical acumen was an inadequate substitute for the vision and
> understanding of Edwards. He grasped the logic of Edwards'

Calvinism, but the contents of Edwards' soul were beyond his capacities.[85] Joseph Haroutunian.

Boldness, freedom and fearlessness are the prime characteristics of Hopkins's theology, It dared attack accepted truths and question their rightfulness to be. It had no shrinking from any consequences that the logic of the premises demanded. It was as strenuous and as able a critique of current beliefs as New England has ever seen. And its influence was great.[86] Williston Walker

Both overstate the case, but both are right, so far at least as concerns that about which they both agree, namely, Hopkins's grasp of Edwards's logic. That Edwards was the more imaginative and original mind is readily conceded by every student of the System. What is arguable is that he realized as completely as did his down-to-earth disciple the doctrinal implications of his metaphysical principles. The fact is, as Henry May says, that "Edwards's idealist metaphysics, his skirting of the edge of pantheism, above all, his fundamentally aesthetic definition of virtue, were not preachable."[87] Neither in the Holy Commonwealth nor in the young Republic was the sixth way of Jonathan Edwards a viable alternative to the old Calvinism and the new infidelity.

Not that there was anything inherently wrong with the principles themselves, at least as far as Hopkins could see. The authority of scripture was still allowed by every Calvinist, as was the conception of God as absolute sovereign. Many there were who, even after the great regeneration controversy had subsided, remained unconvinced that true virtue is benevolence to being in general, but these, he thought, had simply failed to see that Hart's objection to the idea of being-in-general, viz, that it was nothing more than the barest of abstractions, had been effectively disposed of by his redefinition of being-in-general as God and all intelligent creatures.[88] Of course, we with hindsight know that it had not, since there remained the problem of accounting for the balance of nature. But as Hart and his supporters did not press this particular point, it remained for the time unmet.

In the event, the immediate result of the Hopkinsian development was a further polarization within the ranks of the Calvinists and a sundering of Calvinism from unitarianism and universalism. The intelligentsia of New England subscribed to the System in substantial numbers and its clerical adherents grew, according to Park, from a baker's dozen at the outbreak of the Revolution to five score and more by century's end. Hopkinsianism flourished in the seminaries, particularly at Andover, and was propagated in many a sermon and tract, most notably by Nathanael Emmons, until its catastrophic decline occasioned by the introduction at midcentury of the geological and biological theories of evolution.

No one today publicly espouses Hopkinsianism, but wherever profession is made to being born again it lives, since any explanation of the phenomenon of spiritual rebirth or regeneration perforce presupposes either the theory of the immediate operation of the Spirit of God on the awakened heart or some variant etiology of illumination derivative from, or alternative to, that theory. More than this: inasmuch as that theory itself presumes the scriptural conception of God the Father as sovereign and the Son and Spirit as the instrumentalities of that sovereignty, if the born again acknowledge this trinity, to that extent they are logically obligated to accept those doctrines which the System has demonstrated to follow from the trinitarian conception.

Hopkins has been harshly criticized for his emphasis on the total depravity of the heirs of Adam; his belief that one ought to be willing to be damned if that is conductive or necessary to the realization of the greater glory of God has been ridiculed; the contentious character of his reasoning has been greatly resented, particularly by those whose preaching and teaching it has exposed. But none have been so bold as to maintain that his conclusions fail to follow from his first premise, the divine sovereignty. Given this, the unpalatable positions of Hopkinsianism are largely unavoidable. To evade them requires at the very least some modification of the Calvinist conception of God and, Hopkins would add, some justification of this from scripture. His critics sought to provide it, only to provoke thereby the production of yet another and even more thorough system of Calvinist divinity.

Bibliographical Essay

The Works of Samuel Hopkins, D.D., with a **Memoir** of his Life and Character by Edwards A. Park, D.D., in three volumes, edited by Sewall Harding (Boston: Doctrinal Tract and Book Society, 1852; reprinted 1854) is the standard source. It includes the **System of Doctrines** and all of Hopkin's doctrinal and polemical writings with the exception of his **Animadversions on Mr. Hart's late Dialogue.** This last is available, as is the **System,** the biography of Edwards, and virtually everything else of theological significance, on microcards in the Evans American Imprints series. A second edition of the **System,** with chapter numbers and headings altered, was issued in 1811 by Messrs. Lincoln and Edwards of Boston. Hopkins's **Memoirs of the Rev. Jonathan Edwards, A.M.** was published in a separate volume, with numerous emendations, by John Hawksley at London in 1815.

Park's **Memoir.** issued as a separate volume concurrently with the **Works,** is the most recent biography. Park draws heavily on Hopkins's **Sketches of the Life of the Late Rev. Samuel Hopkins,** written by Himself; interspersed with marginal Notes extracted from his Private Diary, etc. (Hartford: Hudson & Goodwin, 1805); and upon John Ferguson, **Memoir of the Life and Character of Rev. Samuel Hopkins** (Boston: Leonard Kimball, 1830); and William Patten, **Reminiscences of the late Rev. Samuel Hopkins** (Boston: Crocker & Brewster, 1843). By modern standards none of these is even marginally adequate. The **Sketches** are just—sketches; Ferguson and Patten are hagiographically anecdotal; Park is too much of one mind with his subject to do even-handed justice to the Hopkinsian theology. His shortcomings as a memorist are discussed at length by George E. Ellis, 'Prof. Park's Memoir of Hopkins,' **Christian Examiner and Relgious Miscellany,** LIV, fourth series, XIX (January, 1853). A fictional Hopkins, barely resembling the historical personage, is portrayed by Harriet Beecher Stowe in her novel, **The Minister's Wooing,** first published in 1859, reissued in 1896, and recently reprinted, with an Introduction by Sandra R. Duguid, by the Stowe-Day Foundation of Hartford in a paperback edition, 1978. The minister of the title is Hopkins as Mrs. Stowe, in the interests of her theological romance, would have him appear in 1791, a bachelor of some forty summers, hopelessly in love with a girl twenty years his junior (in fact, Hopkins; was seventy in 1791, forty-three years married, and the father of eight children). Mrs. Stowe, who had suffered the loss of her son and her sister's fiancee by drowning, and who in consequence had been led to repudiate the high Calvinism championed by Hopkins, here employs her skills as a novelist to the end of justifying a Bushnellian softening of the tenets of Hopkinsianism. A trenchant appraisal of the literary aspects of this employment is provided by Lawrence Buell, 'Calvinism Romanticized: Harriet Beecher Stowe, Samuel Hopkins, and **The Minister's Wooing**,'' ESQ 24 (no. 3, 3rd quarter 1978; no. 92 O.S.), 119-132. The same subject, placed in wider perspective, is treated by Charles H. Foster, **The Rungless Ladder: Harriet Beecher Stowe and New England Puritanism,** New York: Cooper Square Publishers Inc., 1970.

There are no book-length studies exclusively devoted to Hopkins or Hopkinsianism. What we have are chapters and sections of more synoptic works. George Nye Boardman, **A History of New England Theology,** New York: A.D.F. Randolph Company, 1899, retails the contributions of Hopkins to that history in Chapters III, IV, and V. His account is usually thought of as having been superseded by that of Frank Hugh Foster, **A Genetic History of the New England Theology,** Chicago: University of Chicago Press, 1907, a work of wider purport and narrower distinctions. Foster devotes two long chapters to Hopkins, the second of them to the **System,** which he thinks is, "on the whole, for comprehensiveness, thoroughness, high tone, power of reasoning, independence, ethical and spiritual value, and solid contributions to the advancing system of thought...(deserving of) being called a great work—great in comparison with the great systems of the Christian world, and unsurpassed within its own special school." (p.186) Williston Walker includes Hopkins in his **Ten New England Leaders** (New York: Silver, Burdett, & Co., 1901), and finds his system "as strenuous and able a critique of current beliefs as New England has ever seen." (p. 353) This is in contrast to Joseph Haroutunian, **Piety versus Moralism** (New York: Henry Holt, 1932), for whom the "dialectically plausible, but seldom vivid or attractive" theology of Hopkins "marks the transition from Calvinism to moralism." (p. 92).

Of articles about Hopkins there are altogether eight only two of which are recent vintage: Joseph Anthony Conforti, 'Hopkins and the New Divinity,'

William and Mary Quarterly, 34 (1977), 572-589, is a condensation of the author's Ph.D dissertation, **Samuel Hopkins and the New Divinity Movement, 1740-1820:** a study in the transformation of Puritan theology and the New England social order (Providence: Brown University Press, 1975). Conforti is as much and more interested in, and concerned with, Hopkins's impact on the social history of his times as he is with his theology, and the chief value of his study lies in his analysis of the eighteenth century social situation. In similar case is, David S. Lovejoy, 'Religion, Slavery and the Revolution', **New England Quarterly.** XL (June, 1967), 227-263, for whom the importance of Hopkins is his concern for reform and abolition. At the other end of the critical spectrum is Gordon B. Wellman, 'Samuel Hopkins, Rational Calvinist and Mystic', **Review of Religion,** III (March, 1939), 256-276. Wellman thinks to discern mystical tendencies beneath the consistent Calvinist facade, but fails to make a strong case. Oliver Wendell Elsbree, 'Samuel Hopkins and his Doctrine of Benevolence', **New England Quarterly,** VIII (1935), 534-550, views Hopkins as a precursor of Unitarianism insofar as his conception of benevolence approaches the utilitarian. He praises Hopkins for his abolitionism and dismisses his "peculiar" and "antiquated" theology. To complete the group there are four articles published in the nineteenth century. These will be of interest chiefly to specialists in Hopkinsiana. The most helpful of the trio is Edward Beecher, 'The Works of Samuel Hopkins', **Bibliotheca, X.** No. 1, Article III (January, 1853), 63-82. The title is misleading inasmuch as Beecher's essay is actually a sketch and defence of the New England theology in its origins and development, culminating in the system of its great vindicator, Hopkins. For the rest there is Andrew P. Peabody, 'Hopkinsianism', in the **Proceedings of the American Antiquarian Society,** 5 (1888), 437-461; and Alexander V.G. Allen, 'The Transition in New England Theology', **Atlantic Monthly,** 68 (1891), 767-780. The former is mostly devoted to a reprinting of an exchange of letters between Hopkins and Roger Sherman; the latter anticipates the expositions of Boardman and Foster. See also, Enoch Pond, 'Hopkinsianism', **Bibliotheca Sacra,** XIX, 75 (July, 1862), 633-670.

There are three unpublished works worthy of notice. Dick Lucas van

Helsema, **Samuel Hopkins 1721-1803; New England Calvinist,** Ph.D. dissertation, Union Theological Seminary, 1956, reviews the standard materials, but, as one critic has noted, his work "shows some misunderstandings of Hopkins and seems to lack depth of insight." The same should not be said of Hugh Heath Knapp, **Samuel Hopkins and the New Divinity,** Ph.D dissertation, University of Wisconsin, 1971, (University Microfilms #71 28344), for all that he tends uncritically to follow Haroutunian in finding Hopkin's importance to lie principally in his role in the transition from piety to moralism. Lastly, there is William R. Tillman. **The Formation of Samuel Hopkins' Mind,** M.A. thesis, University of Wisconsin, 1967, who argues, mistakenly I think, that Hopkins misunderstood Edwards on the nature of true virtue.

[1] Leonard Woods, **History of Andover Theological Seminary** (Boston: Franklin Press, 1884), 632. Quoting Rev. Samuel Spring.

[2] At the end of January, 1741, writes Park, "and through subsequent days and nights, she had a train of reflections which would *now* be termed Hopkinsian, and which may have been the germ....of Hopkinsianism; for they were, doubtless, soon communicated to the inquisitive and solemn youth who sat at her table and listened to her daily conversation." Quoting now from the diary of Mrs. Edwards, he continues: "I also thought how God had generously given me, for a great while, an entire recognition to his will with respect to the kind and manner of the death that I should die....and how I had that day been made willing, if it was God's pleasure, and for his glory, to die in horror....Upon this I was led to ask myself whether I was not willing to be kept out of heaven even longer; and my whole heart seemed immediately to reply: 'Yes, a thousand years in horror, if it be most for the glory of God....And it seemed to me (considering this) that I found a perfect willingness, and a sweet quietness and alacrity of soul, in consenting that it should be so, and if it were most for the glory of God." **The Works of Samuel Hopkins, D.D.** , in three volumes edited by Sewall Harding with a Memoir by Edwards Amasa Park, D.D. Boston: Doctrinal Tract and Book Society, 1854. I. 22. Hereafter cited as Works by volume number and page number.

[3] **Luke** 13:23-24.

[4] The name and epithet derives from the teachings of the Dutch theologian Jacobus Arminius (1560-1609), and designates those who espoused his views on absolute predestination (he denied it) and universal redemption (he hoped for it). In the lexicon of high Calvinist orthodoxy, the sense is always derogatory, intentionally demeaning and insulting.

[5] Jonathan Mayhew, **Striving to enter in at the strait Gate explain'd and inculcated and the Connexion of Salvation therewith proved from the Holy Scriptures in Two Sermons on Luke XIII: 24.** Boston: Richard Draper, 1761 45-57. Evans 8926.

[6] Ibid., p. 61.

[7] Samuel Hopkins, **An Enquiry concerning the Promises of the Gospel.** Boston: McAlpine and Fleming, 1765. Page 12. Evans 10007.

[8] Ibid., 24.

[9] Ibid., 26-27.

[10] Ibid., 74-75.

[11] Ibid., 78.

[12] Ibid., 78-79.

[13] Ibid., 82.

[14] Ibid., 107n.

[15] Ibid., p. 114. In light of the extensive attention paid in our time by philosophers and religionists alike to the Christian existentialism of Soren Kierkegaard, it is worth noting that the Hopkinsian psychology of despair, as given in **Promises** (110-116), antedates the Kierkegaardian, as offered in **Sickness,** by at least three-quarters of a century.

[16] Ibid., 122.

[17] Ibid., 123-124.

[18] Ibid., 124.

[19] Ibid., 124-125.

[20] Ibid., 128.

[21]Jedidiah Mills, **An Inquiry Concerning the State of the Unregenerate under the Gospel,** containing Remarks on the Tenth Section of the Rev'd Mr. Samuel Hopkins's late answer to Dr. Mayhew's sermon on Striving to enter in at the Strait Gate. New Haven: B. Mecom, 1767 (Evans 10691), 18-19.

[22]Ibid., 23.

[23]Ibid., 14.

[24]Ibid., 16.

[25]Ibid., 7.

[26]Ibid., 113.

[27]Ibid., 114.

[28]Samuel Hopkins, **The True State and Character of the Unregenerate Stripped of all Misrepresentation and disguise; being a reply to Mr. Mill's Inquiry concerning the State of the Unregenerate under the Gospel.** New Haven: Thomas and Samuel Green, 1769 (Evans 11295), p. 5.

[29]Ibid.

[30]William Hart, **Brief Remarks on a Number of False Propositions and Dangerous Errors** which are Spreading in the Country; collected out of sundry discourses lately published, wrote by Dr. Whitaker and Mr. Hopkins, written by way of Dialogue. New London: Timothy Green, 1769 (Evans 11285), p. 49.

[31]Samuel Hopkins, **Animadversions on Mr. Hart's late Dialogue in a letter to a Friend.** New London: Timothy Green, 1770 (Evans 11686), p. 9.

[32]Ibid., 28.

[33]Jonathan Edwards, **The Nature of True Virtue.** Boston: S. Kneeland, 1765, (Evans 9962), pp. 117-118.

[34]Ibid., 118.

[35]William Hart, **Remarks on President Edward's Dissertations concerning the Nature of True Virtue: shewing that he has given a wrong Idea and Definition of Virtue, and is inconsistent with himself. To which is added, An Attempt to shew wherein True Virtue does consist.** New Haven: T. & S. Green, 1771 (Evans 12067), p. 10.

[36]Ibid., 11.

[37]Ibid., 33.

[38]Ibid., 23n.

[39]Samuel Hopkins, **An Inquiry into the Nature of True Holiness.** Newport: Solomon Southwich, 1773 (Evans 12811), p. 14.

[40]Ibid., 13.

[41]Ibid., 12n.

[42]Ibid., 53-54.

[43]Ibid., 82.

[44]Ibid.

[45]Hemmenway had taken exception to remarks of Hopkins made in the latter's reply to Mills, and in **A Vindication of the Power, Obligation and Encouragement of the Unregenerate to attend the Means of Grace** etc. (1772), he undertook to argue anew the case for the spiritual efficacy of actions performed by the unregenerate. Hopkins's answer to him, given in Appendix III to **True Holiness,** drew a snappish response in **Remarks on the Rev. Mr. Hopkins's Answer**

to a **Tract** etc., (1774). The impending Revolution prevented any further exchange, and in any case, Hemmenway had nothing to say that Mills and Hart had not already said.

⁴⁶Twenty years later, in April of 1794, Dr. Samuel Langdon, the President of Harvard College, and doyen of the liberals, raised the regeneration question anew in his **Remarks on the Leading Sentiments of Hopkins's System of Doctrines** (which had been published in 1793). The gospel upon which Hopkins's claim of an immediate operation of the Spirit of God on the regenerate rests, namely, the third chapter of **John**, is, Langdon reminds his readers, concerned much more with the *effect* upon the man made new than with the *agency* of the Holy Spirit. Indeed, there is, he thinks, nothing at all in this chapter to convince us of the necessity for any such immediate operation of and by the third person of the Trinity. The gospel itself, read regularly, suffices to effect that change which is called 'the new man;' to suggest otherwise, argues Langdon, is to suffer that frenzy of enthusiasm which all good Christians and Harvard men will abhor. Hopkins, now in his seventy-fifth year and in poor health, let both criticism and innuendo pass unanswered.

⁴⁷Memoir, **Works** I. 92.

⁴⁸Park, Memoir, **Works** I, 115.

⁴⁹Composed sometime during the 1780's (probably in 1783) the Dialogue was withheld from publication (whether by Hopkins or his prospective publisher is not established) during his lifetime. The hostile reception accorded its posthumous publication in 1804 but confirmed the wisdom of the withholder.

⁵⁰Hopkins, **Works** III, 143-144.

⁵¹Ibid., 144.

⁵²Ibid., 146.

⁵³Ibid., 146-147.

⁵⁴Ibid., 147.

⁵⁵Ibid.

⁵⁶Ibid., 148.

⁵⁷Ibid.

⁵⁸Ibid., 150.

⁵⁹Ibid., 151.

⁶⁰Ibid., 155.

⁶¹Samuel Hopkins, **The System of doctrines contained in Divine Revelation Explained and Defended,** in two volumes. Second Edition. Boston: Lincoln and Edwards, 1811. p. 3. All subsequent references to the System are to this edition, hereafter cited as System with volume and page number. In his Memoir of Hopkins, Edwards Park relates how, when Hopkins was asked, just at the end of his life, whether he would make any alterations in the sentiments expressed in the System, he replied: "No, I am willing to rest my soul on (these doctrines) forever." **Works** I. 232.

⁶²The exception being F.H. Foster, who devotes a chapter of his **Genetic History** to the system.

⁶³Williston Walker summarizes the generally received view when he notes in his chapter on Hopkins in **Ten New England Leaders** (New York: Silver, Burdett & Co., 1901), p. 348, that "The Nature of True Holiness, published in 1773, was his great controversy; in it most of the pecularities of his religious opinions are expressed." Without denying the significance of that splendidly succinct tract, I would argue tht there is more to Hopkins than was there expressed.

[64]**System** I. 5.

[65]Ibid., I. 45-46.

[66]Ibid., I. 3; II. 395.

[67]Ibid., II. 397.

[68]Ibid., I. 49, 50, 51.

[69]Ibid., I. 83.

[70]Ibid., I. 49.

[71]Ibid., I. 84.

[72]Ibid., I. 49, 71, 72, 84.

[73]Ibid., I. 346-347.

[74]Ibid., I. 348.

[75]Ibid., I. 380.

[76]Ibid., I. 438.

[77]Ibid., I. 440-441. As Hopkins understands the matter, the relation is as follows: "The Father gave the Son, and the Son gave himself. He gives himself also in the third person of the Trinity, the Holy Ghost, in renewing and sanctifying the redeemed, and dwelling in them forever." (I. 314-315).

[78]Ibid., II. 102.

[79]Ibid., II. 105. "No command or direction, which is to be found in scripture (he has reference to Mayhew's exegesis of 'Strive to enter in at the strait gate'), can reasonably be understood as prescribing only that which sinners are to do, and may do, while impenitent and disobedient; unless it be expressly said that they are to do it," and Hopkins is confident that no such passage is to be found in scripture. Ibid., II. 106n-170n.

[80]Ibid., II. 106, 108.

[81]Ibid., I. 479.

[82]Ibid., I. 457.

[83]Part II of the System of Doctrines is given over mostly to piety and polity.

[84]**System** I. 510.

[85]**Piety versus Moralism** (New York: Henry Holt and Company, 1932), 82.

[86]**Ten New England Leaders**, 353.

[87]Henry F. May, **The Enlightenment in America** (New York: Oxford University Press, 1976), 59.

[88]**System of doctrines** I. 290-296.

The Thorough Calvinism
Of Nathanael Emmons

"The question among Christians is not, who are probably, but who are certainly right, in their belief of the great and fundamental doctrines of the gospel. There is certainty to be obtained in these points; and all who have obtained it, know that those who differ from them in these points are certainly wrong."[1]

THE THOROUGH CALVINISM OF NATHANAEL EMMONS

> This denomination suppose, that this eminent divine not only
> illustrated and confirmed the main doctrines of Calvinism,
> but brought the whole system to a greater degree of con-
> sistency and perfection, than any who had gone before him.[2]

In the year 1791 appeared the second edition, with large additions, of Miss
Hannah Adams' celebrated **View of Religions,** including a synoptic statement
of the distinguishing tenets of Hopkinsian Calvinism by the Rev. Nathanael
Emmons, minister of the Congregational Church at Franklin, Massachusetts.
She had chosen pre-eminently the right man for the task, since Emmons was
known to the clerisy of New England as a doughty and forceful advocate
of the Edwardsian equation of true virtue with real holiness, and of both
with disinterested benevolence, the proper object of which he, like Edwards
Bellamy, and Hopkins before him, takes to be universal Being, including God
and all intelligent creatures.

Disinterested benevolence, as Emmons understands it, "wishes and seeks
the good of every individual so far as is consistent with the greatest good
of the whole, which is comprised in the glory of God." (H 97)* The operative
phrases here are 'the good of the whole' and 'the glory of God'. To these,
and to what they imply, every Christian must, Emmons insists, consent. With
their implications, as these bear upon the conception of God we will have
more to say below. In the context of this characterization of Hopkinsian
Calvinism, however, the emphasis is on their expression of the law of God,
which is reducible to love to God and to our neighbor as ourselves. The exercise of this love, that is to say, true virtue, is nothing but benevolence acted
out in its proper nature and perfection.

All sin is selfishness, declares Emmons, and adds that this selfishness or
self-love is the foundation of all spiritual blindness, heathen idolatry, and
false religion in the guise of gospel, is indeed, in its whole nature and every
degree of it, enmity against God. Having no true selfless love in their hearts,

*See footnote 2.

those fail in their duty who only attend to the externals of religion, hoping thereby to avoid the eternal damnation which their self-love merits. Emmons forbears to specifically repeat Hopkins' notorious dictum that sinners ought to be willing to be damned for the glory of God, but if all sin really is selfishness it logically follows that sinners unwilling to be damned but confirm their unregenerate state by compounding their sin. Consequently, he does not hesitate to draw the conclusion: "in order to faith in Christ, a sinner must approve in his heart of the divine conduct, even though God should cast him off forever."[3]

Nor is God to be blamed for so ordering his creation that selfishness should prevail and the unregenerate be damned. He is infinitely wise and his knowledge, foresight and view of all possible existences and events is perfect. To assume, therefore, that he actually *preferred* to create a universe totally lacking in moral evil is to assert that the deity is disappointed in the issue of his own creation. But nothing, Emmons argues, can be more dishonorable to God than to imagine that the system actually formed by the divine hand is anything less than the fruit of his original design. Hopkinsians do not doubt that the existence of moral evil conduces to a more perfect and glorious discovery of the infinite perfections of the divine nature than would otherwise have been made to the view of creatures. It must be, then, that the introduction of sin is, upon the whole, for the general good.

Believing firmly that scripture is God's Word, to be taken literally except as common sense dictates otherwise, Hopkinsian Calvinism teaches that mankind became sinners because God was pleased to make a constitution that if Adam sinned, his posterity, in consequence of that sin, should be sinners also. Adam sinned, and we are sinners, but not, Emmons insists, because Adam's sin is transferred to each and all of us. *By* Adam's sin we are become sinners , but not *for* Adam's sin. The *occasion* of his sin is not the *cause* of our sins. The sinfulness of Adam's act is not transferable, because the sinfulness of an act can no more be transferred from one person to another than can the act itself.

The same common sense, Emmons argues, is applicable to the question of the Christian's justification through Christ. "Though believers are justified through Christ's righteousness, yet his righteousness is not transferred to them.

For, personal righteousness can no more be transferred from one person to another than personal sin." The scriptures, as Hopkinsians interpret them, represent sinners as receiving the *benefits* only of Christ's righteousness. We are pardoned and accepted for Christ's sake. This much and no more is the proper scriptural notion of imputation.

For the rest, the Hopkinsians, he tells, us, "warmly advocate the doctrine of the divine decrees, the doctrine of particular election, the doctrine of total depravity, the doctrine of the special influences of the spirit of God in regeneration, the doctrine of the justification by faith alone, the final perseverance of the saints, and the consistency between entire freedom and absolute dependence." To demonstrate the compatibility of these fundamental doctrines with the whole of scripture, and to show how they reasonably and logically follow from, and presuppose, the conception of God as absolute sovereign in whom all creatures live and move and have their being, is the formidable task that Emmons sets himself in the two hundred and sixty-four sermons which comprise his collected works. These sermons, and the five score and more of miscellaneous essays, addresses, sermons for special occasions, and didactic expositions of doctrine that he contributed to various numbers of **The Massachusetts Missionary Magazine, The Connecticut Evangelical Magazine. The Utica Christian Repository, The Hopkinsian Magazine, The Christian Magazine, The Theological Magazine,** and other Calvinist oriented periodicals were, almost literally, his life. Divorcing himself from the chores of daily living, he pursued his sacred calling with a single-minded devotion that later generations would deem fanatic. Like Hopkins,[4] he regularly spent twelve or more hours daily in his study throughout the six decades of his active ministry. "All that a visiter would notice was," according to one such, "that he rose early in the morning, read his Bible, and meditated until the breakfast table was brought into his room; walked from his study chair to his repast, afterwards back to his chair; moved again when the dining table was spread for him....returned in due season to his chosen seat; repeated these journeyings for the evening meal, and before ten o'clock retired to his repose."[5] Like Immanuel Kant, who he resembled in physique if not in visage, the regularity of his habits was such as to serve his neighbors as a clock. He rarely took any physical exercise, and on the infrequent occasions when he was persuaded to leave his study, it was nearly always for necessary pastoral purposes. On his coming to Franklin, he discouraged the social overtures of his new parishioners and declined a generous offer from one of them of room and board, "for fear my acceptance would obstruct my studies." This refusal, he wryly notes, prevented other invitations of the same kind. He married in 1775 and turned over to his wife the management of all household affairs, reserving to himself the general superintendence of his farm, all of which he could survey and did manage from his study.

Weekdays from rising to bedtime he read and wrote. He thought it important to familiarize himself with the writings of both the champions and the critics of the Christian religion, and to this end he immersed himself not only in the exegetical and theological works of his English and American predecessors, but in everything remotely pertinent to his subject appearing in the fields of history, ethics, metaphysics, and civil polity. He even confesses in his Autobiography to having read a few novels "for their beautiful style, lively descriptions, and moral sentiments," albeit he hastens to add that he usually restrained himself from reading for amusement, and put captivating books out of sight.[6]

Fridays and Saturdays he worked on the composition of his sermons, and his method is the mark of the man. Keeping invariably to his principle of preaching on the most important and essential doctrines of the gospel, he would first choose a subject and only then search out a scriptural text fully and clearly adapted to that subject. His subjects were, uniformly, organized by divisions and subdivisions logically developed and culminating in an "Improvement," since he aimed to impress the conscience, as well as to enlighten the understanding, of his hearers. Like Samuel Willard of old and his own mentor Hopkins, Emmons early contemplated the composition of a complete system of divinity in sermons, but unlike these he abandoned the enterprise about half-way through "for no better reason than my inattention and instability." (I. xv)* Volumes IV and V of **The Works**, separately printed as Volumes I and II of **A System of Divinity**, are the product of this contemplation.

This paragon of clerical industry was the product himself of a poor but

*See footnote 1

prolific family of Connecticut farmers. The sixth son and twelfth child of Samuel and Ruth (Cone) Emmons was born on April 20th (old style), 1745 in the township of East Haddam. Both parents were deeply religious. They imbued their children with their own saving faith and were greatly pleased that this youngest son seemed naturally inclined to piety and learning. The death of his mother when he was but twelve may have been a prime cause of his relapse into "a volatile, trifling spirit." In the event, his father changed his mind about making him a scholar and determined to raise him for a farmer. Hating farming and denied the benefits of schooling, young Emmons resolved to educate himself. He purchased a Latin grammar, eventually found a tutor to assist him in his studies, and in due course acquired a proficiency in Latin and literature sufficient to qualify him for admission to Yale College, which institution he entered in 1763. He did reasonably well, although not ranked among the highest in his class, graduated in 1767 and for several months thereafter taught school. He had developed a strong desire to be a preacher of the gospel, and to that end he engaged to study theology, first with a Reverend Strong, who directed him to read through Willard's **Compleat Body of Divinity,** and afterwards with Reverend Smalley, who opened his mind and heart to the Edwardsian New Divinity. Unfortunately for Emmons, the sentiments acquired from Mr. Smalley got him into trouble when the time came for him to be examined for his license to preach. After much debate and soul-searching by his clerical committee he won approval, but one member was moved to vote his dissent in writing, and for a season this document clouded his clerical career. Emmons himself admitted later that as regarded the Old Calvinism of his reverend peers, as distinguished from the New Divinity of Edwards and Hopkins, with which Emmons now fully associated himself, he was "a speckled bird." Even so, he was eventually ordained to the Congregational church at Franklin, which parish he was to serve for fifty-four years until his retirement in 1827. During his tenure as pastor he guided the studies of eighty-seven aspirants to the Congregational ministry and published more than seven thousand copies of some two hundred sermons. His personal life was peaceful but marred by recurrent tragedy. The two children of his first marriage died in childhood and his wife followed in 1778. His second wife, wed in 1780, was the daughter of the second wife of his colleague

Hopkins. She died in 1829 having borne Emmons six children, four of whom died young. He married for a third time in 1831. Predeceasing this wife, Emmons died at Franklin on September 23rd, 1840 in his ninety-fifth year.

II

> There may be therefore room left in divinity and metaphysics, as well as in philosophy and other sciences, to make large improvements. (II. 32-33)

Emmons has no objection to offer to those who, seeking a ready label, identify his theology as Hopkinsian, although in his application of common sense to questions of doctrine, in the rigour of his theological reasoning, and in his continuing inclination to press the implications of scriptural teaching to the bitter or, mayhap, the sublime end he surpasses Hopkins. Forever firm in his conviction that all the teachings of the gospel must be internally harmonious and coherent, he never considers stopping short of following his exposition to whatever conclusions his premises might lead him. That this practice sometimes drives him to embrace positions beyond the hallowed formulas of Calvin himself, Emmons is well aware. He finds the Genevan wanting in thoroughness in his view of the Atonement and illogical in his conception of the connexion between Adam and his posterity. Edwards, whom he greatly admired, and whose disciple he sometimes professed to be, errs egregiously to Emmons' way of thinking in his defense of original sin. Even Hopkins, most of whose positions Emmons inclines to accept as well-taken, fails, he thinks, to see through to the ultimate implications inherent in the Calvinist notion of God.

Indeed, it is arguable that Calvin himself fails to see the implication of his thought when he declares with respect to the knowledge of God the Creator that "no one can look upon himself without immediately turning his thoughts to the contemplation of God, in whom he "lives and moves" **Acts** 17:28). For, quite clearly, the mighty gifts with which we are endowed are hardly from ourselves; indeed, our very being is nothing but subsistence in the one God."[7]

He afterwards tends to restrict his interest in the notion of God to just those characteristics of the deity tending to promote in his reader that sense of "willing reverence" and "earnest fear" prerequisite to "such legitimate worship as is perscribed in the law." Not so Emmons, for all that he too is sometimes strong on the fear of the Lord and not above frightening his congregation into heaven with threats of damnation and hellfire.[8] Like Edwards, he sees nothing incongruous about the application of philosophical notions to the God of the Bible.

That there is, "a first and supreme cause of all that lives and moves and exists in this and every other world" (IV. 404) is, Emmons believes, a plain and obvious truth. "That God is present everywhere, both the light of nature and of divine revelation fully evince. As all creatures....have their being in God, so it is certain to a demonstration, that his presence constantly fills all places throughout his vast dominions....God is equally present with each of his creatures, and with each of his creatures, at one and the same instant." (1. 78; IV. 410). His works are their works, and this "because his works and their works are necessarily and inseparably connected. They live, and move, and have their being in him and he works in them both to will and to do, in all their free and voluntary actions." (IV. 264)

Eternity is one. God is eternal. From this we may deduce, according to our author, that God anterior to his creation is the sole inhabitant of eternity. (IV. 266) We may not deduce, however, that eternity so conceived functions as a foundation or ground. "We cannot conceive of any existence," Emmons admits, "which has no ground or foundation. But the foundation of God's existence is neither before, nor out of himself. For," he argues, "if it were before himself, or out of himself, he could not be the first and self-existent Being. The ground or reason, then, of God's existence must be wholly within himself." (1. 77) Posterior to his creation, God is said to "possess" eternity. "When we would represent the invisible world," says Emmons, "we call it eternity itself, and by going into another world, we always mean going into a boundless eternity." (III. 476) In the same sermon (View of Eternity), he speaks of "that vast eternity which he (God) inhabits," and in which "every human soul shall exist forever, and be forever happy or miserable." (III. 477) The conception of God is throughout one of divine omnipresence. Emmons never tires of quoting **Acts** 17:28, and the context of his quotation[9] regularly suggests that he understands and accepts this particular dictum of scripture, as indeed he accepts all biblical dicta not patently figurative in intent, in a strictly literal sense. Abel Millard, noting this propensity to cite **Acts** 17:28, damns him for a pantheist. Millard, like so many before and after him, has confused pantheism, the doctrine that identifies God and the world as one (which Emmons patently does not do) with panentheism the doctrine which sees God as encompassing the world in the same literal sense is assorted in **Acts** 17:28. Is Emmons, then, a precursor of modern panentheism? We might well so conclude were it not for the fact that no more than Calvin and no less than Aquinas will Emmons allow that the divine perfection is infringed by any taint of material or human deficiency before or after creation. "God is infinitely above all instincts, passions, or affections which proceed from either natural or moral imperfection." (IV. 202) "The plain and important truth (is) that God is perfectly and immutably good, and always acts under the influence of perfect goodness." (IV. 217) The sage of Franklin is one with the orthodox of every Christian generation in his insistence that there is "no natural or necessary connexion between the existence of God, and the existence of anything else in the universe," (IV. 267) and this assertion, of itself, appears to debar any prima facie classification of his theology as panentheistic. Smalley observes the care taken by Emmons to foreclose the inference that God is the only free moral agent in the universe, and deduces from this that he had no pantheistic tendencies.[11] Nor is he, like Edwards, correctly identified as a Christian neo-Platonist. "The works of God are not emanations of his nature, but only the fruits of his power. No created object therefore, bears the least resemblance of the Deity simply because he made it." (IV 351)[12] The divine agency is not the agency of any matter or of man.

Here again, as so many times in the history of Christian theology, we find a philosophically significant conception of God inhibited by a manifestation of the actus purus syndrome,[13] that is, by a devout insistence on the absolute perfection of God to the exclusion and detriment of any real relation to his creatures. On the other hand, attention to the implications of the "exercise" scheme evidences that Emmons' exhibition of the actus purus syndrome may not be as fatal to his implicit panentheism as would at first appear.

To his contemporaries, and to those historians of doctrine who have expounded his views, Emmons is famous primarily because of his insistence that all sin consists in sinning. "Both sin and holiness consist in free, voluntary exercises." (V. 158) The common Calvinist notion, maintained (according to Emmons) by Edwards and popularized by Asa Burton, that a new heart consists in a new taste, disposition, or principle prior to, and the foundation of, holy exercises is mistaken. (V. 128) The truth, Emmons teaches, "is that there is no ground to suppose that a good heart consists in a good taste, or a good principle, or in anything besides good affections." (V. 140) Seeking the origin of these good affections, reason is led to the conclusion that they are the consequence of divine influence, for to deny it, Emmons contends, is to deny that God is absolute sovereign. "Since mankind are the creatures of God, they must be subject to a divine influence in all their free and virtuous exercises," (V. 143) although how God operates on our minds in these free and voluntary exercises passes our comprehension. (IV. 345) The fact of the matter is that God does so operate, and consequently is involved at every moment in every moral act. "Our moral exercises are productions of the divine *power* and not *emanations* of the divine nature." (IV. 350) Which being so, God cannot meaningfully be conceived as actus purus, complete in perfection apart from his creatures, and that because "mind cannot act, any more than matter can move, without a divine agency." (IV. 372)

It has been argued by fatalists (determinists) and Arminians alike that this exercise scheme is inconsistent and absurd, but where, Emmons asks, is the inconsistency?

Who can conceive or explain *how* the Supreme Being exists of himself? or *how* he supports the universe? or *how* he fills all places and surveys all objects at one and the same time? But who, except atheists and skeptics, will presume to deny these truths, or venture to call them inconsistent and absurd? (IV. 344)

Many complain that they have often attempted to reconcile dependence with activity....And to keep themselves in countenance, they bring in Mr. Locke, that oracle of reason,

> who ingenuously owns that he could never reconcile prescience
> in the Deity with human liberty....This, however, will not ap-
> pear strange, if we consider that it belongs not to the office
> of reason to reconcile these two points. Though activity and
> dependence are perfectly consistent, yet they are totally
> distinct....Dependence falls under the cognizance of reason;[14]
> but activity falls under the cognizance of common sense. It
> is the part of reason to demonstrate our dependence on God,
> in whom we live, and move, and have our being. But it is
> the part of common sense to afford us an intuitive knowledge
> of our activity and moral freedom. (IV. 348)

You may find Emmons' argument unconvincing, or then again you may not. That, however, is not the point. What matters to Emmons and to us is the thought that the scriptural conception of God debars any scholastic isolation from the creation even as it reinforces, by its insistence on the ubiquity of the divine influence, a panentheistic interpretation of that conception.

III

> God did not decree things because he saw that they would
> exist; but because he saw that they would not exist without
> his decrees. (IV. 275)

Before the beginning, in the early ages of eternity, God decreed all things that ever have or ever will come to pass. "His infinite wisdom would not permit him to begin the work of creation, until he had decreed the nature, the number, the use and end of all created objects." (IV. 276) Thus he formed and established in his own mind the uniform, consistent, and perfect scheme of the gospel. He foreordained the accuracy of the predictions of those great and distant events which he inspired the writers of the scriptures to record. Among all possible occasions, he determined what should, and what should not, take place. He elected some of his creatures to glory and predestined others to eternal damnation. That these things have happened we know, according to Emmons, from the foreknowledge of God, from explicit declaration of scripture concerning the purposes of God, and from his infinite wisdom.[5]

The truth of the claim that God foreknew all things from eternity is sufficiently established, Emmons believes, by God's foretelling in various places in the Old Testament the coming and death of Jesus, for we cannot suppose that God could have infallibly foretold the great event of Christ's death, with its attendant circumstances, unless he has infallibly foreknown all other events from Adam to Christ.'and if God foreknew all things from Adam to Christ, there can be no question;' Emmons thinks, "but that he foreknew all things from Christ to this day, from this day to the end of time, and from the end of time through the boundless ages of eternity. Indeed, if God foreknew any events, he must have foreknown all events, from eternity." (IV. 265) It may be objected that the argument assumes, what requires to be shown, that is, that God is, if not the immediate author of scripture, at least the source of the inspiration animating his scribes. But the objection, Emmons argues, is self-refuting, for, he asks, "how could God inspire the sacred writers to record these predictions which are contained in the Bible, if he had not foreordained whatsoever comes to pass?" (IV. 277)

Emmons is well aware that this rejoinder itself assumes the doctrine of decrees, but he is clear in his own mind that the assumption is amply justified, and that by attention to the previous question: How could God foreknow all things from eternity? Surely not by information, since there was no other inhabitant of eternity for him to consult. Certainly not from seeing any cause out of himself which should produce the matters foreknown, for no such other cause then existed. Nor can it be that God foreknew all things from eternity merely by knowing the essential perfections of his own nature. "For he was under no natural necessity of exercising any one of his attributes in producing anything out of himself. There was no natural or necessary connexion between the existence of God, and the existence of anything else in the universe. It was, therefore, as impossible for God to foreknow all things by seeing any cause in himself, as by seeing any cause out of himself, of their future existence." (IV. 267) It remains, then, "that the only plain and satisfactory answer to this question is, that God foreknew all things from eternity, because from eternity he had decreed all things." (IV. 267)[16] Which being so, we must also conclude that God's foreknowledge extends no further than that which has existed, now exists, or will exist in some future time. For the fact of the matter is that "God's foreknowledge is not an essential attribute, but the fruit or effect of his decree, as much as the work of his hands. It is altogether owing to men's not making this distinction, that any have supposed that God could foreknow all things without decreeing all things." (IV. 268-269)

For Emmons, as for Calvin before him,[17] this distinction is essential, and that because the result of any denial of the distinction is to make the will of God causally dependent upon something external (the foreknowledge) to that will (the decree) itself. But the will of God is, and for all consistent Calvinists must ever be maintained to be, entirely free. Consequently, Emmons and Calvin alike affirm that God's foreknowledge is in theory ontologically posterior to, and limited by, his decrees, even as they recognize that foreknowledge and decrees tend in fact to coincide.[18]

To those who might incline to think that it makes little or no difference whether one precedes the other or not, Emmons replies that it makes the greatest difference because the doctrine of decrees is the fundamental doctrine of the gospel. "The other essential doctrines of the gospel are founded upon the doctrine of divine decrees, and are supported by it. To deny or disprove this doctrine would be to deny or disprove the whole gospel....The first principle in the scheme of salvation according to the gospel is, that God has decreed all things from eternity. For remove this doctrine, and no doctrine of the gospel can be maintained; there remains no foundation to support the gospel." (IV. 276-277) On this doctrine of decrees depend the moral perfections of God, for we cannot conceive, says Emmons, that these should belong to God unless he exhibits purpose and design. Take from God his decrees, and we cannot believe that he would sustain any moral character, much less a moral character of perfect goodness. The divine inspiration of scripture presupposes God's decree, as does man's freedom to act conformably to the divine purpose. "If the decrees of God prevented men from acting voluntarily, they would indeed destroy their free agency; but since they are consistent with their acting voluntarily, they are entirely consistent with their moral freedom." (IV. 306) Here, it seems, is the real reason why foreknowledge must be distinguished from and subordinated to decrees, for if God's foreknowledge precedes his decree, the assertion of man's freedom becomes logically as well as ontologically indefensible. If God had not first decreed to work in man both to will and to do, he could not have foreknown that men would act to fulfill his purposes. Hence "we must suppose that he always makes them willing to act agreeably to his decrees." (IV. 305) The supposition will perhaps persuade no one not antecedently convinced that God "is the first, the greatest and best of beings, of whom, and through whom, and to whom are all things." (IV. 381) Even so, the proper business of an expounder of Emmons is, as Boynton Smith rightly remarks,[9] with Emmons as he was and not with Emmons as the "improved" ethics and theology of the nineteenth century would wish him to have been.

What God decrees he wills. Hence, Emmons concludes, "we may safely say that the agency of God consists in his will, his choice or volition; and in nothing which is either the cause or consequence of his willing or choosing to produce any effect, or bring about any event." (IV. 378) His knowledge, infinite and unlimited as it is, produces no necessary effect. Nor does his wisdom, by which he has formed the great plan of creation, providence, and redemption. He possesses limitless power, but power also, Emmons reminds us, may exist without any exercise or exertion. "Now if his agency does not consist in his knowledge, nor in his wisdom, nor in his omnipotence, nor in any of his natural perfections, the inference is plain that it must consist in his will, or choice, or volition, and in nothing else." (IV. 379) Such, Emmons preaches, is the activity of God antecedent to, and at the instant of, his creation.

IV

God is the creator, and of course the preserver and governor of the world. As creator he has an original independent right to exercise a supreme and universal superintendency over it....This right....he universally exercises, and actually governs the world as much as it is possible for him to govern it. (II. 458)

The Bible tells us that the universe had a beginning, and that in the beginning God created the heavens and the earth, and this, Emmons avers, must be true, for those who would deny it have no monuments or history so old. The burden of proof is on those who deny divine revelation. "It belongs to them to show how such a revelation as the Bible contains could come down to us without divine inspiration." (II. 17) Moreover, if the Bible was written under the inspiration of divine suggestion, if, as Emmons holds, "every word and sentiment in the Bible was immediately suggested to the sacred penmen by the Holy Ghost," (IV. 85), then, "we must believe that not only all the parts of it are true, but also that all the parts of it are consistent with each other." (V. 346)

The Bible is, he proclaims, free from all human error (IV. 77) and he rejoices in the perfect harmony that runs through all the doctrines of the gospel (IV. 339). Emmons is aware, of course, that there are many ambiguous and variant passages in scripture, aware also of the necessity of justifying his doctrinal interpretations against the cavilling of his Calvinist colleagues, and of meeting the more basic objections brought against consistent Calvinism by its theological and philosophical opponents. Consequently, he is careful to restrict his claim of scriptural inerrancy to the essential and important doctrines. God, he thinks, did not intend that the scriptures should not reveal his will on all religious subjects, nor so clearly reveal it as to prevent all human doubt. With these caveats, however, and believing that "if any passage of scripture will bear a literal sense, we ought to take it literally," (IV. 204) Emmons is prepared to do battle for the consistency and inerrancy of God's word to men.

In considering this "thorough Calvinism" with its ruthlessly logical deductions from scriptural premises, it is important to keep constantly in mind that Emmons does not claim to prove his case by simply adducing scripture appropriate to the particular (and to his critics, peculiar) doctrines he espouses. Every denomination and sect can quote scripture in support of its beliefs, but that for Emmons is beside the point. Thorough Calvinism argues rather from first principles and refutes its opponents by showing forth the specious character of their (alternative) first principles. What these first principles are, apart from the doctrine of decrees above remarked, Emmons doesn't specify.

He does assert that the only proper basis for judging the adequacy of one's theological first principles is reason and common sense. Epistemologically, he is a subscriber to the teachings of Dugald Stewart the Scottish School. For philosophy as a discipline for its own sake, however, he has no time.

V

> God has clearly revealed the mode of his own existence. The doctrine of the Trinity is one of the plainest doctrines in the Bible....This plain and important doctrine has been denied by many, because they could not comprehend it. But let me ask, can this be a good reason for disbelieving what God has plainly revealed? (1. 85)

Attention to scripture leads us to conceive of God as existing in three distinct persons; attention to the word 'person' leads us to the realization that there is no word in any language capable of conveying a precise idea of this incomprehensible distinction in the divine nature. "Let me say, then, the one living and true God exists in such a manner that there is a proper foundation in his nature to speak of himself in the first, second, and third persons, and say I, Thou, and He, meaning only himself....There is a certain *something* in the divine nature, which lays a proper foundation for such a personal distinction. But what that *something* is, can neither be described nor conceived." (IV. 106) Of one thing, though, Emmons is sure: the doctrine of the Trinity implies no contradiction. "It no more implies a contradiction than the doctrine of a true and proper creation. Both are mysteries and both equally incomprehensible. But if we only admit that God is incomprehensible, then we may safely believe that God may be and do what is absolutely above our comprehension." (I. 85) And so we may, if it is permissible to define a contradiction as a doctrine repugnant to reason, as Emmons does (IV. 111), and then rule reason out. Heir, as he was, to the nominalist tradition of Augustine and Ockham, Calvin and Kant, Emmons would see no flaw in any argument presupposing the divorce of faith from reason.

Calvin has decreed that true Christianity knows God only in Jesus Christ. Emmons is not so positive, albeit his intention is impeccably orthodox. His faith embraces the eternal sonship, the mystery of the two natures, the atonement as a propitiation, a literal resurrection, and the union with God and the elect in heaven. Because it tends to set the son below the Father, as a creature is below the Creator, he rejects the doctrine of eternal generation. "There are," he thinks, "no ideas which we can affix to the words, beget, produce, or proceed, but must involve in them an infinite inequality between the three sacred persons of the adorable Trinity." (IV. 114) Thus he feels constrained to reject "such mysteries as cannot be distinguished from real absurdities." (Ibid.)

And yet, there are passages scattered throughout his sermons referent to the person and work of Christ which, taken in the aggregate, tend to emphasize precisely that inequality suggested by the doctrine of eternal generation. In the important sermon "The Scriptural Doctrine of the Trinity not Repugnant to Sound Reason' he distinguishes the superior and inferior offices of the Father and the Son. Referring to the same relation in another context, he notes that "men and angels and even Christ himself have been unacquainted with some of the divine counsels," and adds, "perhaps they never will comprehend them all." (I. 80) Discoursing on the merits of Christ, he denies that Christ merits anything at the hand of God, who is above being bound by any being in the universe (V. 25). He decries the Arian notion of the preexistence of Christ (IV. 601) even as he relates how the Father and the Son "mutually agreed in the counsels of eternity to perform distinct parts." (V. 97) In his curious sermon on **Hebrews** vii:3 (Melchisedec) he undertakes to demonstrate from scripture that Melchisedec, priest of the most high God, without beginning of days, and end of life, is the very same person as Jesus Christ. (VII. 148) The identification is accomplished, it is true, by raising Melchisedec above the status of a mere man. "As Melchisedec he appeared as Jesus of Nazareth, and as Jesus of Nazareth he appeared as Melchisedec. And since there was never any human priest who exactly resembled Christ, it was proper to compare him before his incarnation, to himself after his incarnation." (VIII. 146) The sermon is a splendidly ingenious example of Old Testament Christianizing exegesis, and one wishes that Emmons had pursued further the implications for Christology of this incarnation before the incarnation, but he apparently never did. The fact of the matter is that the persona and work of Jesus Christ present major Christological problems for any theology such as those of Emmons and Edwards which seek to found all doctrine on a metaphysical conception of God as Being in re, or anthropomorphically on the notion of God as Absolute Sovereign. In any trinitarian conception God so defined must be at least primus inter pares. Given God so conceived, Christ is necessarily limited to playing the role of sacrificial lamb whose suffering removes the barrier to God the Father's forgiveness of the posterity of Adam.[20] Which is, indeed, the role that Emmons assigns to him. To say, therefore, that true Christianity knows God only in Jesus Christ is, for a truly consistent Calvinist, to say too much, for given the absolute sovereignty arrogated to God the Father, the role of Christ is necessarily subordinate. Did one doubt that it is so for Emmons, they need only to reflect that of the 264 sermons in the **Works,** six have some aspect of the person and/or work of Christ as their primary subject. A very few others involve the activity of Christ as a substantial secondary consideration, while the balance, some 250 sermons, are concerned with the personal, social, civic, and religious obligations of Christian persons with respect to the goodness, justice, and glory of God the Father Almighty.

With respect to the third person of the Trinity, Emmons has even less to say, and all of it conventional. The eternal procession of the Holy Ghost is denied for the same reason as the eternal generation of the Son, namely, that it implies that the Trinity is not founded in the divine nature but is merely a consequence of the divine will. The Holy Ghost, we are told, is so-called on account of his peculiar office as Sanctifier, and it is not to be supposed that he is essentially more holy than the Father or the Son. (IV 109) His role in the economy of redemption is to renew, sanctify, and bring near to God all regenerate sinners. The rest is mystery.

VI

The dignity of man appears from his bearing the image of his Maker. (II. 24)

The recorders of the Calvinist tradition in America have made much of the Edwardsian and Emmonsite emphasis on the total depravity of mankind, even as they have tended to ignore the reason for that emphasis, namely, the right of God conceived as absolute sovereign to make men what he pleased (IV. 400), and failed to honour the more than equal emphasis of each on the inherent dignity of man. This dignity, for Emmons as for Edwards, derives from the biblical recognition of man made in the image of God. "This allows us to say that man is the offspring of God, a ray from the fountain of light, a drop from the ocean of intelligence. Though man, since the fall, comes into the world destitute of the moral image of God, yet, in the very frame and constitution of his nature, he still bears the natural image of his Maker." (II. 24) As God is spirit, so is man, essentially, spirit, his soul properly understood as "a transcript of the natural perfections of the Deity."

Emmonsism, however, is no pure idealism. Sound reason and philosophy agree that the body is material, the soul immaterial and spiritual, and Emmons supports their verdict. But where some thinkers would have man to be a union of body and soul, and others, secularly minded, decry soul as a chimera, Emmons, keeping ever in view the relation of man to his Maker, teaches that the human soul is not only distinct from and superior to the physical body, but that it can exist in its full vigour and activity in the posthumous state of complete separation. (V. 533) Moreover, he thinks, they are wrong who, like Locke and the learned churchmen who follow his lead, maintain that the soul sleeps until the day of its resurrection. These suppose that the soul may exist after the death without exhibiting any perception, sensibility, reason, or activity, but this is impossible, for a "soul devoid of all such exercises, cannot be distinguished from a mere senseless and lifeless body." (V. 535) Emmons' employment of the term "exercises" reminds us, as it is meant to do, that man as a moral and religious free agent is his exercises, is what his soul does.

That this "exercise scheme" is a precursor of Jamesian pragmatism may be allowed, what must not be conceded, however, is that it is at once Arminianism. This latter, as Emmons understands it, rests on the first principle of a self-determining power in men, to embrace or reject the terms of salvation. "This scheme," he allows, "is very consistent with itself." Its first principle is consistent with the denial of the doctrines of eternal election, final reprobation, and total depravity. "But if its first principle be unscriptural and absurd, then all the doctrines which have been deduced from it have no foundation in scripture, or reason. And it plainly appears," to Emmons' view, "that its first principle is repugnant to the whole current of scripture." (V. 108)[21] Does consistency, then, require that we follow Edwards in his virtual denial of the freedom of the will? Emmons sees no need to do so. Given that God is absolutely sovereign, making totally depraved sinners to be saved by an act of his power, "and if this act of power be special grace, then special grace is as consistent with free agency as common grace." (V. 106)[22] By God's special grace sinful man unwilling to be saved are instantanously rgenerated at the moment they are made willing by an act of divine power. The critics of thorough Calvinism will have it that this specification contradicts free agency, but Emmons will not concede that the postulation of special grace infringes in the least degree upon the sinner's freedom. "It is a dictate of common sense that whatever makes men choose or refuse, is consistent with their liberty; and whatever obstructs or hinders them from choosing or refusing, destroys their freedom. If, therefore, either common or special grace deprived men of the power of choosing or refusing, it would destroy their free agency. But since neither common nor special grace does take away this power, it is evident that neither common nor special grace is repugnant to the freedom of the will." (V. 107)

If true freedom is, as Berdyaev has taught us, freedom not to have to choose or refuse God or any other moral imperative, then Emmons, like Edwards, is properly denominated a determinist. Nor, believing as he does that "mankind have no independent right to their lives, or to any of the blessings of life," (III. 265) would he object to this sense of the characterization. "As the owner of the world, and the giver of every good and perfect gift," God has a right to do what he will with his own. The assertion of this right of God is, for Emmons, nothing abstract or disinterested. The thought is basic to the most eloquently moving of all his sermons. Silence under Affliction, preached at the funeral of his dearly beloved youngest daughter, the hope and dependency of his old age. None who listened that January day in 1823 to their grief stricken aged mentor could doubt for a moment that he whom

God had already bereaved "of father and mother, of brothers and sisters, of one nearer and dearer than either, of several young, tender, fair branches of his family, of all his contemporary brethren in the work of the ministry," believed absolutely and was totally committed to the doctrine that he preached. Like Job on a similar occasion, he accepted discipline and endured; and like Job he had but one request:

> have pity upon me, have pity upon me, O ye my friends; for the hand of God hath touched me. (III. 273)

VII

> My principal aim in these publications was, to explain the meaning, to demonstrate the truth, and to illustrate the consistency of the primary doctrines and duties of Christianity, and thereby distinguish true religion from false. (1. xxxiv)

History has not been kind to Nathanael Emmons. In the judgement of his most sympathetic critic he was a theological curiosity, an anachronism in his own time.[23] Another finds that "just so far as he is modernized, he forfeits the special role which has been ascribed to him in the development of the New England theology."[24] This role itself, according to the ablest historian of that theology, is essentially minor: "to have sharpened somewhat the statement of important truths, to have brought them thus into clearer light, to have made more consistent and effective the practical labors of ministers in converting men, was to him," concludes Frank Hugh Foster, "an adequate aim in life and a sufficient performance."[25] He was, says George Nye Boardman, "the most facile sermonizer that New England ever produced," but as far as his contribution to the New Divinity is concerned, that, he holds, was limited to "an intense development of a single point of Hopkinsianism, and of Edwardeanism," namely, the exercise scheme.[26] Another, more hostile, critic, is of the opinion that in his carrying of Calvinism to its logical conclusion, Emmons created a system of such "harshness and barbarity'" as no Christian would willingly accept,[27] and this was the general judgement of the Nineteenth century, albeit all of Emmons' critics concede with Boynton Smith that "he defined more sharply, and stuck to his definitions better than any preceding New England divine," and that "his main positions are put as tight and tough, as clean and clear, as language can make them."[28]

Were these critics not almost wholly preoccupied with what they take to be aberrations from the generally received position of late Nineteenth century orthodoxy, their conclusions would preclude challenge. As it is, they one and all tend to overlook what to many in this final quarter of the Twentieth century are the two most important contributions of thorough Calvinism, first, its ruthlessly rational systematization of conclusions deductively derived from scriptural premises, and, second, its conception of God and the universe. Attention to the latter suggests the possibility of a panentheistic interpretation which, if allowed, would justify viewing Emmons as a precursor of contemporary process theology, while focus on the former makes most plain the logical and ontological shortcomings of the various attempts by Nineteenth century Christian liberalism to soften the absolute sovereign of scripture into a someone more amiable and benevolent. It is the merit of Emmons to have shown with a consistency and clarity unmatched by any of his predecessors that any such modification of the Calvinist conception of God in the interest of making the doctrines of the gospel socially palatable must end in the subversion of the Christian faith.[29]

Such dogmatism today is not only out of fashion but out of place. However, it is important to keep in mind that the world of Nathanael Emmons was a world universally acknowledged to be slightly less than six thousand years removed from the creation, a world, moreover, which rejoiced in the imminence of the millenium. Like his younger contemporary, Hegel, Emmons was burdened with a conception of the universe which made it difficult, if not impossible, to maintain that God is that Being in whom we literally live, and move, and have our being. He believed it nonetheless, preached it as a mystery of faith, and required that his fellow believers either assent to the system of doctrines conformable to this panentheistic conception or confess that their refusal to assent to such hard doctrine is at once an abandonment of the notion of God as absolute sovereign. Thereby he approximated, insofar as it is possible for a pre-evolutionary era thinker to approximate, the central position of recent and contemporary process theology. To the extent that they understood his position, his critics failed to appreciate or to value it. Indeed, his sermons offer ample evidence that he hardly understood himself the full implications of his preaching. But if we have no license to call him modern, neither have we any coercive reason to rest content with the judgement of the past.

Bibliographical Essay

The primary source is **The Works of Nathanael Emmons,** *D.D.,* in seven volumes, edited by Jacob Ide, D. D. (Crocker and Brewster, Boston, 1842-1850), comprising a Memoir written by himself, an Additional Memoir by the editor, Miscellaneous Reflections of a Visiter upon the character of Dr. Emmons by Edwards A. Park, and two-hundred and sixty-four sermons. Parks' Reflections are an affectionate and judicious account of the man, his mode of life, his standing with the clerisy and in the community, and a lightly sketched overview of those of his teachings which the Visiter finds significant. Park does not take upon himself the responsibility of coming to terms with Emmonsism. He does, however, make the point which the critics of Emmons mostly miss, namely, that the logical rigour of his deductions from his theological principles (all derived from scripture) compels assent to, or refutation of, these principles even as it forbids indifference to them.

A System of Divinity in two volumes, same editor, publisher, and dates, is identical in contents and paging with volumes IV and V of **The Works.** Three additional volumes projected by the editor were aborted for economic reasons. A number of sermons preached on various special occasions have been separately published (see the listing under Emmons in the **National Union Catalog Pre-1956 Imprints** 159, 477-481. Emmons was also associated with, and contributed regularly to, a number of orthodox and evangelical magazines. Ide provides a listing of one hundred and eight of these contributions following Chapter II of the Additional Memoir (**Works** I. lxi-lxii). This periodical material is, in the main, hortatory and didactic, adding but little to the positions developed in the sermons. Two exceptions, requiring notice by the serious student of American Calvinism, are the essays, 'Plain Reasons for being a thorough Calvinist', **Massachusetts Missionary Magazine** III (1805), 212-215; and 'Distinguishing tenets of Hopkinsianism', **The Theological Magazine** (September-October, 1795), 120-125. Most of Emmons' periodical contributions are signed Philonous (his pen name).

Edwards Parks' lengthy **Memoir of Nathanael Emmons,** with Sketches of his Friends and Pupils (Boston: Congregational Board of Publication, 1861) repeats the tribute to the character and ministry of its subject in more detail.

An extended review of the **Memoir** is found in **The American Theological Review**, III,[2] (October, 1861), 632-668. E. Smalley, 'Theology of Dr. Emmons,' **Bibliotheca Sacra?** VII (1850), 254-280, 479-501; and Henry Boynton Smith, 'The Theological System of Emmons', first published anonymously in **The American Theological Review**, XIII (January, 1862), 8-53, and subsequently reprinted as Chapter VI of the volume of Smith's discourses and essays entitled, **Faith and Philosophy** (New York: Scribner, Armstrong, 1877), edited with an introductory notice by George L. Prentiss, expound the system in moderately disapproving detail. Frank Hugh Foster, **A Genetic History of the New England Theology** (Chicago: University of Chicago Press, 1907) treats at length of the relation of the system of Emmons to those of his predecessors and successors, again in a mildly disapproving tone. The Exercise Scheme is subjected to sharp criticism by Laurens Hickok, **Rational Psychology** (Auburn, New York: Derby, Miller, 1849), 459-463.

J.R. Gilmore, 'Nathanael Emmons and Mather Byles, '**The New England Magazine**, N.S. 16 (1897), 732-735, is reminiscence and testimony to Emmons' sense of humor and zest for life. Abel Millard corroborates the latter, even as he abhors the "harshness and barbarity" of Emmons' theology, in 'Nathaniel Emmons, '**American Journal of Theology**, 6 (1902), 17-34. Millard alone, however, among all the foregoing, recognizes Emmons' implicit panentheism (which he, unfortunately, confuses with pantheism). There are no more recent studies.

For the sake of completeness, if for no other reason, mention must be made of Samuel Hanson Cox's interview with Dr. Emmons on August 11th, 1838 at the parsonage at Franklin; subsequently published, presumably verbatim, in his **Interviews Memorable and Useful** (London: Sampson Low, Son, and Co., 1853), 147-201. Cox's principal claim to attention derives from his having, as he thinks, forced Emmons to concede that his metaphysics is in conflict with all the law and the prophets (as understood by Cox). The concession is more apparent than real, and is, in any case, inconsequential. Cox, a humorless and righteous clerical pedant, is oblivious to the fact that Emmons has taken his measure as such, and is humoring his (Cox's) argument. As for that argument itself, the jejeune dogmatism of its presentation neither admits of, nor requires, any theological examinations. Finally, mention ought perhaps to be made of yet another portrait of Emmons, that of Harriet Beecher Stowe, as given in **Oldtown Folks,** XXIX (Boston: Fields, Osgood & Co., 1869), 378-384. This is the popular picture of Emmons (here called Dr. Moses Stern) as seen through the eyes of mid-nineteenth century liberalism and it remains the standard portrait today.

¹The Works of Nathanael Emmons, D.D., with a Memoir of his Life. Edited by Jacob Ide, D.D. In seven volumes (Boston: Crocker and Brewster, 1842; Volume VII published in 1850), I. 193. Citations in text to volume and page of this edition.

²Nathanael Emmons, 'Hopkinsians,' in Hannah Adams, A View of Religions, second edition (Boston: John West Folsom, 1791), 97n. Subsequent editions and reprintings with different pagings, 1801, 1805, 1858, 1874. Hereafter cited in the main body of the text in parentheses as H with page number. Emmons is speaking, of course, of Samuel Hopkins, but the thought is as well, or even better, applied to himself.

³Emmons' own mature view, drawing the logical conclusion from his premise of disinterested benevolence, is that "no person ought to be willing to be cast off forever, simply considered, but only conditionally, if the glory of God and the good of the universe require it", (Works, 287).

⁴"'It is supposed,' says Edwards Park, "that, on an average, Hopkins studied twelve hours a day, for more than half a century....for seventy years,' he adds, "Emmons remained like a fixture in his parsonage study, and like his brethren read "books which are books"." 'New England Theology,' Bibliotheca Sacra, IX, 33 (January, 1852), 191.

⁵Edwards Park, Reflections of a Visiter, Works I, clxx-clxxi.

⁶In his sermon 'Dignity of Man' he discourses at some considerable length on the necessity for reading useful books. "almost any book," he thinks, "if read for use, may be of advantage. We may read amusing and even corrputing books to advantage, if we read them in order to make a good use of them." But, he adds, "we may read all our lives to very little purpose, if we read every book which happens to fall in our way for amusement and not for use." (II. 37) The catholicity of his references in his sermons offers eloquent testimony that as he preached he practiced.

⁷John Calvin, Institutes of the Christian Religion in two volumes. Edited by John T. McNeill; translated by Ford Lewis Battles from the 1559 Latin text. Philadelphia: Westminster Press, 1960.

⁸See his sermon on the Vindictive Justice of God (IV. 234-246), also his sermons on the Future State (V. Part XXIV).

⁹See III. 206, 251, 408, 474; IV. 264, 346, 358, 366, 382, 384, 397, 398, 404, 410, 450; V. 128. 204

¹⁰Abel Millard, 'Nathanael Emmons,' American Journal of Theology 6 (1902), 25.

¹¹E. Smalley, 'Theology of Dr. Emmons,' Bibliotheca Sacra, (1850), 270.

¹²Emmons' sermon 'The Gospel a Scheme of Grace' echos the thought: "the gospel is not an emanation of the divine nature, but a fruit of the divine will....Hence it appears plain and obvious, that the gospel of divine grace must have been a perfectly free and voluntary scheme, which the supreme Being decreed, determined, and adjusted in all its parts, before the foundation of the world." (I. 44)

¹³The character and implications of this aberration are discussed in my article 'Panentheistic Implications of the Ontological Argument,' The Southern Journal of Philosophy, 9 (Summer, 1971), 157-162.

¹⁴If we are to judge Emmons fairly, it is necessary that we be quite clear as to what he understands by this phrase 'cognizance of reason'. In his sermon, Reasonableness of Christianity, he defines it as follows: "by reason, therefore, we are to understand the natural power, faculty or capacity of discerning and investigating truth, as improved by exercise, and assisted by divine revelation". (IV. 93) This last is not to be minimized, for Emmons always assumes that revelation as communicated to us in the Bible is not only perfect truth, free from all human error (IV. 78), but

that all the products of it are perfectly consistent with each other. (V. 346)

[15]The argument supportive of these apodictic assertions is expounded at length in the sermons 'Foreknowledge of God' (IV. 263-274) and 'The Doctrine of the Divine Decrees the Fundamental Doctrine of the Gospel' (IV. 275-285).

[16]Adds Emmons, "it is easy to see that, when God had determined all things, he could foreknow all things. He must have known his own determinations, and, by knowing them, he must have known whatever would come to pass; for he made his determinations in unerring wisdom and perfect goodness, and of course could never see any reason to alter them; and he knew his own omnipotent power to carry into execution all his purposes....His foreknowledge, in this view of it, was founded on his decree, and upon nothing else. If he had not decreed any thing, he could not have foreknown; that the world would exist. If he had not decreed to create angels and men, he could not have foreknown that they would exist....As his foreknowledge was founded on his decree, so it must of necessity be bounded by it. It cannot extend to anything but what is decreed." (IV. 268)

[17]For Calvin the issue arises more particularly in respect to the decree of predestination, but the positions are, in essence, coincident. The distinction in Calvin is discussed by Francois Wendel, **Calvin: the Origins and Development of His Thought** (New York: Harper & Row, 1963), 269-274.

[18]"It is true," writes Emmons, "that God's foreknowledge and decrees are intimately and inseparably connected; and that his foreknowledge as really proves the certainty of all things future, as his decrees. But his foreknowledge has no tendency to make future things certain, which his decrees have. They make future things certain; for it is God's decreeing future things which makes them certain. His decrees fix an inseparable connection between the ends proposed and the means to accomplish them; and this connection produces an absolute certainty of all things which are decreed, and lays the permanent foundation of God's foreknowledge; but at the same time demonstrably proves that the foreknowledge of God and his decrees are entirely different and distinct." (IV. 272)

[19]"The Theological System of Emmons," **The American Theological Review** XIII (January, 1862), 9.

[20]According to Boynton Smith, "Christ has not that control and comprehensive position in this theoretic scheme, which he has in the Scripture, and in the experience of believers. We say in the *theoretic* scheme because we would not for an instant imply that Emmons did not fully believe all that the Scriptures assert about Christ. But his theory obliged him to assign to Christ only the position of removing the obstacle to forgiveness." 'Theological System of Emmons,' p. 41.

[21]"We have shown," writes Emmons, "that God has given a certain number of mankind to Christ; that these, as well as the rest of the fallen race, are totally depraved; that no means or moral motives will make them willing to be saved; and that God only can make them willing, by an act of his power. If these things are true, it necessarily follows that sinners have not a self-determining power, and never will be saved, unless God, by a sovereign and gracious act of his power, bows their wills to the sceptre of Christ." (V. 108)

[22]"The only reason why common grace is universally supposed to be consistent with free agency is," according to Emmons, "because it leaves men free to choose and refuse....obedience to the will of God....But if men are perfectly free under the influence of common grace, because they are capable of choosing and refusing, then for the same reason, they must be equally free under the influence of special grace. For special grace essentially consists in making men willing to do their duty." (V. 106)

200

[23]Park, **Reflections** (I. clxvii).

[24]Boynton Smith, **American Theological Review,** XIII, 9.

[25]**A Genetic History of the New England Theology** (Chicago: University of Chicago Press, 1907), 357.

[26]**A History of New England Theology** (New York: A.D.F. Randolph Company, 1899), 111, 108.

[27]Millard, 18.

[28]Boynton Smith, 10, 11.

[29]"Those, therefore, who now understandingly embrace genuine Calvinism....cannot consistently amalgamate with Arminians, Methodists, Antinomians, Sabellians, Arians, Socinians, or any species of Universalists and Enthusiasts. This is my settled opinion; and therefore I am surprised that so many, who call themselves orthodox, appear so fond of a coalition with other denominations of Christians, who profess to hold systems of theology which are really opposite to, and subversive of genuine Calvinism.' (Autobiography, **Works** I. xxxvi)

The Didactic Calvinism
Of Timothy Dwight

"I think I never knew the man who took so deep an interest
in everything,—the best mode of cultivating a cabbage, as
well as the phenomena of the heavens or the employments
of angels. Attention, stretching his mind in every direction,
made him so great."[1]

THE DIDACTIC CALVINISM OF TIMOTHY DWIGHT

> A principal reason for his success was the sanity with which
> he interpreted the Scriptures. Here was a Professor of Divini-
> ty, with the blood of Edwards in his veins, who stooped to
> testing theological truth by common sense. In an age still
> overfond of debating theological abstractions, Dwight dared
> to proclaim the plain meaning of the Bible to be the true
> meaning.[2]

Herewith he stands as a moderating force against the refusal of Hopkins
and Emmons to soften the harshness of the gospel requirement to the end
of making it more palatable to their restive congregations. He sees clearly,
what they saw at best darkly, that the ascendancy of liberal Christianity and
the rise of Infidelity is not be reversed by dwelling upon the difficulties
inherent in Scripture doctrine. Eschewing their dour approach, he will emphasize, throughout his career as preacher, professor, and president, the practical advantages accruing to the true believer, and, denying metaphysics, display
the literary qualities of, and the historical evidences for, the sacred book.

His very first published pronouncement, **A Dissertation on the History,
Eloquence, and Poetry of the Bible,** delivered at the public commencement
at New Haven in 1772 to an audience accustomed to reserve its critical praise
for the prose and poetry of the ancient Greeks and Romans, exhibits the new
design. "Shall we," he inquires, "be blind to Eloquence more elegant than
Cicero, more grand than Demosthenes, or to poetry more correct and tender
than Virgil, and infinitely more sublime'—that Homer? "Can the matchless
excellence of the sacred descriptions be better illustrated, than by comparing
the sublimest description of a God, in the sublimest of all the prophane writers
of antiquity, with a similar one from the Bible?"[3] The young speaker thinks
not. Neither in eloquence, nor yet as writers of history, are pagan poets and
infidel philosophers the equals, let alone the superiors, of "the sacred
penmen."

Unencumbered by Critical manacles, they gave their imaginations an unlimited range, called absent objects before the
sight, gave life to the whole inanimate creation, and in every
period, snatched the grace which is beyond the reach of art,
and which, being the genuine offspring of elevated Genius,
finds the shortest passage to the human soul.[4]

As for the carping objection that the divine authors of the Bible most often
fail to describe events according to received rules of sound historical method,
Dwight will have none of it. Given that the great end of history is moral instruction, he will have it that every possible method must be used to awaken
that imagination which is the principal inlet to the soul. "What Homer has
done in Poetry, the Divine writers have done in History," [5] and, to Dwight's
view, have done it better.

The objection, however, continued throughout his life to disturb his complacency respecting the historical validity of the scriptures. Twenty years later,
in the augmented[6] **Discourse on the Genuineness and Authenticity of the New
Testament,** he returned to the subject, arguing at length that it was impossible that the divine authors of the gospels should have invented the events which
they describe.

Their character, education, and information, could, in no
degree, qualify them for a successful imposition of this kind.
the truth and accuracy with which they have evidently written....will, to every person, qualified to judge, appear to be
an unanswerable argument of the genuineness of these
writings.[7]

Did it of itself not do so, the references to, and the quotations from, these
sacred books by Catholics, Heretical Christians, and Heathens alone would
suffice "to put their genuineness beyond every reasonable doubt." [8] The fact
that non-Christians as well as Christians have accepted the biblical account
of the events remarked is, for Dwight, enough to establish its authority. Given
that the Historical books of the canon are the foundation on which the re-

mainder rest, it follows, according to our author, that "he, who receives that Historical books are genuine, will find no occasion to question the rest."⁹

Presumably not all of his hearers were persuaded by this argument, since we find him in the closing decade of his life returning once more to the issue in his **Eighteen Lectures on the Evidences of Divine Revelation.**¹⁰ Proceeding from the assumption that a Revelation is absolutely necessary to a proper knowledge of God, and granting that this Revelation is given "in a Book, more ancient, more judicious, and more authentic, even if uninspired, than any other, which has descended to us from early times,"¹¹ Dwight reviews the totality of the various testimonies tending to the confirmation of the several parts of the Pentateuch, and to the claim that Moses was its author, and concludes anew that these must leave the Christian with no doubts whatever respecting the authenticity of the Mosaic history.

However, the matter is not yet entirely settled, for it remains to ask in what sense this and that passage of Scripture is to be understood. To this question, Dwight addresses himself in the very last of his discourses, **On the Manner in which the Scriptures are to be Understood,**¹² written even as the cancer that was to kill him was beginning to manifest itself. To the question posed, his answer was, in his usual manner, direct and forthright: "the sense, in which the various declarations of God in the Scriptures are to be received by us, is the Obvious Sense; or that, which readily presents itself to a plain man, reading them with seriousness and integrity."¹³ For, Dwight reminds us, it is undeniable that a great part of the Bible was written by men who knew no other than plain language, and no other meaning but that which was customary and familiar. Many of them were uneducated men; certain it is that none of them were philosophers. Indeed, delcares Dwight, "there is no more monstrous position, than that the Scriptures are to be so interpreted as to be made consistent with our philosophy."¹⁴ It is no objection against them, that the Scriptures are avowedly mysterious. To the plain men by and for whom they were written these books must necessarily be mysterious. So far is this from being an objection, that it is to be regarded as a matter of course. And in the event, thinks Dwight, there is nothing mysterious or obscure as far as the *declarations* which assert these mysterious things are considered.

> The doctrine of the Trinity would probably be pitched upon
> as the most profound, and difficult of all the scriptural
> mysteries, yet in the declarations, that the Father is God; that
> the Son is God; and that the Holy Ghost is God; and that
> there is but one Jehovah; there is nothing obscure. On the
> contrary, the meaning of them all is entirely obvious; so that
> a plain man will readily perceive it at first sight.[5]

And what is true of the Trinity is, for Dwight, true also of every controverted article of the Christian faith. In sum, "if we allow the Scriptures to be the Word of God; our only duty is to inquire what they say, and to receive it with implicit confidence. What God has said must be true; and all debate concerning its truth is absolutely precluded by the character of its Author."[16]

Such conviction came naturally to the grandson[17] of Jonathan Edwards. At the age of four he had so far mastered the catechism that he could, and did, teach it to the neighborhood Indians.[18] At six he knew himself to be depraved. Sent to study with the master of the local grammar school, he begged permission to begin Latin, and being refused by his father (who thought him much too young for such weighty fare), he managed surreptitiously, with a classmate's text borrowed during daily recess, to twice work through Lilly's Latin Grammar. At eight he was sufficiently advanced in his classical studies to qualify for admission to Yale, but was kept at home until his body should catch up with his mind. We are told[19] that he employed the years to good advantage in his father's well-stocked library. At twelve, having attained the requisite physical maturity, he was sent to study Greek and Latin, and make ready for college, with the Rev. Enoch Huntington of Middletown. A year later he took his entrance examinations, passed handsomely, and in September of 1765 entered Yale.

The story of his college years has been recounted elsewhere,[20] and requires no repeating. After graduation, with the Class of 1769, Dwight stayed on as a resident graduate and, from September 1771 on, as tutor. His regimen in these years, twenty-hour work-days, no exercise, a misconceived vegetarian diet, too little sleep, eyes permanently strained by long hours of study by candlelight, took their inevitable toll. In 1774 he collapsed and was taken home, as he thought, to die. A radical change of habits over a period of fourteen months restored his health, and he returned to his tutorship in the stirring days of spring 1775. While the revolution gathered strength, Dwight wooed a wife and pursued the study of theology. In March 1777 he was married to Miss Mary Woolsey, the daughter of his father's Yale roommate, by his uncle, Jonathan Edwards Jr., and in June, having satisfied his clerical examiners, he was licensed to preach.

A change of administration at Yale in 1777, coupled with the increased recruitment for the Continental Army, led Dwight, fired with patriotism, to seek appointment as chaplain to the First Connecticut Brigade, which office he served until the death of his father forced his return to Northampton in the summer of 1778. As the eldest son, Dwight not only inherited his father's extensive holdings in real estate but also the responsibility for the care of his mother and his twelve brothers and sisters. He became a farmer, on Sundays supplied various neighboring pulpits, and to augment his income, opened a school. He took an active part in town affairs, and for two terms in 1781 and 1782 represented Northampton in the state legislature. He was importuned to run for Congress, but decided that his career lay with the ministry. In May of 1783 he was called by unanimous vote of the congregation to the church at Greenfield Hill (Fairfield), Connecticut. He accepted in July and was ordained in November. His course was set. Henceforward he would be a pastor in Zion, and so it turned out for twelve fruitful and happy years.

In May of 1795 the President of Yale, Ezra Stiles, died, and the Corporation voted to call Dwight as his successor. His Greenfield Hill congregation, loath to lose their beloved pastor, demurred, and the Consociation of his clerical peers being appealed to, refused his request for dismissal. But Dwight was not to be denied. He wanted, the post, had wanted it since 1777, and faced with his determination to accept, and the wish of the Corporation to have him, the Consociation reversed their decision, and his congregation grudgingly permitted him to depart. On August 17th, Dwight formally accepted the Corporation's tender of the presidency, and three weeks later was inaugurated President of Yale College.

II

> It cannot be thought strange, that Infidel Philosophy,
> although destitute of a basis in truth, and of support from
> evidence, should present danger, even from argument. Its
> great object is to unsettle everything moral and obligatory,
> and to settle nothing.[22]

In the course of his dozen years at Greenfield Hill, Dwight's principal avocaiton was that of a poet. His models were Pope,[23] whose style of writing in heroic couplets he assayed to copy in several of his longer compositions, Milton,[24] whose **Paradise Lost** provides the pattern and much of the imagery of Dwight's **The Conquest of Canaan,** and, most important, the Old Testament, from which the setting and the language of virtually all of his religious poetry is drawn. He fancied himself, and was fancied, at least by his friend John Trumbull, as the coming American poet., and if quantity of poetic product alone would have made him such, that he would have been. His muse is fourfold; patriotic, exemplified in **America,** and the **Address;** pastoral, **Greenfield Hill, The Seasons Moralized,** and **Morpheus;** biblical, the aforementioned **Conquest of Canaan, The Tryal of Faith, Message of Mordecai to Esther,** and **the Maniac of Gadara;** and, of most matter as respects his philosophy of religion, polemic, **The Critics,** and **The Triumph of Infidelity.**[25]

The Critics, composed in 1785 as a reply to the generally negative reception accorded **The Conquest of Canaan** by the English reviewers, is Dwight at his polemic best. The reviewers are likened to the mongrel dogs of Cynethe who when,

> "One morn, a greyhound pass'd the street
> At once the foul-mouth'd conclave met,
> Huddling round the stranger ran,
> And thus their smart review began."
>
> No native of the town, I see;
> Some foreign whelp of base degree.

I'd shew, but that the record's
torn We true Welsh curs are better born."

They continue to ridicule the features and character of the greyhound (Dwight) until the goddess Juno; coming upon the scene, turns them for their snarling minds into

"Critics, the genuine curs of men"

condemned forever to rail against,

"Whate'er is great, or just, in nature;
Of graceful form, or lovely feature;
Whate'er adorns the ennobled mind,
Sublime, inventive, and refin'd:
With spleen, and spite, forever blame,
And load with every dirty name."

Dwight must have known that he was overreacting, since he delayed to publish the poem until 1791.[26] But in matters pertaining even peripherally to religion he was not often in such a cool frame of mind. The English reviewers and, for that matter, their American counterparts who presumed to criticize his religious epic were, to his partisan view, all part and parcel of the rising wave of Infidelity which threatened in the name of Reason and Democracy to sweep away the long-cherished virtues and values of Calvinist New England. He could not suffer to remain silent and in 1788 he vented his spleen anew, albeit anonymously, in a poem of forty pages, ironically titled, **The Triumph of Infidelity**.

In view of the fact that Dwight's son is reported[27] as having said that this particular poem was "not acknowledged" by his father, too much perhaps ought not to be made of it. On the other hand, as Howard notes, "his authorship was well known, and the poem survived to embarrass him,"[28] when in later years he turned from New Divinity polemics to Federalist politics. Howard's conclusion is confirmed by Leary[29] and Silverman.[30] The parallels in metre, diction, theme, and phrasing which may be drawn between the **Triumph** and Dwight's later poems, **The Retrospect** and **Greenfield Hill** are, according to the latter, evidence enough to establish his authorship. These parallels, and the testimony of his contemporaries, "taken together, offer," says the former, "evidence too formidable to be broken down by the mere statement that Dwight did "not acknowledge" the production.[31]

Albeit the poem is addressed to Voltaire, he who "light and gay, o'er learning's surface flew,/ And prov'd all things at option, false or true," in the mind of the poet, the instruments of Satan's Triumph are English deists and Scottish skeptics: "in the cobwebs of a college room,/ I found my best Amanuensis, Hume." "My Methodist, brave Herbert, cried,/ And whin'd, and wrote, pretended, pray'd, and lied." And Bolingbroke, "misread, miswrote, misquoted, misapplied,/ Yet fail'd of fame, and miss'd the skies, beside."

> My leaders these; yet Satan boasts his subs
> His Tolands, Tindals, Collinses, and Chubbs.

The old world conquered, Satan turns to the new, only to encounter "in this wild waste, where Albion's lights revive,...a dread race....patient of toil, of firm and vigorous mind."

> But my chief bane, my apostolic foe,
> In life, in labours, source of every woe,
> From scenes obscure, did heaven his (Edwards) call,
> That moral Newton, and that second Paul.
> He, in clear view, saw sacred systems roll,
> Of reasoning worlds, around their central soul:
> Saw love attractive every system bind,
> The parent linking to each filial mind;

> Beneath his standard; lo what number rise, To dare for truth,
> and combat for the skies.

But Satan has his champions here also, the chief of whom in our poet's eyes is Chauncy,[32] whose mind "thro' doctrines deep, from common sense refin'd,/I led, a nice, mysterious work to frame,/With love of system, and with lust of fame." And after him, Mayhew, "in whom my utmost skill/Peer'd out no means of mischief, but the will."

Against these and several others, identified by character but not by name as Satan's votaries, Dwight vents his spleen, his principal objection against one and all being that by making religion an easy way of life they unravel the moral fabric of society, promote social instability and disrespect for the institutions of Christianity, and last, and most reprehensible, mock God. As Silverman perceptively notes, "Dwight knew the distinction between Deists and unorthodox Calvinists; but he saw no difference between Deists and democrats." To him, they were no less than Voltaire, Diderot, Hume, and Chauncy, apostles of Infidelity, "new gates of falsehood open'd on mankind." Unfortunately for the poet's peace of soul, he is unable to report anything more than a battle drawn. At poem's end, Satan retires, "to his cause no friend of virtue won," but neither any foe of God undone."

Retires, but not for long. During the decade 1788-1797 Satan made substantial gains, at least at Yale College, whose students were so far enamoured of the latest French and English fashions in Infidelity as to call each other by the names of the philosophers. In 1795, the year that Dwight took office, the membership of the Church of Christ at Yale had shrunken to two. The faculty, excepting President Stiles, consisted of one professor, Josiah Meigs, a rabid and outspoken anti-Federalist, and as such to be numbered with the devil's minions, and three tutors, whose allegiance was suspect. Dwight promptly cleaned house. Meigs was disposed of by the time-honored academic tactic of securing his election as president of the newly founded University of Georgia. The tutors were replaced, and the requirements for the observance of the Sabbath stiffened.[34] A series of Sunday lectures systematically expounding the New Divinity was begun, and so that no student should retain any doubts whatsoever as to the nature of the enemy, Dwight shortly preached and published two sermons on The Nature and Danger of Infidel Philosophy.

Taking for his text Paul's injunction to "beware lest any man spoil you through philosophy and vain deceit," (**Colossians** 2:8) Dwight begins by reminding his hearers that their duty and interest alike require that they do the will of God, not only because God wills it, but because it is right. As man's whole well-being depends entirely upon his pleasing God, to inquire and determine what God has chosen and requires must ever be the first object of our knowing. But this, Dwight insists, philosophy can never tell us. "The only character of God which can here be admitted is that of Inifinite perfection."[35] But Philosophy, unaided by Revelation, has nothing to say about that. "The designs of a Being infinitely perfect, must be formed to extend through eter nity and immensity; and must embrace all beings and all events together with all their relations and operations."[36] But these, philosophy, which is limited to reasoning from the created evidences, cannot aspire to investigate. Truth, which is of God, is at all times, all in all things, unchangeable. Philosophy, conversely, is constant only as respects its unceasing contrariety. "Among the ancients it was a mere wind of doctrine, varying through all the points of the compass. Among the moderns, also, it has, chameleon like, appeared of many colours."[37]

To prove his point, Dwight offers several pages of propositions purporting to represent views maintained by, among others, Plato, Aristotle, Aristippus, Prophyry, Hebert, Hobbes, Blount, Shaftesbury, Collins, Woolston, Tindal, Chubb, Bolingbroke, and the arch-infidel, David Hume.[38] All of them, as he thinks, exemplars of the fact that Philosophy has been, from its beginnings, "vain and deceitful."[39] "I need only observe further," he afterwards remarks, "that, with respect to the Existence, Character, and Providence, of God, Philosophers differ wholly....Amid such a diversity, and discordance, whom are you to follow; and what are you to believe?[40] Christians believe, he continues,

> that the Scriptures are, and Infidels that they are not, a divine revelation. Neither they, nor we, know; both classes merely believe; for the case admits not of knowledge, nor can it be determined with certainty.[41]

For Dwight, the only question at issue between the Christians and their enemies is: "Which believes on the best evidence?" In matters of religion, he is sure, "Infidels are believers equally with Christians, and merely believe the contrary position."[42]

Failing to see this, Christians have hitherto been content to defend their positions against Infidel attacks. "Infidels have found difficulties, and Christians have employed themselves merely, or chiefly in removing them. Hence Infidels have naturally felt, and written, as if the difficulties lay solely on the Christian side of the debate."[43] Whereas the fact is, Dwight contends, that they lie in no less upon the Infidel philosophy. Had Christians but chosen to carry the attack to the enemy, "they would long since, and very easily, have proved them to be everywhere weak and untenable."[44] To remedy this lack, and reverse the defensive attitude prevailing hitherto, is the principal aim of the second discourse. The discordant and immoral nature of Infidel Philosophy having been exposed to view, it remains to remark and take arms against the Danger.

The attack is opened with a reprise: "Philosophers, as has been remarked, have, from the beginning, changed continually the Infidel system. The doctrines which Herbert and Tindal declared to be so evident, that God could not make them more evident, were wholly given up as untenable, by Hume....Mere Infidelity gave up natural religion, and atheism mere Infidelity."[45] It is said by some that the doctrines of the Scriptures, most particularly those respecting the existence, character, designs, and will of God, are more mysterious than any other, and this is held to be a reproach against these doctrines. But Infidels do not show that these are contrary to anything known, but merely that not all is disclosed. "The difficulties objected to the Scriptures on this score, all arise from what we know not, and not from what we know....they do not shew, that what is disclosed, and believed, is untrue, or improbable; but that it is mysterious or incomprehensible."[46] But this, cries Dwight, instead of being a solid objection against the Revelation of the Scriptures, is a mere exposition of human ignorance: "In this part of their conclusions there is no controversy between them and us."[47] Certainly there are many things of which Infidels are equally as ignorant as Christians. Ignorance is part of the human condition, and it can be no valid objection against the Scriptures that they do not make all things plain. "The mysteriousness of the Scriptures, in several particulars, has been often directly as well as insidiously, objected against their divine origin. To me it appears to be a plain and powerful argument in favour of that origin. Were there nothing in Creation or Providence, which man could not comprehend, one important proof that they were works of God would be taken away."[48] Objections of this nature, then, arising as they do from ignorance, have no real force, and this is so whether we have regard to the Word of God or to the circumstances in which it was proclaimed.

Passing from the negative to the positive, Dwight discerns another argument, drawn from the comparative character of Christians and Infidels, which, he believes, "may be alleged with a force incapable of being obviated."[49] This is the argument from moral superiority, and runs thus: "the weight of virtue has been wholly on the side of Christianity. Nothing can be more properly or more forcibly contrasted....than the opposite lives of Christians and Infidels. The life of St. Paul alone, puts all Infidelity out of countenance"[50] "So evident, thinks Dwight, "is the want of morals on the part of Infidels, in this country, generally, that to say—'A man is an Infidel'—is understood, of course, as a declaration, that he is a plainly immoral man."[51]

The insolence and ridicule universally visited by Infidel writers upon their Christian adversaries is, to Dwight's view, a final indication of the weakness of their cause and the insufficiency of their arguments."A strong man is usually mild, and civil; a weak one, to conceal his weakness, is often petulant and blustering."[52] That this might seem at least to the philosophers calumniated in the discourses, as a prime case of the pot calling the kettle black, would disturb Dwight not at all. Nor would it concern him that philosophers would not consider his reasoning logically coercive or sufficiently conclusive against their Infidelity. For Dwight is not addressing himself to the philosophers but to impressionable students who are, in his eyes, in mortal danger of succumbing to the "guilty pleasures" of "this unhappy Philosophy." Consequently, he feels no obligation to apply himself to a detailed consideration of those objections from logic or experience that rise to challenge his vision of changeless truth. If their objections should prove decisive, "if their wishes should be accomplished, the world," he is convinced, "will be converted into one theatre of falsehood perjury, fraud, theft, piracy, robbery, oppression, revenge, fornication, and adultery."[53] With these consequences in mind, and

with the blessings of Christianity in view, he abjures his audience to leave
to the Infidel his peculiar gratifications, and that without a sigh.

> You will not, therefore, repine, that you cannot shine at a
> horse-race, bet at a cockpit, win at a gaming table, riot at
> the board of intemperance, or drink deep at the midnight
> debauch, or steal to infamous enjoyments at the
> brothel....The course of sin, begun here, may continue forever.
> The seed of virtue, sown in the present world....may be destin-
> ed to growth immortal....What the natural eye thus sees with
> dim and probable vision, Christianity, possessed of superior
> optics, discerns, and promises, with clear prophetic certaini-
> ty.[54]

Yale College, now thoroughly dominated by Dwight, remained enlightened
by the superior optics of Christianity, even as the philosophical Enlightenment came more and more to engage the mind of the world outside.

In this same year, John Robison, Professor of Natural Philosophy in the
University of Edinburgh, published his **Proofs of a Conspiracy against the
Religions and Governments of Europe, Carried on in Secret Meetings of Free
Masons, Illuminati, and Reading Societies.** These purported to document the
existence of an international organization of free thinkers dedicated to the
overthrow of Christian society and religion, and they were shortly confirmed
by the publication at Hartford of an English translation of the first volume
of the Abbe Barruel's **Memoirs, Illustrating the History of Jacobinism.** The
latter dealt in detail with what the author was pleased to call 'The Anti-
Christian Conspiracy', which, it was feared, was about to be exported to
America. Dwight, whose abhorrence of Infidel philosophy had conditioned
him to believe the worst, devoured both works, and afterwards happening
upon Helen Maria Williams' letters describing A **Residence in France during
the Years 1792, 1793, 1794, and 1795,** his conviction of the imminent danger
to the Christian way of New England was confirmed. The public, he realized, must be warned, and soon. Thus when opportunity, in the form of an
invitation to deliver the annual Fourth of July oration to the citizens of New

Haven presented itself in the new year, he seized the occasion to sound the alarm.

What his fellow-citizens thought of his conception of The Duty of Americans at the Present Crisis[55] is not readily determinable at this distance in time. Howard tells us[56] that the democrats among them were outraged, and well they might have been, since the discourse is an overblown diatribe against all things French, republican, and secular. Taking for his text, **Revelation** 16:12-16, the account of the pouring out of the sixth vial,[57] which Dwight thinks to have been under way for about one hundred years (roughly, the period of the rise and triumph of Infidel philosophy), he seeks to relate the scriptural prediction of the rise of false doctrines and impious societies to the activities of the satanic organization described in Robison and Barruel:

> With unremitting ardour and diligence the members insinuated themselves into every place of power and trust....entered boldly into the desk (pulpit), and with unhallowed hands and satanic lips, polluted the pages of God, inlisted in their service almost all the booksellers, and of course the printers, of Germany; inundated the country with books, replete with infidelity, irreligion, immorality, and obscenity; prohibited the printing, and prevented the sale, of books of the contrary character; decried and ridiculed them when published in spite of their efforts....and in a word made more numerous, more diversified, and more strenuous exertions, than an active imagination would have preconceived.[58]

And what they have done in Germany, and afterwards in France, and most lately in England and Scotland, that, Dwight is convinced, they now propose to do in these newly united States.

What must the Christian do in the face of this rising tide of unholy secularism? Observe the Sabbath. "Christianity cannot fall, Dwight avows, but by the neglect of the Sabbath."[59]

> The Sabbath, with its ordinances, constitutes the bond of union to christians; the badge by which they know each other; their rallying point; the standard of their host. Beside public worship they have no means of effectual discrimination. To preserve this is to us a prime interest and duty.[60]

Given his gloomy sketch of the awful powers of the satanic host, the Sabbath would seem a slender rod of defence, but Dwight is of the opinion that it alone will suffice, for his only other advice to his fellow-citizens is that they separate themselves from the enemy, who, the balance of his discourse implies, is revolutionary France and those who, like Jefferson, would identify their views with her politics and philosophy. Shun the French, he beseeches them. Shun them, or "you cannot otherwise fail of partaking in their guilt and receiving of their plagues."[61] "Will you," he inquires, "rely on men whose principles justify falsehood, injustice, and cruelty? Will you trust philosophists?"[62]

> I am a father. I feel the usual parental tenderness for my children. I have long soothed the approach of declining years with the fond hope of seeing my sons serving God....But from cool conviction I declare in this solemn place, I would far rather follow them one by one to an untimely grave, than to behold them, however prosperous, the victims of philosophism.[63]

But lest you be alarmed by these dire portents, I am, he concludes, warranted to declare that neither France, nor all Europe, can subdue these United States so long as we resist the seductions of philosophists and put our trust in the Lord our God.

III

> If we allow the Scriptures to be the Word of God; our only duty is to inquire what they say, and to receive it with im-

plicit confidence. What God has said must be true; and all debate concerning its truth is absolutely precluded by the character of its Author.[64]

As Dwight's tenure lengthened, so did his influence outside the College. He became a person to be reckoned with in clerical affairs and in Connecticut politics.[65] Nationally, he espoused the platform of the Federalist Party, believing with them that what the country needed most was a strong central government dedicated to the continuation of the economics and social tie with England, the severance of same with France, and a sound currency. He counted himself, and was counted, as one of "the saving remnant" devoted to the defence of religion against its cultured despisers, and of the propertied class against those commoners[66] who, with Jefferson, championed secularism and democracy. Attention to these issues brought him into contact with politicans, educators, journalists, and various men of affairs, and these acted collectively to exert a moderating and broadening influence on his sermonizing. The lectures and discourses delivered after 1800 display a mind more restrained and judicious in its judgments, and reveal an advocate reliant more on reasoned argument than on scoring debating points. he sees now, what the author of **The Triumph** and The Duty of Americans did not, that denominational interests must give way to a concern for the Christian common cause.

During his years at Greenfield Hill he had composed and delivered more than once a sequence of sermons on the major doctrines of Christian theology. At Yale he had continued the practice, preaching each Sunday morning in term time on some particular aspect of the churches' teaching, following this up each Sunday afternoon with an "Improvement" of his morning lecture. This sermon-cycle, revised and corrected at each repetition, and written out over a period of years by his various amanuenses, was posthumously published in five volumes under the title, **Theology; Explained and Defended in a Series of Sermons.**[67] If Dwight deserves to be remembered for any reason other than for his contribution to the development of Yale, it is for this work.

As before, in the sermon-systems of Bellamy, Hopkins, and Emmons, so here too, the Explanation and Defence presupposes a Scriptural authority unquestioned. For Theology, as Dwight defines it, *"is the science of the will of God concerning the duty, and destination, of man."*[68] and what the will of God concerning these subjects is, cannot, he thinks, possibly be known, unless he is pleased to disclose it.

> When thus revealed, it can never be safely added to, diminished, nor otherwise in any manner altered by man. To him, whatever God is pleased to withhold must be unknown. By him, whatever God is pleased to reveal must be unalterable....As, therefore, the Scriptural System of Theology could not have been invented by man; so neither can it possibly be amended by man.[69]

In the Sacred Text, mankind are commanded to listen to the things spoken by the Wisdom of God, because they are right and excellent things. So far as the purposes of the Scriptural System are concerned, it is of no consequence whether we suppose them to have been revealed by the wisdom of God, literally understood, or by Christ. "The things here referred to (in the **Theology**) are the things contained in the Scriptures. All these were spoken by the Wisdom of God."[70]

What this Wisdom is we know. It is that Obvious Sense of the Sacred Text in which God's declarations are received by the common man.[71] This has to be the case because, as earlier noted, the Bible was written by plain men who knew no other language than that of the common people, and no other meaning than that which was familiar and customary. "Our Savior spoke almost everything which he said, to the common people. Matthew wrote his Gospel for the Hebrew Christians at large. Mark, Luke, and John, wrote their's for the Christian world at large. To the same persons were addressed the Acts of the Apostles,"[72] and so on. "From this fact, it follows irresistibly, that these parts of the Scriptures were written in language which the people could understand."[73] Indeed, "it cannot for a moment be admitted by common sense, or common decency, much less by a spirit of piety, that God has revealed his will to mankind, and yet that the language in which the Revelation is made, is such, that those, to whom it is peculiarly addressed, should be unable to understand its meaning."[74] We cannot believe that our Saviour and his Prophets and Apostles should address mankind in phrases unintelligible.

But if that is so, what, then it will be asked, are we to make of the fact that much of the language of Scripture is figurative, and therefore obscure? I concede, Dwight replies, that Scripture is extensively figurative, but this is not to admit that it is obscure, let alone unintelligible. "The figures, employed in the Scriptures, are those of mere nature; and are, therefore, generally at least, easily explained by the mind of everyone who knows the language of nature. The figurative phraseology in the Bible, which is obscure, is, ordinarily not that which the writers intended to use; but that which is made figurative by those, who comment on their writings."[75] Even so, the objector replies, many of the doctrines of Scripture are profound and mysterious, and demand assent beyond the capacity of human understanding. I confess it, says Dwight, but let us keep in mind that 'all such difficulties arise, not from the thing revealed, but from the philosophical curiosity with which it is investigated by ourselves. Let it ever be remembered that the decisions furnished by this investigation, are never matters of faith....and that the investigation itself is very often....mischievous and well as useless."[76] To think that the Scriptures must be so interpreted as to accord with our philosophy is monstrous. The scriptural evidence which we are required to believe presumes the veracity of God, and, adds Dwight, "he who will be contented to take his Maker at his word, will rarely find himself embarrassed."[77]

The organization of the **Theology** repeats the pattern, if not the peculiarities of Willard's **Compleat Body,** Bellamy's **True Religion,** and Hopkins's **System.** The existence of God is premissed and proved, his attributes are delineated, his sovereignty declared, and his relation to mankind through the Law and the Mediator is spelled out in minutest detail. Such departures as Dwight makes from the positions taken by his predecessors are, in the main, dictated by the circumstances of his times, the growth of a European literature critical of the claims of religion and, in his own country, the emergence of liberal cum unitarian Christianity.

Dwight wastes no ink on prefatory pieties, but comes immediately to the point. "The existence of God is the basis of religion....Happily for us, and accordably with his own wisdom, God has not.....*left himself without* ample *witness.*"[78] In addition to Scripture there is the evidence from his works. Given the authority of the former, and allowing that the latter is governed by the principle of cause and effect, no objection, he maintains, can prevail against the cosmological and teleological arguments as these have been formulated by Locke and Berkeley. As for Hume's critique of causality, that, he thinks, finds no support even in its author:

> The necessity of causes to all the *changes* of being is, so far as I know, universally admitted. *Mr. Hume* particularly, talks as commonly, or rather as uniformly, in this manner, as any Christian does; and not only argues from cause to effect, and from effect to cause, as much as other men, but *discusses* this subject abundantly....Indeed, without admitting it, neither he, nor any other man, could argue at all.[79]

Similarly, as regards the objections of the atheists, these are, one and all, either self-contradictory, as in their argument from the eternity of the material world (an infinite casual series is impossible), or vitiated by a failure to face plain fact, as in their argument from the casual (chance) character of existence (the state of things refutes it). Nor, Dwight concludes, is the atheist objection from the imperfection of the world in any better case, for it is certain that God can do very few things we can comprehend and a great many that we cannot.

The first thirteen sermons composing the **Theology** are devoted to the existence, unity, and attributes of God. In all of this, there is nothing novel, nothing to give offense to the orthodox, unless it be the preacher's tendency to play down the harsher side of the divine sovereignty. Thus even as he extols the immutability of God, this disposition to accommodate his teachings to the sentiments of the new age leads him to disavow the imputation of inexorability. For Dwight, God is "immutably exorable,"[80] and he does not pause to justify this compounding of incommensurables, nor does he see any contradiction in his assertion of God's foreknowledge of contingent acts.[81] A similar ambivalence is present in his view of the forgiveness of sins. God, he allows, is merciful, but we cannot conclude from this that he will forgive the sins of mankind.[82] The tendency is pronounced in his thought respecting the damnation of infants:

> The situation of infants and the dispensation of Providence towards them, I acknowledge to be, in many respects, mysterious, to a degree, beyond my ability satisfactorily to explain. But I utterly question the ability of any objector to show, that they suffer more than they deserve.[83]

Of one thing, however, he is certain: "if we please to be saved, we shall *now* be saved....There is nothing which prevents us from being saved, but our own inclination."

This salvation being accomplished through the Atonement of Christ and the work of the Holy Spirit in Regeneration (of which more below), assumes the truth of Trinitarianism, and no member of the Standing Order was more sensitive to the challenge to the truth of that assumption emanating from Boston and Cambridge than the President of Yale. The controversy over the appointment of Henry Ware Sr. to the Hollis Professorship was still fresh in his mind, as was the election of the liberal, Samuel Webber, to the presidency of Harvard in 1806, and the final triumph of the liberals in the subsequent election of his dynamic successor, John Kirkland, in 1810. Hopkins was dead, and Emmons buried in a country parish. In was left to Dwight, as the most prominent of the surviving heirs of Edwards, to provide the required defence, and thus it is that three of the most important sermons of the **Theology** are dedicated to the meeting the objections of the Unitarians, offering counter-objections, and taking exception to the unitarian conduct of the controversy.[85]

The first and principal objection of the Unitarians to the doctrine of the Trinity is that it is self-contradictory, that three persons in one God is either tritheism or unintelligible, but neither, Dwight contends, need be, or are, admitted by Trinitarians. Trinitarianism is not tritheism because no Trinitarian understands 'person' to signify three beings, nor does the alleged unintelligibility of the doctrine follow from the fact. "The nature of the thing declared is absolutely unintelligible; but the fact is, in a certain degree, understood without difficulty,"[86] Thus, says Dwight, "if I am asked, as I probably shall be, what is the exact meaning of the word *Person* in this case, I answer, that

I do not know.... I further answer, that the term in dispute serves to convey, briefly and conveniently, the things intended by the doctrine; viz. that the Father is God, the Son is God, and the Holy Ghost is God; that these are Three in one sense, and One in another."[87] One, in the sense that they share in common all the attributes of God and are alike self-existent, eternal, omniscient, omnipotent, and possessed of the same boundless moral excellence; Three, insofar as they are distinguished in holy scripture. "The sense in which they are three and yet one, we do not, and cannot, understand. Still we understand the fact; and on this fact depends the truth, and meaning, of the whole Scriptural system."[88] Should it be objected further that this is tantamount to an admission of unintelligibility, Dwight would deny it. Unitarians can no more deny the truth of the proposition than Trinitarians can affirm it, since it simply is not an object of intellectual discernment or philosophical inquiry. Why, then, do Trinitarians adopt it as part of their creed? "Because," answers Dwight, "God has declared it."[89]

Granting that it is so, the question remains as to just what it is that God has declared, and in their answer the Unitarians profess to see a second objection, namely, that the doctrine of the Trinity is anti-scriptural. For Scripture exhibits Christ as inferior to the Father in knowledge (**Mark** 13:32) in goodness (**Matthew** 19:17), and in power (**Mark** 15:31-34), and justifies no higher status for him than that of a delegated God. Not so, rejoins Dwight. The Scriptures, properly understood, no more warrant the Arian view of Christ as a delegated god than they do the Socinian view of Jesus as a mere man, as is evident in **Matthew** 11:25 and **John** 8:23, 17:4. Should any further evidence of the falsity of the Unitarian interpretation by demanded, we have but to remember that their view requires that we renounce the scriptural account of Christ's role in the work of redemption, his Atonement, our depravity, the impossibility of Justification by our own righteousness, and regeneration by the Spirit of God. In short, Unitarianism entails the renunciation of Scripture itself! Seen in this light, can it, he asks, be doubted that Unitarianism is "an immoral influence," serving only to promote Infidelity?

Unitarianism being, as he supposes, disposed of, and the deity of Christ and the Holy Spirit vindicated, the explanation and defence of the New Divinity continues with a series of sermons on the Priesthood of Christ, the

224

theologically most important of which are the three sermons on the Atonement. Dwight's exposition develops along the familiar lines laid down by Bellamy and Hopkins. The Government of God is a moral government which can only be preserved by a continued obedience to its laws. By virtue of their disposition to depravity[90] derived from Adam, mankind is lost to sin, and as such deserving of eternal punishment. Were God to absolve the penitent, were the penalties of the law not to be inflicted upon its transgressors, God's government would be disregarded and his glory diminished. Consequently, an atonement must be made for all mankind,[91] and that by one who has perfectly obeyed the law, is empowered to act, and vicariously suffers in the room of sinners for their sake.

This atonement, Dwight reminds us, is not to be thought of as a literal ransoming. "We are not, in the literal, sense, *bought,* or *purchased,* at all. Nor has Christ, in the literal sense, paid any price, to purchase mankind from slavery or death."[92] Thus such phrases as, 'he bought our salvation with his blood,' or, 'he ransomed us, or redeemed us,' are to be taken simply and solely in a figurative sense. God's pardon of Christ for us does in no way expiate our sin. We were sinners before his Atonement, and remain sinners after. He has, figuratively, redeemed us from the *curse* of the law, but not from the law as such. "No man is pardoned merely because of the Atonement made by Christ; but because of his own acceptance, also, of that atonement by faith. The way is open, and equally open, to all; although all may not be equally inclined to walk in it."[93]

As before, in the case of the deity of Christ, so here also Dwight seeks to justify the Atonement against its philosophical critics. These would have it that a vicarious atonement for sin is inconsistent with the dictates of right reason, because the sin is ours, and any atonement or expiation ought to be made by us. Why should an innocent (Christ) have to suffer for our sins? To say that God's glory demands it is to demean God. Surely, the more honorable path would be for God to forego the sacrifice and forgive the penitent? Dwight will not concede it: "To these questions, I answer, that it ill becomes a creature of yesterday to employ himself in contriving a government for the Universe."[94] Why should we, whose faculties are barely adequate to understand the existing state of things, presume to question the decisions of God. It is enough for us to know what Scripture has told us, that Christ's suffering was voluntary and his Atonement acceptable to God.

That we can know even this much, presupposes the restoration of our souls to holiness by the Spirit of God.[95] The great proof for the necessity of such a regeneration is, for Dwight, found in the depravity of our nature. "In our flesh or native character there dwelleth no good thing....I shall consider this point as being actually proved."[96] and "take it for granted, that mankind are, in some instances, really regenerated."[97] Given then, the necessity and reality of regeneration, it remains to consider its nature and its evidences.

To this task, Dwight devotes a further sixteen sermons, but the essence of his view is expressible in sixteen words: Regeneration is the instantaneous and imperceptible communication to the regenerate of a relish for spiritual objects. Or, as he puts it,

> In regeneration, the very same thing is done by the Spirit of God for the soul, which was done for Adam by the same Divine Agent at his creation. The soul of Adam was *created* with a relish for Spiritual objects. The soul of man who becomes a Christian is *renewed* by the communication of the same relish.[98]

This is not to say that the Spirit of God creates in the regenerate a volition they did not previously possess. The change involved is no change of character. The disposition to depravity remains. All that has happened is that a consciousness of holiness has been raised in those who are the recipients of God's grace, and that not immediately, for all that the change is instantaneous, since this consciousness, as Dwight conceives it, is ordinarily imperceptible by its beneficiaries.[99]

Thus it is no indication that one *is not* regenerate because they can offer no account of the exact time or place of this event. Conversely, the experience of "an unspeakable joy," preceded by a conviction of sin, is no sure evidence of one *is* regenerate, since such emotions are sometimes excited by natural causes.[100] Nor is zeal in the cause of religion, or exactness in the performance of religious duties, or even suffrance of persecution for religion's sake, any indisputable evidence of regeneration. Certainly, our confidence that we are sanctified is no such evidence of regeneration. Nor does the belief and opinion of others that we are entitled to the name of Christian make it so. Of such evidences at these, delcares Dwight, Scripture knows nothing, but always and only teaches that "by their fruits shall ye know them." "The truth is," he concludes, that "the infusion of a relish for divine things...is...perceivable only by its effects."[101]

The thirteen sermons on the Law, and the thirty more on the Ten Commandments that follow directly upon these, mark a subtle but significant departure from the Edwardsian metaphysics of morals and Bellamy's theology of the Great Commandment. What has intervened is the rise of Utilitarianism. Dwight has studied Paley[102] and read enough of Godwin[103] to be appalled by the latter's understanding of the greatest good for the greatest number, and in his sermon, Utility the foundation of Virtue, he seeks to appropriate the principle of Utility to the service of consistent Calvinism.

He begins properly with a definition. "By the word, Utility, I mean a Tendency to produce Happiness."[104] What is it that produces Happiness? Glorifying God. "It is therefore true in the proper sense, that virtuous persons, by voluntarily glorifying God, become the objects of his delight; or, in other words, the means of happiness or enjoyment to him."[105] That this is not utilitarianism of the sort envisaged by Paley or Godwin, Dwight is well aware. the notion that Utility per se is the measure of virtue is summarily denied. The utility that matters to theology is what is useful to God for the realization of his purposes. "To us, Utility, as judged of by ourselves, cannot be a program of moral conduct."[106] Not Utility as such, but the Bible, and the Bible alone, is, for Dwight, "the only safe rule by which moral beings can, in this world, direct their conduct."[107]

We are commanded by Scripture to love God in a spirit of disinterested benevolence. Thus far Dwight is at one with his predecessors. But he sees nothing in the Great Commandment that implies the denial of a proper creaturely pursuit of happiness. The belief of Sarah Edwards and Samuel Hopkins[108] that true Christians ought to be willing to be damned for the greater glory of God is no scriptural injunction. Christian resignation does not require that we should be willing to suffer Perdition. It is, he argues, only by a grammatical quibble that **Exodus** 32:32-33 and **Romans** 9:3 are reinterpreted as enjoining voluntary damnation. With such extremes real religion has nothing to do. In real religion the great essential is the heart's confidence in the moral character of God, and the pursuit by the soul[109] of that holiness or moral excellence which is most pleasing to Him. "Real Christianity is the Energy, or Active power, of the soul, steadily directed to that, which is believed to be right, and thus directed to it, merely because it is right."[110]

That his undergraduate hearers should be left in no doubt as to the specifics of that right action required of them, Dwight devotes the last eighty sermons of his series to the system of duties (Sermons 91-162) and dispensations (Sermons 163-171) devolving upon Christians from their public profession of the Covenant[111] to the final accounting before God after death of their conduct in life.[112] Seventeen Yale classes were exposed to the complete cycle.[113] An unknown, but certainly large, number of seminarians studied some or all of them in one way or another of the twelve editions of the **Theology** that appeared before the Civil War. For two generations after its author's death, the standard of the New England Theology was the system of Timothy Dwight.

IV

> It was the glory of this great man that he had no love for innovation. He did not believe that theology was, like philosophy, left in such a situation that ages might pass on during which the honest inquirers in the church would be necessarily and invincibly ignorant of its fundamental truths. Nor did he think it proper to sacrifice common sense to metaphysics.[114]

He might well have been writing with perfect accuracy about himself, for the qualities Dwight sees in Edwards were exactly those his supporters saw in him. His refusal to be pinned down to exact theological positions and his tendency to soften hard doctrines was taken by them as evidence of his prudence and moderation. His vigourous partisanship in the Federalist cause was accounted patriotism, while that domination of the Standing Order which won from his critics the derisive epithet "Pope"[115] was viewed by the members as clerical statesmanship. Posterity, however, has not been so kind. The virtually undiluted admiration accorded Dwight by his students and colleagues has faded in our cynical century to a hardly veiled contempt. He has been damned for an opportunist, and stigmatized as a man whose mind never grew![116] Of those who in our time have studied his life and works with care, only Cuningham really likes him—warts and all. Parrington's verdict, delivered more than half a century ago, still stands:

> A great college president Timothy Dwight may very well have been; he was worshipped by his admirers only this side of idolatry; but a great thinker, a steadfast friend of truth in whatever garb it might appear, a generous kindly soul loving even publicans and sinners, regardful of others and forgetful of self, he assuredly was not![117]

The judgment is reaffirmed by Howard:

> He saw the apocalyptic beast and heard things that go bump in the night where there was nothing but social change in the mask of anarchy and rumbling challenges to human intellect....and most of his public utterances, during the last two decades of his life, survive as nothing more than vivid reminders that no man can flounder more wildly than the one who hangs his clothes on a hickory limb and refuses to go near the rising tide which engulfs him![118]

It would perhaps be saying too much to claim that these appraisals are mistaken. Dwight is not a great thinker, if by that be meant a contributor of original and epoch-creating ideas and values. His was the prickly personality of an eighteenth century oligarch, as such naturally antagonistic to the shibboleths of Jeffersonian democracy. So fervid an admirer of the philosopher-president as Parrington could hardly be expected to dispense the milk of kindness to one who stood squarely against everything that Jefferson stood for. Howard's judgment, however, is another story.

To the modern mind, even to the modern religious mind, John's vision of the four beasts (**Revelation** 4:6-9) is something quaint and archaic. It was not so to Edwards, nor to his first disciples, nor yet to any Christian who, like Dwight, presupposes that the canon of scripture is the Word of God. Thus when Howard suggests that this vision of the apocalyptic beasts is akin to an overactive imagining of things that go bump in the night, he not only trivializes that particular scripture, but makes plain in his conviction that Dwight's presupposition is wrong. If that is indeed the case, then Dwight's elitist faith, founded as it is on scripture, "Strait is the gate and narrow the way, which leadeth into life, and few there be that find it." (**Matthew 7:14**) must be misplaced, most certainly so when placed in opposition to that secular egalitarianism which Howard's judgment presupposes, and against which so many of Dwight's public utterances are directed. It may well be that Dwight erred in hanging his clothes on the hickory limb of Holy Scripture. Our modern understanding of these matters makes possible that he did. But I doubt that Dwight himself would have been convinced of it, for what should a defender of the faith do, if not defend the faith!

In any age, including our own, this is not a task which makes for popularity in intellectual circles. Dwight makes no secret of his contempt for the pretensions of reason, but this is not to say that he abandons it. He is not anti-intellectual for all that he fulminates against the attempts of the philosophers to deny mankind their hope of heaven. He abhors Infidelity not because of its logic, but because it is folly "that Infidelity naturally and necessarily becomes, when possessed of the control of the national interests, a source of evils so numerous and so intense as to compel mankind to prefer any state to these evils."[119] If he emphasizes the moral at the expense of the metaphysical it is because he believes with all his heart and mind and soul that Infidelity unchallenged tends inevitably to immorality and the unravelling of the very fabric of society. Dwight's crowning achievement is to have persuaded the next generation that the preservation of society as we know it and value it is contingent upon the triumph of scriptural morality, and to have trained up the man who would prove it so.

230

Bibliographical Essay

Dwight's **Theology:** explained and defended, in a series of (173) sermons, with a Memoir of the Life of the Author (by his sons, Sereno E. and William T. Dwight), five volumes (Middletown, Connecticut: Clark and Lyman, 1818-1819), early became a standard text, used in orthodox seminaries and church schools throughout the nineteenth century. Barely thirty years after Dwight's death, it had gone through twelve American editions, been reprinted twice at Glasgow and four times at London. It was reprinted in the decades following the Civil War, and again at London as recently as 1924. Except for slightly altered pagination, the differences between these various reprintings and editions are insignificant, typographical rather than textual. The two discourses on **The Nature and Danger of Infidel Philosophy** (New Haven: George Bunce, 1798) are preserved in the Evans American Imprints Series (Evans 33657), as is the **Discourse on the Genuineness and Authenticity of the New Testament** (New York: George Bunce, 1794), Evans 26924. With this last should be read the anonymous discourse **On the Manner in which the Scriptures are to be Understood, Panoplist and Missionary Magazine,** XII, nos. 5, 6 (May-June, 1816), 193-203, 249-256. Of somewhat lesser theological import, but worth a look, are the two volumes of **Sermons** (New Haven: Howe, Durrie, and Peck, 1828), and the unsigned **Eighteen Lectures on the Evidences of Divine Revelation, Panoplist and Missionary Magazine,** III, IV, IX (1810-1813). For the student who has these volumes, the pagings are easily found. He who perseveres to look them up will find a ragbag of archaeological, literary, and mythological evidences tending, in the author's opinion, to the confirmation of the history recorded in the Bible. See also the discourse on **The Dignity and Excellence of the Gospel** (New Haven: J. Seymour, 1812). Delivered at the ordination of his old pupil and amanuensis, Nathaniel W. Taylor.

   The Major Poems of Timothy Dwight, facsimile reproductions with an Introduction by Williams J. McTaggert and William K. Bottorff (Gainesville, Florida: **Scholar's Facsimiles & Reprints,** 1969), includes **America, The Conquest of Canaan, The Triumph of Infidelity, Greenfield Hill,** and **A Dissertation on the History, Eloquence, and Poetry of the Bible.** Dwight's **Travels**

in New England and New York is available in a splendid new edition, edited with an Introduction and notes by Barbara Miller Solomon, with the assistance of Patricia M. King, four volumes (Cambridge: The Belknap Press of Harvard University Press, 1969). Those sections in volume four on the Learning, Morals, and Religion of New England, are particularly pertinent to a proper understanding of Dwight's theological position. In a similar vein is Dwight's defense of the United States against the criticisms of Robert Southey, in his **Remarks on the Review of Inchiquin's Letters, Published in the** (English) **Quarterly Review, Addressed to the Right Honorable George Canning, Esquire** (Boston: Samuel T. Armstrong, 1815). Inchiquin the Jesuit was a fictional traveler whose favorable opinions of America, in letters written to correct what his creator, Charles Ingersoll, had deemed to be derogatory remarks made by various English visitors. Southey, the English poet and man of letters, had reviewed Ingersoll's book unfavorably, and Dwight, enraged by what he too considered demeaning criticisms, leaped to defend his country. A rather more complete account is given in Howard (392-396). A detailed listing of the various printing and editions of most of Dwight's works may be found in **The Bibliography of American Literature,** compiled by Jacob Blanck. Six volumes (New Haven: Yale University Press' 1957). 519-530.

As the most prominent and influential citizen of his state in his era, Dwight early attracted the attention of biographers. The Memoir, by his sons, which serves as a preface to **Theology** is filiopietistic. The several sketches of Dwight by his contemporaries (see Cuningham, 356) are uniformly hortatory and fulsome, as are the materials in William B. Sprague, **Annals of the American Pulpit** (New York: Arno Press, 1969), II, 152-165. Moses Coit Tyler, **Three Men of Letters,** viz. Bishop Berkeley, Joel Barlow, and Dwight (New York: Macmillan, 1942, is scholarly, pedestrian, and thorough, except as regards the **Theology,** which is sketched in a paragraph (327). However, the author supplies a comprehensive bibliography of manuscripts, printed works, sketches, memoirs, tracts, and articles by and about Dwight and his times. Shorter, but measurably more interesting for the student of Dwight's didactic Calvinism, is Leon Howard's perceptive and erudite study of four of **The Connecticut Wits,** viz. John Trumbull, Timothy Dwight, David Humphreys, and Joel Barlow (Chicago: University of Chicago Press, 1943), each and all of them, according to Howard, indelibly molded by their years at Yale. Only two chapters are specifically devoted to Dwight, but these are required reading. The author provides a compendious "check list" of writings by each of his subjects, together with detailed bibliographical notes for each chapter. Of smaller compass, focusing most particularly on the lterary side of his subject, is Kenneth Silverman, **Timothy Dwight** (New York: Twayne Publishers, 1969). Silverman outdoes Cuningham by devoting but half a paragraph to **Theology** (112), but managing in that brief compass to misconceive the significance of Dwight's doctrine of regeneration. The most recent study is that of Stephen Edward Berk, **Calvinism versus Democracy, Timothy Dwight and the Origins of American Evangelical Orthodoxy** (Hamden, Connecticut: Archon Books, 1974). This is a retitled reworking of the author's Ph.D dissertation, University of Iowa, 1971. Berk sees Dwight's "moderate evangelical Calvinism" as ushered from "a rising humanitarian spirit," based upon "one major principle, that of utility in producing human happiness." In this view, I suspect, he has been strongly influenced by Haroutunian, but that, after all, is not a bad influence. Complete with bibliography and notes.

The balance of the secondary literature pertaining to Dwight's life and thought is a mixed bag, including nothing of particular pertinence to his formulation of consistent Calvinism. Ralph Henry Gabriel, **Religion and Learning at Yale, The Church of Christ in the College and University, 1757-1797,** includes a very readable chapter on Dwight, placing his subject in the context of his times and remarking his relation to the revival of 1802. Gabriel does not entirely approve of his subject: "with all his gifts, Dwight never rose above the fighting partisan. He never transcended the Federalist's contemptuous attitude toward the common man." (57). An earlier study, on which Gabriel may have drawn, Franklin B. Dexter, 'Student Life at Yale under the first President Dwight 1795-1817,' **Proceedings of the American Antiquarian Society,** 27 (1917), 318-335, offers a glimpse of Dwight as pedagogue, but nothing more substantial. Robert Edson Lee, 'Timothy Dwight and the Boston Palladium,' **The New England Quarterly,** XXXV, no. 2 (June, 1962), 229-239, researches Dwight's relation to, and publications in, a conservative periodical, while Lewis Leary, 'The Author of the Triumph of Infidelity', **The New England Quarterly,** XX (September, 1947), 377-385, explores the question of

Dwight's authorship and concludes, contrary to the testimony of Dwight's son (Cuningham 356), that Dwight is probably the author.

There are, so far as I am aware, but three dissertations on, or cognate to, Dwight's religious thought: Paul T. Shiber, **'The Conquest of Canaan' as a youthful expression of Timothy Dwight's New Divinity and Political Thought** Ph.D. dissertation, Miami, 1972; Lewis E. Buchanan, **Timothy Dwight, Man of Letters,** Ph.D dissertation, Wisconsin, 1941; and Wayne Conrad Tyner, **The Theology of Timothy Dwight in Historical Perspective,** Ph.D dissertation, North Carolina, 1971. The one of the three that I have seen (Tyner's) lives up to its title, placing Dwight's life and thought in the political and religious context of his times. Tyner's study breaks no new ground, relying almost entirely on previously published studies, but it is fair to its subject, judicious, and clearly written. Includes a detailed bibliography of primary and secondary sources.

[1]Nathaniel William Taylor in a letter to William Buell Sprague, in **Annuals of the American Pulpit** (New York: Arno Press, 1969; reprint of the 1866 edition, II, 161.

[2]Charles E. Cuningham, **Timothy Dwight 1752-1817, A Biography** (New York: Macmilan, 1941), 319.

[3]Dwight, **A Dissertation on the History, Eloquence, and Poetry of the Bible** (New Haven: T. & S. Green, 1772), 3, 15. Evans 12380.

[4]Ibid., 4.

[5]Ibid., 7.

[6]'A little more than half of what is now published was delivered from the desk.' From the Advertisement.

[7]Dwight **A Discourse on the Genuineness and Authenticity of the New Testament** (New York: George Bunce, 1794), 13. Evans 26924.

[8]Ibid., 24.

[10]All of them published sequentially in **The Panoplist and Missionary Magazine United,** volumes and pagings as follows: Lecture I, Vol. III (June-July, 1810), 14-19, 57-64; Lecture II, Vol. III (August, 1810), 101-111; Lecture III, Vol. III (September, 1810), 164-169; Lecture IV, Vol. III (October, 1810), 201-208; Lecture V, Vol. III (December 1810), 295-300; Lecture VI, Vol. III (January, 1811), 351-356; Lecture VII, Vol. III (February, 1811), 389-396; lecture VIII, Vols. III, IV (March-June, 1811), 441-46, 5-11; Lecture IX, Vol. IV (July, 1811), 56-63; Lecture X, Vol. IV (August, 1811), 106-112; Lecture XI, Vol. IV (September, 1811), 155-160; Lecture XII, Vol. IV (January, 1812), 345-354; Lecture XIII, Vol. IV (March, 1812), 436-444; Lecture XIV, Vol. IV (May 1812, 529-536; Lecture XV, Vol. IX (June, 1813), 4-11; Lecture XVI, Vol. IX (July, 1813), 49-56; Lecture XVII, Vol. IX (August, 1813), 111-117; Lecture XVIII, Vol. IX (December, 1813), 529-536. The passage from Vol. IV to Vol IX is a typographical error. For reasons unknown to me, the editors changed the numbering of their volumes.

[11]Dwight, **On the Evidence of Divine Revelation,** Lecture I, Vol. III, no. 2 (July, 1810), 64.

[12]Dwight, 'On the Manner in which the Scriptures are to be Understood', the **Panoplist and Missionary Magazine,** Vol. Xii, nos. 5, 6 (May-June, 1816), 193-203, 249-256.

[13]Ibid., 194.

[14]Ibid., 255.

[15]Ibid., 255.

[16]Ibid., 256.

[17]His mother was Mary Edwards, third daughter of Jonathan and Sarah. She married Major Timothy Dwight, the third of the name, in 1750. The Dwights and the Edwardses were Northampton neighbors. Major Dwight's father, Colonel Timothy Dwight, was one of the few leading citizens of the town to stand by Jonathan Edwards in the affair of his dismassal. The fourth Timothy, first of the thirteen children of Mary and Timothy Dwight, was born at Northampton on May 14th, 1752. Timothy Dwight (1828-1916), the fifth to bear the name, Professor and President of Yale (1886-1898), was our Timothy's grandson.

[18]The tale is told by Cuningham, who got it from Benjamin Woolsey Dwight's notebook. 'Biographical Hints and Facts respecting the late Rev'd Timothy Dwight'. See Cuningham, 1, 363.

[19]Cuningham, 16-18.

²⁰In the Memoir, afterwards by Sprague, more recently by Howard (see bibliographical essay), and at length by Cuningham, 20-32.

²¹President Naphtali Daggett, with whom Dwight had worked in harmony throughout the years of his tutorship, resigned and was succeeded as President by Ezra Stiles, whose educational philosophy and theological learnings were at some variance from those of Dwight. Dwight himself had briefly nurtured presidential hopes, and had gone so far as to prepare a petition of application, when second thoughts intervened aand persuaded him not to submit it.

²²Dwight, **The Nature and Danger of Infidel Philosophy exhibited in two discourses addressed to the candidates for the baccalaureat in Yale College,** September 9th, 1797 (New Haven: George Bunce, 1798), 50. Evans 33657.

²³Alexander Pope (1688-1744), English poet and essayist. Dwight's *nom empreunte,* Scriblerus, signed to several of his periodical contributions, is taken from Pope's **Memoirs of Martinus Scriblerus** (1741)

²⁴John Milton (1608-1674), English poet and Puritan political essayist.

²⁵**The Major Poems of Timothy Dwight,** facsimile reproduction with an Introduction by William J. McTaggert and William K. Bottorff (Gainsville, Florida: Scholars' Facsimiles & Reprints, 1969), includes **America, The Conquest of Canaan,** and **Greenfield Hill. The Tryal of Faith, The Seasons Moralized, Message of Mordecai to Esther, Columbia** and the **Address,** are included in Elihu Hubbard Smith, **American Poems** (Litchfield, Connecticut: Collier and Buel, 1793); a facsimile reproduction with an Introduction, Notes, and Index by William K. Bottorff (Gainesville: Scholars' Facsimiles and Reprints, 1966.)

²⁶In **The Gazette of the United States,** of July 13th, 1791. Reprinted in Smith **American Poems,** 70-75.

²⁷Cuningham, 356.

²⁸Howard, 218.

²⁹Lewis Leary, 'The Author of **The Triumph of Infidelity,**' **The New England Quarterly,** XX (September, 1947), 377-385.

³⁰Kenneth Silverman, **Timothy Dwight** (New York: Twayne Publishers, 1969), 81-94, 157-158.

³¹Leary, 385. It has been suggested, in view of Dwight's scholastic turn of mind, that his statement that he did "not acknowledge" the poem, meant no more than that he did not claim authorship, since to "not acknowledge" is the same as to deny outright.

³²Charles Chauncy (1705-1787), pastor of the First Church of Boston for sixty years, and prolific author. His defence of Universalism in **The Mystery Hid from Ages and Generations made manifest by the gospel Revelation: or, the Salvation of all Men the grand thing aimed at in the Scheme of God** (1784), is characterized in **The Triumph of Infidelity** as a work designed "to wound the eternal cause with deepest harms."

³³Timothy Dwight, 87.

³⁴Yale students were required to attend morning and evening prayers, forenoon and afternoon worship, and during the balance of the holy day (beginning at sundown on Saturday) remain in their rooms. Walking abroad on the Sabbath, or admitting other students to their rooms for social purposes, was regarded as profanation, and as such strictly prohibited. See Franklin B. Dexter, 'Student Life at Yale College under the first President Dwight (18-795-1817)', **Proceedings of the American Antiquarina Soceity,** 27 (October, 1917), 334. See also, Ralph Henry Gabriel, **Religion and Learning at Yale** (New Haven: Yale University Press, 1958), Chapter 4.

236

[35]Dwight, **The Nature and Danger of Infidel Philosophy exhibited in two discourses addressed to the candidates for the baccalaureate in Yale College, Sept. 9th, 1797** (New Haven: George Bunce, 1798), 17. Evans 22657.

[36]Ibid.

[37]Ibid., 67.

[38]As Howard notes (348), Dwight had but little firsthand knowledge of these thinkers. The propositions he cites and the arguments he presents are borrowed from a variety of secondary sources, principally John Leland's **A view of the Principal Deistical Writers,** Joseph Priestley's **Observations on the Increase of Infidelity,** and Philip Skelton's **Deism Revealed.** Dwight himself acknowledges in a footnote that his summary of Hume's teachings is taken verbatim from Bishop Horne's **Summary of Mr. Hume's Doctrine's, Metaphysical and Moral.**

[39]**Nature and Danger,** 18.

[40]Ibid., 35.

[41]Ibid., 57.

[42]Ibid.

[43]Ibid., 70.

[44]Ibid.

[45]Ibid., 83.

[46]Ibid., 52.

[47]Ibid.

[48]Ibid., 52-53.

[49]Ibid., 82.

[50]Ibid.

[51]Ibid.

[52]Ibid., 84.

[53]Ibid., 42.

[54]Ibid., 92-93.

[55]**The Duty of Americans, at the Present Crisis,** Illustrated in the Discourse preached on the fourth of July, 1797 (New Haven: Thomas and Samuel Green, 1798), Evans 33656. Hereafter cited as **Duty** with page reference.

[56]**The Connecticut Wits,** 350-351.

[57]According to Dwight, "by the ablest commentators the fifth vial is considered as having been poured out at the time of the Reformation." If the pouring continued as supposed for 180 years (the average vial-pouring length), its termination was in the year 1697. "In the sixth great division of the period of providence, denoted by the vials filled with divine judgments and emptied on the world, the wealth, strength and safety of the Anti-christian empire will be greatly lessened, and thus effectual preparation will be made for its final overthrow." **Duty,** 7.

[58]**Duty,** 13.

[59]Ibid., 18.

[60]Ibid., 19.

[62]Ibid., 23.

[63]Ibid., 26.

[64]Dwight, 'On the Manner in which the Scriptures are to be Understood,' **The Panoplist and Missionary Magazine,** XII, no. 5 (May-June, 1816), 256. Hereafter cited as **Scriptures Understood** with page reference.

[65]In a privately printed pamphlet published in 1799, John Cosins Ogden, one of Dwight's harsher critics, notes that, "President Dwight is making great strides after universal controul (sic) in Connecticut, New England, and the United States, over religious opinions and politics. He is inspiring his pupils with political prejudices against some of our best fellow citizens, in warm and unbecoming language. He is seeking to establish the Edwardean system of doctrines and discipline, from pride for his grandfather's (President Edwards) talents and fame, while but few indeed of that deceased gentleman's dependants believe in his tenets. With a large salary paid from public bounty, he is maintained in his place, and excites and perpetuates party designs." **An Appeal to the Candid, upon the present state of Religion and Politics in Connecticut** (Stockbridge, 1799), 9.

[66]For all of his disdain for the common man, it says something for Dwight's sense of values that under his administration the rating of students by social standing, rather than by intellectual achievement, was abolished at Yale.

[67]As delivered to five generations of Yale undergraduates, the sequence consisted of 160 sermons, forty each academic year, continued over the four years of the undergraduate course. The sequence as published consists of 173 sermons, the additions presumably representing further specification of the doctrines discussed.

[68]Dwight, **Theology; Explained and Defended, in a Series of Sermons, with a Memoir of the Life of the Author** (Middletown, Connecticut: Clark and Lyman, 1818-1819), Sermon XXXIX (II, 134). Hereafter cited as **Theology** with a sermon number (Roman) and volume and page number in parentheses.

[69]Ibid.

[70]**Theology,** Sermon CLXXII (V. 552).

[71]**Scriptures Understood,** 194.

[72]Ibid., 195.

[73]Ibid.

[74]Ibid.

[75]Ibid., 200.

[76]Ibid., 202.

[77]Ibid.

[78]**Theology,** Sermon I (I. 3).

[79]Ibid., Sermon I (I. 7-8).

[80]**Theology,** Sermon V (I. 88).

[81]Ibid., Sermon XV (I. 250-251).

[82]Ibid., Sermon XII (I. 195).

[83]Ibid., Sermon VIII (I. 138).

[84]**Theology,** Sermon XV (I. 253).

[85]Dwight here has in view the case for Unitarianism as presented in Joseph Priestley's **Notes on all the Books of Scripture,** and in various writings of Richard Price and Thomas Belsham.

That he was aware of an emerging American Unitarian movement, as represented in various articles in **The Christian Disciple** and in the early sermons of William Ellery Channing, may be assumed, but by the time this movement attained its maturity Dwight was dead.

[86]**Theology**, Sermon XXXIX (II. 139).

[87]Ibid., 137-138.

[88]Ibid., 138.

[89]Ibid., 139.

[90]"'The human character,' notes Dwight in his sermon on the degrees of depravity, "is not depraved to the full extent of the human powers." (Sermon XXXI. I. 525). True, sin does come into the world by Adam, but Adam's sin is not imputed to mankind. Just how, then, it might be wondered, is mankind implicated in the original sin? Dwight does not pretend to know. "I now observe further, that I am unable to explain this part of the subject. Many attempts have been made to explain it; but I freely confess myself to have seen none, which was satisfactory to me; or which did not leave the difficulties as great, and, for aught I know, as numerous, as they were before." (Sermon XXXII. II 5).

[91]"'If Christ did not make an atonement for sin, it will be difficult; I presume it will be impossible; to point out, or to conceive, in what respect his advent was of such importance, either to the glory of God, or to the good of mankind." (Sermon LV. II. 388).

[92]**Theology**, Sermon LVII (II. 412).

[93]Ibid., Sermon LVI (II. 407).

[94]Ibid., Sermon LV (II. 385).

[95]Dwight is here assuming that his refutation of Unitarianism has established that the Holy Ghost is not, as they declare, an Attribute of God, but rather a Person, "God, employed in his most wonderful work; that of restoring holiness to the soul of man." Sermon LXX (III. 5).

[96]Sermon LXXIII (III. 48-49).

[97]Sermon LXII (III. 33).

[98]Sermon LXXIV (III. 64).

[99]For those who might wish for some elaboration and clarification of this position, Dwight has none to offer: "I shall not attempt, here, to describe the Metaphysical nature of the work of regeneration, nor to define, precisely, the manner in which it is accomplished; nor the exact bounds of the Divine, and human agency is this great concern. Of these subjects I have not sufficiently distinct and comprehensive views." Sermons LXXIV (III. 67-68).

[100]Dwight has in mind here the celebrated conversion of St. Augustine, in consequence of his having overheard a passage of Scripture as he passed by. He confesses to some degree of skepticism with respect to cases of this sort. See Sermon LXXXVIII (III. 267-269).

[102]William Paley (1743-1805), English clergyman and Utilitarian philosopher. Author of **The Principles of Moral and Political Philosophy** (1785); **Horae Paulinæ**, in defence of the New Testament against the fable hypothesis (1790), **View of the Evidences of Christianity**, arguments contra deism (1794); and **Natural Theology** (1802), which contains the famous version of the design argument based upon the analogy of the watchmaker. Dwight may have read all of these works, it is certain that he is familiar with the first.

[103]William Godwin (1756-1836), English philosopher, novelist, and sometime dissenting minister. Author of the **Enquiry Concerning Political Justice and its Influence on General Virtue and**

Happiness (1793). It was this work, presumably, which aroused Dwight's ire.

[104]Sermon XCIX (III. 440).

[105]Ibid., (III. 449).

[106]Ibid., (III 451).

[107]Ibid.

[108]The greater part of Sermon XCV (III. 374-379) is apparently directed aganist the Hopkinsianian doctrine of damnation.

[109]In Sermon XXIV, The Soul of Man not a Chain of Ideas and Exercises, Dwight takes issue with Emmons, "the ablest philosopher among all those whom I have known to adopt this (exercise) scheme on this side of the *Atlantic*." It is, he argues, contrary to the natural conception of mankind in that it destroys personal identity (by assuming attributes conceivable apart from substances), implies the denial of reward and punishment, virtue and guilt, and annihilates the influence of motives.

[110]Sermon LXXXIXJ (III. 285).

[111]A thorough review of the nature of the public covenant of the Israelites with God impels him to the conclusion that, "the Members of the Christian Church are, in my view, required to enter into the same Covenant, in the same public manner." CXLIX (V. 156).

[112]Dwight holds that "the soul after death returns immediately to God, to give an account of its conduct in the present life." In this account, he believes, "will be unfolded, alike, the state of the thoughts, and that of the external conduct. Of course, the soul will be furnished with the power of recollection, sufficiently capacious to comprehend all that it has done, and will be compelled to declare it without disguise, enhancement, or enasion." Sermon CLXIV (V. 431-432). Following this account, the Sentence of God is pronounced, in consequence of which, the soul immediately enters upon a state of reward or punishment.

[113] Sermons CLXXII and CLXXIII, taking as their text, **Proverbs 8:6**, consist of General Remarks recapitulating the teaching of the whole.

[114]Dwight, **Travels in New England and New York,** 4 volumes. Edited by Barbara Miller Solomon with the assistance of Patricia M. King (Cambridge: The Belknap Press of Harvard University Press, 1969), IV. 229. Hereafter cited as **Travels** with volume and page number.

[115]"At this time," according to John Cosins Ogden, "Connecticut is more completely under the administration of a Pope than Italy....President Dwight, elected by ecclesiastics who maintain their own succession, and pay obedience to no authority on earth....is a more formidable character than the Pope of Rome." **An Appeal to the Candid upon the Present State of Religion and Politics in Connecticut** (Stockbridge: n.d.), 14. Evans 34267.

[116]Silverman, **Timothy Dwight,** 152.

[117]Vernon Louis Parrington, **Main Currents in American Thought** (New York: Harcourt, Brace and Company, 1930), I. 363.

[118]Howard, **The Connecticut Wits,** 401.

[119]**Travels,** IV. 272.

The Moral Calvinism
Of Nathaniel William Taylor

"The question is not, what subjects do; but what has the moral governor done? It is not what is the conduct of subjects under the system but what is the system under which they act."[1]

THE MORAL CALVINISM OF NATHANIEL WILLIAM TAYLOR

> The sinner must be willing to accept of the salvation of the gospel—to accept it as it is, not in some of its parts, but as a whole....this implies the absolute and unqualified renunciation of our own righteousness, a deep conviction of our own depravity and guilt, and consequence desert of the wrath of God. No man can be willing to accept of salvation....who has a word to say about his good deeds, or his own efforts of any sort. All these must be abandoned as the ground of acceptance, and he must be willing that God should have *all the glory* of his salvation.[2]

On April 8th, 1812, Nathaniel William Taylor[3] was ordained and installed as pastor of the First (Center) Church and Congregation in New Haven. The Charge was given by the Rev. James Dana, his predecessor once removed; the Right Hand of Fellowship was extended by Samuel Merwin, pastor of the adjacent United Church, and the ordination sermon, inordinately long,[4] was preached by his mentor and patron, President Dwight.

Dwight and Taylor had met for the first time in 1800 on the occasion of the latter's admission to Yale. Following his graduation in 1807[5] he had lived in the President's house while studying for the ministry. During this time he earned his keep by service as a secretary to the half-blind Dwight, reading to him, taking his dictation, and editing the proofs of his various works in process. Taylor it was who presumably transcribed much, if not most, of the sermons comprising **Theology: Explained and Defended.** Their friendship thus begun was enduring. Taylor's admiration and respect for his teacher was reciprocated by Dwight's trust in the integrity and theological soundness of his sometime student. With the President's warm approval he was elected to a Yale tutorship for the academic year 1809-10, but declined, preferring to continue his theological studies. In 1810 he was licensed to preach, began to supply vacant pulpits, and married the companion of his childhood, Rebecca Marie Hine, the daughter of the New Milford innkeeper. Proffered the pastorate of the Center Church a year later, he at first declined, feeling himself unready and unworthy, but at the urging of his patron Dwight, whose influence had worked to secure him the initial invitation, he accepted a second call, and in 1812 took his place among the leaders of New Haven.

His performance in the pulpit was to prove that Dwight had made no mistake in thinking that his protege had the makings of a champion in the crusade against Infidelity. The sermons preached by the young minister during the decade of his tenure at the Center Church reveal a mind dedicated to the principles of orthodoxy and a voice eloquent in its defence, albeit one which even in these early productions shows forth an originality of thought which disturbed not a few of his brothers in Christ. The sovereignty of God delighting in his law and glory,[6] the vicarious Atonement of His Son, to the end that those who heed his call might be restored to the favor of the Father,[7] the depravity of the human heart,[8] the necessity of regeneration by the intercession of the Holy Spirit[9], an insistence upon true holiness,[10] are as much a part of the New Haven theology as ever they were of that of Northampton, Newport, or Franklin. No less than Edwards, does Taylor shrink from the conviction that it is no fault in a minister to frighten sinners out of hell:

> if ministers would preach the truth, they must thunder an
> alarm in the ears of sleeping guilt, and rouse the stupid to
> a sense of a judgment and a damnation that lingereth not![11]

In sermon after sermon he inveighs against complacency and abjures his hearers to heed the call to repentance. He never tires of telling his congregation that the whole life of man ought to be, indeed must be if he is to escape damnation, a continual act of religion. For, he insists,

> It is one thing to profess to believe that there is a God, and
> another to believe that he is what he is. Many there are who
> would not deny the divine existence, yet who do deny the
> divine character. They deny that he is the righteous gover-
> nor of the moral world. Their language is, either that he is
> indifferent to the actions of men, or that he is too merciful

to punish any of his creatures. But to believe in a God who will make no discrimination between characters—who regards the holy and unholy with equal approbation—who will dispense no future rewards or punishments, is substantially the same thing as to say, *There is no God.*[12]

What does sound reason pronounce concerning the man who says such? Just this, replies Taylor: he who thus subverts the sovereignty of God, impugns his right of legislation, by his unbelief makes God a liar, and deprives himself of all real good in this world and all comfort in the next. If there is no God, no danger is encountered, no loss sustained.

But, if there *may be* a God, who can measure the folly of firmly denying his being, and all that system of truth which it involves, and acting accordingly? The speculative and practical atheist is undone. There *may be* such a God as the Bible reveals. The bare statement of the case makes the reflective mind shrink back with horror from the thought. To deny the being of a God, when there *may be* one, to live in this world as if there were no God; and enter eternity, there to have, for the first time, the full conviction, by meeting the awful reality?[13]

Not that Taylor himself ever haboured any such doubt. His sermon on The Habitual Recognition of God defines a conception of the deity identical in all respects with that of orthodoxy. His Lectures testify to his unwavering belief in the divine origin of Holy Scripture, the credibility of miracles, and a creation by fiat somewhat less than 6,000 years ago. Even so, the suspicion grew in the minds of the more conservative of the Connecticut clerisy that brother Taylor was dubious in doctrine. The prejorative epithets 'Arminian' and 'Pelagian' began to be heard in reference to his preaching, particularly as that respected the matters of regeneration and free-will. His opposition to the literalist interpretation of **John** 3:3-5, his insistence that the Biblical account of regeneration as a new creation, a being born again, must be understood

244

as "wholly figurative,"[14] was thought by the more partisan among the advocates of the new divinity to betoken a falling away from the position of Edwards and Hopkins. And to a degree it was.

In his sermon on The Sinner's only Duty to make himself a New Heart, Taylor defines the work of the Holy Spirit in regeneration as,

> that influence or operation by which he brings the sinner, in the free, unconstrained use of his own moral powers, to fix his heart on God.[15]

Shall we, he asks,

> be told that the work of the Spirit is a literal creation of some new mental property—some new constitutional taste, relish, or something that nobody can tell what; and that it is heresy—damnable heresy—to deny it? And is it so?—the work of the Holy Spirit in regeneration, the literal creation of a new soul, either in whole or in part? You may as well say that the work of the Spirit is building the Tower of Babel. The work of the Holy Spirit is not such a work![16]

To his Hopkinsian critics, committed as they were, to the notion of regeneration as an immediate and instantaneous change of heart wrought by the Spirit of God upon the previously totally corrupt and wholly unregenerate sinner, Taylor's definition, apparently denying any sharp distinction between regenerate and unregenerate, was manifest apostasy. Nor were they reassured by his explanation that,

> the influence of the Spirit is that mysterious influence that moves upon, softens, and wins a rebel heart to the love of God—an influence under which the sinner, in the free exercise of his own adequate powers, loves, believes, and obeys God his Saviour.[17]

In the free exercise of his own adequate powers." Could this be anything other than Arminianism of the worst sort? Actually it could, and was, as Taylor strove to make plain in a sermon not preached, but published under the title **Regeneration the beginning of Holiness in the human Heart.**

The sermon proper (excluding the Remarks appended to it) is an extended variation on a familiar theme, i.e., the declaration of the scriptures that the whole of the human race is divided into two classes;

> those who belong to one class are denominated saints, the righteous, friends of God, children of God; the other, are called sinners, the wicked, enemies of God, children of the devil. A third class cannot be found in the scripture. No one can belong to both classes at once. Those who belong to one class, it has been proved (by reference to scripture), are born again; those who belong to the other are not![8]

We recur again, says Taylor, to **John 3:3-5**

> Except a man be born again, he cannot see the kingdom of God, Regeneration, then, is the dividing line between those who are accepted and those who are condemned. All who die on this side of regeneration, will be saved; all who die on the other side will be lost. But all will be saved who have the least degree of holiness; none will be lost but those who are utterly destitute of holiness![9]

What, then, he inquires, can be the condition of those who, if such there be, possess some degree of holiness and are not regenerated, or who, conversely, are regenerated but have no holiness? The former, not having been born again, cannot be admitted to heaven; the latter cannot be saved since they lack any degree of holiness. "Will our opponents tell us there is a purgatory?" he asks, and does not deign to answer. Hopkins himself could not have put the matter plainer. As respects the *substance* of the doctrine of regeneration, Taylor is at one with his predecessor.

Still, as will subsequently become evident, there is a difference between their respective positions, and that sufficient to lead Taylor's biographer to insist that neither he nor his exemplar, Dwight, are properly understood as continuors of the line of Consistent Calvinists. According to Sidney Mead,[20] both of them are rather the "theological heirs" of the Old Calvinists inasmuch as their positions on "the divine permission of sin, man's ability and freedom of choice under the gospel appeal, the status of "unregenerate doings," the "use of means" to bring men to God, and the use of the term "self-love" to designate natural and neutral powers in unregenerate men"[21] recapitulate the positions, and even the language, of this school. This conclusion leads him to suppose

> that we may soon be called upon to revise radically our common view of the development of religious thought in New England. Recent studies, as for example, the work of Perry Miller, indicate that the Calvinism of the New England Puritans was already greatly modified by their "Covenant Theology." In this view it also appears that the pre-revolutionary Old Calvinists, not the Edwardeans or consistent Calvinists, were the direct theological descendants of the Puritans. It seems, then, that the line can be drawn from Puritanism to Old Calvinism to Taylorism, each the system of the dominant party in its era. It is possible, in brief, that Edwardeanism or Consistent Calvinist was never *the* **New England theology.**[22]

The thesis is bold and deserving of a far more detailed treatment that our purpose here allows. Suffice it to say, then, that it is possible, but not, I think, likely, given *all* the evidence.

To begin with, the distinction between Old and Consistent Calvinism itself is necessarily imprecise since both are in agreement on the substance of doctrine respecting the sovereignty of God, the authority of scripture, the atonement of Christ, the election of some and the damnation of others, and the work of the Holy Spirit in regeneration. Where they differ, on Mead's own accounting, is in lifestyle and outlook (most Old Calvinists served urban rather than rural or village congregations) and attitude, they tended to follow the "old steady order of things," eschewed enthusiasm, and saw no need to explain or to explain away difficulties in doctrine. A prototypical example, according to Mead, was Taylor's grandfather, the revered and influential pastor of the church at New Milford, and "the man under whose patriarchical influence Nathaniel William Taylor spent the first fourteen years of his life." "We may suppose," Mead writes,

> that Nathaniel, just fourteen, however unformed his religious ideas may have been, must have ridden down the Derby road that day thrilled at the prospect of entering Yale College and thoroughly imbued with the idea that he was not of the New Lights, not of those who made "enthusiasm and metaphysics" the order of the day and brought "divisions and fierce disputations," but of the sober, industrious people who were the "friends of the old steady order of things."[23]

Whether we may suppose that young Taylor was so "thoroughly embued" or not, in the event his viewpoint was certainly enlarged as he came more and more under the influence of Edwards' grandson. Mead is constrained to concede that Dwight was "by birth and training an heir of the Consistent Calvinists;" but he thinks to save his thesis by arguing that "he had stepped out of their ranks to adopt the Old Calvinist conception of the use of "means."[24] Granting such a departure in this one isolated instance[25] and allowing that 'means' means for Dwight precisely what it meant in the lexicon of Old Calvinism,[26] does it follow that Taylor came to the ministry as a friend of the old steady order of things? Attention to the Remarks appended to the 1816 sermon on regeneration no more supports this supposition than does the substance of doctrine of that sermon.

Regeneration, he reminds his hearers, "is an essential doctrine, because it declares the necessity of a radical change of moral character or of the production of holiness in the human heart, which before this change is utterly destitute of holiness."[27] He decries the opinion of the Wesleyans and Episcopalians, who would have us believe that man's power to perform good

248

works, lost in Adam, is restored in Christ.

> As to the restoration of lost powers, I ask what powers were
> lost? Did all the posterity of Adam, by the fall, lose the
> powers of moral agency?....Did they become incapable of sin-
> ning?....If they could not sin, why was a Saviour needed?[28]

The truth is, says Taylor, that the Savior was promised for a race that could
and did have the powers of moral agency, that could and did sin. "For nothing
is plainer, than that man may be a complete moral agent, and yet be entirely
sinful; nay, he cannot be entirely sinful, unless he is a moral agent."[29] Possessing these powers, man sins, and will continue to do so until his obstinacy
in sin is subdued by divine grace. "But this is holiness; and if this be im-
planted, the man is regenerated."[30]

As for the view advanced by the Episcopal bishop, Hobart, that regeneration so conceived differs only verbally from that Renovation effected by baptism into the ranks of the visible Church, Taylor will have none of it.

> No, my Brethren, it is not so. *We* believe Regeneration to be
> the beginning of holiness in the human heart; that there is
> no evangelical faith, no sincere repentance, no holy love, no
> holiness, previous to a change of heart by the Spirit of God.
> *We* believe that every child of Adam is in a state of enmity
> against God, under condemnation to eternal death, with no
> claim to God's favour, until his heart is changed by the Ho-
> ly Ghost.[32]

So far, he is at one with Edwards, Bellamy, and Hopkins. However, in a lengthy
review of Gardiner Spring's[33] **Dissertation on the Means of Regeneration** ex-
tending over four numbers of the **Quarterly Christian Spectator** for 1829.[34]
his position is explicitly qualified. Now he sees, as in the earlier sermon he
had not, that a proper understanding of man as a moral agent under the Moral
Government of God must include in the process of regeneration that act of
will and disposition of heart whereby he expresses an intelligent preference

for his Maker to every other subject, and consecrates himself to His service and glory.

For Hopkins, regeneration is that *simple* and singular act of grace whereby the Holy Spirit grants the sinner a new heart. Consequently, he is impelled to deny the claims of Mayhew, Mills, and Hart respecting the use of "means." Herein, thinks Taylor, he errs, and that by reason of his failure to recognize that regeneration is *complex* in that it admits of a wider, *comprehensive* sense, the sense, that is, in which it includes the act of the sinner making God rather than the world the object of his choice, as well as the *restricted* sense heretofore distinguished.[35] Is this to revert to the position of Mayhew, Mills, and Hart? Not at all, declares Taylor, for they too err insofar as they maintain that the pre-regenerate acts and doings of the sinner, good works, church attendance, and edifying reading, constitute a sanctioned use of means.[36] Both sides, Taylor believes, are led into error by their common confusion, derivate in Hopkins' case from Edwards, of *selfishness* with *self-love*. In truth, argues Taylor, the motive governing the one is different in scope and kind from that operative in the other.

Self-love, as Taylor defines it, is that constitutional desire of happiness which is an original principle of our nature.[37] It is that choice of the superior good (God) to all inferior (worldly) goods. In *selfishness*, the heart is fixed upon a definite (worldly) object; in *self-love*, as here defined, the heart is wholly focused upon God as man's ultimate means of happiness. Indeed, for Taylor, the phrase 'using the means of regeneration' refers specifically and exclusively to those acts which are dictated, not by selfishness, but by self-love.[38] Thus Hopkins is right to denounce Mayhew, Mills, and Hart for sanctioning *selfish* acts, but wrong in his failure to see that the choice of God over the world is motivated by *self-love*. For in regeneration man is not, as Hopkins would have it, a passive recipient, but "an active being, transferring his affections from the world to God as the object of his supreme regard."[39] In the complex act of regeneration God secures by his immediate intervention. "in a manner which we can never comprehend, an entire and permanent change in the *choice* which we make between himself and the world."[40] Even so, Taylor argues, "it is obvious that such a change can never take place except in the view of motives, of divine truth contemplated by the mind; or, in other words, that there are *means* of regeneration."[41]

Should the Hopkinsians still be inclined to insist upon the passivity of the recipient in regeneration, Taylor will appeal to authority. "In respect to the *mode of divine operation* in producing a change of heart, we are averse to indulging in speculation. The scriptures, however, authorize us to assert generally, that the *mode* of divine influence is consistent with the moral nature *of this change as a voluntary act of man; and also that it is through the truth and implies attention to truth on the part of man*."[42] Consider, for example, the following: I *thought* on thy ways, and *turned* my feet until thy testimonies."[43] Can anyone doubt, he asks, that this text, and others that he is prepared to exegete,[44] imply and require a precedent act of the part of the sinner to the action of the Holy Spirit in the complex process of regeneration? Taylor thinks not, but is willing to rest his case on **Luke 13:24**.

> The mental process which we have denominated using the means of regeneration, consists of the very acts in the commencement of a religious course, which are distinctly recognized, and expressly comprised, in this divine injunction, "strive to enter in at the strait gate."[45]

In other words, "our principle is simply that of Edwards: 'God produces all and we *act* all.' "[45]

Were it not for this invocation of the revered name of Edwards, a motif recurrent in Taylor's essays and lectures, the reader who has followed the exposition thus far might well conclude that Mead is right to suppose that the line of descent in the New England theology is from Puritanism through Old Calvinism to Taylorism. The latter's vindication of the use of means, coupled with his disinclination to speculate with respect to the mode of the divine operation in regeneration and his employment of the notion of self-love, seem to track directly the Old Calvinist tradition. Still, matters are not always what they seem, and the clue that this is so in Taylor's case is—again—his reference to Edwards.

He has taught us to regard true virtue as love to being in general and to God our sovereign in particular, while his disciple Bellamy has made plain the purport of the great commandment. Both, it is true, define the love that

God requires as the antithesis of self-love. But it is necessary to note that the self-love which they reject is precisely that which Taylor calls selfishness, and that what he names self-love, i.e., man's instinctive and constitutional desire for ultimate happiness, is more closely akin to what Edwards calls benevolence and Hopkins names true holiness. In short, the term as here employed means not *self*-love but rather the love of the self for God.

So too, as regards the denotation and connotations of the term 'means': to use "means," we are told, is to exert oneself in various ways sanctioned by the Standing Order; Mead cites "reading and hearing read the Bible, meditating on it, praying for mercy, church attendance, and avoidance, of sinning knowingly,"[47] these being exactly the "means" approved by the Old Calvinist, Moses Hemmenway.[48] As respects reading or hearing the gospel, Taylor is in full agreement. Without using this particular means of regeneration the sinner, he maintains, will never be regenerated, whereas by adhering to it he just may be. For the rest of Mead's "means," however, he holds no brief. What are the acts, he asks, that constitute the means of regeneration?

> We answer, that by *using the means of regeneration* we do not understand any acts which either precede or are to be distinguished from regeneration itself, when this term is used in its more common popular import; but we understand *those acts which, together with another act are in the more popular use of language included under the term regeneration.*[49]

What are these acts? Taylor never tells us in so many words, but his subsequent exposition makes it clear that he is here referring to that state of mind in which the sinner chooses God, and that action on the part of the Holy Spirit whereby God reciprocates. Which notion, again, is close to, if not indistinguishable from, the position of Edwards as expressed in his Dissertations.

For Taylor himself, the issue here raised as to whether his theology and that of his mentor Dwight are in the right line of Edwards or, as Mead would have it, Old Calvinist in inspiration and expression, is no issue at all. What matters to him, and, I suggest, should matter more to us, is the truth of those teachings common to Calvinists of every shade of opinion.

Among Calvinists there are minute differences of opinion. They entertain, for example, different views of the mode of the Holy Spirit's operation on the heart in regeneration, and yet entirely agree in the general fact of his agency, in proclaiming this moral transformation. A similar remark applies to the different and more specific statements of the doctrine of human depravity....What Calvinism is, then, is to be determined, not by these minute points of explanation and hypothesis....but by those general doctrines, in which as a class they agree.[50]

II

We are often compelled to complain, that the opponents of Calvinism, never fairly attack its doctrines....We are sometimes disposed to wonder,—if this system of doctrines be really so absurd, and dangerous, and 'blasphemous' too,...why it cannot be shown to be so, without resorting to misrepresentation,—and why those who undertake to expose its enormities, are not content sometimes to hold it up, just as it is actually professed and believed.[51]

As the nineteenth century passed into its second decade, the clerisy of New England came more and more to realize the importance of replacing the old system of training up candidates for the ministry through private study with an established pastor, by a more formalized curriculum of theological education. Andover Seminary had been established with the blessing of Dwight and the orthodox clergy of Connecticut in 1808, and in 1818 a group of Yale students and professors had begun to meet informally to pursue substantially the same course of studies as that followed at Andover. By 1822 this "school of theology by voluntary association" had developed to the point of a demand for the establishment of a theological department in the College. A petition was duly drawn and presented by fifteen students, supported by the faculty,[52] and by the generosity of Timothy Dwight Jr. who subscribed five thousand dollars toward the endowment of a chair in honor of his father. From the onset, it was generally agreed that the Dwight Professorship of Didactic Theology should go to Taylor. The governing Society of the Center Church, loath to lose him, objected vigourously, and only yielded, grudgingly, to the decision of an ecclesiastical council that it was the duty of the church to resign him. This being accomplished, in November of 1822, Taylor entered upon the duties that would occupy most of his working hours for the thirty-six years remaining of his life.

Theologically, it was a peculiarly contentious time. The liberal Christianity of Chauncey, Mayhew, and the senior Ware was flowering into an explicit Arminianism cum Unitarianism heralded by the publication in 1819 of William Ellery Channing's Baltimore Sermon.[53] His "leading principle," that scripture is to be interpreted in the light of our realization that "the Bible is a book written for men, in the language of men, and that its meaning is to be sought in the same manner as that of other books,"[54] coupled with his conviction "that God, when he speaks to the human race, conforms....to the established rules of speaking and writing,"[55] undercut the orthodox assumption of an inspired revelation and, in the eyes of Taylor and his party, promoted the spread of Infidelity. Moses Stuart, the professor of sacred literature at Andover, spoke for them all in rejecting the Unitarian allocation of final authority to reason. Channing's principles, he thinks, must eventually lead most men who approve of them to the conclusion, that the Bible is not of divine origin, and does not oblige us to belief or obedience."[56] Nor, he adds, will your own well-attested personal piety serve to prevent those who have not your education from reaching bolder conclusions. Indeed, Channing's own conclusion is bold enough. The new principles of biblical exegesis, he argues, make plain the absurdity and falsity of much of Calvinist doctrine, resting as we have seen that it does, as much and more on the Old Testament as on the New. For Channing, on the contrary, the Christian religion "lies chiefly in the New Testament.

> The dispensation of Moses, compared with that of Jesus,
> we consider as adapted to the childhood of the human race,
> a preparation for a nobler system.[57]

We object, he continues, "to that system which arrogates to itself the name of Orthodoxy," insofar as in its various shapes "it casts dishonor on the Creator," in that it teaches that God brings us into life with such a constitution "as to render certain and infallible the total depravity of every human being from the first moment of his moral agency."[58] We abhor that doctrine which asserts the election of some, and the liability of all, including infants, to everlasting damnation. We believe that true holiness "has its foundation in the moral nature of man, that is, in conscience, or his sense of duty," and that "no dispositions infused into us without our own moral activity are of the nature of virtue, and therefore we reject the doctrine of irresistible divine influence on the human mind."[59] By these remarks, he is quick to add, "we do not mean to deny the importance of God's aid or Spirit; but by his Spirit we mean a moral, illuminating, and persuasive influence, not physical, not compulsory, not involving a necessity of virtue."[60] Thus, having to the entire satisfaction of himself and his hearers cast down the pillars of Calvinism, he proceeded to instruct the ordinand in the performance of his ministerial duties.

Ten years earlier, in a review of a work purporting to treat of the "gross errors" of Orthodoxy, Channing had allowed that,

> the general argument against Calvinism, in the General View of Christian Doctrines, is the *moral argument,* or that which is drawn from the inconsistency of the system with the divine perfections. It is plain that a doctrine which contradicts our best ideas of goodness and justice cannot come from the just and good God, or be a true representation of his character.[61]

To the view of "common and unperverted minds," it must, he declares, appear impossible that reasonable men can continue to maintain that mankind, fallen in Adam, are under God's wrath and curse, that a certain number are elected to salvation even as the rest are left to corruption and the eternal pains of hellfire, yet holding all the while that God is good and his justice equitable.

> Is it probable that a religion having this object (of manifesting God as perfect benevolence and bringing men to love and imitate him) gives views of the Supreme Being from which our moral convictions and benevolent sentiments shrink with horror, and which, if made our pattern, would convert us into monsters?[62]

Were a parent to form himself on the Universal Father as described by Calvinism, "that is, were he to bring his children into life totally depraved, and then to pursue them with endless punishment, we should charge him with a cruelty not surpassed in the annals of the world."[63] I am aware, says Channing, that it will be said that this characterization of the moral tendency of Calvinism takes no account of the famous distinction between *natural* and *moral* inability. But, he adds, "with due deference to its defenders, it seems to us groundless and idle, a distinction without a difference."[64] Yet even as he decries the distinction, Channing is quick to reassure the orthodox that he intends no disparagement of person. "We have aimed to expose doctrines, not to condemn their professors. It is true that men are apt to think themselves assailed when their system only is called to account. But we have no foe but error."[65] So too will Andrews Norton[66] contend, but unlike Channing he had no gift for disarming his theological opponents. In truth, Norton was everything that Channing was not. Proud to the point of arrogance, self-righteous, as quick to take offence as to give it, egotistic, learned to a fault, in sum, the professorial type at its most obnoxious; such was the formidable man whose proclaimed contempt for Calvinism Taylor was now called to counter.

In that same summer of Channing's declaration of Unitarian independence, Norton was inaugurated as Dexter Professor of Sacred Literature in the Divinity School at Cambridge. His inaugural discourse, preached to an admiring audience of mostly liberal Christians, echoes Channing's emphasis on the importance of a reasoned religion and, by implication, denigrated the revivalist tendencies and experimental piety of Connecticut Calvinism. The "consummate theologian," as Norton conceives him, will be a man of the highest intellectual acquisitions and endowments, learned in the languages of scripture, a philologist well acquainted with the principles of biblical criticism,

a philosopher well-versed in the classics, a scholar ever ready and able to subject to the strictest logical scrutiny those "words and expressions which often
deceive us, and often mock us with only a show of meaning. He must," the
lecturer continues, "engage in complicated and difficult processes of reasoning, in which the terms of language divested of all their usual associations,
become little more than algebraic symbols." That this characterization, by
its omissions, must serve to deny to most, if not all, Trinitarians and Calvinists,
the right to wear the mantle of theology, Norton knows full well, and that
his opponents might be left with no doubts as to his meaning and intent,
he concludes with a challenge:

> if anyone refuses to submit to the decisions of our natural
> reason, and the dictates of our natural feelings; if he come
> to us teaching what he calls incomprehensible propositions
> and truths above reason: if he maintains doctrines abhor-
> rent to all our best sentiments respecting God and his moral
> government; and if he requires us to believe the system which
> he has received; we have a right to require of him in return,
> what are his qualifications to discuss these subjects?....Is
> theology, the most profound and extensive of sciences, the
> only one in which ignorant presumption may be allowed to
> dogmatize[68]

The language was calculated to offend the evangelicals, and in that it was
successful. Beecher seethed,[69] and Taylor undertook to rebut. Eighteen months
later the **Quarterly Christian Spectator** carried his unsigned review of an Inaugural Discourse.

He could not gainsay the merit of Norton's call for an educated ministry,
and he did not try. That, he thought, was not the point at issue.

> We ask, with a confidence not to be shaken, that the affir-
> mative must be conceded to us, are not a love of the truth,
> purity of intention, spiritual discernment, and a heart renew-
> ed until holiness, quite as indispensable? Intellectual and

spiritual accomplishments *united.* make the real 'consummate theologian'.[70]

The fact of the matter is that,

> some of the truths of the Bible are so contrary to our natural
> views, or so humiliating to our natural feelings, that it is only
> through the medium of regeneration that they are conveyed
> to the heart and seen in their real beauty and glory.[71]

Philosophy and Philology are all very well in their place, but "the divine character of the (bible) must, from its nature, impose a restraint on the feelings of men, and it certainly ought to repress the presumption, that would treat it as though it were merely a human production."[72] The philological enterprise must not be so conducted "as necessarily to excite the suspicion in uneducated people, that something may yet be elicted from the bible of a character essentially different from what has been known."[73] The point is, that we are simply "not permitted to approach that book with our critical analysis."[74] A catastrophe must be expected to ensue if that theology only shall be allowed which, instead of making us new creatures, is satisfied to elevate our minds and improve our natural feelings.

> Our author's system of religion, so far as he discloses any,
> is too meager for creatures that need all the riches of divine
> mercy in their forgiveness and salvation. It is too cold to af-
> fect a heart so insensible as the sinner's. It is too wrapt up
> in generalities and abstractions, to point us to our duties,
> to adminster to our wants, or even to inform us that we have
> any.[75]

As it happened, Norton had already anticipated the general drift of Taylor's response in his Thoughts on True and False Religion. "Can you believe," he asks his reader, "that the doctrines of Calvin have had much tendency to develop the higher powers and better affections of men?"[76] Taylor would have it that Calvinism alone answers to the cry of the sinner of salvation, whereas its tendency in truth is to demoralize the young and terrify their elders. "Whatever may be the worth of true religion, it surely does not follow, that this system of blasphemy must also be of great value."[77] A proper regard to the moral tendency of Calvinism must enforce the conclusion that it has no very beneficial effects.

Taylor's reply, given in yet another review, was to call in question the fairness and accuracy of Norton's characterization of Calvinism. Why is it, he inquires, that those who undertake to expose its absurdities and enormities are not content to exhibit it just as it is actually professed and believed? If our creed is so horrible and blasphemous, why is it taught in every established church in Christendom? Taylor concedes that Calvinism is not without fault and flaw:

> We do not indeed apprehend that all of Calvin's views of metaphysical subjects were either clear or correct. His was not the age of philosophical precision. His system of theology was derived chiefly from the Scriptures. In adapting it to the received system of philosophy at his time, he sometimes erred: and many who followed him became still more erroneous. Neither in metaphysics nor in theology do we call him or any man Master, But he was very far from maintaining those blasphemous doctrines which are so often attributed to him by ignorant or designing men.[78]

As indeed, maintains Taylor, we are from holding the simplistic view of Calvinism attributed to us by our Unitarian critics.

Professor Norton would have us believe that Calvinism is of little value and totally lacking any beneficial effect, but what sort of logic is it that would infer the nature and tendency of a doctrine from its effects on those who disbelieve it! "When it is admitted that the Bible contains a revelation from God, it hardly seems reasonable that we should reject its doctrines....until we are satisfied of the effect which each will produce on the heart and character of the believer."[79] In short, the argument from moral tendency cuts both ways—for those who claim, as the Unitarians do, to believe that the Bible is God's word to man.[80]

Whether Norton was offended by the aspersion cast upon his logic, or by the reviewer's insinuation that his position also was vulnerable, or, as he said, by "the charge made against me in very coarse language of having wilfully and knowingly misstated the doctrines of Calvinism,"[81] he was stung to the point of immediately composing an intemperate letter to the editors of the **Quarterly Christian Spectator.** It was the sort of letter that one dashes off in the heat of the moment, and later cooling off, tears up. Only Norton mailed it. Indignantly denying any misstatement whatever, he challenged his reviewer, this "anonymous scribbler without truth and without shame," to show the misstatement in the following passage from **Thoughts:**

> what shall we say of a religion, which teaches that he (God) has formed men, so that they are by nature wholly inclined to all moral evil; that he has determined in consequence to inflict upon the greater part of our race the most terrible punishments; and that unless he has seen fit to place us among the small number of those whom he has chosen out of the common ruin, he will be our eternal enemy, and infinite tormentor; that having hated us from our birth, he will continue to exercise upon us forever his unrelenting and omnipotent hatred.[82]

"I have not," Norton writes, "in the passage quoted asserted that the doctrines in question are doctrines of Calvinism. I do now assert it; and in proving the truth of this assertion, shall prove the truth of what I have said."[83] Whereupon he proceeds to cite a variety of passages from the Westminster Larger Catechism and Confession, the Synod of Dort, and the works of Calvin and Edwards, all of them, he insists, tending to confirm the statements made in the passage quoted.

The root issue, both Norton and the Editors are agreed, relates to the doctrine of depravity, specifically to two propositions implicit in the passage in question:

1. That God creates a sinful nature in man.

2. That this nature necessarily (i.e., by a physical necessity)
   makes them the objects of his vengeance.[84]

Norton argues that the numerous citations given from Calvinist writings clearly confirm that both propositions are correct statements of Calvinist doctrine. The Editors vigourously deny it,[85] maintaining that nothing in Calvin himself or in his followers evidences either that *God creates* man's sinful nature or that this created nature is what it is by a *physical* necessity. Norton grudgingly concedes that the propositions are not explicit in Calvin or Edwards or Westminster, but insists that they arc "a fair and necessary inference" from these, and snidely adds that it is not his business to reconcile the contradictions and absurdities of Calvinistic writers. "I have never had any doubt that such contradictions and absurdities might be found in abundance in their works....In my letter I have proved it to be a doctrine of Calvinism, that men from their very nature, *without reference to any actual sins,* are odious in the sight of God, and objects of his vengeance,"[86] and, he adds, "I expect the whole of this letter to be inserted without alteration or omission in your next number....If you do not insert it....I shall use every means in my power go give it publicity."[87] The Editors, of course, were not about to be thus intimidated into any such publication, and Norton's expectation, as he must have anticipated, failed of realization. Still, he could not have been unduly disappointed. He had achieved his primary purpose of holding Calvinism up to ridicule, and he did not deign to notice Taylor's review of his **Views** when it shortly appeared.

Or if he did, he may have concluded that silence was the better option. For to call Taylor's rejoinder a "review" is to do it less than justice, since what we have now to take account of is the definitive statement of what Calvinism is and means both in its historical context and in its nineteenth century mode of expression. As our author remarks at the onset, the enquiry to which we are now led by the pamphlet before us is: What is Calvinism, especially on the article of depravity? The specification is important, the more so as "belief or rejection of this doctrine involves the belief or rejection of the whole

Gospel."[88]

Professor Norton has made a great play of parading the views of Calvin, Edwards, and the Westminster divines, to the end of demonstrating that these worthies are as one in holding the doctrine that God *creates* man with a sinful nature. Consequently, Taylor realizes, any adequate answer to the previous question must begin by showing that none of the passages cited by Norton, or indeed any that might be brought forward, stands as evidence of such a view. To the contrary, a careful reading of Calvin confirms that his position was that we, as the descendants of Adam, are *not* born as God has formed us. We have from our birth that which is not created in us by God. "The nature may be from God, but the corruption is from ourselves."[89] "Our nature is not as it was *created* by God, but as it was *Vitiated* in Adam."[90] It will be, indeed it has been, objected that Calvin is inconsistent, but, Taylor replies, Calvin's inconsistency, or yet the inconsistency of Edwards or the Westminster divines, is not what is here in question. "We are sitting not in judgment upon his abilities as a reasoner, but enquiring concerning his faith as a divine."[91] Norton has charged Calvin and his disciples with holding that God *creates* man's sinful nature, but the fact is that he and they specifically and consistently deny the charge throughout their manifold works. And even if they did not, the Calvinism of the present age does not hold to the view charged upon it by Professor Norton. "The creed of dead men we leave to Unitarians to adjust and controvert as they please."[92]

With respect, then, to the article of depravity, Taylor will have it that the Calvinism of the present age is not to be identified with everything believed and taught by Calvin, or by any pre-nineteenth century Calvinist author.

> The reason is obvious and substantial; neither Calvin, nor any Calvinist author is implicitly followed on this article of faith, by all who are denominated Calvinists. What Calvinism is, then, is to be determined, not by those minute points of explanation and hypothesis which are subjects of difference among Calvinists themselves, but by those general doctrines, in which as a class they agree.[93]

What are these "general doctrines"? "All who take the denomination of Calvinists, will," Taylor answers, "agree that,

> mankind came into the world in such a state that without
> the interposition of divine grace, all as soon as they become
> moral agents, sin in every accountable act.[94]

No one who should admit this statement, argues Taylor, would be rejected from the Calvinist community by his brethren on the ground of heterodoxy.

> At the same time, were this proposition to include any things
> more specific respecting the origin of sin than it does, many
> among Calvinists would not subscribe to it....The general
> truth thus stated, is regarded by the whole class as an essen-
> tial truth of Christianity; anything beyond it, as a point of
> speculative philosophy which may be believed or disbeliev-
> ed, without affecting the real doctrine of Calvinism.[95]

"So if Calvin, and the Westminster divines, and Edwards, and Hopkins, and Smalley, and Dwight, and Emmons, differ in the minute explanations of the doctrine of depravity, still they agree in the general doctrine itself,—that all men though complete moral agents do, unless divine grace intervene, commit sin in their first and in every subsequent moral act. Let *this* then be their Calvinism on this point; and thus the pretended difficulty vanishes."[96]

And so it does, *if* all those named are absolved from the requirement of specifying just when and how it is that mankind become moral agents.[97] For Taylor, as we shall see when we come to consider his view of the moral government of God, this absolution poses no real problem. So too for Emmons and those who with him subscribe to the dictum that all sin lies in the sinning, the minimal definition proposed will serve well enough; for the rest, he will remind us that the creeds of dead men do not signify. "What Calvin believed and taught, and what any modern Calvinist authors have taught, are questions of no real importance in the present discussion, any farther than their opinions are proved to be prevalent in our times and in our own country."[98]

As for Norton's strictures respecting necessity, there is, Taylor concludes, no cause for concern, "for if it be a doctrine of Calvinism that men sin as moral agents, it is *not* a doctrine of Calvinism that men are subject to a necessity which destroys moral agency."[99]

III

> In representing the depravity of man, preachers should use much caution. There has been much erroneous and injudicious preaching on the enmity of the heart towards God. It is too generally considered to be *overt hatred of God*....The Bible never so represents the matter. You must adopt the Bible sense of the words hate, enmity.[100]

Taylor's sermon **Concio ad Clerum,** preached in the chapel of Yale College on September 10th, 1828, is by far the best known of his discourses, mainly because it was then and afterwards conceived by some as a defense of a new doctrinal departure called "Taylorism" or the "New Haven theology." Actually, the departure, such as it was, was nothing really new. The doctrine of depravity expounded in the **Concio** is substantially the same as that defended in the 1816 sermon and in the various replies to Norton. As Taylor remarks in his foreword: "The author of this discourse has no reason to believe, that the views which it contains, are in any essential respect diverse from those of his brethren, who heard it....he is not aware of any change in his own views....since he entered the ministry; nor of any departure in any article of doctrinal belief from his revered instructor in theology, the former President of the College."[101]

Scripture teaches that we were and are by nature the children of wrath, or, in Taylor's words, "that the entire moral depravity of mankind is by nature." In what, then, shall we say that this moral depravity consists? Not, according to our preacher, in any essential attribute or property of the soul, nor yet in any thing created in man by his Maker. Not in a nature corrupted, as Edwards says, by its being one with Adam, nor by any constitutional propensity, nor "in any *disposition* or *tendency* to sin which is *the cause of all sin*"[102]

Albeit with respect to this last, Taylor would distinguish between "a *disposi-tion* or tendency to sin which is prior to *all* sin, and a *sinful* disposition."[103] The distinction is subtle, so subtle that Taylor's critics will fail to see here any distinction at all, but his intent is, I think, plain enough. For even as he admits that, (1) there is a cause of *all* sin, and (2) a cause of each particular individual sin subsequent to the cause of *all* sin, he insists that the term 'cause' is not to be taken as signifying either efficient causation or a *physical* cause. "I am not," he tells his hearers, "saying that there is not, what with entire propriety may be called a disposition or tendency to sin, which is the cause of *all* sin; nor that there is not, as a *consequence* of *this* disposition or tendency, what with equal propriety may be called a *sinful* disposition, which is the true cause of all *other* sin, itself excepted. But I say, that which is the cause of *all* sin, is not itself sin."[140]

> The cause of all sin, itself sin! Whence then came the first sin? Do you say, from a previous sin as its cause? Then you say, there is a sin before the first sin....And what sort of philosophy, reason or common sense, is this—a sin before the first sin?—Do you say there must be *difficulties* in theology? I ask must there be *nonsense* in theology?[105]

Certainly not. But the question remains: "What is this moral depravity for which man deserves the wrath of God?"

> I answer—*it is man's own act consisting in a free choice of some object rather than God, as his chief good;—or a free preference of the world and of worldly good, to the will and glory of God.*[106]

Will you call this "Taylorism"? If so, says, Taylor, Calvin himself, the Westminster divines, Bellamy, Edwards, and saints Paul and James are Taylorites, since attention to their various writings on this topic shows each and all echoing in their several ways the position here stated. And what they have said, Common Sense confirms.

Take any action which common sense would call a sinful action; what, asks Taylor, is the sin of it? And answers, that state of mind which prefers some selfish interest to the glory of God. "This preference then of some private interest, object or end, rather than God, common sense decides to be the sin of all that we call sinful action, and strictly speaking, the sum total of all sin."[107] This state of mind or private interest, and not any previous thing as the cause of it, is the sinful disposition bespoke. "This forbidden choice of worldly good, this preference of the low and sordid pleasures of earth to God and his glory—this love of the world which excludes the love of the Father—*this—this* is mans's depravity."[108]

The Bible says[109] that this depravity of mankind is by nature, and we accept its authority. But what are we to understand when it is said that our depravity is *by nature*? The Arminians argue that sin is a matter of circumstance and all Calvinists will agree that "there can no more be sin without circumstances of temptation, than there can be sin without a nature to be tempted." Why, then, Taylor inquires, ascribe sin exclusively to nature? Because, he replies, such is the nature of mankind, "that *they will sin and only sin in all the appropriate circumstances of their being.*"[110] Whatever the circumstances may be, "place a human being any where within the appropriate limits and scenes of his immortal existence, and such is his nature, that he will be a depraved sinner."[111]

Just so, but this, Taylor insists now, as earlier he had insisted against Norton and Spring, is not to say that the nature of mankind is of itself sinful; neither is it to say that their nature is the *physical* or *efficient cause of their sinning;*

> but I mean that their nature is the occasion, or reason of their
> sinning:—that such is their nature that in all the appropriate
> circumstances of their being, they will sin and only sin.[112]

On this distinction, between nature as efficient or material cause, and nature as *occasion* or *reason*, everything depends; for if it be disallowed, then it must perforce be admitted that God, the ultimate cause of nature, is the original cause of sin! Consequently, as Taylor clearly sees, we must hold, with Emmons and Dwight, that all sin consists in sinning, in other words, that nature is the *occasion* and not the *cause* of sin![113]

Should you incline to doubt it, Taylor would have you consider the words of the Apostle in **Ephesians** 2:1-3. He does not say, nor can he mean to say, that the nature of man is of itself sinful. In this passage he is assigning the cause of sin, and remarks that it is *by nature* "If you say that he teaches that the *nature* itself is *sinful,* then as the cause must precede its effect, you charge him with the absurdity of asserting that there is sin, before sin."[114] Obviously that cannot be what he means. "The Apostle doubtless conforms his phraseology to common usage, and must mean simply that such is their nature that uniformly in all the appropriate circumstances of their being, they will sin."[115] All scripture confirms that it is so. "God in his testimony, from the beginning to the end of it, asserts this appalling fact,—the absolute uniformity of human sinfulness, throughout the world and throughout all ages. Not a solitary exception occurs....One character then, if God's record be true, prevails with absolute unvarying uniformity, from the fall in Eden till time shall be no longer. Let the circumstances of men be what they may, the eye of God sees and the voice of God declares that "there is no difference,—all are under sin."....If then the absolute uniformity of an event proves that it is *by nature,* then does this uniformity of human sinfulness prove that man is depraved by nature."[116]

It is consistent with this conviction that infants too must invariably sin. "The very birth of a human being is an event which involves the certainty of entire moral depravity, without the supernatural interposition of God to prevent it."[117]

> Do you ask, when will he begin to sin? I answer, I *do not know* the precise instant. The Scriptures do not tell us,— and I can see no possible use, in saying that we *do* know, what it is most palpably evident we do *not* know. Is it then said, that we sin before we are born? But there is no such thing as sinning without acting![118]

Again, Taylor appeals for confirmation to his predecessors. Dr. Emmons, he notes, espouses the same position, as does President Edwards. "That sin or guilt pertains exclusively to voluntary action, is the true principle of orthodoxy. We have seen that the older orthodox divines assert this principle, and that they abundantly deny that God is the creator or author of sin. Will you then charge them, as some have charged me,[19] with being a heretic? "Is the man who believes and teaches the same thing a heretic?"[120]

There were in Connecticut a conservative band of clerics prepared to press the charge. Their spokesman, the Rev. Joseph Harvey,[21] pastor of a church in Westchester, in a review[122] of **Concio** published in the following year, finds Calvin, the Westminster divines, Edwards, Bellamy, Dwight, and saints Paul and James, failing to support the new New Haven divinity. Not one of these authorities, as the reviewer reads them, are interpretable as saying that there is no native sin. Taylor would have us believe that the question at issue is simply and solely whether every actual sin is voluntary, but that, Harvey argues, does not reach to the point to be settled, "which is, can there be no other sin, than that which consists in a voluntary transgression of known law?"[123] Does the entire moral depravity of mankind, he inquires, consist in just this, and in nothing else? To reply in the affirmative would be, he avers, to allege the existence of an effect without a cause, to say, otherwise, that sin has no cause, as it is the *occasion* of sin, but, says Harvey, if that is all we mean by cause, then he has relinquished the certainty of the effect, inasmuch as 'occasion' implies a dependence on circumstances, and this, by Taylor's own definition, is Arminianism!

Should he, shunning this consequence, be disposed to retain the certainty of the effect (as in fact he was), "then," Harvey argues, "he is bound by every sound principle of reasoning to admit, not only the efficiency, but the sinfulness of nature as a cause."[124] The alternatives are exclusive and the dilemma is complete. "Either nature is the efficient and criminal cause of actual sin, or is merely an occasion, affording opportunity and facility to external circumstances."[125] Taylor must perforce opt for one or the other. To attempt to combine them, so as to ascribe a certain uniform effect to a contingent series of occasions would be absurd. "And to ascribe it to any cause which is inadequate to its production, is the same as to ascribe it to no cause. Actual sin then, if it be a certain and exclusive effect, must result from a cause which is sinful. This mode of reasoning is sanctioned by the scriptures....this mode of reasoning has always been considered correct by Edwards and other standard writers on divinity."[126] Taylor's attempt to evade this acknowledgement by seeking to disengage the notion of causation from its physical or efficient identity is, to the reviewer's way of thinking, "calculated to bewilder rather than to enlighten." Disallow the evasion, and, he reminds us, Taylor is left with the proposition that Nature is not the efficient cause, but only and nothing other than, the occasion or reason of sin; left indeed with all the contradiction this proposition entails.

However, Harvey is not yet done with what he perceives to be the subversion by the proponent of **Concio** of the truth once given to the Old Calvinist churches. He finds him fundamentally unsound in his view of the moral condition of newborn infants, God in his moral government, he reminds his reader, has always treated infants as sinners subject to salvation through Jesus Christ, and he professes to understand the sermon as denying that it is so. In similar fashion, his reviewer saddles Taylor with the sentiment that God could not prevent sin, and he "recoils" at passionate length from this "appalling thought."

Underlying these criticisms, as well as the effort to impugn Taylor's conception of causation as occasion, is, of course, the Old Calvinist conviction that God having spoken in Scripture, any attempt to rationalize, or even to gloss, His Word is to darken counsel. Consequently, the preacher's concern to mitigate the odiousness of the doctrine of depravity by a moralization of the divine sovereignty, constitutes an attempt to explain that which Scripture itself, in the person of the Lord censuring Job, tells us were better left unquestioned. As Harvey, speaking for his faction, puts it:

> We do not know what is necessary for the greatest good, we do not know what God can, or what he cannot do, we do not presume to give counsel to Jehovah in these concerns, we are of yesterday and know nothing. All we pretend to know or assume, concerning God and his ways, is, what he has revealed of himself, and what he actually does.... From these fixed points we turn our attention to what really ex-

ists. We find moral evil or sin existing in the divine government. And what shall we say respecting it, as matter of fact? Shall we undertake to say, it is on the whole a defect in the divine government....This we think, would be an impeachment of the wisdom and goodness of God, or a denial of his supreme and controlling power. In doing this we should darken counsel by words without knowledge. Rather let us say and feel, "Shall not the Judge of all the earth do right." "The Lord reignth let the earth rejoice, let the multitude of isles be glad thereof."[127]

To these piously modest professions, Chauncey Goodrich, a disciple and colleague of Taylor, replied in the next issue of the **Quarterly Christian Spectator** with a forty page **Review of Taylor and Harvey on Human Depravity.**[128] He had little to add to what already has been said except to reiterate in forceful terms his mentor's conviction that while our native propensities are the ground or reason or occasion of our sinful actions, they are no more to be thought of as efficient or physical causes of those actions than are the motives or acts of will which impel them.[129] Taylor himself, apparently more agitated by Harvey's ascription to President Dwight of the teaching that sin pertains to our substantial or essential nature than by any of the arguments directed against the preachments of the **Concio,** promptly produced a pamphlet[130] refuting this scurrilous interpretation of Dwight's teaching, and in a Postscript reiterated the argument of his sermon. Since neither of these rejoinders, nor Harvey's subsequent reply to Goodrich,[131] added anything new or substantial to the previous discussion, we may safely leave them to the mercies of those who fancy theological minuitiae.

From the position thus forged in the fires of controversy, i.e., that there is no sin before the occasion of sin, Taylor never retreated. In his later lectures on Human Sinfulness the doctrine is elaborated to the point of redundancy. As for the consistency of it with that other doctrine of Election which as a professed Calvinist he was obligated to maintain, that he is prepared to allow on authority. "I do not suppose," he notes, "that any exhibition of this doctrine, however clear and consistent it may be, will be sufficient in actual fact to put an end to all caviling and objection."[132] The fact is that the

Scriptures contain a doctrine of Election, and since all Scripture is profitable, it behooves he who bears God's commission to publish God's counsel in this matter, lest "the lightning of his indignation" descend upon him. The simple truth, "in which all who are not Universalists, and who believe in the necessity of God's grace to renew the heart, must agree, is this:

> That God has eternally purposed to renew and sanctify, and save a part only of mankind.[133]

Herein, he contends, is comprised the entire doctrine of Election. Yet even as we confess this, we must, he adds, admit: (1) that Christ died as truly for the non-elect as for the elect; (2) that the promise of life is sure to all who repent and believe; (3) that all men are capable of such repentance since *all* men are free moral agents: (4) that it is God's will that all men should come to repentance. "I am not saying," he tells them,

> "*that God will change the appointed system of influence,* or....do those things which may be necessary to secure the repentance of the non-elect sinner. To do this....would be worse than to leave the sinner to his choice under the influence appointed. It would result in more evil than good."[134]

Moreover, it must be remembered that no man, elect or non-elect, will come to compliance with God's terms for life without his grace. "Abundant as is the provision for the salvation of all....abundantly able as they are as moral agents to comply with the terms of salvation....not one will do it. Left to themselves, each and all of them will persist in rejecting Christ, and by their own choice plunge into perdition."[135]

Faced with this prospect, God interposes with the purpose of Election. Preferring that all should repent and live, and unwilling that his beloved Son should die in vain, he purposes that some shall be saved as his wisdom permits. To this end he creates a moral system peopled by moral subjects capable of preferring doing right to doing wrong. It will be said that God could have done better, that he could have produced more holiness than his establishment of a moral system can or will produce, but, rejoins Taylor, the supposition is false. To hold that God might have produced more happiness and holiness than his moral government does actually is to deny that the moral system is the best system, and this Taylor will not and cannot concede. God had adopted

> *a moral system as the only and best means of accomplishing the high ends of infinite goodness;* he has adopted it notwithstanding he foresaw that some moral agents would pervert their high powers of moral agency....he purposed these results rather than not adopt the best system....consistently with securing the perfect holiness of the greatest number; and doing it with the most unqualified preference of the holiness and happiness of all, to the sin and misery of any....and at last giving up the incorrigible to their merited doom![136]

Could he, consistent with these objectives, have saved more, he must have done so. "An infinitely benevolent God would secure such a result were there no such impossibility. To deny such impossibility is to say that God might produce more happiness than he does produce, and this," Taylor is convinced, "is to deny his benevolence. Here then we must rest. Here all do rest who believe that evil exists and God is good."[137]

IV

> You say it is impossible that God should adopt such as system as I have described. I show you that you cannot prove it, and have therefore no right to say it. Confess the possibility of such a system, and so take back your objection and I am satisfied. My argument will then remain in unimpaired force![138]

Taylor was forty-two when he preached **Concio,** and he had thirty years yet of living and lecturing remaining to him. In this last long segment of his life he would compose the essays on the Trinity, Election, and Human Sinfulness, and twice repeat to his students in the theological department the cycle of thirty-five lectures on the Moral Government of God. In their scope and marshalling of detail these last far surpass all that had gone before, and yet, curiously, they have received a minimum of attention from Taylor's expositors. That his contemporaries took so little notice is explained by the fact that the lectures were published posthumously, and by the time of his death the New Haven Theology had long since ceased to command general attention. As for the near total lack of recent interest,[39] that may well have to do with the realization that nothing really new has been added in these lectures to the notion of moral agency and governance asserted in the controversies with the Unitarians and the Tylerites.

Then, as later, Taylor is attempting to establish from the Scriptures the general fact of God's moral government, as instanced in the Books of Moses. Now, as earlier, his teaching is,

> generally speaking, that the Scriptures exhibit God as administering over men a perfect moral government under an economy of grace.
>
> A perfect moral government, as before defined, *is the influence of the rightful authority of a moral governor on moral being, designed so to control their action as to secure the great end of action on their part through the medium of law.*
>
> Law, in this general forensic import, is *an authoritative, perfect rule of moral action, fully sustained in its authority by the requisite sanctions.* In this general forensic import of the word, law is essential and common to every form of a perfect moral government![40]

The law, thus understood, is an clear for Taylor as ever it was for Edwards, Emmons, and Hopkins: "a moral being must be good, or he must be wicked. He must be for the greatest good, or against it. He must be benevolent or he must be selfish."[141]

A moral being must act, and that action is in every case dictated or prompted by his elective preference for the highest good, benevolence, or for some inferior worldly good. "The law of a perfect moral government absolutely and universally requires benevolence and benevolence only, and absolutely forbids selfishness."[142]

To Taylor it is obvious that such a requirement presupposes and assumes man's ability or power to obey God. "Until man has *power* to *obey,* it is absolutely inconceivable that he should obey, for the act of obedience is *his own* act, done in the use or exercise of *his own power* to obey."[143] To say, with Augustine, that all mankind, as they were created one moral person in Adam, had this power but that they utterly lost it by their participation in his Fall in absurd, inasmuch as it is to say that the power which is essential to the beginning of moral obligation is not necessary to its continued existence. Nor, he argues, is the Edwardian theory of inability in any better case. "Such *an inability* furnishes not the slightest evidence, that when one wills morally wrong, he has not in the proper and true sense of language, power or ability to will morally right; nor that when he has willed morally wrong, he has not the power or ability to will morally the next moment."[144] If the moral government of God is to function properly, mankind must have the power and ability to obey divine law, and that without the interposition of grace. To Tyler and Harvey, such a view marks its holder for a Pelagian, but in this, Taylor thinks, they are mistaken.

> The error of Pelagius is, not that he maintained man's ability to obey God without grace, but that man does *actually* obey God without grace. Some, who would seem to think themselves to be well-read theologians, appear not to know the difference between affirming that man *can* obey without grace, and affirming that he *does* or ever will obey without grace. I affirm the former and deny the latter. I suppose a *necessity* of grace, not to constitute men moral agents, or able to obey God, but to influence those to obey God who can, but from willfulness in sin never will obey him without grace.[145]

Every moral government presupposes moral agents; the moral government of God can assume no less, but it differs in that it incorporates an economy of grace, a revelation of *"favor to sinners*—to moral beings who can and who ought, and yet who in fact never will obey God without the supernatural grace of his Holy Spirit."[146]

Is there, Taylor asks, "any way to magnify the grace of God in this world's redemption from the power and doom of sin, except by unfolding his rightful authority as a lawgiver?"[147] And answers, no. The authority of the divine law must be established by confirming the authority of Him whose law it is, and this entails our recognition of the distributive justice of God in the punishment of sinners. "Thus he shows his supreme approbation of obedience, by conferring the requisite reward on the obedient subject, as the necessary and only means in this case of sustaining his authority. Thus he shows his supreme disapprobation of disobedience, by inflicting the requisite penalty on the disobedient, or by providing an atonement, as the necessary and only means in this case, of sustaining his authority."[149]

However, Taylor would not have us think of the Atonement as God's act of abnegation. The sacrifice of Christ, as he understands it, does not negate the Father's right and duty to punish the transgressor. But if God's justice, under an atonement, does not compel the pardon of sinners, neither does it require their condemnation. It may, he allows, "do either the one or the other as the general good shall dictate or demand. What the atonement does, and all that it does as an atonement, is to render it *consistent* with justice to pardon the sinner, by fully sustaining even in such a case, the authority and justice of the lawgiver in the best manner possible to him."[150] For Taylor, as for all Edwardians, God is sovereign, and his moral government will serve his glory. He claims and will have the perfect and uninterrupted obedience of his subjects, and it makes no difference that this claim never has been, nor ever can be, satisfied. "It is immutable like its author, and so long as he is what he is, and his subjects are what they are, there can be no satisfaction for one violation of this high and holy claim of this eternal and immutable and perfect rule."[151]

V

> We must have a sound, deep philosophy, and yet it must be
> common sense philosophy, such as all the world can under-
> stand if we would defend orthodox theology.[152]

Sydney Ahlstrom has reminded us of the indebtedness of Taylor and his
mentor Dwight to the common sense realism of Thomas Reid and Dugald
Stewart,[153] a realism whose plainest expression is found in the late sermon,
What is Truth? The answer, says our preacher, is that "truth is the reality
of things," specifically, *"that reality of things which the Gospel reveals."*[154]
This reality, otherwise defined, comprises the nature, relations, and the fitness
of things, which fitness, it is argued, is the ground or reason why God has
done what he has done, and will do what he will do through all eternity. From
these common-sensical premises follows all that has been said before concerning the penalties and rewards resultant from the operation of God's moral
government in the room of the depraved by nature. Obviously, this account
leaves no leeway for any philosophical quibbling as to the status of the real,
nor does it allow for any critical analysis of the content of scripture. We are
bidden to take the world as it is and the Word as revealed.

Unfortunately for Taylor and his school, as the nineteenth century wore
on into its middle decades the progress of philosophy and physical science
was such as to preclude the retention of the simplistic verities of Scottish-
American common-sensism. The appearance of Lyell's **Principles of Geology**
in 1830 put paid to the possibility of believing that the world was something
short of six thousand years duration, even as the speculations of Wallace and
Darwin inhibited further serious discussion of the relation of mankind to
Adam. The authority of Reid and Stewart was already giving way in Taylor's
day to the hegemony of Kant and Hegel. Ahlstrom suggests[155] that the Edwardsian era in New England theology may justifiably be considered to have
ended with the death of Taylor in the centenary year of the founder's passing, and if one requires a *terminus ad quem* of essential Edwardsianism, 1858
will do well enough, but this is not to say that the quest for a consistent

Calvinism ends here.

The liberalization of orthodoxy begun in Dwight's emphasis on the practical aspect and continued in Taylor's insistence on the moral prospect, opened the way for the theological efforts of Park, Hickok and Harris. It is arguable that Taylor went as far as any Calvinist could go without betraying the basic principles of his illustrious predecessors, and this reaching out, together with his success in denaturing the doctrine of depravity and elaborating the moral dimension of the sovereignty of God, keeps the quest in being. Then too there in his achievement as a revivalist.

Mead and Pope have stressed this last, suggesting that it is as a preacher of the second great awakening that Taylor best served the cause of Calvinism. As Mead sees him, Taylor was never so much concerned with building a coherent system of thought as he was in getting results![57] In one sense this is absolutely correct. The pragmatic moment is as present in each quest for a consistent Calvinism as it is in any other systematization of thought. That Taylor preached to preserve orthodoxy in New England, and enjoyed considerable success in his endeavours, is a matter of record. But no more than Edwards should he be judged on the basis of his reputation as a master of homiletics. If he deserves to be remembered, it is because in his Essays and in his Lectures he continues and builds upon Edwards' True Virtue and Hopkins' True Holiness.

Bibliographical Essay

The nearest thing to a Collected Works are the four volumes of essays, lectures, and sermons published at the behest of Noah Porter and Taylor's Yale colleagues by Clark, Austin and Smith in 1859. Subsequently reissued as a set, these comprise: **Practical Sermons,** thirty-two sermons delivered during Taylor's tenure as minister of the Center Church., **Essays, Lectures, etc. upon Select Topics in Revealed Theology,** including five lectures on the Trinity, fourteen discourses on Human Sinfulness, two essays on Justification, four sermons on Election, and the sermons **Perseverance** and **What is Truth?** and two volumes of **Lectures on the Moral Government of God.** Regrettably, the interest of the editor and publisher did not reach to the reprinting of Taylor's important essay, 'Review of Spring on the Means of Regeneration,' **Quarterly Christian Spectator,** I, Nos. I-IV (February-December, 1829), 1-40, 209-234, 481-508, 692-712; **American Periodical Series** 1800-1850, Film 1585, Reel 230. Nor do the four volumes include Taylor's reviews of Norton (see below) or any of his various and mostly anonymous contributions to the **Christian Spectator** and other periodicals. A catalogue of these is provided by Franklin Bowditch Dexter, **Yale Biographies and Annals 1805-1815,** Sixth Series (New Haven: Yale University Press, 1912), 159-163.

The Unitarian Controversy begins with Andrews Norton's **Inaugural Discourse, Delivered before the University in Cambridge. Aug. 10th, 1819** (Cambridge: Hilliard and Metcalf, 1819). Reviewed by Taylor, **Quarterly Christian Spectator,** III, No. 2 (February , 1821), 74-83 (note: the volume numbers of this periodical are repeated (see above); in a new series); Film 1585, Reel 195. Rejoinder by Norton, 'Thoughts on True and False Religion,' **Christian Disciple and Theological Review.** II, new series, no. 11 (September-October, 1820), 337-365: Film 1585, Reel 78. Reviewed by Taylor, 'Review of Erskine's Remarks on the Internal Evidence for the truth of Revealed Religion; Thoughts on True and False Religion by Andrews Norton,' **Quarterly Christian Spectator,** IV, No. V (May, 1822), 249-264 (on Erskine); No.VI (June, 1822), 299-318 (on Norton); No. VIII (August, 1822), 445-448 (editorial reply to Norton's letter); No. XII (December, 1822), 667-668 (further correspondence); Film 1585, Reel 195. Defence and documentation of his charges, by Norton, 'Views of Calvinism,' **Christian Disciple,** IV, new series, No. 22 (July-August, 1822), 244-280; Film 1585, Reel 78. Reply by Taylor, 'Review of Norton's Views of Calvinism,' **Quarterly Christian Spectator,** V. No. IV (April, 1823), 196-224; Film 1585, Reel 196. Hilrie Shelton Smith, **Changing Conceptions of Original Sin** (New York: Scribner's, 1955), 88-96, gives an account of this controversy, as does Mead (see below), 173-194.

Taylor's 1816 sermon, **Regeneration the Beginning of Holiness in the Human Heart** (New Haven: Nathan Whiting, 1816), drew a forty page review by the Rev. Menzies Rayner, an Episcopal clergyman whose main concern is to defend his bishop (Hobart) against Taylor's "unfair quotations and gross misrepresentations." The celebrated sermon, **Concio ad Clerum** (New Haven: Hezekiah Howe, 1828), is criticized by the Rev. Joseph Harvey, **A Review of a Sermon delivered in the Chapel of Yale College, September 10th, 1828 by Nathaniel W. Taylor, D.D.** (Hartford: Goodwin & Co., 1829). A vindication of the sermon against its critic is offered in an unsigned review ascribed to the Rev. Chaucey Goodrich, 'Review of Taylor and Harvey on Human Depravity,' **Quarterly Christian Spectator,** I, No. 11, Article XI (June, 1829), 343-384; Film 1585, Reel 230. With this should be read the **Postscript** to **An Inquiry into the Nature of Sin as Exhibited in Dr. Dwight's Theology. A Letter to a Friend** by one Clericus (Taylor) (New Haven: Hezekiah Howe, 1829). For the details of the Taylor/Tyler controversy and much else, see Zebulon Crocker, **The Catastrophe of the Presbyterian Church in 1837, including a full view of the recent Theological controversies in New England** (New Haven: B. & W. Noyes, 1838) As a reasonably objective contemporary observer of the events and controversies he describes, Crocker is an invaluable witness, and fortunately for his reader the very soul of lucidity, brevity, and wit. These virtues are not so much in evidence in Bennet Tyler, **Letters on the Origin and Progress of the New Haven Theology** (New York: R. Carter & E. Collier, 1837), but the book is important as an account of the viewpoint of Taylor's conservative orthodox opposition.

The one substantial published study of Taylor and his times is Sidney Earl Mead, **Nathaniel William Taylor 1786-1858, A Connecticut Liberal** (Chicago: University of Chicago Press, 1942). Much more than a life of its subject, or even an exposition of his "peculiar views," it ranges over the entire battlefield of doctrine and church polity current in the first third of the nineteenth century. Mead is so much concerned with the parts played by Timothy Dwight and Lyman Beecher in the continuing controversy between Old and Consistent Calvinism, and in the warfare of both with Unitarianism and Episcopalianism, that he occasionally loses sight of his primary subject. Lively and well-written, this book is essential to a proper understanding of the main currents of early nineteenth century religious thought, albeit its theses, the identification of Taylor with Old Calvinism, of both with the mainstream of the New England theology, and of revivalism as the essence of that theology, are debatable. Complete with an Appendix listing the articles and reviews on the Taylor/Tyler and other Taylorite controversies compiled by Chauncey Goodrich under the title, **The New Haven Theology,** and a catalogue of the manuscript sources in the Yale University Library. Supplementing this is the excellent study by Earl Aurel Pope, **New England Calvinism and the Disruption of the Presbyterian Church,** Ph.D dissertation, Brown University (Department of Religious Studies), 1962: University Microfilms 63-1048. From this Professor Pope has mined a two-part article, 'The Rise of the New Haven Theology,' **The Journal of Presbyterian History,** 44 March-June, 1966), 24-44, 106-121. On the controversy between the Unitarians and the Calvinists, see C.H. Faust, 'The Background of the Unitarian Opposition to Transcendentalism,' **Modern Philology,** 35 (1937-38), 297-324. Theodore Thornton Munger, a doyen of the New Theology, who was a student under Taylor, offers a respectful view of his old instructor in 'Dr. Nathaniel W. Taylor, Master Theologian,' **Congregationalist and Christian Advocate,** XCIII (1908), and there are further biographical recollections by Noah Porter, Taylor's son-in-law, in the volume celebrating the semi-centennial of the Divinity School of Yale College, and in William Chauncey Fowler, **Essays, Historical, Literary, Educational** (Case, Lockwood and Brainard, 1876). Leonard Bacon, **Memorial of Nathaniel Taylor, D.D. Three Sermons** (by Bacon, Rev. S.W.S. Dutton, and Rev. G.P. Fisher) (New Haven: Thomas H. Pease, 1858), consists of eulogies delivered at Taylor's funeral.

[1] Nathaniel William Taylor, **Lectures on the Moral Government of God,** two volumes (New York: Clark, Austin & Smith, 1859), I, II, 198. Hereafter cited as **Lectures** with volume, section, lecture, and page number.

[2] N.W. Taylor, 'Salvation Free to the Willing', in **Practical Sermons** (New York: Clark, Austin, & Smith, 1858), 318. Hereafter cited as **Sermons** with title and page number.

[3] The fourth of his line to bear the name, Taylor was born at New Milford, Connecticut, on June 23rd, 1786. The Rev. Nathaniel William Taylor (1722-1800), pastor of the Congregational church at New Milford, Yale Class of 1745, and a member of the Yale Corporation from 1774 until his death, was our Nathaniel's grandfather and, according to Mead, the prime influence on him in his formative years. Nathaniel W. Taylor (Yale Class of 1785) was as his uncle. His father, Nathaniel W. Taylor (1753-1818) was a well-to-do farmer and apothecary; his mother, Anne Northrup, came from a prominent New Milford family. He received his primary education in the New Milford common school and was prepared for college at the academy run by Rev. Azel Backus, Bellamy's sucessor at Bethlem. In the fall of 1800, aged fourteen, he entered Yale, beginning what was to be a lifetime association.

[4] Timothy Dwight, **The Dignity and Excellence of the Gospel** (New York: J. Seymour 1812), 34pp.

[5] Halfway through his freshman year Taylor suffered a debilitating eye disorder and was forced to withdraw from college. Upon his return a year later the affliction recurred necessitating another lengthy convalescence. In all, Taylor fell three years behind his original classmates. It is arguable that Dwight and Taylor were drawn together as much by their common misfortune as by the convergence of their theological views.

[6] "He delights in his law, as the transcript of his nature; he delights in his Son, as the express image of his person, in the whole plan of salvation, as unfolding the riches of his goodness and wisdom....As God thus delights in the manifestation of himself—that is, in his own glory, so all his acts....are directed to this end." Holiness alone fits for Heaven', **Sermons,** 204.

[7] "Merely to provide salvation for men, and to make the offer of it, would, we believe, have never brought the Son of God to die on the cross. We must look for some further and higher end....This end is the actual restoration of a part of mankind to the favor of God." 'The Atonement a Pledge to the Christian for every real good', **Sermons,** 92.

[8] 'The Goodness of God designed to reclaim', **Sermons,** 239.

[9] "What is the work of the Holy Spirit in changing the sinner's heart? It is that influence or operation by which he brings the sinner, in the free, unconstrained use of his own moral powers, to fix his heart on God. It is not the creation of any new mental power or property, but it is an influence which secures simply and solely, in a complete moral agent, the right use of powers already possessed." 'The Sinner's Duty to make himself a new Heart', **Sermons,** 406. Herein, we have a significant departure from the position of the early Edwardsians, but of that more below.

[10] "*No Man,* be he who he may, whether high or low, rich or poor, learned or ignorant, honorable or mean;—*no man,* whatever religion, or virtue, or profession, or creed, or works, or prayers he may boast of, without holiness, shall be admitted into the presence of God....Were God to admit the unholy into his blissful presence, it would be a full and decided declaration, that sin and holiness were things without a difference....that the whole work of redemption....was at most only a mighty farce. But will the great Eternal thus tarnish his glory, and demolish the foundations of his throne? Or, must the unholy in this world be unhappy in the next? 'Holiness alone fits for Heaven', **Sermons,** 204-205.

[11]"Sinners hate the light", **Sermons,** 183.

[12]"Practical Atheism", **Sermons,** 160.

[13]Ibid., 163.

[14]"A new creation is not a new birth, nor is it a resurrection from the dead. Indeed, if the change be truly and literally any *one* of these three things (the third being a new birth), then it cannot be truly and literally either of the others....Plainly the language is wholly figurative, since otherwise it must be contradictory and false." 'The Sinner's Duty to make himself a New Heart', **Sermons,** 238, 399.

[15]Ibid., 406.

[16]Ibid.

[17]Ibid.

[18]**Regeneration the beginning of Holiness in the human Heart,** A Sermon (New Haven: Nathan Whiting, 1816), 7. The sermon contains a prefatory note in which the author (Taylor) remarks his purpose in publishing as the removal of misunderstanding concerning his opinion, and the opinions of the positions he here opposes.

[19]Ibid., 9.

[20]Sidney Earl Mead, **Nathaniel William Taylor 1786-1858, A Connecticut Liberal** (Chicago: University of Chicago Press, 1942). Hereafter cited as **Mead.**

[21]**Mead,** viii.

[22]**Mead,** ix. Zebulon Crocker, **The Catastrophe of the Presbyterian Church in 1837, including a full view of the recent Theological Controversies in New England** (New Haven: B. & W. Noyes, 1838), supports Mead to a degree when he notes that "they who formerly condemned Hopkinsianism, are now arranged in a party, which receives its chief countenance and sympathy in New England, from Hopkinsians of the highest school. While they whose heresy is an object of alarm (i.e. the Taylorites) agree much more nearly than their opponents, with the Old Calvinists." Hopkinsian disinterestedness,: he remarks in a footnote, "God's efficiency in the production of sin,—concreated *actual* sin,—sin the necessary means,—on all these points the New Haven divines depart from Hopkins towards Calvin and the Westminster divines. The Hopkinsians say that infants suffer and die because of their own personal sin; New Haven and Princeton agree in saying that it is in consequence of Adam's sin." "The difference, however, between the New Haven divines and their opponents, he (Crocker) regards as trivial, compared with the great doctrines of the gospel, all of which they hold in common; nor does he see the least cause, on the ground of theological sentiment, for strife or alienation." iv-v, 295-295n. Nor, indeed, do I. Hereafter cited as **Crocker** with page reference.

[23]**Mead,** 23.

[24]Ibid., 27. The "means" here referred to is in substance that which Mayhew, Mills, and Hart stressed in their controversy with Hopkins concerning the character of regeneration. See Chapter IV, section II.

[25]Mead offers no other evidence in this context, albeit he does argue in another context (pp. 119-120) for the sinner's use of the "means of Grace."

[26]To say precisely what "means" means to Old Calvinists is difficult because "means" meant any means whereby a change of heart was induced and the sinner saved. Thus where the opponents of Hopkins spoke of means, they meant, primarily, the reading and preaching of the Gospel. Others of their way of thinking would include as "means" good works and the example of saintly persons.

[27]**Regeneration the beginning of holiness in the human Heart,** 11.

[28]Ibid.

[29]Ibid., the Great Commandment, he reminds us (12n) presupposes man's ability to love the Lord his God, and that not with God's soul and strength and mind, but with his (man's) own.

[30]**Regeneration the beginning of holiness in the human Heart,** 18.

[31]The main thrust of the Remarks appended to the sermon is a contravention of Hobart's view, which Taylor, "effectually to repel the charge of misrepresentation," (41n) quotes at length and disputes point by point. The significance of this extended discursus is, of course, Taylor's assumption that he is here defending the Calvinist doctrine of regeneration against its cultured despisers.

[32]**Regeneration the beginning of holiness in the human Heart,** 18.

[33]Gardiner Spring, like his classmate Taylor, was a protege of Dwight. A member of the Yale Class of 1805, his clerical life was spent as pastor (1810-1859) of the Brick Presbyterian Church in New York City. The Dissertation which Taylor purports to be reviewing serves him simply as a point of departure for the expression of his own view of regeneration. There is, to be sure, some pro forma criticism of Spring's position in the first section of the review, but in the main, writes Taylor, "we have intentionally dwelt chiefly on those points, which Dr. Spring was led, by the nature of his design, to leave untouched."

[34]**The Quarterly Christian Spectator,** I, No. I, Article I (March, 1829), 1-40; No. II, Article I (June 1829), 209-234; No. III, Article VI (September, 1829), 481-508; No. IV, Article VIII (December, 1829), 692-712. **American Periodical Series,** Film 1585, Reel 230. The four articles, as per the custom of the **Quarterly,** as unsigned. For another account of these articles, see **Mead,** 227-228.

[35]Taylor devotes several pages of his review (488-494) to exploding the Hopkinsian notion that regeneration is a physical change effected by an immediate operation of God qua Spirit on the regenerate without the intervention of the preliminary moral acts denominated "means". "It is," writes Taylor, "a truth often overlooked, in theological discussion, that God as a moral governor, can be glorified only by the love and service of beings who are intelligent as well as voluntary." Review of **Spring,** 494.

[36]To Taylor's view, all of these, and whatever other acts not done directly from the motive of self-love, are as sinful and as deserving of condemnation as ever Hopkins pronounced.

[37]Review of **Spring,** 20, 32, 210, 222, 226, 494.

[38]Ibid., 218.

[39]Ibid.,. 209.

[40]Ibid.

[41]Ibid.

[42]Ibid., 17. Taylor's italics.

[43]**Psalms** 119:59. Taylor's italics.

[44]Specifically, **Matthew** 6:21 and 22:37.

[45]Review of **Spring,** 222.

[46]Ibid., 702-703. Subsequently, the Rev. Bennet Tyler, the pastor of a Congregational church in Portland, Maine, published **Strictures on the Review of Spring** (Portland, 1829), arguing that although he (Taylor) "has not formally denied any one doctrine of the orthodox system, he has

adopted principles, in his statements and explanations, which will lead, by inevitable consequence, to the denial of important doctrines; and that his speculations will pave the way for the gradual influx of error upon the American churches, disastrous to the interests of evangelical religion.'' (8) Despite the fact that there was in this criticism no issue of substance, Taylor replied in an interminably detailed 'Review of Dr. Tyler's Strictures on the Christian Spectator,' **Quarterly Christian Spectator,** II (March, 1830), 147-200, thus setting off the war of pamphlets known as the Taylor/Tyler Controversy. Crocker (299) lists the sequence of the ensuing publications.

[47]**Mead,** 117n.

[48]Hemmenway, together with the Rev. Samuel Cooke of Stratford, and the Rev. Nathaniel Taylor of New Milford, are cited by Mead as exemplars of Old Calvinism.

[49]Review of **Spring,** 16. Taylor's italics.

[50]Review of Norton's **Views of Calvinism, Quarterly Christian Spectator,** V, No. 4 (April, 1823), 217, 219. **American Periodical Series** Film 1585, Reel 196. The review is unsigned.

[51]Review of Erskine's Remarks on the Internal Evidence for the Truth of Revealed Religion; Thoughts on True and False Religion by Andrews Norton,' **Quarterly Christian Spectator,** IV, no. VI (June, 1822), 303. **American Periodical Series,** Film 1585, Reel 195. Hereafter cited as Review of Erskine and Norton with page reference.

[52]As Mead notes (151n) they put their money where their hearts were, subscribing between them thirty-five hundred of the twenty thousand dollars deemed necessary to secure the endowment. In addition to their contribution to this sum, Professors Chauncey Goodrich and Eleazer Fitch bound themselves by promissory note for five thousand dollars more.

[53]**Unitarian Christianity:** Discourse at the Ordination of the Rev. Jared Sparks, **in The Works of William E. Channing, D.D.** (Boston: American Unitarian Association, 1903). Hereafer cited as Channing, **Works,** with page reference.

[54]Channing, **Works,** 367-368.

[55]Ibid., 368.

[56]Stuart, **Letters to Dr. Channing on the Trinity,** in **Miscellanies** (Andover, 1846), 167. A detailed and lucid account of the Channing/Stuart exchange is provided by C.H. Faust, 'The Background of the Unitarian opposition to Transcendentalism.' **Modern Philology,** 35 (1937-38), 297-324.

[57]Channing, **Works,** 367.

[58]Ibid., 377.

[59]Ibid., 380.

[60]Ibid.

[61]The Moral Argument against Calvinism, Illustrated in a Review of a Work entitled "A General View of the Doctrines of Christianity, designed more especially for the Edification and Instruction of Families, in Channing, **Works,** 461.

[62]Ibid., 467.

[63]Ibid.

[64]Channing, **Works,** 460. Mead (178) sums it up best: "belief in the doctrines of Calvinism is morally degrading; therefore, those doctrines cannot be true."

[65]Channing, **Works,** 467.

[66]An exact contemporary of Taylor, born in 1786 at Hingham, Massachusetts and educated at Harvard (Class of 1804), Norton's career at Harvard paralleled that of Taylor at Yale. Both began

284

as tutors, both were famous controversialists, Norton perhaps the more so inasmuch as he stood in theology squarely against Calvinist orthodoxy on the one hand and against Emersonian transcendentalism on the other. His major work was his three-volume study of **The Evidences for the Genuineness of the Gospels** (1837, revised and corrected, 1844), albeit his **Statement of Reasons for not believing the Doctrines of the Trinitarians, concerning the nature of God, and the person of Christ** (a book-length expansion of his 1819 lecture of the same title, published in 1833) was more widely read and discussed. Norton died in 1853, predeceasing Taylor by five years. Charles Eliot Norton (1827-1908), the well-known editor, and author of various historical and literary studies, is his son.

[67]Andrews Norton, **Inaugural Discourse, Delivered before the University in Cambridge, August 10th, 1819** (Cambridge: Hilliard & Metcalf, 1819), 8.

[68]Ibid., 39-40.

[69]An account of Lyman Beecher's role in the Unitarian controversy is provided by Mead, Chapters VIII and XI.

[70]Taylor (unsigned), **Review of an Inaugural Discourse delivered before the University in Cambridge, August 10th, 1819: by Andrews Norton, Dexter Professor of Sacred Literature, Quarterly Christian Spectator,** III (Febraury, 1821), 76.

[71]Ibid.

[72]ibid., 79.

[73]Ibid., 78.

[74]Ibid., 79.

[75]Ibid., 83.

[76]Andrews Norton (unsigned), 'Thoughts on True and False Religion', **The Christian Disciple and Theological Review,** II, new series, no. 11 (September-October, 1820), 362.

[77]Ibid., 340.

[78]Review of Erskine and Norton, 448.

[79]Ibid., 299.

[80]As Mead notes, "this turns the argument from tendency back on the Unitarians by insinuating that the tendency of their views is toward the outright rejection of revealed religion," (182) which, as the later apostasy of the transcendentalists demonstrated, it certainly did.

[81]Andrews Norton to the Editors, **'Quarterly Christian Specttory,** IV, No. VIII (August, 1822), 446. Reprinted with comments and documentation in Norton, 'Views of Calvinism', **The Christian Disciple and Theological Review,** IV, new series, no. 22 (July-August, 1822), 247-264.

[82]Norton, 'Thoughts on True and False Religion', **Christian Disciple,** II, new series, no. 11 (September-October, 1820), 340.

[83]'Views of Calvinism', **Christian Disciple,** IV (August, 1822), 248.

[84]Propositions as formulated by Norton, 'Views of Calvinism', 270.

[85]Given his direct interest, as the reviewer, and his close association with the Quarterly, it is reasonable to assume that the Editors include Taylor, or, at least, that their view of the matter is coincident with his. Their reply to Norton is given in the **Quarterly Christian Spectator,** IV, (August, December, 1822), 445-448, 667-668.

[86]'Views of Calvinism', 271, 276. My italics.

[87]Ibid., 264.

[88]Taylor, 'Review of Views of Calvinism by Professor Norton,' **Quarterly Christian Spectator,** V, no. 4 (April, 1823), 196. Hereafter cited as 'Review of Views' with page reference.

[89]'Review of Views,' 200.

[90]Ibid., 205. My italics.

[91]ibid., 198.

[92]Ibid., 221.

[93]'Review of Views,' 219.

[94]Ibid., 217. Taylor's italics.

[95]Ibid.

[96]'Review of Views,' 220.

[97]This minimal Calvinism could not, and as things turned out did not satisfy everyone. Bennet Tyler, the Hopkinsian president of Dartmouth College, and a Yale classmate of Taylor, ws particularly disturbed by what he took to be a falling away from true Calvinism to what he called Taylorism. A war of articles and pamphlets, the Taylor/Tyler controversy, ensued, ended only by the death of the participants in the spring and summer of 1858. I forbear to burden the reader with an exposition inasmuch as the issues raised by Tyler and responded to be Taylor are not so much matters of theology as they are of church polity. As Mead rightly remarks: "the significance of the so'called "Taylor and Tyler" controversy is not primarily theological at all, in the sense that it led to changes and developments in theological thought. It was rather political, that is, a controversy over whether or not the New Haven version of Calvinism was to be permitted to continue in the Congregational churches of Connecticut." **Mead, 222.**

[98]'Review of Views,' 220.

[99]Ibid., 222.

[100]Taylor, **Essays, Lectures, Etc. upon Select Topics in Revealed Theology** (New York: Clark, Austin, & Smith, 1859), 138-139. "See," he continues, "**Deuteronomy** 21:15; **Matthew** 6:24; **Luke** 14:26; **Proverbs** 13:24; **Matthew** 1:3, **Romans** 9:13: and **John** 12:25, where hate is used in the sense of a *lesser degree of love."*

[101]Taylor, **Concio ad Clerum, A Sermon delivered in the Chapel of Yale College, September 10th, 1828** (New Haven: Hezekiah Howe, 1828). His reference is, of course, to Timothy Dwight. Hereafter cited as **Concio** with page reference.

[102]**Concio,** 6.

[103]Ibid., 7.

[104]Ibid.

[105]Ibid.

[106]Ibid., 8. Taylor's italics.

[107]**Concio,** 11.

[108]Ibid., 13.

[109]**Ephesians** 2:3.

[110]**Concio,** 13.

[111]Ibid., 14.

[112]**Concio,** 14.

[113]To see here, as some do, a difficulty with respect to the free-agency of mankind, is, Taylor

argues in a lengthy footnote, to have misapprehended the terms involved. "When we speak of the depravity or sinfulness of man *by nature,* no one, who correctly interprets the language, can understand us to mean that *nature* is the *physical* or *efficient cause* of sin, operating by an absolute and irresistible compulsion. All that can be properly understood is, that *nature* is the *occasion* of sin, as a free act. The very nature of the predicate, *sin,* requires the restriction of the phrase to this import....The Apostle cannot be understood to mean....that nature is a *physical cause* of which *sin* is a *physical effect*....But if *nature* is not a *physical cause* of sin, but simply the *occasion* of sin, then since nothing but *physical* influence or efficiency can be supposed in the present case to be inconsistent with moral freedom, the consistency between sinning by *nature* and sinning freely, is apparent....if nature is simply the *occasion* of man's sinning, why may he not sin freely?—Why not, as well as if *circumstances* or *motives* were the occasion?" **Concio,**16n. A similar result appears to follow if we allow that the casual character of nature is no more than a *formal* casuality, a possibility which Taylor's text imples, and which nothing in his other lectures and discourses appears to rule out.

[114] **Concio,** 15.

[115] Ibid.

[116] **Concio,** 16-17.

[117] Ibid., 23.

[118] Ibid., Taylor's italics.

[119] The charge had been made publicly in the course of a sermon by the former pastor of the Congregational church at Fairfield, Connecticut, the Rev. Nathaniel Hewit. According to Hewit, who was speaking in opposition to an earlier plea for funds to support the establishment of a professorship of sacred literature in the theological department at Yale, Taylor and his colleagues were guilty of heresy with respect to their views of the nature and extent of human depravity, regeneration, divine influence, decrees, and election. Taylor in particular was castigated as a Pelagian and an Arminian. The theological department itself, Hewit thundered, not only ought not to be supported, it should be abolished as a nuisance. Taylor, on being informed of these accusations, prepared **Concio** as a reply, and preached the sermon first at Fairfield. A full account of this and related matters respecting the controversies involving Taylor and his school is given in Crocker's, **The Catastrophe** etc. Chapters XII-XX.

[120] **Concio,** 26.

[121] Joseph Harvey, born 1787, educated at Yale, Class of 1808. He too served as an amanuensis of Dwight until his call to the Congregational church at Goshen, Connecticut in 1810. Subsequently pastor at Westchester (1827-35) and the Presbyterian church at Thompsonville (Enfield), Connecticut (1838-56). Harvey outlived his old adversary by many years, dying at the ripe age of eighty-six in 1873.

[122] Joseph Harvey, **A Review** (Hartford: Goodwin & Co., 1829). Hereafter cited as **Review** with page reference.

[123] **Review,** 5.

[124] **Review,** 28-29.

[125] Ibid., 28.

[126] Ibid., 29.

[127] **Review,** 34-35.

[128] **Quarterly Christian Spectator,** I, no. II, Article XI (June, 1829), 343-384. For a detailed ac-

count of Goodrich's criticisms of Harvey, see **Crocker, 127-130.**

[129]Of course, it can be argued that motives and acts of will are themselves efficient causes, indeed Harvey implies as much.

[130]**The Nature of Sin as Exhibited in Dr. Dwight's Theology, A Letter to a Friend** (New Haven: Hezekiah Howe, 1829). The pamphlet is signed by one Clericus, subsequently identified by Taylor (**Essays, etc.,** 216) as himself.

[131]**An Examination of Dr. Taylor's Sermon on Human Depravity** (Hartford: Goodwin & Co., 1829). Herein Harvey, persuaded to a degree by Goodrich and Taylor, abandons his notion of depravity as inherent from Adam, maintaining rather that mankind come into the world with a voluntary will to sin. Presumably Taylor found this new statement of position so indistinguishable from his own view as to obviate the necessity for any further argument.

[132]Taylor, **Essays, etc.,** 375.

[133]Ibid., 374.

[134]Ibid., 377.

[135]**Essays, etc.** 378.

[136]Ibid., 385.

[137]**Essays, etc.,** 384.

[138]**Lectures,** I, I, VIIIm 180.

[139]Mead mentions the **Lectures** only in passing. Haroutunian sees in them the shift away from a consistent Calvinism based upon the presupposition of the absolute sovereignty of God to a consistent Calvinism grounded in the divine moral government, but his notice is merely incidental to the central thesis of his book. See **Piety versus Moralism,** 252-254.

[140]**Lectures,** II, III, VII, 129.

[141]Ibid., I, I, II, 26.

[142]Ibid., I, I, III, 47.

[143]**Lectures,** II, III, VII, 133.

[144]Ibid., 134. The argument whereby Taylor arrives at this conclusion is at once too extended and too intricate to admit of ready redaction or concise quotation. The point of it is that the Edwardian distinction between natural and moral inability fails of its purpose of preserving the power of the moral agent to obey the divine command because of an inherent ambiguity in the terms. Taylor suggests, but presumably in deference of Edwards does not say, that this ambiguity amounts to a contradiction.

[145]**Lectures,** II, III, VII, 132n.

[146]Ibid., 139.

[147]Ibid.

[148]By this phrase 'distributive justice' Taylor understands "justice as the attribute of a moral governor, which involves the particular disposition to maintain his authority by means of legal sanctions." The legal sanctions here envisaged are the natural good promised for obedience and the natural evil threatened for disobedience to God's law. See **Lectures,** II, Appendix I, Part II, 283.

[149]**Lectures,** II, III, VII, 145.

[150]**Lectures,** II, III, VII, 147.

[151]Ibid., 148.

288

[152]Taylor to William Chaucey Fowler, in Fowler, **Essays: historical, Literary, Education** (Hartford: The Case, Lockwood & Brainard Co., 1876). 62.

[153]Sydney E. Ahlstrom, **A Religious History of the American People** (New Haven: Yale University Press, 1977), 355-356. For a more detailed account see Ahlstrom, 'The Scottish Philosophy and American Theology', **Church History,** 24 (September, 1955), 257-272.

[154] Taylor, **Essays, etc.,** 461, 464.

[155] Sydney E. Ahlstrom, Theology in America (Indianapolis: Bobbs-Merrill, 1967), 211.

[156]**Earl Aurel Pope, New England Calvinism and he Disruption of the Presbyterian Church.** Ph.D. dissertation, Brown University (Department of Religious Studies), 1962. University Microfilms 63-1048. Except for Mead, whose intrpretation of Taylor Pope inclines to endorse, this is the only detailed study of the New Haven theology in its larger context.

[157] **Mead,** 99.

The Conciliatory Calvinism
Of Edwards Amasa Park

"He so admired and reverenced Edwards that he believed himself at every point a follower of the master. Why he thought so is one of the great mysteries of the subject. He was himself a greater mind than Edwards."[1]

THE CONCILIATORY CALVINISM OF EDWARDS AMASA PARK

All sacred rhetoric is but a new arrangement of the materials
of theology.[2]

In the winter of 1834-35 Nathaniel Taylor lectured on the Atonement, and among his hearers was a young minister named Edwards Park. The year previous, an affliction of the eyes, aggravated by a general physical debility, had forced Park to abandon his pastoral duties, and he had spent the intervening months in travel and introspection. Now restored to health, he came to New Haven in the hope of recovering a faith beset by nagging doubts. His confidence in the system of doctrines which he had absorbed as a student at Andover Theological Seminary under the guidance of the redoubtable Abbot Professor of Systematic Theology, Dr. Leonard Woods, had been disturbed and eroded by the pallid performance of Woods in the latter's celebrated controversy with Harvard's Henry Ware Senior. However, as he listened to Taylor's conciliatory apologetics, Park felt his faith reviving. The following spring he resumed his career, taking a professorial appointment at Amherst, and a year later, the position he really wanted having become vacant, he accepted a call to Andover to take up the duties of the Bartlet Professor of Sacred Rhetoric.

The opening sentences of his Inaugural Address made it plain to the Andover community that he understood his office to involve something more than simple exposition of the rules of sacredotal rhetoric. The preacher, he informs them, must first be a theologian, and that because theology comprehends all other sciences as its tributaries, and by them is connected with every art—including homiletics. Pulpit eloquence presupposes intense theological study; lacking this it lapses into rodomontade. A meagre system of theology will suffice for the preacher who is satisfied to make conversions, but God, Park believes, is not glorified unless we love theology itself. "The Deity is not glorified by conversions, but by conversions to the truth."[3] Therefore, he concludes, "a complete theologian, one who takes in the essence and the bearings, and the inspiration and the life of theology, is the only model of pulpit eloquence."[4]

In a companion article published in the same year he addresses himself to the mode of exhibiting theological truth. We must, he thinks, pay scrupulous attention not only to the matter but also to the manner of our preaching. Harsh doctrine (Park is thinking here of the severities of Calvinism as preached by Hopkins and Emmons) should be preached in a mild and seemly manner. To insist upon the letter of the sterner truths to excess is to darken understanding, the more so since the theological truth, as Park conceives it, is the great and free original of which orthodoxy is the cramped epitome. "The Bible," he insists, was never designed to supersede the exercise of ingenuity, or of original thought."[5] Which being so, "we are to preach not to the man as he was, but," Park teaches, "to the man as he is. A sermon which penetrates through the intellect to the heart, which is drunk up by the heart as the thirsty earth drinketh up the rain; a sermon which is so timely that it seems to be the counterpoint of the heart itself, each being imperfect without the other; which in familiar phrase goes to the very spot, and is just the thing, this is a true sermon."[6]

"We need and crave," he writes in a subsequent exposition of the duties of the theologian, "a theology as sacred and spiritual as his (Edwards'), and moreover one that we can take with us into the flower-garden, and to the top of a goodly hill, and in a sail over a restful lake, and into the saloons of music....and to all those harmonizing scenes where virtue holds her sway not merely as that generic and abstract duty of a "love to being in general," but also as the more familiar grace of a love to some beings in particular."[7] But lest he be thought to be retreating from the principles laid down in Edwards' exposition of True Virtue, he is quick to remind his reader of his allegiance to the New England divinity, "the principles of which shall always live. The more it is opposed as heresy and "new light," so much the more closely will we bind it to our hearts; for it is the fruit of sound sense and severe thought, and, above all, deep devotion."[8] "Let us then," he exhorts his reader, "give heed to ourselves and the doctrine; be first pure and always peaceable. And may our great Teacher make us cautious like Edwards, scrutinizing like Hopkins and Bellamy and Strong; honest like Emmons....and above all may we be humble as the child who asks for bread, and as God is true, shall never receive a stone."[9]

These orotund and elevating sentiments came naturally to Park,[10] who could with propriety speak as one born to the succession. His father, Calvin Park, had studied as a young man with Nathanael Emmons, and the sage of Franklin was a frequent visitor in the Park home. "I was," Edwards Park tells us, "at ten years of age somewhat of a theologian, and a rigid Calvinist; had a great reverence for Dr. Emmons and Dr. Hopkins."[11] Their influence eventually led him to Andover and to the task of formulating a theology true to their teaching, if not to its more extreme forms of expression.

At Andover he wore himself out with rigourous study and in 1830, diploma in hand, he accepted a call to the Congregational church at Braintree, Massachusetts which parish he served until compelled by ill-health to resign in 1833. From 1836, when he received his call to Andover, until his retirement in 1881, he was the dominant member and principal ornament of the faculty, first as Bartlet Professor (1836-1847) and afterwards as the successor of Woods in the Abbot chair. In September of 1836, his career course set, he married Miss Anna Maria Edwards, a great-granddaughter of both Jonathan Edwards and Benjamin Franklin. In 1842 he suffered a recurrence of his eye problem, and again sought relief in travel, this time in Germany. There he consulted eye-specialists, worked away at the language, and made the acquaintance of several prominent theologians, among them Neander, Tholuck, and Hengstenberg. His health once more restored, he returned to Andover and his professorial duties. Unfortunately for his future health, he did not know how to husband his energies. He carried a heavy teaching load, preached regularly, and served as President of the Faculty. To these duties he added in 1844 the editorship of the journal **Bibliotheca Sacra**, continuing in that office until his retirement. Inevitably, his health again deteriorated, and again he sought surcease in travel, to Germany in 1863-64, and again to Germany and the Holy Land in 1869-70. His later years at Andover were marred by increasing controversy with the younger and more liberal-minded faculty. In 1893 Mrs. Park died after an exceptionally happy marriage of fifty-seven years. Park never really recovered from the loss. He lingered on in the old brick house at Andover where all of their life together had been spent, dying in his sleep on June 4th, 1900.

294

II

Natural Theology teaches the total depravity of man, the
decrees and the justice of God; and is thus a fit preparative
for that more glorious Theology which unfolds the gracious,
the redeeming, the electing, the regenerating love of the triune
Jehovah.[12]

In their joint essay on Natural Theology, ascribed to a Society of Clergymen
(actually, a society of two), Park and his dear friend and Andover colleague,
Professor Bela B. Edwards, address themselves to the prevailing indifference
to the subject on the part of those Congregationalist and Presbyterian clergy
who, in the opinion of the authors, ought to be its most devoted students
and defenders. For the province of Natural Theology, they are agreed, is one
of the greatest extent, comprising as it does, "that class of truths which relate
to God, his being, perfections, government and purposes; all considered
without a prominent reference to the duties and destination of man."[13] The
definition is broader than most philosophical theologians would allow. But
it is necessary that the definition be so broad since it is the one principal aim
of our authors to show how Natural Theology augments and justifies the
revealed Word.

The value of all studies, claims Park, may be measured by their tendency
to awaken our enthusiasm for the examination of the sacred oracles. "This
is a preeminent advantage of Natural Theology. It reveals to us the mercy
of God, and thus excites our curiosity to learn how he can pardon sin. It con-
vinces us of our future existence, and thus makes us inquisitive to ascertain
what will be the precise condition of the soul in the eternal world. It discloses
many truths which are essential to our moral welfare, but leaves so many relations of these truths unexplained, as to enkindle an intense desire to understand the word which bringeth life and immortality to light."[14] "The chief
use of Natural Theology," adds Edwards, "is that it forms the basis on which
all written revelation rests."[15]

It does so, he and Park think, by its proofs confirming the existence of
the God who reveals himself in scripture. For, they aver, "it will not be ques-

tioned that the logical order of our processes is to believe in the existence
of a being before we consider the truth or falsehood of his declarations....When
it is said, therefore, that the revealed system must be founded on Natural
Theology, it is meant, in part, that we must prove the existence and attributes
of the supreme Being from what he has done, before we can prove the truth
of the declarations purporting to be his."[16] That these proofs, specifically the
arguments from efficient causation and design, are valid, our authors do not
doubt. Park takes the principle of causality as an ultimate given, and that
despite the strictures of Hume as presented in his "remarkable Dialogues."
These last Park simply discounts. "It were," he thinks, "easy to prove by a
process of *reductio ad absurdum,* that we have no knowledge of an efficiency
in nature, if we have none of the Efficient Cause of nature."[17]

But the benefit is not all in the direction of revealed theology. As Natural
Theology contributes to our understanding of scripture, so much more does
that which has been revealed throw light on that which has been justified.
"There are," Park reminds us, "many dark passages in the volume of nature,
which are illustrated by the book of inspiration. The teachings of the former
volume are so far confirmed by the latter, so many of its deficiencies are supplied, that the right-minded student of the one will feel his knowledge to be
incomplete without an acquaintance with the other. Wherever the Bible has
been studied, Natural Theology has been cultivated, not because it could not
have been cultivated without the Bible, but because this book has reflected
so much light upon nature, as to make the lessons easy and alluring, which
were previously more difficult and repulsive. We feel a quickened interest in
the Bible, from the fact of its explaining so many enigmas in the creation."[18]
Why not, then, remain with the authority of scripture and let the proving
go. Because, says Park, not all men are to be won by the simple exhibition
of evangelical doctrine. "The internal evidence of scriptural truth is sufficient to convince honest inquirers, but for such as are not honest, more tangible
proofs are needed."[19] Thus, he concludes, "every preacher who would silence
gainsayers, especially everyone who aims to instruct the heathen, must be
familiar with the system of truth which the opposers of revelation feel compelled to believe."[20]

The theme is echoed in his inaugural address, On the Religious Influence of Theological Seminaries, delivered to the students and faculty of Andover on the occasion of his assumption of the Abbot Professorship. "The original law of our constitution," he tells them, "is that feeling shall follow perception, and in obedience to this law the heart is often enlarged as the under standing is expanded."[21] Given that it is so, the purpose of a seminary education is, he thinks, twofold: first, to acquire a large view of divine truth, and concurrently with that, to develop a capacity for holy love. Here again, as in his earlier exposition of the Duties of a Theologian, Park is suggesting that any truly adequate theology must do justice at once to the claims of the heart and the mind. Three years later he was invited to give the Convention Sermon at the annual meeting in Boston of the Congregational ministers of Massachusetts, and he seized the opportunity to clarify his conception of the nature and relation of the two modes of theology.

III

One chief benefit of theological controversy is, that it manifests the comparative *necessity* which the disputants feel for misrepresenting each other. He who has the greater need of this malpractice has the weaker cause.[22]

In New England ministerial reputations have been made, and sometimes ruined, by addresses delivered to Boston audiences. So it was with Edwards, Emerson, Channing, and Parker; so it is with Edwards Park on the occasion of his notable discourse on The Theology of the Intellect and that of the Feelings. The audience assembled in the Brattle Street Meeting House that May morning in 1850 was the usual clerical mix. Old Calvinists sat cheek by jowl with Hopkinsians, and both fraternized, for the duration of the sermon, with their Unitarian brethren. A conciliatory preachment was in order, and Park, very much aware of the diversity of doctrinal views represented by his hearers, had every intention of avoiding controversy. Unfortunately, as he tells us in a footnote appended to the published version of his sermon, "he was led into a course of thought which he was aware that some clergymen of Massachusetts would not adopt as their own, and for the utterance of which he was obliged to rely on their liberal and generous feeling." in this he was to be surely disappointed.

To illustrate his two modes of theology he offers two texts:

> The strength of Israel will not lie or repent: for he is not a man that he should repent. **I Samuel** 15:29.

> And it repented the Lord that he had made man on the earth, and it grieved him at his heart. **Genesis** 6:6.

The former exemplifies, according to Park, the theology of the intellect. The latter instances that of feeling, and, he contends, the two passages do not contradict one another.

> In order to make us feel the strength of God's aversion to sin, it (the second passage) declares that he has repented of having made our race, has been grieved at his heart for transgressors, weary of them, vexed with them. But it does not mean that these expressions which, as inflected by times and circumstances, impress a truth upon the soul, be stereotyped into the principle that Jehovah has ever parted with his infinite blessedness; for in order to make us confide in his stability, it (the first passage) denies that he ever repents, and declares that he is without even the shadow of turning.[24]

In brief, the first passage is supposed to be taken literally, the second figuratively. The first, to Park's view, is prose, the second, poetry. The first is truth, the second, faith. And should you ask how Park knows for certain that it is thus and so since biblicists may differ and the passages do not themselves advertise their status, he would reply:

> Has man been created with irresistible instincts which impel him to believe in a falsehood? Or has the Christian been inspired with holy emotions which allure him to an essen-

tially erroneous faith? Is God the author of confusion;—in his word revealing one doctrine and by his Spirit persuading his saints to reject it? If it be a fact, that the faithful of past ages, after having longed and sighed and wrestled and prayed for the truth as it is in Jesus, have at length found their aspirations rewarded by any one substance of belief, does not their unanimity indicate the correctness of their cherished faith, as the agreement of many witnesses presupposes the verity of the narration in which they coincide?[25]

For his part, Park has no doubt that consensus suffices to confirm doctrinal truth in most cases. That is because in some respects, but not in all, the theology of feeling coincides with that of intellect as regards the *substance* of truth,[26] as the figurative most frequently coincides with the literal in its root meaning.

Given this coincidence, the two modes of theology tend to coalesce, and Park himself allows that in those cases where they differ, "the intellect must be the authoritative power, employing the sensibilities as indices of right doctrine, but surveying and superintending them from its commanding elevation."[27] Noting this, Blau[28] and Cecil[29] argue that we have here to do, not with two theologies, nor yet with two forms of one theology, but with two forms of language. And certainly there are passages in the sermon which suggest that this is the fact of the matter. Thus Park, referring to the theology of feeling, speaks of, "the language of emphasis, of impression, of intensity....no more at variance with the intellectual theology than with itself."[30] and asks, "who calls this language an exaggeration of the truth? If interpreted by the letter, it does indeed transcend the proper bounds; but if interpreted as it is meant, as it is felt, it falls far short of them."[31]

Be it so, Park would deny that his two modes of theology are no more than two forms of language, and rightly, for his critics have tended to overlook the metaphysical foundation of the theology of feeling, namely, the Hopkinsian doctrine of regeneration by the immediate operation of the Holy Spirit. Throughout it is assumed "that man, with no extraordinary aid from Divine grace is obstinate, undeviating, unrelenting, perservering, dogged, *fully set* in those wayward preferences which are an abuse of his freedom. His unvaried wrong choices imply a full, unremitted, natural power of choosing right."[32] The *unrenewed* heart, he tells his hearers, is like a stone, needing to be exchanged for flesh, which God giveth as it hath pleased him. The substance of doctrine discerned in feeling must be right, for, says Park, "it is precisely adjusted to the soul, and the soul was made for it."[33] The theology of the feeling is anthropomorphic, intuitive, metaphorical, imprecise, poetic. It is free to be discordant, here affirming, there denying. But this is far from fitly being represented as nothing more than a figurative form of language. Its words, protests Park, cannot be called "*merely* figurative, in the sense of arbitrary or unsubstantial. They are the earliest, and....the most natural utterances of a soul instinct with religious life."[34] They are, in short, the outpourings of a regenerate heart.

Granting there really are, as Park claims, these two distinct modes of theology, the question remains: to what purpose is the distinction made? To the purpose, certainly, of providing a vehicle for the explanation and amelioration of the harsher doctrines of that Hopkinsianism which Park himself professes. In the course of his sermon he repeatedly impresses the theology of the feelings into this service. Are there difficulties as regards the logic of the Atonement? The theology of the feelings dissolves them.[35] Does the intellect allow the salvation of all men as a logical inference or question the imputation of the crime of one man to his millions of descendants?[36] Park advises reliance on the feelings. Does consistent Calvinism convey the impression that the divine government is harsh, pitiless, insincere, and oppressive? Put your trust rather in the feelings.

"So far as any statement is hurtful," writes Park in a paragraph omitted from the sermon as delivered, "it parts with one sign of truth. In itself," he continues, "or in its relations it must be inaccurate, whenever it is not congenial with the feelings awakened by the Divine Spirit. The practical utility, then, of any theological representations is one criterion of their propriety."[38] Practicality and propriety become one with the religious feelings when we recognize that "the dissonance of pious feeling, with the mere generalities of speculation or with any misapplied fragments of truth, tends to confine them within their appropriate, which is their usual sphere. In this light," he concludes, "we discern the necessity of right feeling as a guide to the right proportions of faith."[39]

The sermon was widely reviewed and, with one notable exception, the reviewers were kind. Park's leaning to liberalism was applauded, and such reservations as his critics confessed had more to do with his "rich rhetoric" than with the substance of his discourse. The exception was Charles Hodge, the redoubtable editor of, and principal contributor to, **The Biblical Repertory and Princeton Review.**

His career closely paralleled that of Park, or rather, Park's followed narrowly on that of Hodge, as the latter was the elder by eleven years, having been born at Philadelphia in 1797. Educated at the College of New Jersey and the Princeton Theological Seminary, Hodge, like Park, was offered a professorship at his clerical alma mater at the age of twenty-five, and, like Park at Andover, he would spend his entire professorial career at Princeton Seminary. Like Park, he helped to found a major theological journal and, like Park, he remained its editor for more than forty years. He traveled in Germany as a young man, met several of the same theologians Park was to encounter a decade later, and, again like Park, succeeded in due course to the principal professorship at his seminary. The span of his service was slightly longer, sixty-six years at Princeton, to Park's sixty-four at Andover. The parallelism extended even unto the beginning, length, and end of their lives: both had been born in the month of December, both lived to the age of eighty-two, and both died in the month of June.

In the area of theological scholarship, however, the two were hardly comparable. Hodge far surpassed Park in both the quantity and quality of his published work,[40] and in his lifetime was the more widely respected as a controversialist. As the principal Nineteenth Century champion of the Old Calvinism, he defended the pre-Edwardsian tradition against New Divinity schismatics and Unitarian heretics for sixty years. His most famous aphorism, quoted ad nauseam with glee by his Andover adversaries and by liberals who mistakenly thought it the epitome of fundamentalism, was that Princeton had never originated, nor ever would originate in his lifetime, any new idea. What he meant, of course, and professed lifelong, was the faith of our fathers, living still, in spite of Edwards, Hopkins, and Park.

In this peniultimate decade of the twentieth century, with its proliferation of denominations and chaos of cults, the substance of doctrine separating the Old Calvinism from the New Divinity is extremely dificult to determine with any precision. The similarities between Hopkins' **System of Doctrines** and Hodge's **Systematic Theology** far outweigh the differences they express, and the same may be said of the credos of Hodge and Park. Both are faithful in spirit to the dicta of Dort and Westminster. Each conceives of God as absolutely sovereign, and acknowledges the authority of his Word as given in Scripture. They are virtually as one in allowing that the sense of that Word is not always to be taken literally. And yet, Hodge feels himself obliged to speak of Park's Convention Sermon as "inimical to the authority of the word of God," and professes to see in it "such an attack on doctrines long held sacred as must make it right in those who believe these doctrines to raise their protest against it."[41]

That our author does not *intend* such an attack in his exposition of the two modes of theology, the reviewer[42] readily allows.

> We are far from supposing that the author regards his theory as subversive of the authority of the Bible. He has *obviously* adopted it as a *convenient* way of getting rid of certain doctrines, which stand out far too prominently in scripture and are too deeply impressed on the heart of God's people to allow of their being denied.[43]

As if one innuendo was not enough, Hodge adds a second:

> There is another advantage of this theory of which the Professor *probably* did not think. It enables a man to profess his faith in doctrines which he does not believe.[44]

So much, thinks Hodge, for motivation, and proceeds to "a brief analysis of the Convention Sermon.

He begins by calling the reader's attention to the two texts, **Genesis 6:6** and **I Samuel** 15:29. Here, he reminds us, are two assertions in direct conflict, God repented and God cannot repent. Both, given that Scripture is authoritative, must be true. But how are they to be reconciled? By assigning

302

the former to feeling and the latter to intellect, says Park. Hodge disagrees. "The texts do not belong to different categories; the one is not the language of feeling and the other of intelligence; the one does not affirm what the other denies."[45] The fact is, says Hodge, that both are figurative, both are intelligible. "The one, in its connexion, expresses God's disapprobation of sin, the other his immutability. The one addresses the sensibilities as much as the other; and the one is as much directed to the intellect as the other."[46] The point is, "that such language, when interpreted according to established usage, and made to mean what it was intended to express, is," Hodge insists, "not only definite in its import, but it never expresses what is false to the intellect."[47] The truth of the matter is that the feelings themselves are the intellect in a certain state. "In every case it is the truth as understood that is felt."[48] The texts in question, indeed, every passage cited by Park as an illustration of modes of expression which he holds the intellect would not adopt, is, to Hodge's way of thinking, really the product of that theology. Thus when Park tells us that the theology of the intellect would not originate the phrase that the soul expired, nor that "God the mighty maker died," when he assures us that "it would never suggest the unqualified remark that Christ has fully paid the debt of sinners, for it declares that this may be justly claimed from them, nor that he has suffered the whole punishment which they deserved, for it teaches that this punishment may still be righteously inflicted on themselves; nor that he has entirely satisfied the law, for it insists that the demands of the law are yet in force,"[49] he is, Hodges claims, substituting speculations of his own mind for the mind of God.

> Entirely irrespective, therefore, of the validity of our author's theory, we object to this sermon that it discards as the language of emotion, historical didactic argumentative statements, and in short everything he is not willing to receive, as far as appears, for no other reason, and by no other rule than his own repugnance to what is thus presented.[50]

As for Park's theory *qua* theory, it is, Hodge avers, predicated on an erroneous psychology. The theory assumes a distinction amounting to a dualism of the emotive and cognitive faculties beyond anything that experience warrants. "The very idea of a theology of feeling as distinct from that of the intellect, seems to take for granted that there are two percipient principles in the soul."[51] It supposes, as a matter of fact, two conflicting intelligences in each of us, the one judging a Bible text true, the other adjudging it false, and neither in contradiction. But the familiar fact that men may at one time judge a doctrine true and at another think it false is no proof of a theology of the intellect as distinct from that of the feelings. "Such vacillating judgements are really what they seem—contradictory apprehensions of the intellect."[52] The truth is, Hodge declares, "that all religious language is false to the intellect, is profane to the feelings and a mockery of God."[53] It makes no difference whether one finds such language in hymnal, homily, or confession. "Men may no more sing falsehood to God, than speak it in a sermon, or profess it in a creed."[54]

Stung by this contemptuous dismissal of what he had honestly intended as a gesture of conciliation,[55] and angered as much by the attacker's cloak of anonymity as by his *ad hominem* rhetoric, Park shortly repaired to his study, and in the next issue of **Bibliothecs Sacra** there appeared **Remarks on the Biblical Repertory and Princeton Review**. The article is deliberately dispassionate in tone. Park is acutely sensitive to the fact that he has little to gain and much to lose by engaging Hodge on his own low ground. The position taken is that the review is a caricature to be endured with patience, and he patiently sets about correcting the reviewer's "misstatements."[56]

Such mis-statements do not deserve or require refutation, claims Park, and proceeds to devote thirty-three pages to them. The charge that his sermon implies a dualism of faculties in the soul is met with a flat denial and a counterclaim: "the Reviewer's charge of dualism rests on his own oversight of the difference between *distinct* and *separate*," whereas "the sermon specifies two diverse *methods* of representing our personal identity."[57] "Throughout the sermon the distinction is between the "*intellectual statements* of doctrine," and the more "*impressive representations of it*," i.e., of the same doctrine."[58] Therefore, writes Park, softly turning the other cheek, "we will not borrow his own indecorous language, and say of his reasoning on the subject, that it "indicates a most extraordinary confusion of mind;" we only say that it makes a confusion of mode with essence, the forms of a thing with the thing itself?"[59]

There is one criticism, however, not so easily tolerated, and that is Hodge's claim that the sermon preaches Pelagianism. Outraged by this impugnation of his orthodoxy, Park is impelled to set forth at some length, and in the clearest terms, his teaching with respect to the dogmatic truths of Calvinism, and inasmuch as this is as specific a statement as may anywhere be found in his published writings, it merits extended quotation. According to Park:

> The author of the sermon has never doubted but firmly believes that in consequence of the first man's sin all men have at birth a corrupt nature, which exposes them to suffering, but not punishment, even without their actual transgression; which, unless divine mercy interpose, secures the certainty of their actual transgression, as soon as they can put forth a moral preference, and of their eternal punishment as the merited result of this transgression; a corrupt nature, which must be changed by the supernatural influence of the Holy Ghost before they will ever obey or morally please him; and therefore the author believes that men are by nature, i.e., in consequence, on account of it, sinners, and worthy of punishment "for all have sinned."
>
> The author of the sermon has never doubted but fully believes, that all converted men will be, on the ground of Christ's death, not only saved from punishment but raised to happiness, will be not only pardoned but justified, not only treated in important respects as if they had been positively and perfectly holy....
>
> It is a solemn truth, distinctly avowed in the discourse, that "There is a life, a soul, a vitalizing spirit of truth, which must never be relinquished; for the sake of peace even with an angel. There is....a line of separation which cannot be crossed between those systems which insert, and those which omit the doctrine of Justification by faith in the sacrifice of Jesus. This is the doctrine which blends in itself the

theology of intellect and that of feeling....'And, again, the author of the discourse avers, in the most prosaic language, that "the atonement has such a relation to the whole moral government of God, as to make it *consistent* with the honor of his legislative and retributive justice to save all men, and to make it essential to the highest honor of his benevolence or general Justice to renew and save some....

The author of the sermon believes, and has never implied the contrary, that Christ's death being vicarious, his sufferings being substituted for our punishment, we are literally unable, after having once sinned, to be saved without him; that we are not only redeemed from eternal punishment by his propitiatory sacrifice, but, even after we have been regenerated by his Spirit, we are entirely dependent on his grace in sending the same Spirit to secure our continuance in holiness; and, moreover, that we are every instant preserved in being by his Almightly power, so that without him we literally *cannot* even exist.[60]

In all of the above there is nothing significantly discordant with the tenets of Consistent Calvinism as codified by Hopkins and certified by Emmons. Of course, Hodge would have it that the whole Edwardean succession is suspect, but Park is more than willing to bear responsibility for his predecessors if only the reviewer and his readership will recognize that

although the sermon was designed to be homiletical rather than doctrinal, yet it incidentally teaches the dogmatic truths of Eternal Punishment, the Resurrection, the General Judgment, man's Entire Sinfulness, his Native Corruption, his need of Regeneration by the interposed influence of God, the Vicarious Atonement and "the doctrines which concentrate in and around it; and it repeatedly represents all Christian truth as that "which God himself has matched to our nicest and most delicate springs of action, and which, so highly

> does he honor our nature, he has interposed by miracles for
> the sake of revealing in his written word."[61]

This, Park thinks, still rankling from the reviewer's insinuation that his theory is subversive of and inimical to the proper authority of the Bible, should dispose once and for all of the reviewer's *argumentum ad captandum vulgus.*

Hodge professes not to understand what Park can possibly have in mind by such an invidious characterization of his argument. "We wrote a review which we intended to make a sort of model of candor and courtesy....to guard against discourtesy we resolved to abstain from all personal remarks and to confine ourselves to the theory under discussion."[62] Be that as it may, his resolution in his response to Park's **Remarks,** published in the very next number of the **Biblical Repertory,** is much more in evidence. His concern, however, is largely with the theory as such, rather than, as Park would prefer, with the specifics of the theory, because, says Hodge, "having failed to understand the Sermon, we shall not be presumptuous enough to pretend to understand the reply. It is not our purpose, therefore, to review it in detail."[63]

What his purpose is, he promptly makes plain. The main point at issue, he now contends, is nothing more than this: "Is that system of doctrine embodied in the creeds of the Lutheran and Reformed Churches, in its substantial and distinctive features, true as to its form as well as to its substance? Are the propositions therein contained true as doctrines, or are they merely intense expressions, true not in the mode in which they are there presented, but only in a vague, loose sense, which the intellect would express in a very different form."[64] True as doctrines, Hodge replies, realizing that this does not resolve the issue since attention to the history of Christianity reveals two great systems of doctrine in perpetual conflict.

> The one begins with God, the other with man. The one has as its object the vindication of the Divine supremacy and sovereignty in the salvation of men; the other has for its characteristic aim the assertion of the rights of human nature. It is especially solicitous that nothing should be held to be true, which cannot be philosophically reconciled with the liberty and ability of man.[65]

As he proceeds to the cataloging of the principles of this latter system, and
to a comparison of these with the principles of the former, a task which takes
him thirteen pages, it becomes apparent that the system which begins with
God is that Old Calvinism which Hodge himself champions, whereas the
system alleged to take its rise from man is the New Divinity of Park and his
theological predecessors.

This last, asserts Hodge, is characteristically rational. It seeks to explain
everything so as to be intelligible to the speculative understanding. Not so,
however, the former. It is confessedly mysterious.

> The Apostle pronounces the judgment of God to be un-
> searchable and his ways past finding out.... The origin of
> sin, the fall of man, the relation of Adam to his posterity,
> the transmission of his corrupt nature to all descended from
> him by ordinary generation, the consistency of man's
> freedom with God's sovereignty, the process of regeneration,
> the relation of the believer to Christ, and other doctrines of
> the like kind, do not admit of "philosophical explanation."[66]

It is, he claims, an undeniable historical fact that this former (Old Calvinist)
system expresses the position of the Church through history. Unfortunately,
In our own age and country, this system of doctrine has had to sustain a renewed conflict. It has been assailed by argument, by ridicule, by contempt. It
as been pronounced absurd, obsolete, effete, powerless....Still it stands. What
then is to be done? Prof. Park, with rare ingenuity answers, "Let us admit
its truth, but maintain that it does not differ from the other system. There
are two theologies, one for the feelings, the other for the intellect, or, what
may be made to mean precisely the same thing, two forms of one and the
same theology.[67]

To Park's reiterated remonstrance that he does not teach two theologies, Hodge
replies:

> It is perfectly immaterial whether Professor Park teaches that

there are "two theologies," or "two forms of one and the same theology." His readers understand the former expression precisely as they do the latter, after all his explanations. The former is the more correct, and has the usage of all ages in its favour. One great difficulty in regard to this sermon is, that its author wishes to change the established meaning of terms, and call new things by old words." [68]

Now, says Hodge, reverting to the previous question, the issue is not which of the two systems (two theologies) is true, or even whether either is true. "Nor is the question, which of the two Professor Park believes....The point to be considered is not so much a doctrinal one as a principle of interpretation....The question is whether there is any correct theory of interpretation by which the two systems above referred to can be harmonized?" [69] Park says they may and must, and his sermon is designed to that end. It was intended to, and does, teach that the "two theologies" though differing in form, agree in substance. "And further," says Hodge, "it is said expressly, "One aim of the sermon was to show that *all creeds which are allowable* can be reconciled with each other." " [70]

Here, he thinks, we strike the nerve of the matter. "We do not overlook the word *allowable*....We did not understand the sermon to advocate entire scepticism, and to teach that whatever may be affirmed, can with equal propriety be denied. Nor was it understood to teach that all religions are true....Nor did we understand our author to advocate that latitudinarianism which embraces and harmonizes all nominally Christian creeds....The sermon, therefore, was not regarded as a plea for Socinianism as an *allowable* form of Christianity. But it was understood to teach that "all allowable creeds can be reconciled with each other," [71] that is to say, the creeds and confessions of Lutheranism and the Reformed Churches.

This means, Hodge argues, if it means anything, that Old Calvinism, here taken as synonymous with the historic creeds and confessions, is reconcilable with the New Divinity, and certainly Park would not deny that his version of Calvinism is, to this extent, conciliatory. But Hodge will not have it so. "Can it," he asks, "be necessary to show that the differences between the two systems brought into view in this sermon, are substantial differences of doctrine and not a mere difference in words?"[72]

> The one system (Old Calvinism) says, the sin of Adam is imputed to his posterity. The other (New Divinity) says, the sin of Adam is *not* imputed to his posterity. ....The one system asserts, that the nature of man since the fall is sinful anterior to actual transgression. The other says, All sin consists in sinning, a passive nature existing antecedently to all free action cannot be sinful.[73]

These, Hodge insists, are real differences, not to be papered over by introduction of a theology of feeling. Either an inherent corruption exists anterior to voluntary action, or it does not, and the creeds of Christendom confirm that it does. "The whole Latin Church, the Lutheran, all the branches of the Reformed Church, unite in the most express "nicely measured" assertions of faith in this doctrine (of a prior inherent corruption)."[74] And should you beg leave to doubt it, Hodge is ready to confirm his claim with a wealth of citations from these same confessions and creeds.

To say that the sin of Adam is imputed to his posterity is to express a different thought, a different truth, a different doctrine, from what is expressed by saying, as does Park, the sin is in the sinning.

> The one of these statements is not merely an intense, figurative, or poetic expression of the thought conveyed by the latter. The former means that the sin of Adam was the judicial ground of the condemnation of his race, and therefore that the evils inflicted on them on account of that sin are of the nature of punishment....There is here a real distinction. These two modes of representing our relation to Adam belong to different doctrinal systems.[75]

That Park should think otherwise is, declares Hodge, owing to his having confused a truism, "figurative language is not to be interpreted literally," with the philosophical claim that, "right feeling may express itself in diverse, conflicting, and therefore in some cases, in wrong intellectual forms."[76] And what is this, he asks, if not to claim that religion consists essentially in feeling, and what is that if not an American version of the claim of Schleiermacher?

Hodge knows in his heart, of course, that Park, for all his emphasis on the religious role of feeling, is not so easily classified as an American Schleiermacher. "We do not mean to attribute to Professor Park anything more than the *principle* that religion consists essentially in feeling; we do not wish to be understood as ever insinuating that he holds either its adjuncts or its consequents."[77] Certainly, he ought to hold them. Given his equation of religion with feeling, it is only fair that he should teach the philosophy of the religion of feeling, and, Hodge believes, fair too that he should be taxed with the adjuncts and consequents.[78] Therefore, having voiced the disclaimer, he devotes the next several pages of his reply to an exposition of the Schleiermacherian theology, and concludes that "such, to the best of our understanding of the matter, is the theory to which the *radical principle* of Professor Park's sermon belongs."[79]

Having thus effected the reduction of Park's theology to that of Schleiermacher in its most simplistic form, Hodge finds fair game in Park's unguarded ascription of theological error to the confounding of poetry with prose. "Was it," he innocently inquires, "with this penny-whistle he discoursed such music as stole away the senses of a Boston audience?....Did he persuade the shrewd Athenians of America, that it was a feasible matter to interpret the Westminster Confession as a poem, and that men would never have peace until that feat was accomplished?"[80] He seems, Hodge muses, "to labor through this whole reply to persuade his readers that this is all he meant."[81]

Not so, Park replies. "The attempt of the Reviewer....to prove that there is another and a "German" theory, can serve no other purpose that to link the sermon with the (to many persons) "*hard name*" of Schleiermacher. It is an unworthy attempt. Had he given a fair exhibition of either the German theory or the sermon, he could not have failed to show their antagonism. He pretends that the sermon grows out of the indirect idea that "right moral feeling may express itself in wrong *intellectual* forms," by which he means, *false statements literally understood.* No such thing. The contrary is asserted throughout the discourse."[82] And Park adds, with this failure of the Reviewer to connect "a theory of Schleiermacher which has no more connection with the Sermon or Reply than it has with an acute-angled triangle,"[83] with the theology of the discourse, goes his attempt to find an irreconcilable difference between Old Calvinism and New Divinity. "But let us not plunge into extremes. Let us not infer that pious men....must either become latitudinarian and care nothing for their differences, or else denounce each other as Pelagian, and magnify their minor disagreements."[84] Let us recognize that the New Divinity is as much, if not more, concerned to proclaim the divine sovereignty as its Old Calvinist counterpart, and take heed instead of the Unity amid Diversities of Belief, even on Imputed and Involuntary Sin.

The title of this reply to Hodge's second article announces Park's new thesis: some of those who dispute on behalf of opposing allowable systems may sometimes be more harmonious than their creeds. Having established the thesis with respect to the systems of his and Hodge's theological forebears (given its generality and the careful qualification 'some at sometime,' he could hardly have failed in this endeavour), Park undertakes to apply the thesis to the doctrines of imputed and involuntary sin. "These doctrines," he tells us, "are singled out for various reasons. First, they have been imagined to be *the* fundamental doctrines of the Bible. Secondly, it is more difficult to reconcile the New England with the old Calvinism[85] on these subjects than on any other. If we can succeed here, we can succeed everywhere; and above all, on the doctrines of imputed righteousness, atonement, inability."[86] It is no coincidence, of course, that these last and imputed sin are precisely those doctrines in which Hodge finds the New Divinity particularly defective, and Park's purpose becomes clear when he tells us, thirdly, "the style of the old Calvinistic writers....and the manner in which they often explained it may illustrate the meaning of the phrase "theology of feeling." "[87]

Subsequently, the largest part of the fifty-three pages of **Unity amid Diversities** is given over to arguing that no substantial differences of doctrine can be predicated on a figurative language. The writings of Calvin and his European disciples are ransacked to prove their recognition of the figurative, as are Hodge's other works relating to the subject of original sin. The substance of Park's argument, in the main a textual criticism and reinterpretation of loosely related passages drawn from articles and books composed over a period of thirty years to the end of showing that Hodge himself has inconsistently indulged in figurative language indistinguishable in meaning from that remarked in the Sermon, defies compression. Suffice it to say, that he has little difficulty in making his case, since not even Hodge is capable of a perfect consistency of doctrinal statement over such an extensive tract of time.

> It is a plain case. There is no help for our Reviewer. He must agree with us so long as he does not retract his reiterated concessions (to the figurative). Here it stands. Is sin a transgression of the law? Yes. What law was addressed to our nature before our birth? No law except that addressed to our nature in Adam. Then there was no real sin, except as we were once in Adam. But our Adamic life was figurative, as our critic admits; then the resultant sin is figurative; and this is our passive sin. How can there be a literal transgression of a figurative law?[88]

If there cannot, and logic no less than common sense says that there cannot, then the theory of a passive state of sin anterior to the act of sinful transgression must be given up, and with it Hodge's claim of a real difference between the two allowable systems.

It remains, then, to renew the plea of conciliation, and Park thinks to find in Zwingli's suggestion that original sin as it exists in Adam's descendants is not properly a sin but a disease,[89] the model for the reconciliation of the two systems. Could we but agree on this formulation of the issue, Park supposes, our substantive difference would be resolved.

> This is our aim. With this design was an humble sermon preached on "the one theology in two forms." It was intended not to shield such men as Pelagius from the charge of heresy, but such men as our Reviewer, from the charge of remaining *steadfast* and *uniform* in an absurdity. It was meant to be an olive branch of peace.[90]

Hodge took due note of the "absurdity" (as Park surely intended he should), and secure behind the walls of Gibraltar and Ehrenbreitstein[91] scorned the olive branch.

By now Hodge was growing weary of the controversy, or so he says, for weary or not, the next issue of the **Princeton Review** carried his harshest judgment yet on Park and his Convention Sermon. He accuses him of not having understood the question at issue, and worse of "evasion and playing with words."[92]

There is not in the whole long article under consideration," he maintains, "any frank or manly discussion of principles. His (Park's) great object seems to be to elude pursuit by a copious infusion of ink."[93] Hodge objects to "the personal character he has given to the discussion"[94] (the pot calling the kettle black, this), and suspects "that when our author wrote his Convention Sermon he had no developed theory whatever."[95]

> There probably floated into his mind the simple principles, that men often say things in an excited state of the feelings, which mean more than their sober judgment can approve; that good people agree much nearer in experience than in their creeds; and that a man often changes his faith with his varying states of mind; and he thought he could, out of these principles, construct a scheme of union of all allowable creeds, and do away with the inconvenient obstructions of sound and unsound theology. But in the excitement of the work, his Pegasus ran away with him, and carried him over into the German camp, and when a friendly hand had to rouse him up and tells him where he has got to go, he insists he is still safe at home.[96]

This was condescension enough, but what really riled Park was Hodge's claim that in the articulation of these principles he had put himself "in special opposition to the faith of the New England churches," and to the teachings of its "venerable father" the sainted Edwards.[97] "It is," he cries, "Professor Park, and not we, who is the assailant of New England theology,"[98] and with that final barb he thought to have closed the controversy.

Park thought otherwise. The insinuation that his critic was closer in spirit, and even in doctrine, to Edwards and the New England theology, certainly must have rankled, the more so since he took enormous pride in the deference paid to him as the recognized heir of Edwards and Hopkins, and he quickly assayed to set the matter right. He begs leave, therefore, to explain the term 'New England theology', and to show that the theology of the Convention Sermon is faithful to its principles. "That sin consists in choice, that our natural power equals, and that it also limits, our duty,"[99] on these principles, says Park, Edwards, Bellamy, Hopkins, and Emmons are agreed, and so too is Park himself. To these principles, he notes, have been added those others which, since the time of Edwards, have marked their expositors as advocates of the New Divinity. Among these Park singles out the truth, "that an entirely depraved man has a natural power to do all which is required of him."[100] This old truth made new in the writings of Edwards and his disciples, taken in conjunction with the "three radical principles" above remarked, properly defines Calvinism it is improved form. "It does not pretend," says Park, "to be a perfect system....Neither does our system profess to be original in its cardinal truths....It is not new Calvinism, but it is consistent Calvinism."[101] And for fifty pages he descants on the differences between the creed which draws its life from Edwards, Bellamy, and Hopkins, and the "brittle theology" of Princeton, to the presumed detriment of the latter. No new argument in defense of the two modes of theology is offered, unless one regards the identification of these two modes with the New England theology as such, and the article drew no reply.

So it ended, as had the earlier controversies between Hopkins and Hart, Woods and Ware, and Taylor and Tyler, with each side feeling vindicated. That each could in good conscience think so was owing, in the main, to the narrowness of the doctrinal differences separating them. Unlike their predecessor controversialists, Hodge and Park are not fundamentally at odds on any major article of faith. That Hodge is able in all seriousness to claim a closer tie to Edwards than that of the professed Edwardeans, points up the closeness of their respective positions. Park himself concedes as much when he represents as merely verbal "the difference between our theory and that which our Reviewer adopts in those better hours, when he abandons the old

Augustinism.''[102] Both are loyal to Westminster and Savoy, as one in their orthodox views of Election and Atonement, differing only in some details of their notions of native depravity. Both stand squarely on the authority of the Bible. Both assume without question that it is trustworthy with respect to those portions of the Word intended by God to be taken literally. Both allow that much in scripture is properly to be treated as figurative or metaphorical. They differ incidentally insofar as Hodge will not agree that the figurative or metaphorical passage *may be* as Park affirms, *literally* false. To save the appearances and preserve consistency, Park proposes his theology of feeling. Consistency does not matter to Hodge; he will have it that both the figurative and the literal are true, each in their respective spheres, however inconsistent they may appear, since such consistency is a mystery Christians should not seek to penetrate. They are both theologically thin-skinned. Each never fails to take the measure of the innuendo of the other. Hodge is clearly the superior polemicist, and sheltered by the shield of an uncritical faith intuitively justified, his position is invulnerable. Park is at the greater risk, but has the better case, for all that he is no more willing than his predecessor Woods to accept Unitarianism as an ''allowable'' version of the gospel. As matters turned out, neither was destined to prevail, although that was not apparent at the time.

IV

> If any man will start, as did Edwards and Hopkins, with
> Biblical results, he will find at once, as they did, that these
> results are the germs of a true and comprehensive
> philosophy.[103]

Posterity has so far identified Park with the Convention Sermon that it has tended to overlook the fact that in 1850 the largest part of his production still remained to be written. The Memoirs of Hopkins and Emmons, the Introductory Essay to **The Atonement,** his commentary on the Andover Associate creed, and the bulk of his editorial work and compositions for the **Bibliotheca Sacra,** all follow upon the Theology of the Intellect and that of the the Feelings. In this last half-century of his life he would attain the zenith of his powers and influence as a pedagogue, and confirm his reputation as "the last of the consistent Calvinists," but never more would he aspire to break new theological ground. Never again would he venture into the uncharted realms of doctrinal speculation. The advent of Darwinism, which roused Hodge to battle, left Park strangely unmoved. The growing liberalism of the New England clergy only intensified his own commitment to orthodoxy as defined by Westminster and Andover. In the thirty years remaining of his academic career he would confine himself in classroom and in print to the defence of the faith once given to Edwards and Hopkins.

The opportunity, not to say the necessity, to do so arose almost immediately in consequence of the publication in the **Princeton Review** of a review article on Archibald Alexander's **Outlines of Moral Science.** The piece was unsigned, but the polemical style of the reviewer, who in praising his teacher Alexander took it upon himself to denigrate the moral philosophy of Edwards and his followers, left little doubt that Hodge had returned to the fray. His target here is the Dissertation on the Nature of True Virtue, which work, unlike that of the recently deceased Alexander, Hodge suggests Edwards would not wish to defend in going to confront his Maker. The Edwardean identification of true virtue with absolute benevolence or love to being in general appears to Alexander cum Hodge as a form of the false ethics of Utilitarianism.

This somewhat remarkable conclusion is arrived at by way of an identification of benevolence with happiness. From which, according to the reviewer, it follows that absolute benevolence equals general happiness. But general happiness, we are reminded, is at once the goal of Utilitarianism and the ultimate end envisaged by Edwards. Ergo, the moral philosophy of Edwards is Utilitarianism.

Nonsense, replies Park, the reviewer has confused Edward's use of 'ultimate' with his sense of 'last'. He does teach that the general happiness is the final object which righteous men aim to secure, that it is their 'ultimate end'...:"He calls an end *"ultimate*," because it is the last in a chain where a man's aim rests....Now because Edwards believes that the will of good men regards, ultimately in point of time, the general happiness, the **Princeton Review** accuses him of believing that this general happiness in the *only* good; just as if, because one good is the *last* which is sought, it is therefore the greatest, and because it is the *final* it is therefore the only good! Because there is to be a *last* day, can we infer that there is to be only one day?''[104] Obviously not, answers Park, and concludes that the Edwardean theory is neither that form of utilitarianism which represents happiness as the sole good, nor is it that which regards the happiness of creatures as the great object of pursuit. ''The greatest good in the universe is holiness, although in point of time the last goal aimed at is the general happiness....In point of dignity and worth, the chief end, which is a good in itself, is the love of the general holiness; but in the order of development, the final object of pursuit, the last but not the best, is the general happiness.''[105] That the reviewer has failed to see what, as a good biblicist he ought to have noticed, namely, that the Edwardean theory of virtue is that of the Son of God himself as given in **Matthew 22:37-40** is owing to the fact that his (and Alexander's) theory of virtue is based not, as it ought to be, on the scriptures, but on unaided reason! This was a low blow, and not entirely fair to the reviewer, but it was certainly no lower a thrust than the reviewer's insinuation that the dying Edwards would not care to defend his dissertation at the throne of God.

As for Park, he was prepared to defend the Edwardean cause in any venue. He was most particularly concerned that the doctrine of the Atonement be properly understood, and to that purpose published in 1859 a volume of some five-hundred plus pages of discourses and treatises on the Atonement by various of his predecessors and contemporaries, the whole prefaced by an Introductory Essay. This Essay is entirely devoted to the Christological views of the authors of the several treatises, which are beyond our purview to rehearse, and in any case it is not necessary that we do so since Park's own view of the doctrine is succinctly stated in his pamphlet, **The Associate Creed of Andover Theological Seminary.**

This work had its genesis in the effort of a number of the younger Andover professors and their supporters to soften the doctrinal requirements for election to an Andover professorship. The chief of these, in force from the foundation of the Seminary in 1808, specified that every candidate on the day of his inauguration publicly make and subscribe a solemn declaration of his faith in Divine Revelation, and in the fundamental and distinguishing doctrines of the gospel as expressed in the Associate Creed. Park himself had gladly made such profession, and had repeated it, as required by the rules, every five years. Succeeding generations, however, faced with increasingly liberal theological tendencies, had found themselves unable to subscribe in good conscience fully and faithfully to each and every article and, consequently, had proposed a "new departure," namely, that no higher standard of orthodoxy should be required of an Andover professor than that demanded of any Congregational or Presbyterian pastor. A publicly professed commitment to "the substance of the doctrines" of the creed should, they thought, suffice. Otherwise, they argued, the time will soon arrive when no professor will consent to subscribe to such an antiquated and obsolete confession of faith.[106] Park's retort was typical of the man. Should that day come when all of the Calvinistic ministers of New England have begun to hesitate,

> the Seminary is free to invite its professors and visitors from the Presbyterian Church, north, south, east, or west; and when the whole Presbyterian Church in America has departed from its Confession, the Seminary can import its professors from Scotland; and, when Scotland has declined, there will be ample time for considering what to do next![107]

Those who are for us will adopt the Creed; those who are not we do not need.

To simplify understanding of what is here involved, Park distinguishes four doctrines, "because their practical importance is easily seen, and because their truth has been recently denied or doubted:"[108]

> The first of these four doctrines is: The Bible, in all its religious and moral teachings, is entirely trustworthy![109]

> The second of the four doctrines is: All the moral actions of every man, before he is converted by the Divine Spirit, are opposed to the divine law, and are sinful![110]

> The third of these doctrines is the atonement; and this in-

cludes the following facts: The Son of God took upon
himself the office of High Priest, and offered his blood as
a sacrifice for all men; his sacrificial pains and death were
inflicted by his Father, were representative of the penalty
which the Father had threatened to men, were substituted
by the Father, for the actual punishment of believers, were
equivalent to that punishment in honoring and vindicating
the Father's holiness, distributive justice, and law; were needed, first of all, on God's account and in order that he may
forgive the sins of the penitent; and accordingly the crucifix-
ion of the Lamb of God, and the sufferings preparatory to
it, and implied in it, are the sole and exclusive ground on
which the penitent are saved: and therefore the grace of
Christ, as manifested in his sacrificial pains, is the brightest
of all his glories![11]

The fourth doctrine is: the present life is the only state of
probation; the future state is a state, not of probation, but
of punishment: the punishment of incorrigible transgressors
begins as soon as they die, and continues forever![12]

To each of these four doctrines, and most particularly and in greatest detail
to the third, Park subscribed without reservation. In these doctrines he was
educated in his early youth.

I believed them before I ever saw the walls of Andover, and
I was more deeply convinced of their truth while I was a student in the Seminary and have been still more profoundly
convinced by my intercourse with two of the divines (Emmons and Woods) who helped to insert these doctrines into
the Associate Creed. From the fact that I have occupied my
chair with the *consciousness of accepting* all these doctrines,
it is an illogical inference that other persons may occupy

320

> chairs of instruction in the Seminary while they have the *con-*
> *sciousness of not accepting* all these doctrines.[113]

When the time came for him to retire, Park nominated his sometime student and disciple, Frank Hugh Foster, as his successor, and his disappointment when his candidate was passed over in favor of a proponent of the "new departure" must have been extreme. The defeat of his nominee he could, and did, as Foster himself tells us, "accept in silence."[114] But as far as the "new departure" was concerned, he felt duty-bound to oppose it with all his might, and he did so to his dying day.

V

> Of course, his most ardent admirers would not think of placing him in the same rank with the great pioneers in theology....Yet among the choir-leaders of the New England theology since Edwards, he has hardly been surpassed in acumen, and it is he who closes the series.[115]

Subsequent generations have taken for granted Fisher's conclusion, echoed by Foster, tending thereby to overlook and undervalue the later contribution to consistent Calvinism of Samuel Harris. However, if Park was not, strictly speaking, the last of the consistent Calvinists, he was generally perceived to be the champion of a creed outworn. Hodge had long since gone to his reward, and the "new theology" was not disposed to emphasize the logic of the divine sovereignty. Even so, this perception is hardly just to one who, as Cecil rightly remarks, "was in the best sense a mediating theologian."[117] That it prevailed is, I suspect, largely owing to the readiness of students of the period to take as gospel Frank Hugh Foster's two surveys of Park's system, first in 1906 in the **Genetic History** and thirty years later in the **Life**. After all, who would know better the true worth of that system than Park's own choice of a successor. Unfortunately for Park's later reputation, Foster's understanding of his old teacher is that of an uncritical admirer ("He was himself a greater mind than Edwards.") long since disenchanted with his old teacher's theological viewpoint. Moreover, it is a judgment based not so much on Park's published writings as on Foster's notes and recollections of classroom lectures delivered extempore.[18] This is not to imply that Foster falsifies Park. The doctrines that the pupil attributes to his master, Park certainly maintained. The question is rather one of emphasis and whether a theologian is more properly assessed on the basis of his published work rather than as the professor of an unwritten system of doctrines.

Park's works, obviously, are not to be classed with those of Edwards, or even with those of Hopkins and Emmons. In this much, George P. Fisher's judgment is absolutely correct. He is not in the same rank with the great pioneers of theology. It is not as an original thinker that he deserves to be remembered, but rather as a sharp and dedicated advocate of the New Divinity, and in that lesser supporting role his importance is undeniable. He successfully indoctrinated two generations of Congregationalist clerics in the tenets of Hopkinsianism, and his prowess as a polemicist postponed the "new departure" for the better part of a third. Had he been able to keep his health and, more important, had he continued to develop his thinking along the lines laid down in the Convention Sermon, the transition from the New Divinity to the Darwinian world of the New Departure would have been accomplished much earlier and easier.[19] For Park, contrary to the prevailing impression, was no enemy to evolution. He had long been aware of the literal falsity of the six days of creation, had read and favorable reviewed Lyell's **Principles of Geology,**[20] and, unlike his great opponent Hodge, he remained undismayed by the impact of Darwinism on theology. But he was very tired, and the state of his health left him with little energy for the good fight. He continued to repair regularly to his study with the end in view of reworking his lectures into a system of doctrines, but nothing came of the effort and the times simply passed him by.

Bibliographical Essay

Park left no system. In his retirement he projected putting into systematic form the bits and pieces of theology scattered throughout his published addresses, articles, discourses, essays, memoirs, memorials, reports, reviews, and sermons, and in his unpublished notes and lectures, but failing eyesight and a general deterioration of his health prevented his bringing the project to fruition. In the event, it would have been a monumental, if not impossible, task for any septuagenarian of whatever state of mental and physical fitness considering that the total number of his publications, exclusive of book-reviews, exceeded two hundred. All of these, together with a representative selection of some seventy-four of his four hundred book-reviews, are listed in Anthony Clay Cecil Jr., **The Theological Development of Edwards Amasa Park: Last of the Consistent Calvinists,** unpublished Ph.D dissertation, Yale University, 1973 (Ann Arbor: University Microfilms, #73 16768, pages 271-337). A model of what a dissertation should be, but rarely is, Cecil's prose is eminently readable and his scholarship is superior. It is greatly to be regretted that this work remains unpublished since it is the better of any of the secondary sources remarked below.

There are two collections of sermons: **Discourses on Some Theological Doctrines as Related to the Religious Character** (Andover: Warren F. Draper, 1885), and **Memorial Collection of Sermons** (Boston: Pilgrim Press, 1902). This latter includes the famous Convention Sermon, The Theology of the Intellect and that of the Feelings, originally published in **Bibliotheca Sacra,** VII, No. XXVII, Article VI (July, 1850), 533-569, and subsequently reprinted several times, most recently in Joseph L. Blau (editor), **American Philosophical Addresses 1700-1900** (New York: Columbia University Press, 1946). Of the articles that antedate the Convention Sermon, the most important for the understanding of Park's theological perspective are: the Bartlet Professorship Inaugural Address, 'Connection between Theological Study and Pulpit Eloquency', **American Biblical Repository,** X, No. XXVII, Article VIII (July, 1837), 169-19; 'The Mode of Exhibiting Theological Truth', **American Biblical Repository,** X, No. XXVIII, Article X (October, 1837), 436-478; the Address to the Theological Society of Dartmouth College on the 'Duties of a Theologian',

American Biblical Repository, Second Series, No. IV, whole number XXXVI, Article VI (Octobr, 1839), 347-380; and 'Natural Theology,' **Bibliotheca Sacra,** III, No. X, Article 11 (May, 1846), 241-284. This last "furnished by a Society of Clergymen" (actually, Park and his colleague Professor Bela B. Edwards).

The theological implications of the Convention Sermon as viewed from the Old Calvinist or Princeton perspective are anonymously held up to critical view by Charles Hodge, 'Professor Park's Sermon,' **The Biblical Repertory and Princeton Review,** XXII, No. IV, Article VII (October, 1850), 642-674. Park was provoked to reply with 'Remarks on the Biblical Repertory and Princeton Review,' **Bibliotheca Sacra,** VII, No. XXIX, Article IX (January, 1851), 135-180. This, in its turn, prompted a further spate of criticism from Hodge, '**Remarks on the Princeton Review,** Vol. XXII, no. IV, article VII by Edwards A. Park,' **The Biblical Repertory and Princeton Review** XXIII, No. II, Article VI (April, 1851), 306-347. Stung by this continuing drumfire of hostile criticism, and by Hodge's insinuations of heresy and worse, Park published 'Unity amid Diversities of Belief, even on Imputed and Involuntary Sin,' **Bibliotheca Sacra** VIII, No. XXXI, Article VII (July, 1851), 594-647. But Hodge would not let the matter rest, and there shortly appeared 'Unity amid Diversity of Belief even on Imputed and Involuntary Sin; with Comments on a Second Article in the Princeton Review relating to a Convention Sermons,' **The Biblical Repertory and Princeton Review,** XXIII, No. IV, Article VII (October, 1851), 674-695. Park, however, had the last word in the controversy with 'New England Theology, **Bibliotheca Sacra IX,** No. XXXIII, Article VII (January, 1852), 170-220. Hodge greatly disapproved, but forebore to reply; thereafter Andover and Princeton would remain in the antipodes of Calvinism in America.

Another article in the exchange between Andover and Princeton, unrelated to the Hodge/Park controversy, but important for the light it throws on Park's subscription to the Edwardsian ontology, is the unsigned essay ("It cannot with truth be ascribed to any one individual") by Park and his Andover colleagues concerning 'President Edwards's Dissertation on the Nature of True Virtue,' **Bibliotheca Sacra,** X, No. XL, Article III (October, 1853), 705-738. This is essentially a straightforward defense of the Hopkinsian interpretation as opposed to the utilitarian interpretation favored by Princeton.

Every five years Andover required of its professors that they publicly subscribe to a statement of beliefs prepared by the Hopkinsian founders of the seminary. Park's own interpretation of this statement of New Divinity principles is justified in detail in **The Associate Creed of Andover Theological Semianry** (Boston: Franklin Prss, 1883) and further attested to in the anonymously published **A Declaration of Faith** (Boston: Thomas Todd, 1884).

Park's principal biographical works, in addition to the book-length Memoirs of Hopkins and Emmons, include the studies of his colleagues, Professors Leonard Woods and Bela B. Edwards. **The Life and Character of Leonard Woods Jr.** (Andover: Warren F. Draper, 1880), and **Memoir** in **Writings of Professor B.B. Edwards,** 2 vols. (Boston: John P. Jowett, 853), I, 1-370. Also the Memoir of his sometime pupil at Amherst and Andover, W.B.Homer, in **Writings of the Rev. William Bradford Homer,** second edition (Boston: T.R. Marvin, 1849), 13-136. **The Atonement, Discourses and Treatises,** edited with an important introductory essay, 'Rise of the Edwardean Theory', by Park (Boston: Congregational Publishing Society, 1859) comprises materials on the subject by Edwards Jr., Smalley, Maxey, Emmons, Griffin, Burge, and Week. By Park also are the entries in the **Schaff-Herzog Encyclopedia** for New England Theology, Hopkinsianism, and the individual entries for Jonathan Edwards, father and son. Joseph Bellamy, Eliphalet Pearson, John Smalley, Samuel Spring, Nathan Strong, Moses Stuart, Stephen West, and Samuel Worcester.

The secondary source materials are a mixed bag. Frank Hugh Foster's chapter on the theology of Park, a revised version of his article, 'Professor Park's Theological System', **Bibliotheca Sacra,** LX (April, 1903), 672-697, is largely localized to a consideration of Park's attempts to circumvent the difficulties inherent in the Edwardsian doctrine of the will. His **Life of Edwards Amasa Park** (New York: Fleming H. Revell, 1936) is essentially a rhapsody of praise from a former student who, ironically, no longer finds it possible to believe in his teacher's theology. Moreover, Foster has relied heavily on the eulogy of Dr. R.S. Storrs, **Edwards Amasa Park, Memorial Address** (Boston: Samuel Usher, 1900) **Pupils** (Boston: Samuel Usher, 1899) for his anecdotes. At the other extreme are the articles by Charles Hodge listed above.

The serious student of Park's theology will want to take note of the following articles: Newman Smyth, 'Orthodox Rationalism', **Princeton Review,** LVIII, No. IV (May, 1882), 294-312; John Williams, 'New England Theology', **Church Review and Ecclesiastical Register,** V No. III (October, 1852), 349-360, and VI, No. I (April, 1853), 82-100; Jeremiah Eames Rankin, 'Edwards Amasa Park', **Bibliotheca Sacra** LX (April, 1903), 201-222; and George P. Fisher, 'Professor Park as a Theologian', **The Congregationalist,** LXXXV, 24 (June 14th, 1900).

There are in addition to Cecil two dissertations: Kenneth Elmer Rowe, **Nestor of Orthodoxy, New England Style: A Study in the Theology of Edwards Amasa Park,** Ph.D dissertation, Boston University, 1969, and Gary Dale Long, **The Doctrine of Original Sin in New England Theology: from Jonathan Edwards to Edwards Amasa Park,** Ph.D dissertation, Dallas Theological Seminary, 1972.

326

[1]Frank Hugh Foster, **A Genetic History of the New England Theology**, 258-259.

[2]Edwards Park, 'Connection between Theological Studies and Pulpit Eloquence', **American Biblican Repository**, X no. XXVII, Article VIII (July, 1837), 191. An address delivered on the occasion of his inauguration as Bartlet Professor.

[3]Ibid., 188.

[4]Ibid., 182.

[5]Edwards Park, 'The Mode of Exhibiting Theological Truth', **American Bibilical Repository**, X. no. XXVIII, Articles X (October, 1837), 463.

[6]Ibid., 447. For a further elaboration of Park's view of the nature of a "true sermon", see his essays, 'Power in the Pulpit', **Bibliotheca Sacra**, IV, no. 13 (February, 1847), 96-117; 'Dignity and Importance of the Preacher's Work', **Christian Review**, IV, no. 16 (December 1839), 581-603; and 'Plainness as a quality of Sermons', **Christain Review**, V, no. 20 (December, 1840), 481-510.

[7]Edwards Park, 'Duties of a Theologian', **The American Biblical Repository**, Second Series, no. IV, whole no. XXXVI, Article VI (October, 1839), 374.

[8]Ibid., 380.

[9]Ibid.

[10]Edwards, the second of the four sons of Calvin Park, Professor of Moral Philosophy at Brown, and Abigail Ware (Park), was born at the family home in Providence on December 29th, 1808. He attended town schools in Providence and afterwards the academy at Wrentham. It was, he recalled in later life, a very poor school. However, the boy was precocious and disposed to hard study, and his father's tutelage overcoming the shortcomings of his formal schooling, he qualified for admission to Brown, which he entered at the early age of thirteen, graduating in 1826 several weeks before his eighteenth birthday. For a brief period thereafter he taught school, and then, forming the purpose of training for the congregational ministry, studied theology for a year with his father, who had himself been ordained some years earlier.

[11]Quoted by Frank Hugh Foster, **The Life of Edwards Amasa Park** (New York: Fleming H. Revell Company, 1936), 31.

[12]'Natural Theology', **Bibliotheca Sacra**, III, no. X, Article II (May, 1846), 273. All but the last eight pages of the article, which are the work of Edwards, are rightly ascribed to Park.

[13]Ibid., 246.

[14]Ibid., 273.

[15]Ibid., 276.

[16]Ibid., 276, 277.

[17]Ibid., 259.

[18]Ibid., 273-274.

[19]Ibid., 275n.

[20]Ibid., 275.

[21]Edwards Park, 'On the Religious Influence of Theological Seminaries', Introductory essay in the **Writings of William Bradford Homer** (Boston: T.R. Marvin, 1849), xiv.

[22]Edwards Park, 'New England Theology', **Bibliotheca Sacra**, IX, no. XXXIII, Article VII (January, 1852), 173n.

[23]Edwards Park, 'The Theology of the Intellect and that of the Feelings', **Bibliotheca Sacra**, VII, no. XXVII, Article VI (July, 1850), 533n. Hereafter cited as Convention Sermon with page number.

[24]Ibid., 537.

[25]Ibid., 544.

[26]"The theology of the intellect and that of the feelings tend to keep each other within the sphere for which they were respectively designed, and in which they are fitted to improve the character. Both of them have precisely the same sphere with regard to many truths, but not with regard to all. (Ibid., 550-551)

[27]Ibid., 545.

[28]Joseph L. Blau, **American Philosophical Addresses 1700-1900** (New York: Columbia University Pres, 1946), 640.

[29]Anthony Clay Cecil Jr. **The Theological Development of Edwards Amasa Park: Last of the Consistent Calvinists,** Ph.D. dissertation, Yale Univesity, 1973 (University Microfilms #73 16768), 99.

[30]Convention Sermon, 549.

[31]Ibid.

[32]Ibid., 548.

[33]Ibid., 544-545.

[34]Ibid., 538.

[35]Ibid., 535.

[36]Ibid., 545,535.

[37]Ibid., 545.

[38]Ibid., 555.

[39]Ibid.

[40]His major works are his **Commentary on the Epistle to the Romans** (1835), **The History of the Presbyterian Church in the United States** (1840), a best-seller (35,000 copies sold), **Way of Life** (1841), his magnum opus, **Systematic Theology** in three volumes (1871-1873), and the anti-evolutionist tract, **What is Darwinism** (1874). Like Park he was a prolific contributor to periodicals, publishing more than 130 articles and numerous reviews.

[41]Charles Hodge, 'Professor Park's Sermon', **The Biblical Repertory and Princeton Reveiw,** XXII, no. IV, Article VII (October, 1850), 646.

[42]The article was unsigned, although Park and, presumably, much of the readership of the **Princeton Review** readily discerned the author by the style and pattern of his argument.

[43]'Professor Park's Sermon', 646. My italics.

[44]Ibid., 646. My italics.

[45]Ibid., 652.

[46]Ibid.

[47]Ibid.

[48]Hodge, 'Professor Park's Sermon', 668.

[49]Park, Convention Sermon, 535.

[50]'Professor Park's Sermon', 535.

[51]Ibid., 660.

[52]'Professor Park's Sermon, 660.

328

⁵³Ibid., 665.

⁵⁴Ibid., 666.

⁵⁵"The title of the sermon was selected as a deferential and charitable one. It was designed to mitigate prejudices by conceding somewhat to them." Park, 'Remarks on the Biblical Repertory and Princeton Review,' **Bibliotheca Sacra,** VIII, no. XXIX, Article IX (January, 1851), 140. Hereafter cited as **Remarks** with page number.

⁵⁶"The Repertory mis-states the very object of the discourse. It describes the sermon as advocating not two different forms but two essentially antagonistic "**kinds** of theology," two opposing sets of "*doctrine*," both equally correct. it recognizes no difference between an image or symbol, and a truth. As many of its reasonings are directed against a wrong subject, they spend themselves like arrows aimed at the wrong target." **Remarks,** 142. Park's italics.

⁵⁷Ibid., 147, 148.

⁵⁸Ibid., 143.

⁵⁹Ibid., 148.

⁶⁰Ibid., 15-66-167, 168, 169. The quoted passage inside the quoted material is from the Convention Sermon, op. cit. 559.

⁶¹Ibid., 171-172. The quoted passages inside the quoted material are from the Convention Sermon, op. cit. 561-544.

⁶²Charles Hodge, 'Remarks on the Princeton Review, Vol. XXII, no. IV, Article VII by Edwards A. Park,' **The Biblical Repertory and Princeton Review,** XXIII, no. II Article VI (April, 1851), 306-307.

⁶³Ibid., 307.

⁶⁴Ibid.

⁶⁵Ibid., 308-309.

⁶⁶ibid., 317-318.

⁶⁷Ibid., 319.

⁶⁸Ibid., 337n.

⁶⁹Ibid., 320.

⁷⁰Ibid., 322. Quoting Park, **Remarks,** 175. My italics.

⁷¹Ibid., 322.

⁷²Ibid., 327.

⁷³Ibid., 325.

⁷⁴Ibid., 324n.

⁷⁵Ibid., 327-328n.

⁷⁶Ibid., 333.

⁷⁷Ibid., My italics.

⁷⁸"Professor Park may ask, what has all this to do with his convention sermon? That discourse does not teach that all religion consists in feeling, nor does it advocate the view of revelation and inspiration deduced from the principle. Very true. But it does teach one of the main principles of the theory in question. It does teach that right feeling may express itself in inconsistent intellectual forms." Ibid., 346.

⁷⁹Ibid., 336. My italics.

[80]Ibid., 341.

[81]Ibid., 341n.

[82]Park, 'Unity amid Diversities of Belief, even on Imputed and Involuntary sin, with Comments on Second Article in the Princeton Review relating toa Convention Sermon,' **Bibliotheca Sacra,** VIII, no. XXXI, Article VII (July, 1851), 596n.

[83]Ibid., 646n.

[84]Ibid., 594.

[85]Not to be confused with the Old Calvinist position as maintained by Hodge. The Old Calvinism and old Calvinistic writers to which Park refers are the European antecedents of himself and Hodge.

[86]'Unity amid Diversities,' 607.

[87]Ibid., 607.

[88]Ibid., 640.

[89]'Zuingli (sic), in his **De Peccato Originali Declaratio,** says that he will not contend about a word, that he will permit men to call our native tendency to self-love by the name of sin....but he insists that so far forth as it is passive and inborn, it is "not sin but a disease"." Ibid., 644.

[90]Ibid., 647.

[91]the reference is to Hodge's footnote "**Remarks,** 319n): "The New York Independent, in a notice of our former review (of Park's sermon), objected to the tone of confidence with which we wrote on this subject. How can we help it? A man behind the walls of Gibralter, or of Ehrenbreitstein, cannot, if he would, tremble at the sight of a single knight, however gallant or well-appointed he may be. His confidence is due to his position, not to a consciousness of personal strength."

[92]Hodge, 'Unity amid Diversity of Belief and even on Imputed and Involuntary Sin; with comments on a Second Article in the Princeton Review relating to a Convention Sermon,' **The Biblical Repertory and Princeton Review,** XXVII, no. IV, Article VII (October, 1851), 687.

[93]Ibid., 694.

[94]Ibid., 688.

[95]ibid., 693.

[96]Ibid.

[97]Ibid., 684.

[98]Ibid., 694.

[99]Park, 'New England Theology,' **Bibliotheca Sacra,** IX, no. XXXIII, Article VII (January, 1852), 175.

[100]Ibid., 177.

[101]Ibid., 184.

[102]Ibid., 219n.

[103]Park, 'President Edward's Dissertation on the Nature of True Virtue,' **Bibliotheca Sacra,** X, no. XL, Article III (October, 1853), 725. W.F. Draper's **Index to the Bibliotheca Sacra** (Andover: Warren F. Draper, 1874) credits the article to Park, albeit the author indicated on the title page is "An Association".

[104]Ibid., 719.

[105]Ibid., 723.

[106]Their presentiment was fulfilled. Andover did close it doors, although not until long after Park had passed from the scene.

[107]Park, **The Associate Creed of Andover Theological Seminary** (Boston: Franklin Press, 1883), 97.

[108]Ibid., 3.

[109]Ibid.

[110]Ibid.

[111]Ibid., 4.

[112]Ibid., 5.

[113]Ibid., 86.

[114]Foster, **Life of Edwards Amasa Park**, 239.

[115]George P. Fisher, **Congregationalist**, LXXXV (June 14th, 1900), 24.

[116]He "closes the series" of the New England divines. The system collapsed after his resignation of the Abbot chair and during his lifetime." **Life**, 253. Foster is technically correct. The system did collapse in Park's lifetime if one includes in that the years in retirement during which Samuel Harris was writing and publishing his neglected trilogy.

[117]**Theological Development of Edwards Park**, 267.

[118]Foster, **Genetic History**, 503.

[119]According to Blau, 'Park's emphasis on the emotional and moral side of religious life makes the (Convention) sermon stand out as one of the precursors of such a "new" theology as did in fact develop out of the thought of his contemporary Horace Bushnell.' Joseph L. Blau, **American Philosophical Addresses 1700-1900** (New York: Columbia University Press, 1946), 625-626.

[120]Park, Review of Sir Charles Lyell, **Principles of Geology**, 11th revised edition, **Bibliotheca Sacra**, XXXI (October, 1874), 785-790.

VII LAURENS PERSEUS HICKOK

"Theology cannot triumph in the adoption of a philosophy which gainsays it." — Laurens Hickok[1]

> Canst thou by searching find out God? canst thou find out
> the Almighty unto perfection? It is as high as heaven; what
> canst thou do? deeper than hell; what canst thou know?....
> I know that thou canst do every thing....things too wonder-
> ful for me, which I knew not."[2]

In eighteenth century America that answer passed for sound philosophy. The authority of Locke lent it credence: if there was no knowledge transcendent of sensation, he would be a fool indeed who would presume to formulate a metaphysics of the supernatural. Better to believe with Edwards, Bellamy, Hopkins, and Emmons in the absolute sovereignty of an arbitrary God, and trust for the rest, to the harmony of doctrine ready to hand in scripture. What the senses left in doubt, revelation would make good. So they thought, and as yet there was no one in America to call in question the truth of their presupposition.

In Europe it was, as usual, a different story. The comfort which the more intellectual among the faithful had gained from Locke's conviction of the reasonableness of Christianity was, owing to Hume, long since lost. Nor did the efforts of Kant suffice to reestablish their ebbing confidence in the arguments of the orthodox. The faith the Critiques of this latter had made room for was not such as any Calvinist could rest easy in. And there was worse to come. The post-Kantians moved quickly to positions no biblicist could aspire to share. The authority of the Bible itself was impugned by successive waves of German critics. Inevitably, their works found shelf room in American college and seminary libraries. Young men whose fathers had been brought up on Dwight's **Theology Explained** now were faced with the challenge to the faith posed by the new German infidelity. Most failed the test, but here and there a questing spirit, undeterred by barriers of language and undismayed by alien ideas, began to read and to wonder. One such was Emerson; Theodore Parker was another; a third, earlier, and in some ways more dedicated to the new philosophy than his Unitarian contemporaries, was Laurens Perseus Hickok.

His forebears were colonial stock, several generations resident at Danbury (and its suburb, Bethel), Connecticut. There, on the next to the last day of the year 1798, Hickok was born. He attended local schools, and in 1820 was graduated from Union College. He taught school and studied for the ministry with Bennet Tyler, a Calvinist firmly committed to the doctrines of total depravity, the federal headship of Adam, and the absolute sovereignty of God. Presumably young Hickok subscribed to each of these, for in 1823, having been duly examined and approved by the local consociation, he was ordained to the Congregational Church at Kent, Connecticut. Here he remained until 1829, when, heeding a second call, he removed to the church at Litchfield. In 1836 he abandoned the pastorate for a position as professor of theology at Western Reserve College. From 1844 to 1852, when he returned to Union College[3] as vice-president and professor of mental and moral science, he occupied the chair of Christian Theology in the Auburn (New York) Theological Seminary.

His address, **Theology as a Science,** delivered on the occasion of his inauguration to this chair, at once proclaims his commitment to consistent Calvinism and anticipates the character of the argument of his later works. It is, he maintains, fully as much in accordance with God's will that there should be a thorough science of the Christian Religion, as it is that there should be a coherent science of nature. "Both fields are full of God, and each exhibits the most astonishing traces of the magnitude and the minuteness of his superintending wisdom, and each should be studied, both in their facts and their laws...."[4] The authority of Dwight notwithstanding, we need not and should not settle for allowing that the facts and laws of our Christian religion are of a mysteriousness precluding philosophical investigation. To the contrary, we must philosophize, and that because, as Kant has taught us,

> "Facts, alone, give mere appearance; Principles, alone, give
> mere theory: facts, in combination with their principles, give
> valid science. In getting facts, we merely *observe*; in attaining principles, we merely *speculate*; in binding facts by principles into systems, we first of all *philosophize*."[5]

Wherefore we may say that "A Philosophy of Nature no more legitimately exists, than there may exist a Philosophy of the Christian Religion."[6]

In treating of Theology as Science, the facts to be subsumed under principles divide, according to Hickok, in three portions, the ritual, the doctrinal, and the spiritual. The first of these need not detain us, for all that our speaker, cognizant of the interest of his audience, spends several pages of his text discussing that principle of symbolism[7] which gives consistency and system to all the facts in the ritual of religion. Nor need we dawdle over the principle of the doctrinal, i.e., the complete harmonizing of righteous authority with mercy, since that too is of small account when set against the principle of the spiritual of religion.

> Both the ritual and the doctrinal may be fully comprehended in their facts and principles, and if the spiritual be excluded all is worthless and vain. Formality is worthless; and dead orthodoxy is worthless; all of religion is worthless; except as the spiritual is diffused through it, and interpenetrates and quickens every part."[8]

Religion to be known must be studied as a living product, a life everywhere quickening in the regenerate. We seek the law or principle in this life, and we find it, says Hickok, in that grandest of principles, *"faith in the Son of God."*[9]

In company with Edwards, Bellamy, and Hopkins, Hickok holds fast to the conviction that the essence of all spiritual life is love, but where they emphasize the duty of disinterested benevolence, he stresses worthiness. "*Worthiness to be happy* is the ultimate end and aim of love. And here, the only way to secure this end is by the cross of Christ."[10] Nothing else will do it.

> "Education; philosophy; social association; sacraments, administered by such as have no matter how direct a succession from the apostles, or even by apostles themselves; scrupulous formality; orthodoxy in doctrine; all; all, except a living faith in Christ, are utterly powerless and lifeless here."[11]

In this world dead in sin there is no other way. "from a race" dead in trespasses and sins, "there can no spiritual life be engendered, by any other possible principle."[12]

This being the case defines, for Hickok, the true limits within which philosophical speculation about religious matters is admissible. "That speculation which applies principles to facts, and retains no theory which the facts do not warrant, needs no apology. It may," he concedes, "boldly demand for itself a right to be, and not ask for mere toleration."[13] But when theory outruns facts, and for Hickok the facts of Scripture are not in question, the true church of Christ must discriminate between the theorist and his theory, the man and his book.

> When the man is right in fact, but wrong in his theory, then
> let the man be loved, while his theory is exposed and refuted;
> if both the man and his book are wrong in fact and theory,
> though not fundamentally so, put them both over into the
> denomination to which they belong, but let Christian chari-
> ty still bear with them. If the book only be fundamentally
> wrong....and the man truly, though inconsistently, stops short
> of the fundamental error; then let his book be burned....but
> let the man "himself be saved; yet so as by fire." Of course,
> if both are heretical, let both be condemned together."[14]

In his subsequent works this echo of Edwardsian hell-fire is no longer to be heard, and indeed it would be unfair to judge the man and his work solely on the basis of a single hyperbolic statement made in the coda of an address to an audience of conservative clerics. In the event, Hickok's later writings, most particularly the **Rational Psychology** and its sequel the **Rational Cosmology,** are very different in tone and content, for all that the contention implicit in each is that the theory there proposed is not contradictory of any *essential*[15] scriptural fact.

II

"There must somewhere be a position from whence it may

clearly be seen that the universe has laws which are necessarily determined by immutable and eternal principles."[16]

Where are we to find this position? Apparently not in Philosophy, for that
has been declared to be synonymous with Infidelity. And yet, not entirely
out of philosophy either, since our concern is with the principles behind the
facts. But what is that discipline which is at once philosophical and not
Philosophy as such? Psychology, or the Science of Mind.[17] As understood by
Hickok, this is divisible into Empirical Psychology[18], the science of experience
and its organization, and Rational Psychology, the science of those *a priori*
conditions which give the necessary and universal laws to experience, and by
which intelligence itself is alone made intelligible. So far as this latter science
is made to proceed, it will, says Hickok,

> "give an exposition of the human mind not merely in the
> facts of experience, but in the more adequate and comprehen-
> sive manner, according to the necessary laws of its being and
> action as a free intelligence. It will, moreover, afford a posi-
> tion from which we may overlook the whole field of possi-
> ble human science, and determine a complete circumscrip-
> tion to our experience; demonstrating what is possible, and
> the validity of that which is real. In it is the science of all
> sciences, inasmuch as it gives an exposition of intelligence
> itself."[19]

The language recalls Kant; the scope of Hickok's "science" is Hegelian, nor
is it to be denied that what the former sought in his Critiques of Reason and
Judgment, and the latter found in his Phenomenology and Logic, Hickok
seeks and finds in the conclusions of his Rational Psychology. Withal, it would
be a mistake to think that we have here to do with nothing more than an
inferior American imitation of these German classics. Hickok is no Kantian,
nor yet an Hegelian, for all that he derives his method from the one, and
the magnitude of his task from the other. He will not admit the limitation
of our thought to the phenomenal; he will not concede that Spirit is no more

than Nature in its Truth as Mind. These idealistic pantheisms, as he will call them, are no less to be combatted by the Rational Psychology than that skeptic sensationalism which is the death of all sound philosophy and true religion, and that materialistic pantheism which Emerson and his school have misnamed Transcendentalism. All, he holds, are forms of Infidelity, whose limitations and errors a comprehensive Rational Psychology must lay bare. Herein it subserves the interests of the Christian Faith and vindicates that notion of Divine Sovereignty which, for Hickok, as for his predecessors in the quest for a consistent Calvinsim, is the beginning and the end of everything.

Knowledge begins with experience. This, Hickok assumes, all will admit. How, then, does the knower come to know objects out of, and at a distance from, himself. Locke will have it that the object makes an impression upon the organ of perception, which latter, by its nervous susceptibility, perpetuates the impression and communicates it to the brain where it is translated into an idea representative of the object outside. The difficulty with this (correspondence) theory, as Hickok points out, is that it can offer no assurance whatever as regards the correctness of our perceptions. "If we say the representative is like the object, it can only be a mere assumption, inasmuch as no comparison can be instituted between them, for the representative only is given....Yea, inasmuch as the representatives are all that the intellect possesses, how is it possible that we may know that anything other than the representatives really exist?" (*2 RP 30*)* The answer provided by Berkeley is, of course, that it is impossible. Nor is this answer, Hickok argues, to be successfully controverted by adopting the alternative theory of Hobbes. If mind and its objects are alike matters in motion, what is to represent? And what is it that is represented?

Knowledge begins with experience. If it also ends with it, if the whole is left to rest upon the affirmations of the senses, the philosophical ultimate is--skepticism. The last word on the epistemological problem is that of Hume. The desperate attempt of Reid[20] to save the appearances by making perception out to be an immediate something confirmed by common sense is to no avail.

*See footnote 19.

"Unless we can transcend all knowledge from sensation, and attain to these notions as wholly new conceptions in reflection, and verify them in the higher functions of an understanding as having a valid reality of being, we cannot exclude the skeptic from his logical right to doubt whether even he must not doubt universally....If we can come to the knowledge of the understanding in its conditioning laws of operation, and determine to the intellect, in its process of thinking in judgements, an equal validity as before in its process of perception; then may we from such results demonstrate also the validity of their being for the substances and causes of the understanding, as before for the phenomena of the sense. And such verification of the being of substances and causes, and their uniformity as universal laws in the connections of nature, will be an annihilation of all skepticism of mind or matter, and do away with all apparent conflict between consciousness and reason. And most surely such a consummation is hopeless, in any other manner than through an *a priori* method of investigation."
(2 RP 44-45)

The validity of experience can only be demonstrated by that which is not of experience. "The physical can find no law of exposition save in the metaphysical." (2RP 24) The natural finds its meaning nowhere save in the being of the supernatural.

It follows, then, Hickok believes, that the quest for a consistent Calvinism must fail to the degree that it deliberately avoids the formulation of a metaphysics of the supernatural. Lockean sensationalism and Hegelian rationalism are positions equally untenable for the Christian philosopher. The former, he avers, tends ever to materialism and culminates at last in atheism; the latter leads at first to absolute idealism and utimately, as the systems of Fichte, Schelling, and Hegel himself testify, to idealistic pantheism.[21]

"May we then betake ourselves to a process of *Eclecticism*, in this variety and great contrariety of philosophical thinking and its results? Such a method of building up a system anticipates that there is truth in all philosophizing, though more or less partial, distorted and obscured and the process is to sift the truth from the error, and with this pure residuum of all systems build up the only and altogether true....But how to go on with this sifting process, and detect all the pure truth and take it from all other systems? Certainly in no other manner than by first taking a stand-point upon some system, which in its law of construction is comprehensive of all so far as they are true, and which at once vindicates its own right to be by embracing the truth of all, and thus demolishing them in building up itself." (RP 70-71)

But with this we have already passed beyond the perspective of eclecticism! To philosophical supernaturalism? The Mystic and Transcendentalist will not admit it. Renouncing vain philosophy, the former waits for inspiration to inform him of the being of God, and never, Hickok reminds us, pauses to reflect that this inspiration may be nothing more than the excited workings of his own inner being. The Transcendentalist meanwhile pursues a different course.

"He rises quite above the philosophy of sensation and empiricism, and is clearly aware of the empty and dead material mechanism in which that must terminate. He admits apriori truth, and contends strenuously for the authority and validity of rational investigation, and the soundness of the demonstrations thereby affected. In this process, the intellectual functions of judgment and forms of all thinking are correctly attained; and the laws of nature, as universal and necessary, are fairly expounded....But this is the "ultima thule" of philosophical attainment....The standpoint of this *partial Transcendentalism* is wholly within nature. It transcends the phenomenal in sensation, truly and philosophically, and such is its deservedly great praise; but to it the supernatural is darkness." (RP 74-75)

For all that it speaks in lofty terms of soul and Oversoul, it honors a deity unworthy of the name of God.

Skepticism or supernaturalism: when all is said, these are the philosophical alternatives. No one of the middle ways mentioned or mentionable is tenable since all such must somehow beg the question of the existence of that Person whose activity it is that ultimately makes experience meaningful. Nor, Hickok contends, is this conclusion to be evaded by any willingness on our part to settle for one among the somewhat less than personal deities proposed by the several varieties of pantheistic rationalism. For all that they bear his name, these are not God.

> "God is not phenomenon, nor substance and cause connecting phenomena: He is beyond all this, for this is nature only and is God's creature. He thus as truly transcends the understanding as he does the sense, and cannot possibly become objectively known but by the higher faculty of the reason. All philosophy is most absurdly denominated Rationalism, which makes its ultimate conclusions to be in nature, and denies that there is any thing which may be known as the supernatural. It is a Rationalism discarding the very organ and faculty of reason itself." (RP 83)

True rationalism is rather supernaturalism, and its instrument is that of Rational Psychology, "which having given the laws of intelligence in the functions of the sense and the understanding, now completes its work in the attainment of the conditional laws of the faculty of the reason," thereby subverting skepticism and laying "the foundation for demonstrating the valid being of the soul in its liberty, and of God in his absolute Personality." (RP 85)

III

> "Man can intelligibly expound his own intelligence, and philosophically interpret his own philosophy; and in this con-

sists the science of all sciences, viz: a rational exposition of
our psychological being and agency." (RP 105)

The epistemological claims of empiricism and idealism having been examined and found wanting, the way is open for the consideration of the question
which troubled Kant as it troubles Hickok, and after him all who take
philosophy seriously, the question, that is, of the organization of the manifold
of phenomena into the object sensed. With Kant, Hickok holds that it is mind
which gives order to nature and organizes the chaos of sensation into things
and events. Mind it is which conjoins, connects, and comprehends phenomena
as such and in their causes. That it is so must be, Hickok thinks, manifest
to anyone capable of introspection. The world does not come to us ready
made. There are no facts save as the faculty of Sense determines its data to
be such; there is no order to things save as the faculty of the Understanding
ordains it; there is no meaning to nature save as the faculty of Reason
prescribes it. Which being so, it follows, Hickok argues, that a rational
psychology exhibiting the subjective Idea and objective Law of each of these
faculties in turn is propaedeutic to any ontology or theology aspirant to acceptance by reasonable men.

In such a rational psychology each of the faculties just mentioned will,
therefore, display its essential Idea and Law, the one, subjective, being attained by an *a priori* process of investigation, the other, objective, being determinable by an induction of the facts proper to the faculty in question.

> "An Idea is, thus, a systematic process in pure thought by
> which it is possible to secure a specific result. When that pro-
> cess appears objectively in actual facts, we term it Law. And
> when the Idea and Law accord, we have Science." (RP
> 542-543)

This accord being demonstrated, the rational psychology of each faculty finds
its completion in the recognition of the error of those philosophies
predominantly or exclusively subjectivist or objectivist in their orientation,
for the truth is--both in correlation. Hence, in what follows, we shall, for each

faculty in turn, remark the detail of Hichok's deduction of its Idea, after which notice is to be taken of that induction demonstrative of that Law which is the Idea's counterpart in nature. Only then shall we be in a position to understand and to appreciate that conception of God which is for Hickok the source and meaning of the whole.

There is an *a priori*. Kant did not doubt it and neither does Hickok. Nor is there any essential difference between them as regards the nature of this *a priori*. For both, sensation is transcended with the realization that all experience presupposes Space and Time. These, considered in abstraction from the objects they define, are, for Hickok as for Kant, forms of intuition. Of themselves, they are pure forms, known as such by primitive intuition. Both, it is contended, are given in an *a priori* cognition, which latter clearly evidences our possession of a higher faculty than Sense, for "if all cognition must be of that only which is first given in the sensation, then certainly the primitive intuition of pure space and time must be an impossibility." (RP 130) Since this primitive intuition is a fact, and since pure space and time are not, of themselves agents able to collect and fix precise limits within themselves, it follows that "some agency *ab extra* must make such conjunctions, and give such limits." (RP 145)

Into the modes of *a priori* intellectual operation whereby this agency effects the construction of the phenomenal under the forms of space and time we need not enter. Suffice it to say that Hickok conceives this agency to embrace both the subjective and objective aspects of all cognition. However, since this agency could hardly accomplish its work of conjoining diverse points and instants in unity in the absence of some light, we must, he holds, here add to our schema, consciousness, "for the light of which we are here speaking is the very thing we mean by consciousness." (RP 168)

> "The pure object is put within this light, and thus the mind possesses it in its own illumination, and this is the same as to say that the object stands in consciousness. Not as an act, but as a light; not as a maker—for that is the province of the intellectual agency—but rather as a revealer." (RP 169)

The distinction is important, since otherwise we might be tempted to identify the consciousness with the self, whereas the latter is, for Hickok, that transcendent unity of agency and illumination which is forever subject and never object even to itself. "The agency as process of conjoining may go on within the primitive intuition, and the pure product as quantity constructed may also stand out in the consciousness; but the self in which the conjoining agency and revealing consciousness have their unity must of course lie back of the primitive intuition." (RP 177) Which is to say, that while we may come to the conviction *that* a self is, we cannot here determine *what* the self is, "inasmuch as all the agency for knowing which we have yet attained is simply that of conjoining in unity and attaining to the forms for phenomena, while the self cannot be phenomenon nor be constructed in the shapes of space or the successions of time." (RP 177)

How, then, it might be asked, do we awake to this conviction of the being of the self? If the self is, as Hickok suggests, analogous to a mirror, how does the mirror come to know itself a mirror? Apparently by some sort of immediate apprehension of self as distinct from not-self, for there is, we are told, a spontaneous agency which constructs its product in space and time, which product becomes the object in consciousness. This (spontaneous agency) is, he continues,

> "distinct from the constructing agency, and both it and the process of its construction are in the immediate intuition, and thus in the light of consciousness they are diverse from each other. The agency and the consciousness are referred in their unity to one self, which is the *unity* of self-consciousness, but the object cannot be so referred; that is other than self; and this discrimination between what is from *self* and what is from *not-self*, is the *finding of myself.*" (RP 178)

Thus, according to Hickok, do we attain an *a priori* position as regards the *subject* of any and all sense experience.

What then of this object that is other than self? It too, he teaches, is immediately beheld.

"When a content in the sensibility gives the matter for some phenomenon as quality, and this is brought directly within the light of consciousness, this also we immediately behold; but inasmuch as this is empirical and not pure object, so the distinction is made for it by calling it *empirical* intuition. In all perception of objects in the sense this content in the sensibility is given, and as the *matter* of the phenomenon, its apriori investigation is as necessary to a complete idea of the sense as the process of its construction into form." (RP 180)

We have, therefore, now to attain the subjective Idea of the Sense in the empirical intuition, and this not, as before in the case of pure intuition, by a process of abstraction ("an abstraction of all content from the sensibility would be a void of all matter for phenomenon, and thus the nihility of all empirical intuition"), but rather by an anticipation (prolepsis) of the nature of content in general. "An anticipation of such content in general, as condition for any and all perception of phenomena, and in the conception of which an occasion may be given for determining what intellectual operation is necessary universally for bringing such an anticipated content under an empirical intuition, will give us our determined apriori postion." (RP 181) Since the content may exhibit all possible diversity of kind and variety, an agency is demanded which is capable of distinguishing amid the manifold varieties and kinds of sensation. Analysis of this operation of distinction discloses first that something rather than nothing appears, second, that it is something particular, specific real as distinguished from Reality as such, and third, that it has a quality peculiar to itself.

"It is, moreover, apriori manifest, that not only must all complete distinction include the elements of reality, particularity, and peculiarity, inasmuch as nothing can be distinctly apprehended except as a reality which is particular from all others and peculiar in itself; but also that no operation of distinction can have more than these three elements, for when the appearance is apprehended in its reality, particularity and peculiarity it is completely discriminated, and no work of distinguishing can be carried forward any further....This operation of distinction, as an intellectual work bringing the diverse sensation into a precise appearance in consciousness, may properly be termed *Observation*. The completed result as precise appearance in consciousness is *Quality*. (RP 189)

In a subsequent anticipation, this Quality is contemplated as having Quantity and both are further discriminated until we have determined the possibility of ordering sensation in all the forms which the phenomenon may assume.

Thus far we have remained shut up within the realm of the purely subjective. Still wanting is that conviction which enables us to assume a correlation between the internal Idea and the external fact. This correlation Hickok now assays to provide, and that by hypothesizing "that all the facts in the process of perception must stand within the law which demands the *intellectual operations of Distinction of quality and Conjunction of quantity*; and consequently that where this law is complied with in its demands, there is clear perception." (RP 237-238) Induction, he contends, reveals that it is so, and with this recognition the rational psychology in reference to the Faculty of the Sense is complete.

"We have attained its *apriori Idea* both for the pure and for the empirical intuition, and found it in this--that a content must be given in sensation, and that this must be Distinguished in its matter, and Conjoined in its form, as conditional for all possible phenomena in perception. This apriori idea has not only been attained as a *void thought*, but we have assumed it hypothetically, and questioned actual experience largely under its direction, and have gathered a wide induction of facts which are manifestly held in colligation by it, and from which it would be safe to make the deduction, that this law in the facts induced, as correlative with our ideal hypothesis in which the facts have been bound up, is a *general Law* for all the further facts of perception that any experience may give to us....We know the appearance not only, but the *knowing* of that appearance. In this is science; and from its apriori demonstration is transcendental science; and thus a *rational*, and not merely an *empirical* or inductive Psychology." (RP 279-280)

We know that there is something in the senses and something of mind, and we know moreover that Kant was right to hold that concepts without percepts are as empty as percepts without concepts are blind. "The occuring (sic) of the sensation is wholly from the without, the constructing of the sensation is wholly from the within; but the subjective agency in constructing is wholly conditioned by the objective content which affects the sensibility." (RP 306) This we know, and knowing it we know also that Materialism and Idealism are true as regards what they affirm and false in what they deny. Nor, thinks Hickok, is this to admit with the skeptic that each cancels out the other and leaves the knower with no surety at all. "That the inner development of thought is real, and that sensation is an affection of the sensibility as mental, both are valid; but that all valid being is thus subjective, and that the content in sensation is not wholly *ab extra*, is erroneous." (RP 316) Erroneous, because it is not true that consciousness and reason contradict each other as regards their respective accounts of perception. It is true, as consciousness asserts, that we immediately perceive the content of sensation; it is equally true that what is perceived is not the source of that sensation.

"Consciousness affirms one thing, an immediate perception of qualities; and reason does not at all contradict this; but affirms and *a priori* demonstrates it. Reason also affirms one thing--whatever it may be which is under or back of the qualities, and is causality for their coming within the sensibility that they may thus be brought by the intellectual agency into the light of consciousness--that this causality as thing in itself can not be immediately perceived." (2RP 383-384)

With this distinction, Hickok claims, skepticism is overthrown, for certainly consciousness may very well testify for its immediate perception of the phenomena as quality without thereby contradicting reason's denial of an immediate perception of the object as thing in itself. What the skeptic fails to realize is that the object for the sense (the quality) is not at all the same as the object for the reason (the sources of the quality); therein he is guilty of the fallacy *figurae dictionis*, which being recognized, his case is lost. The alleged contradiction having been shown the rest upon a fallacy, the validity of the position as thus far rehearsed remains unimpeached. We have thus a valid being of the external material phenomena against Idealism; and an equally valid being of the inner spiritual phenomena against Materialism; and a complete subversion of that Universal Skepticism which denies that we may have either. What we do not have, however, is any assurance that these phenomena are collected into things and events in such wise as to constitute a whole of nature. "If we may know other than isolated phenomena in their separate places and periods, a higher faculty than that of conjunction in sense is necessary." (RP 324) This higher faculty is the Understanding, and as before with the faculty of Sense, so here too we have first to deduce *a priori* its subjective Idea and consequently, by induction, to show forth its counterpart as the empirical law of the objective.

The intellectual agency supplies two sorts of relations in consciousness. One sort, the conjunction of phenomena, has already been accounted for by the operations of the faculty of Sense; the other, "where the elements are held together by an inherent bond and all coalesce in one whole," is the function of the faculty of Understanding. What Sense constructs, Understanding connects, and this is no other possible maner than by a discursus.

> "That I have the sensation of warmth may be given in the
> sense, and when, and how much; but all this will be isolated
> sensation and not connected experience, except as I can con-
> nect that sensation with other sensations in their common
> grounds and sources, and say the sun or the fire warms me.
> But in order to such judgment in experience that the sun
> warms me, I must apriori assume the notions of both ground

and source, and discursively through these conclude upon the judgment in experience. The experience does not and can not give the notion, the notion is conditional for the connected experience." (RP 337)

The ordering of the manifold of sensation into a connected pattern of things and events is, therefore, owing entirely to the operation of the notion. "Phenomena will be conjoined by phenomena, but can be connected only by the notion....The same intellect *conjoins* the diversity--and this is the faculty of the sense--which *connects* the phenomena--and this is the faculty of the understanding." (RP 333)

Pure thinking is thus nothing but this connecting of phenomena in their notion. "The whole work is thus entirely intellectual. The anticipated content is constructed in the sense when there is no actual sensation, and is thus a conceived phenomenon only; and the notion, as connective, is wholly supplied by the understanding as pure conception also; and thus the whole process, though combining both intellectual conjunction and intellectual connection, is wholly a mental conception and therefore pure thinking." (RP 334) What we call a train of thought is simply this notional in process; when the thought has as its object the connection of phenomena into things and events, it becomes "an order of experience." As in Kant, so with Hickok, the law and order that men have sought in nature is to be found in the faculty of understanding. "The intellectual process is ever from one sense-conception to another by a discursus through an understanding-conception, and the judgment resulting is wholly synthetical--adding the necessary connection of the phenomenal in the notional--and thereby giving universality to the ultimate judgment, as, that all phenomena must stand in some ground, or must originate in some source. And the great question is--how verify this synthesis?" (RP 340)

According to Hume it cannot be done because there is no proof possible of necessary connection, and if his assumption that habit only induces the conviction of such a connection is correct, then his conclusion inevitably follows. We cannot, therefore, simply assume a necessary connection. It is not to be thought of as an invariable order of sequence, nor yet as an ultimate fact of common sense. We are not to take the understanding-conception on trust, nor merely because we need it as our connective conditional for all possible thinking....nor are we to assume it merely as the condition and law of our subjective thinking." (RP 343) By no intuitive process of any sort is a determination of connection to be reached. Rather must we take those media common to both a construction of phenomena in the sense, and a connection of phenomena into things and events as experience in the understanding, and by means of these discursively determine this necessary connection. Such media, according to Hickok, are space and time. "And now, the design is to show, in the use of space and time, how it may be determined that constructed phenomena may be connected into things and events in an order of objective experience, and how only this may be done, and which will be the Understanding in its Idea." (RP 346)

What is it that connects phenomena in space and time? From what has gone before we know that it cannot be that the phenomena are given in perception as connected. As for the supposition of some Idealists that space and time, as thought in a whole of all space and all time, may themselves determine the connection of phenomena in an experience, a brief analysis of what such a supposition must involve suffices, he thinks, to destroy its cogency. There remains, then, only one other supposition possible, namely, that phenomena are connected by a space and time-filling force determinative of each place and period in a whole of time and space.

> "This space- (and time) filling force is altogether a notion, and impossible that it should be other than an understanding-conception, and yet it is manifest that it may be an occasion for phenomena as appearing in consciousness....It cannot itself become appearance but thought only, and yet it may manifest itself through a sensibility in all possible quality....It thus determines its own content in all sensibility as conditioning the constructing agency, and secures its phenomena to be objective in each, and itself as ground the same object to all." (RP 361-362)

In ensuing chapters Hickok calls it Substance, and conceives it as perduring through all modifications, as the standard by which time is measured. "Whether substance itself may begin....is," he feels, "a question for quite another faculty than the understanding." (RP 391) In any case, it is, from the standpoint of the understanding, inconceivable that anything should exist except as grounded in a permanent substance. "There can be no change but in a permanent which neither alters nor varies." (RP 394) In short, there can be no chance.

Except as phenomena stand connected in their permanent substance, there can be no determination of them in the one immensity of space and the singular eternity of time. "The operation of connection must, therefore, be universally conditioned upon the notions in an understanding of Substance as ground in space, and of Substance as source in time; which last, as modified for succession, becomes Cause; and again modified for concomitance, becomes Reciprocal Causation." (RP 381)

Just how this modification comes to pass Hickok does not tell us; the implication is, as we shall see, that it is the consequence of the activity of the Absolute as revealed in the operation of the faculty of Reason. For the present, however, he contents himself with the specification of those understanding-conceptions (Substance, Cause, Action and Reaction) through, which, as he thinks, the phenomena of nature are connected in a universal spatio-temporal whole of experience. From this *a priori* demonstration of connection we have, he concludes, "the valid synthetical judgements in their universality and necessity of comprehension--that qualities must inhere in their substances--events must depend on their sources--effects must adhere through their causes--and all concomitant phenomena must cohere in their reciprocal influences." (RP 411) Such, in sum, is the complete *a priori* Idea of the faculty of Understanding.

This idea it is that is now to be taken as a hypothesis and applied "to actual facts in a sufficiently broad induction to induce full conviction, that our necessary and universal idea has its counterpart in a veritable law of intelligent action." (RP 472) Needless to say, this ingathering of the facts confirms the hypothesis that we never determine experience in one universal space or time, in any totality of places in space or moments in time, except in the thought of a connective notional. As earlier in the Sense, so here in the Understanding, the hypothesis is seen to be the law in the facts.

> "And inasmuch as we have now found the law in the facts comprehensively for all determination of phenomena in place and in period, and can now see that the law in the facts is precisely the correlative of our apriori idea of an understanding; we may unhesitatingly affirm, that here is a true and valid psychological science. We know the Understanding completely, both in its transcendental Idea and in its empirical Law." (RP 519)

Here, it would seem, we might rest, for if Hickok's argument is sound, the nature of things as they exist has been shown to be "an intelligible Universal System."

> Not an accumulation of atoms but a connection of things; not a sequence of appearances but a conditioned series of events; not a coincidence of facts but a universal communion of interacting forces. Nor is such a conclusion merely assumed; nor the credulity induced by habitual experience; nor the revelation of an instinctive prophecy; but a demonstration from an apriori Idea and an actual Law which logically and legitimately excludes all skepticism." (RP 530)

And yet, even as we proclaim this result, we are, notes Hickok, forced to recognize that it is only in virtue of our possession of a comprehending faculty of Reason that we have been able to subject the operations of the Sense and the Understanding to this *a priori* examination. "In the use of reason we have thus come to a science of both the sense and the understanding. In the sense we *perceive*; in the understanding we *judge*; but in the reason we have *overseen* both the process of perceiving and the process of judging." (RP 534) What we have now to determine is the process by which the reason may come to know and comprehend itself as overseer.

The difficulty in arriving at this determination lies, of course, in the necessity of attaining a standpoint outside of both the phenomenal and the notional. No longer is it permitted to us to appeal to intuition in space and time, for what we now seek cannot be constructed. No more may we find help in the notional, for what we demand cannot be connected in the conditions in the conditions of substances and causes. "The overseer of nature must not be shut up within nature. We are to comprehend nature and this is not to be effected by any connecting of things in nature." (RP 535-536)

We have, in short, to do with the supernatural, and with the reason as organ for attaining to a comprehension of the supernatural, and the question is: how to do it? Let us, Hickok suggests, begin by positing a pure Ideal, the same to be thought of as that aim or end which nature *per se* subserves. That we are justified in making such a postulation follows, he thinks, from our recognition that nature itself requires to be explained. "In some way, reason must find an agent....in whom....the substance of nature may find an origin." (RP 560) This agent when found must prove to be absolutely self-sufficient and unconditioned by anything whatever, for such alone can stand above nature and condition nature without the reciprocity of a conditioning back upon itself from nature. What shall we call this unconditioned agent? Let us, proposes Hickok, "give to this conception of a supernatural being the high name, which must be his own prerogative and incommunicable possession--THE ABSOLUTE." (RP 561)

As the understanding-conception of the notion is above the idea of the phenomenal, so is this reason-conception of the Absolute above the idea of the notional; let us, then, says Hickok, distinguish it from its predecessors by naming it the Ideal.

This ideal of the absolute is to be the compass for comprehending nature, as the notional was the medium for connecting phenomena in a nature of things. In this we are to determine how it may be known, as a synthetical proposition, that nature must have its author; as in that it was determined how it might be demonstrated, that phenomena must be inherent in substance, adherent in cause, and coherent in

354

reciprocal influence....

And yet still farther, as we found the very essence of
substance in its causality be a space-filling and time-enduring
force....so now we must find the very essence of the absolute
to be a spaceless and timeless *personality*, who, as above all
the modes of expansion in space and duration in time, may
be not nature but supernatural; not thing but person." (RP
563-565)

As person it is pure activity, "but such pure activity is the conception of *pure
spontaneity*; and this must stand as our first element of Personality." (RP 569)
The second element, as deduced by Hickok, is pure autonomy, for "that spontaneity may become *personal* activity, and thus a will which may *behave*--i.e.,
have possession and control of its own agency—it must possess an end in
itself, and thus impose law upon itself, and thereby be autonomic." (RP 574)
This second element in interaction with the first now manifests itself as will,
herein is characterized as pure liberty, and with this third element the Ideal
completes itself. "These three, Spontaneity, Autonomy, and Liberty are all
the elements which determine Personality; and, as in the Ideal of the Absolute, determined in his personality, we are to comprehend universal nature,
so in these, we have the apriori Elements of an operation of Comprehension."
(RP 604)

At this point it is, Hickok warns us, necessary to recall that we have here
to do exclusively with a reason-conception of the supernatural, that is, with
a conception of Personality entirely removed from that which Sense and
Understanding denotes as person. Thus if on occasion we employ terms borrowed from the world of nature in reference to the supernatural, "we are by
no means to allow ourselves to come under the delusion, as if with the terms
there had come up the things of nature, and that such supernatural causation had any connection with nature's causes in their necessitated conditions.
If the words are sometimes borrowed, the meanings must never be confounded." (RP 607) The language with which we characterize the Absolute is always
analogical. Between the Ideal Personality and that creation which his will
in liberty brings to pass there is a gulf complete. For Hickok, no less than

for St. Thomas Aquinas, the Creator is absolutely independent of that creation which is utterly dependent upon him.

How, then, one might wonder, does Hickok propose to account for the existence of man and the ten thousand things, the more so as the assumptions of the **Rational Psychology** hardly permit him to evade the problem of creation by proclaiming it to be a mystery of faith. His answer is, to say the least, ingenious. Allow that we have made abstraction of all distinguishable phenomenal and notional force, retaining only that which is most simple and ubiquitous, i.e., the force of gravity. We have in this, Hickok believes, "all that is necessary for an apriori representation of a universal nature of things *in itself,* and not in phenomenal appearance." (RP 556) For whatever center of force we consider at any point will be revolving about some center of gravity, it will be force in counteraction. "Can the reason take its stand upon some central point, around which the universe shall revolve, and find an author and primal originating source for it, without needing any higher point of antagonism? Such ultimate point we now assume in conception...." (RP 556)

That we may be clear as to just what is involved in the reason-conception of this central force upon which the universe allegedly reposes, Hickok invites our consideration of the following analogy:

> Conceive of two congealed pencils, such that when their points are pressed in contact the pressure shall equally liquify them both, then will this liquefaction accumulate itself about the point of contact; and if no external disturbing force be present it will perfectly ensphere itself there, the sphere enlarging as the pressure continues and the accumulation increases. If now we will abstract all that is phenomenal in this, and retain only that which is the space-filling as thing in itself, we shall have the pure conception of force as generated in antagonist action....Let the antagonism at the center be adequate to fill the space the universe occupies, and the essential space-filling substance of the universe is a necessary conception. So, it is manifest, a universal space-filling substance may be." (RP 557-558)

356

Whence comes this antagonism? "In what source may we find these acts which counteract, to become identical? All force, and thus all nature is a genesis in a *duality*; in what may this find a primordial and abiding *unity*?" (RP 559) Reason, he thinks, cannot evade the question, nor is it answerable save as reason postulates a will in liberty wholly above and separate from all force in nature.

> He (the Absolute) may originate simple acts which, in their own simplicity, have no counter-agency....From his own inner capacity of self-determination he may designedly put simple acts in counter-action and at their point of counter-agency a force begins which takes a position in space and occupies an instant in time....Above that point of counter-agency all is simple activity--unphenomenal and unsubstantial....in, and below that point all is force--phenomenal in the perception of the sense, and substantial and causal from its antagonism in the judgment of the understanding....The Deity needs but to will the counteraction in its perpetuated force, and universal nature finds its equilibrium in the repulsion from the center and the reflex pressure to the center, and holds itself suspended on its own conditioned forces, without the possibility of any weariness or exhaustion to its maker....in short, the whole formal arrangements of the universe are given in the very points where the primordial forces have their genesis." (RP 608-611)

Since this divine will is wholly external to its product (God apart from the world), it follows that it must be, as Calvinism contends, absolutely sovereign in all its operations. Such is the Ideal of the faculty of Reason; it requires only an induction of the various classes and categories of cosmological fact to establish the accordance of this Ideal with the objective law of the reason, and this, thinks Hickok, is easily enough done. "This is all that we have proposed to ourselves, and in this we have a complete (Calvinist) philosophy of the human mind--a *Rational Psychology*." (RP 712)

IV

"This system of Rational Psychology, necessarily, either
deifies the human reason or else undeifies God."²²

For a decade following the appearance of his big book Hickok basked in
the approval of his clerical and professorial colleagues. Auburn and Andover
took solid comfort from his exposure of the inadequacies of Emersonain
transcendentalism. Union College called him to be vice-president and professor of mental and moral philosophy. Tayler Lewis wrote a long and
laudatory account of the Rational Psychology for **Bibliotheca Sacra**.²³ The
appearance of its sequel, **Rational Cosmology**,²⁴ in 1858 prompted the editors
of this same periodical to begin a lead article summarizing Hickok's
philosophy with the declaration that these volumes, together with the textbooks, **Empirical Psychology**²⁵ and **A System of Moral Science**,²⁶ "represent
the highest attainments in speculative thought which the American mind has
yet reached." The conclusion of their lead article was no less complimentary:

"the deeply seated feeling of an increasing number, that his
writings satisfy a want not otherwise supplied; the comprehensive range of his principles, and the facility with which
their application can be carried to the highest problems
respecting nature, the soul, and God, as well as the singular
accordance which his philosophic direction is seen, as soon
as it is pointed out, to have with the profoundest drift of
American activity in other respects, emboldens the prediction that, if American philosophy is to have a history, the
course of its stream and the bulk of its waters can appear
in no other channel than the one he has indicated."²⁷

In 1861, even as the armies formed, a second edition of **Rational Psychology**
appeared. As if reflecting the spirit of the times, it was attacked by an
anonymous critic in the **Princeton Review** in terms that must have astonished
the editors of **Bibliotheca Sacra**, had they not been aware, as Hickok also was,

of the fundamentalist bias of that journal and its sponsor seminary. Hickok's criticisms of the epistemological adequacy of common sense were ridiculed. The very possibility of a rational psychology was dismissed as an undertaking "both impossible and absurd."[28] Hickok himself was reviled as a partisan of that very pantheism which he had been at considerable pains to refute. The period of approval was over. The theological war had begun.

The basic objection of the critic, the Rev. Edwin Hall, is well taken. He sees, as Hickok does not, that a reason capable of ascending *a apriori* to the principles governing the functions of divinity must end by deifying itself. "The reason that can discern *a priori* the necessary, unmade, physical principles of the universe, can, " he admits,

> "indeed make a Rational Cosmology. It can tell *how* to create, and what creation *must be*, and so have whatever "position" this affords for making a Rational Psychology. If it can then see *a priori*, as well, the "necessary, external, and unmade principle" which must condition the Creator in making intelligent beings, then it can indeed make a Rational Psychology. The Creator has no choice, and can exercise no wisdom, save only whether, and how long, to put his acts in counteraction, and to supply forces. Unmade principles "condition all power," and determine the rest, whether God will or not....Were it not so, then a Rational Cosmology and a Rational Psychology must both be impossible; that is, the Rational Psychology necessarily either deifies the human reason or undeifies God."[29]

If it intends the former, then, Hall argues, Hickok is a pantheist *malgre lui*; if it tends to the latter, then his claim to have provided a consistent Calvinism must be given up.

There is no room for the Only Living and True God in a universe made on this scheme. He could not exercise wisdom, taste, or goodness. Unmade principles conditioned all his power; he had only one choice and one function- -to put his acts in counteraction. Such a being is not God.[30] Did not Hall conveniently choose to ignore Hickok's carefully drawn distinction between the natural and the supernatural, did he not as carefully avoid taking cognizance of Hickok's oft-repeated ascription of perfect freedom and absolute sovereignty to reason's God, his case would command our support. Even so, he has a point, for while Hickok has safeguarded the sovereignty of God by insisting on His externality to the world His simple act creates, he has not, as Hall goes on to point out, any very reasonable explanation to offer as regards the manner and motive of the original creation.

> "We never knew--we cannot conceive--that it is possible for a spirit to put its pure acts into counteraction. What is it? The *substance* of the spirit pressing against its substance with a physical forceful impingement? Impossible. Thought pressing physically against thought? Impossible! Moreover, if we suppose the pure act of a pure spirit--what is it? and what is the result, save the spirit itself in action? On this plan, the" impenetrable substance "which is made, is simply the creator impinging against himself; the pure spirit himself in action is himself the world he makes; and so we end in Pantheism."[31]

That this last is what he really finds distasteful about the **Rational Psychology** his subsequent remarks make clear. Hall stands foresquare on the Bible, which he thinks must be impugned by any psychology exalting reason to the detriment of common sense. "What is it," he asks, "that the reason here sees *a priori*, in her search after her own existence; and without seeing which she cannot comprehend universal nature, nor prove herself a faculty of reason? Why here are all the great facts of Trinity, Incarnation, and Atonement; all seen by the reason without the Bible," and before man can ever know the Bible even as an existing outward thing! "...Why was Paul....not an apostle of the Reason!....Why had he not discernment to see that the deepest mysteries of revelation, --Trinity, Incarnation, Propitiation, --are all open to the *a priori* view of the transcendental reason!"[32] Demonstration, Hall avows, "can never go beyond an intuitive truth, or direct beholding."[33] Wherefore, then, should Christians trust to revelation to make good that which common sense holds doubtful. What was good enough for the Eighteenth century is still, so it seems, good enough for the Rev. Hall.

That it was not, however, good enough for any thinker capable of recognizing the latent contradiction in a theology combining empiricism and supernaturalism, Hickok's friend and colleague, Tayler Lewis, undertook to demonstrate in an article[34] defending the *a priori* school of philosophy against that *a posteriori* school whose teachings are presupposed by Hall. If reason is as much a gift of God as sense, why is it, he inquires, irreverent or presumptuous to argue *a priori* the ways of Deity? The Reviewer (Hall) is shocked at the boldness of the man who would hold that there are principles unmade conditioning Divinity; what he ought to be shocked at are those who, like himself, think so little of God as to suppose Him "a power and a will, a blank, conceptionless, idealess being, living in a blank eternity."[35] They only lower their own position, Lewis believes, who laugh at those who, in company with the greatest theologians of the Church, do not hesitate to say that God observes the law he has ordained.

Hickok's own reply to Hall is no less contemptuous: "The article (in question) manifests throughout that the writer of it has an entire want of discernment of the philosophical distinctions between phenomena and things in themselves. ....the natural and the supernatural....and in this discrimination is," Hickok contends, "the full evidence that he has not yet taken the first step in that long path which philosophy has for so many ages been traveling. To him all objects are just what and just as the senses give to us, and all investigation of them can attain to nothing other than that which the analysis and deductions of the logical faculty can make out of them. The speculation pursued in the **Psychology** is often misconceived, more often entirely beyond his apprehension, and the only answer to the **Review** that is practicable would be that for which there is not found a sufficient inducement, viz., the pointing out item by item the perpetual failures to attain the rational meaning of the work which the Reviewer has taken in hand."[36] Evidently Hickok did not for long retain this attitude of superiority, for in the very next issue of the same journal we find him embarked upon a detailed exposition of Hall's "mistakes and fallacies" to the end of dispelling the suspicions of those who had interpreted his first statement to mean that Hall's review was really unanswerable.

As Hickok sees it, Hall's critique enshrines three fundamental errors of interpretation, which errors, he thinks, account for three further and separate instances of sophistical reasoning. To begin with, Hickok claims, Hall has confused his (Hickok's) view with that of Skepticism; he (Hall) has assumed, moreover, that the **Psychology** proposes to explain all that mind can do; finally, he has interpreted Hickok's claim to have found the clear conception of what reason is and does to mean that there is no reason at all until so found. On these mistakes his critique builds; on these his refutation and ridicule of the system is founded. Their error being shown, the refutation of the refutation is accomplished.

Hickok begins by reminding Hall and his readers of what it is that really has been presupposed in the *Psychology*:

> "The **Psychology** proceeds upon the assumption that there are rational principles, true in themselves, unchangeable and forever; not so made and might have been otherwise made, but antecedent to and controlling all making that is righteous and wise. It supposes that all action without the guidance of such principle is irrational, and all action against such principle is wrong. That God, who is absolute reason, guides his omnipotence by such rational principle, and could in no other manner be holy or wise. That these principles are given in the absolute reason, and are not thus out of God, but because God is, so they are, and therefore his ends of action are ever found within himself, and all he does is for his glory, or for his name's sake."[37]

Is this ground of procedure, as Hall contends, derogatory to God? Hickok vehemently denies it. The sophistry of Hall's contention is, he believes, seen in the critic's false assumption that God is thereby forced to conform to a principle which man has found, which principle, Hall assumes, is human and not divine. "The only answer that is needed to this is," says Hickok, "that the idea in God and man is the same, and is in truth only the Divine idea which the finite mind has been able to apprehend, as alike in kind though less complete in degree."[38]

A similar sophistry, Hickok argues, is evident in the Reviewer's claim that the wisdom of God is annihilated by the assumption of such eternal principles conditioning His action; for that God can be, and yet be abstracted from the possession of unmade principles and eternal ideas, is a notion that the Reviewer himself has repudiated insofar as he has assumed that God is power and wisdom omnipotent. But there is, Hickok adds, still a third, stranger, sophistry inherent in Hall's argument, for the latter insists that with the presence of these unmade principles God cannot choose; he is by them deprived of free agency.

> "The sophistry lies in supposing that the alternatives (between contrary choices) are excluded by the necessity of the principle and not by the perfections of the divine Agent. An unmade, necessary principle may admit of the alternative of its violation and the power of the disobedient agent may refuse to be conditioned by it, but the perfections of God forbid that there can ever come the tempting occasion for him to violate it. He is absolute Reason, and the supposition of his violation would at once make him to become Unreason. ....His perfections secure that what might admit of violation in itself, yet will never admit of the actual fact of violation, from the impossibility that there should ever arise an occasion for it. God will ever choose to stand by his own glory."[39]

Does such a view end, as Hall insists, by deifying reason and undeifying God? If Hickok's rejoinders have been to the point, the answer to this question begins with the recognition that these two, the deification and the undeification, are not, as Hall supposes, obverse sides of a single intellectual operation. For if Hall is wrong to assume that God's freedom is abolished by His acting in accordance with principle, then God is God whether reason be deified or not!

Is reason deified in the **Psychology**? Hickok nowhere specifically denies it. God is here sometimes, and in the later books quite frequently, described as Absolute Reason. The Idea is, we have been told, the same in man and God. It seems reasonable to infer from these and other evidences scattered throughout the works that deification of the reason is permissible insofar as its object is a clear conception of a perfect will in liberty, impermissible insofar as it is the deification of reason in nature. Similarly as regards the undeification of God; if by God we understand no more than reason in nature, we indeed undeify divinity. If, however, by God we mean "a will in Liberty carried up to Absolute personality, we have," Hickok assures us, "a truly rational Psychology in which is the only door of escape from pantheism and a philosophical entrance upon a pure Theism."[40] We have, in sum, a truly consistent Calvinism.

V

"As it appears it is a system almost entirely rationalistic in its tone and method though in his own mind it was a biblical system."[41]

Like Kierkegaard, whose way of faith he would have vigourously disavowed if he had known of it, Hickok was, from the beginning, "a religious author". The whole of his writing is dedicated to the vindication of the sovereignty of God. To forget this is at once to lose sight of the motive generating the development of the **Rational Psychology** and its six sequels. It is, then, as a religious author that he requires to be judged. His "constructive realism"[42] may be, indeed I think that it is, the grandparent of that critical realism which is not yet out of vogue in American philosophy; his descriptions of the operations of the intellect may be, as I believe they are, of value still; withal, his importance is owing neither to these nor yet to those interpretations of the data of astronomy, physics, chemistry, and biology which many in his own day found so valuable. If he deserves to be remembered it is rather because he saw, as the Edwardsians did not, that supernaturalism finds its justification in rationalism and its contradictory in common sense empiricism.[43] That he is today forgotten by virtually all save the historians of psychology is owing to the fact that his supernaturalism is of such a sort as no modern rationalism cares to defend.

The Absolute Spirit can, Hickok tells us in his *Creator and Creation*, originate force with unequal impulses, and this must immediately generate motion. the force moves, but the Mover does not move, and in this force motion begins. Later in the same work, in a chapter explanatory of the origin and relation of the soul to its body, we are told that,

> "material (antagonist) and ethereal (diremptive) forces originate in God, and are put out from him in an overt experience by his immediate creative act, but they are not in his likeness. God is not force, neither antagonist nor diremptive, though he is the direct Maker of them both."[44]

In brief, creation *ex nihilo* is presupposed. Here, and throughout his writings, all is made to fit the facts as **Genesis** relates them, and those that will not fit, Hickok will expose as contradictory and absurd. Thus, he writes, "what has been called "natural development," or "law of evolution" to account for the origin and perpetuation of species is utterly unphilosophical because wholly destitute of reason." (CC 312)* Reason, as Hickok sees it, teaches that life and mind is the result of a superinduction by the Creator of appropriate instincts and purposes upon ethereal (spiritual) forces. The gradations of species, he believes, are not to be accounted for by any theory of natural selection but are in truth the consequence of a supernatural arrangement. On this last everything depends. The Unmoved Mover sets in motion--forces, but how or why He does it Hickok does not pretend to know. No more than his predecessors in consistent Calvinism is he prepared to apply a rationalist analysis to the divine Sovereignty.

In the works of his later years, as in the **Psychology**, the problem of the relation of these imcompossibles, supernatural and natural, simple act and complex force, God and universe, continues unresolved. The former member of each pair is, he is sure, independent of the latter. The theological position is, throughout, orthodox.[45] The ingeniousness of Hickok's solutions to the various problems of Christian theology, his speculations concerning the nature

*See footnote 44.

of the Trinity (CC 241ff), his resolution of the soul-body problem (CC 342-349), his reconciliation of geological fact with the activity of the six days of **Genesis** (RC 386-389)*, all these are conditioned upon his uncritical acceptance of the conception of God as Absolute Sovereign.

There are passages, not frequently encountered but scattered throughout his works, where he seems to recognize the logical impossiblity of his conception of the God-universe relation. One such occurs in his first reply to Hall, when, following a passage remarking the harmony of true Platonism with the Bible, he concedes that "the Theism of the Bible is in an important and most sublime sense a Pantheism."[46] In the Scriptures, he continues,

> "God is made to be "All in all." "By him all things consist." We "live and move and have our being in God." He is the All in such a sense that all things come from and stand in him, and a withdrawal of his energy in anything must be followed by its instant annihilation."[47]

This sounds suspiciously like panentheism, or at least like that panentheism which the theology of Edwards has been alleged to be, and perhaps Hickok was aware of this revolutionary character of his thought since his orthodoxy leads him to qualify it immediately.

> "But the distinction between the Bible and all heretical pantheism is broadly marked in this; the Bible starts with an absolute will in Liberty, and thus with a proper personality, and this personal God "in the beginning creates the heavens and the earth." ....All heretical Pantheism starts with an impersonality, a germ of physical or logical energy, which is the same in its being at the beginning as at its close and merely changes its modes of manifestation....The last is always and everywhere nature; the first is wholly supernatural, above time and irrespective of space, and both nature and nature's space and time are the products of his originating activity."[48]

*See footnote 16.

Can God guide nature without it being in Him or He in it? Again, in **Creator and Creation**, Hickok's first impulse, based on his awareness of the Aratean declaration (**Acts** 17:28), is to answer—no. Thus, he muses, "all must live, and move, and have their being *in* Him; and yet intelligibly they must stand *only in* Him, but *out* of each other; all immediately within God-consciousness but only mediate to any other consciousness." (CC 159) Again, fearful of the charge of pantheism, he suppresses the thought with his very next sentence: "The Absolute Spirit was, while yet the material worlds were not." (CC 159-160)

In the **Rational Cosmology** the same thought occurs again, and is suppressed in the rising of the further thought that the "In God," taken literally, must impugn the absolute personality. Biblicist that he was, it seems never to have occurred to Hickok that the "proper personality" of infinite being might be something extra-anthropomorphic. In its usage of the findings of science and philosophy his system far surpasses that of Edwards; in the sophistication of its conception of the relation of God to the world, it falls somewhat short of Emmons; which is to say, that while we might, with reason, characterize Hickok as the Kant of consistent Calvinism, we should mistake his achievement were we to call him its Hegel.

Bibliographical Essay

The student of Hickok should begin with **Rational Psychology, or, the Sub-**jective Idea and the Objective Law of all Intelligence (Auburn: Derby, Miller & Company, 1849). The same is available in a facsimile reproduction with an Introduction by Ernest Harms (Delmar, New York: Scholar's Facsimiles and Reprints, 1973). Harm's Introduction emphasizes Hickok's contributions to psychology (the book is published as a volume in the History of Psychology series edited by Robert I. Watson). A revised edition, with some sections drastically shortened and others extensively rephrased was published in 1861. The former, restated as a philosophy of nature, comprises **Rational Cosmology,** or, the Eternal Principles and the Necessary Laws of the Universe (New York: D. Appleton, 1858; second edition, revised, 1859, 1861). Applied to the problem of the relation of God to the world, it constitutes **Creator and Creation,** or, the Knowledge in the Reason of God and his work (Boston: Lee & Shepard, 1872). **The Logic of Reason, Universal and Eternal** (Boston: Lee, Shepard, and Dillingham, 1875) consists of a survey of those various philosophies of logic which serve as prolegomena to that ontology of logic which is the system of rational psychology restated as a logic of Absolute Being. Antedating all but the first of the above are the two textbooks, **A System of Moral Science** (Schenectady: G.Y. van Debogert, 1853) and **Empirical Psychology,** or, the science of mind from experience (New York: Ivison, Blakeman, Taylor & Company, 1854). Both of these works were widely used in American college classrooms throughout the latter half of the nineteenth century, and both ran through several editions. However, neither is especially pertinent to Hickok's psychological Calvinism.

The theological foundation of the Rational Psychology is laid rather in Hickok's Address on the occasion of his inauguration to the Chair of Christian Theology in the Theological Seminary at Auburn on January 8th, 1845, entitled, **Theology as a Science** (Auburn, New York: H. & J.C. Ivison, 1845). Copies of this are rare and hard to come by, but one is found in a **Collection of Lectures and Sermons 1823-1845** (compiler and publisher unknown) in the Virginia Library of the McCormick Theological Seminary (shelf number BV4241/C697). The important article, 'Evolution from Mechanical Force,'

Princeton Review (March, 1878), 567-605, exposes the "contradictions and absurdities" of mechanical (Spencerian evolution; rejects the theory of evolution by natural selection on the grounds of lack of evidence, and plumps for superinduction by God as the only safe way to account for the proliferation of species and the ascent of man. A projected edition of Collected Works, presumably to include all of the above, was announced for publication in 1875, but seems never to have been carried to completion, nor have I been able to confirm the existence of that book-manuscript on which, according to **The Presbyterian** (issue of May 12th, 1888), Hickok was supposed to be working on at the time of his death.

The earliest notice of **Rational Psychology** in the periodical literature is the review and appreciation by Hickok's friend and Auburn colleague, Rev. Tayler Lewis, 'Hickok's Rational Psychology,' **Bibliotheca Sacra**, VIII (1851), 181-217. This was followed, after an interval of several years, by an even more fulsome, albeit unsigned, account of the entire system as sequentially presented in **Empirical Psychology, Moral Science, Rational Psychology, and Rational Cosmology,** by Edwards Amasa Park, 'Dr. Hickok's Philosophy,' **Bibliotheca Sacra,** LXII (April, 1859), 253-278. Park's article remains the best synoptic overview of Hickok's philosophy, marred only by the completely uncritical attitude of the reviewer. At the opposite extreme from Park, is the anonymous review (by Edwin Hall) of the Revised edition of **Rational Psychology, Princeton Review,** XXXIII (1861), 577-610. Tayler Lewis defends Hickok's "constructive realism" against Hall's "naive realism" in, 'Two Schools of Philosophy,' **American Theological Review,** IV (1862), 102-134. The same volume contains Hickok's own replies to Hall, 'Modern Philosophy Pantheistic,' 199-227, and 'Psychology and Skepticism,' 391-414, together with Hall's rebuttal, 'The Rational Psychology and its Vindications,' 611-642.

[1]Laurens Hickok, 'Modern Philosophy Pantheistic', The American Theological Review, IV (1862), 221.

[2]Job 11:7-8, 42:2-3

[3]Upon the death of Eliphalet Nott in 1866, Hickok succeeded to the presidency of Union, which post he retained until his retirement in July of 1868. Thereafter he lived at Amherst in the house of his nephew, Professor (later President) Julius Seelye. There, on May 7th, 1888, he died.

[4]Hickok, Theology as a Science. An Addess, on the occasion of his inauguration to the Chair of Christian Theology in the Theological Seminary at Auburn, January 8th, 1845 (Auburn: New York: H. & J.C. Ivison, 1845), 7-8.

[5]Ibid., 8.

[6]Theology as a Science, 8.

[7]"The true principle....is this—The ceremony is a divinely appointed symbol for presenting and enforcing some spiritual truth." Ibid., 21. This appointment is by the grace of God through the agency of the Holy Spirit.

[8]Ibid., 28-29.

[9]Ibid., 31.

[10]Ibid.

[11]Ibid., 31-32.

[12]Ibid., 31.

[13]Ibid., 34.

[14]Ibid., 35.

[15]The qualification is necessary since it is no part of Hickok's purpose to justify every last fact in Scripture. No more than his predecessors is Hickok to be counted as a fundamentalist.

[16]Hickok, Rational Cosmology (New York: Appleton, 1859), 3. Hereafter cited as RC.

[17]This answer, perfectly reasonable in Hickok's day, when Psychology was commonly conceived as a branch of Philosophy, is, of course, none such as any modern psychologist would assent to without substantial qualification.

[18]See Hickok, Empirical Psychology, or, the Science of Mind from Experience (New York: Ivison, Blakeman, Taylor & Co., 1854).

[19]Hickok, Rational Psychology (Auburn: Derby, Miller & Co., 1849), 21-22. Hereafter cited as RP. A second edition of this work, with some sections considerably shortened and others partially rewritten or rephrased was issued in 1861. The argument of the original, however, remained unchanged. "Some modifications have thus been made of particular parts, but not in the general method." Nor yet, he might have added, in the specific conclusions, since these too "had been too comprehensively thought out to admit of any change." (Preface, v). Subsequent references to this edition are cited in the text as 2RP with page number.

[20]Thomas Reid (1710-1796), founder of the Scottish, or common-sense, school of philosophy, professor at Aberdeen and later at Glasgow (1764-1781). His reply to Hume is given in his Inquiry into the Human Mind on the Principles of Common Sense (1763).

[21]Here, I would submit, Hickok has missed the mark, for Hegel, at least, is no pantheist, if by that is meant the interchangeability of the notions 'God' and 'Universe'. What he is, is a panentheist! See my 'Hegel as Panentheist', Tulane Studies in Philosophy, IX (1960), 134-164.

370

²²Review of the revised edition of **Rational Psychology** (2RP), **Princeton Review**, XXXIII (1861), 598. The review is unsigned. I assume, following the generally received opinion, that it was written by Edwin Hall.

²³Tayler Lewis, 'Hickok's Rational Psychology', **Bibliotheca Sacra**, VIII (1851), 181-217.

²⁴Hickok, **Rational Cosmology**; or, the eternal principles and the necessary laws of the universe. (New York: D. Appleton, 1858), 2nd edition revised, 1859, 1861.

²⁵Hickok, **Empirical Psychology**; or, the science of mind from experience. (New York: Ivison, Blakeman, Taylor and Co., 1854; Schenectady: G.Y. van Debogert, 1854; 2nd edition 1855; reprinted 1859, 1862, 1863, and subsequently through the 1880's.

²⁶Hickok, **A System of Moral Science** (Schenectady: G.Y. van Debogert, 1853). This text too was to be reprinted many times by various publishers and run through several editions to the end of the century.

²⁷'Dr. Hickok's Philosophy', **Bibliotheca Sacra**, XVI (1859), 253.

²⁸Ibid., 278.

²⁹Hall, **Princeton Review**, XXXIII (1861), 600-601.

³⁰Ibid., 601.

³¹Ibid., 602.

³²Ibid., 605-606.

³³Ibid., 610.

³⁴Tayler Lewis, 'The Two Schools of Philosophy', **American Theological Review**, (1862), 102-134.

³⁵Ibid., 123.

³⁶Hickok, 'Modern Philosophy Pantheistic', **American Theological Review**, IV (1862), 202.

³⁷Hickok, 'Psychology and Skepticism', **American Theological Review**, IV (1862), 399.

³⁸Ibid., 400.

³⁹Ibid., 404.

⁴⁰Hickok, 'Modern Philosophy Pantheistic', 227.

⁴¹F.H. Foster, **Genetic History**, 341. Foster has reference in the passage cited not to Hickok but to Emmons. Nowhere in his **Genetic History** does he even mention Hickok. It is entirely possible that it never even occurred to him to count Hickok a defender of the New England theology. Most probably he had not read Hickok's books; they would not have been required reading in the clerical circles in which Foster moved. Nonetheless, his omission of Hickok is, from the standpoint of scholarly thoroughness, inexcusable. He ought to have known how well his estimate of Emmons fitted the Auburn professor. Indeed, had he not viewed his subject too narrowly, he must have seen that Emmons was no rationalist at all!

⁴²Constructive realism differs from naive, or natural, realism in denying that we know immediately, or by representation, the external cause of our sensations. For it there is no common sense object; rather is it that what we take to be the object common to our own and other's senses is, in truth, an object of common reason. The position is similar to that maintained by Berkeley, although Hickok thinks it not so extreme as that of the Bishop, whom he takes as having taught that there is no world at all independent of perception. For himself, of course, Hickok does not doubt that an external world exists apart form his perception of it. The **Psychology**, he notes, "anticipates that, in order to any knowledge in sense, organs of sense must be possessed and that these organs must in some way be affected and induce a sensation. No organ, or an organ

vacant of all content of sensation, and there can be no perception." 'Psychology and Skepticism,' 394-395.

[43]If Hickok is right then Edwards was wrong, at least to the degree to which he presupposed a Lockean epistemology. Of course, it is arguable that what attracted Edwards to Locke was as much and more the latter's predisposition to an intuitive faith in the God of English Calvinism.

[44]Hickok, **Creator and Creation**; or, the knowledge in the reason of God and his work (Boston: Lee & Shepard, 1872), 166. Hereafter cited in the text as CC with page number.

[45]That is, the same as was indicated by Figure 1 (the first way) as noted in our analysis of Edwards' conception of God See p. 62.

[46]Hickok, 'Modern Philosophy Pantheistic,' 223.

[47]Ibid.

[48]Ibid. See also RC 400-403.

The Philosophical Calvinism
Of Samuel Harris

"However far science may advance, it can never transcend Theism, which recognizes perfect Reason as the ultimate ground of the universe, and its truths, laws, ideals and ends as the archetypes which the universe is progressively expressing."[1]

THE PHILOSOPHICAL THEISM OF SAMUEL HARRIS

> Here is no provincial theologian, under the influence of one
> restricted current of theological thought....You have here a
> theologian drawing his material from the whole world.[2]

By nineteenth century standards Samuel Harris[3] was a learned man. He had a gift for languages, and what is more important, the urge to use them. Of all the champions of a consistent Calvinism none was as well or as widely read in the literature of philosophy. His books bespeak a large familiarity with all of the major currents of European thought. More than Park, he had a cleric's knowledge of Greek and Latin, read French easily, and knew something of Spanish and Italian. The German theologians were his staple diet; for relaxation he read English poetry.

Like Edwards, he had been in the morning of his career a scholar-minister. From 1838 until 1841 he served as principal of Washington Academy in East Machias, Maine. In this latter year he was ordained to the ministry of the Congregational Church and subsequently held pastorates at Conway, Massachusetts and at Pittsfield resigning this last to accept the chair of systematic theology at Bangor Seminary. Henceforward he would be an academician. In 1867 he was offered, and accepted, the presidency of his alma mater, Bowdoin College. Four years later, having realized his mistake (the students were unruly, and he was at best an indifferent and unwilling disciplinarian) he eagerly welcomed an offer of appointment as Professor of Systematic Theology in Yale Divinity School. His first book, a collection of his seminary sermons,[4] was published in 1874; his first major scholarly work, **The Philosophical Basis of Theism,*** appeared in 1883. By then Harris was well past the age at which our modern practice decrees retirement. In happy ignorance of this he continued to teach and to write. In 1887 he published **The Self-Revelation of God,** and in 1896, at the age of eighty-two, brought

---

*Citations to this volume and its sequels are indicated in the body of the text by initials, i.e., PBT, SRG, and GCL with chapter (Roman capitals) and page number.

forth the first two volumes[5] of his systematic theology under the title, **God The Creator and Lord of All.** His labours done, he resigned his chair and retired to his summer home at Litchfield to await with equanimity the death that came for him on June 25th, 1899.

For all that his books are of a size and style appropriate to the presentation of a systematic theology, Harris's purpose and program is consistently homiletic. His rationalism, such as it is, is ever in the service of evangelism. The evangelical fervor which impelled him into the ministry shines through all his work. No more than Hopkins and Emmons does he doubt that the Bible records the historical truth, albeit his understanding of the nature of that truth is rather less fundamentalist and more philosophically informed than that of his eighteenth century forebears. To the end of his life his faith in the authenticity of God's revelation of himself to the authors of scripture remained unaffected by the strictures of nineteenth century biblical criticism. He will allow that the Bible is not "a mere book-revelation, a book of sentences, an arsenal of proof-texts, in each dictated by God and declaring a truth and rule of life for all persons in all places and all times."[6] "We must," he concedes, "have regard to the literary character of the Bible. It contains history and biography, didactic and preceptive teachings, proverbs, poetry, rhetorical figures, parables and fables, peculiar national and oriental coloring of thought, symbol and types, apocalyptic imagery, inspired prophecy. The interpreter must take note of these peculiarities. and they are to be interpreted according to the reasonable principles and laws of interpreting language." (GCL I. 13) Withal, the revelation communicated through these media is not to be denied. Reason no less than scripture, he maintains, confirms the fact that God has spoken to man. "Every science in its sphere discloses God revealing himself to men, and so is tributary to God's revelation of himself in Christ, perpetuated in the Holy Spirit, which is the highest form of his Self-revelation." (GCL I. 15) The facts observed no less than the vision proclaimed bear witness to the universal reign of law. "Theology therefore begins, like all science, in the observation of facts. God's revelation of himself is by his action in the constitution and evolution of the physical universe; in the constitution and history of man; and pre-eminently in his action redeeming man from sin, and developing his kingdom, recorded in the

Bible and continued through all subsequent ages in the Holy Spirit....Theology....brings the observed facts into the light of reason to ascertain their causes and laws, their relations to one another, and the unity in a system, only in the recognition of God, the absolute and universal Reason." (GCL I. 14-15) In this conception of deity as absolute Reason it rests, for herein Theology defines itself and discovers that in, by, and through which all questions are answered and all difficulties overcome.

II

> In defending theism it must never be forgotten that belief in a divinity wells up spontaneously, like the belief in the outward world, and is as well-founded. (SRG9)

Of realisms in philosophy there are no end, nor will there be as long as curiosity about the world outside our body persists. But does this curiosity demand a theory of knowledge to account for the existence of that which common sense never doubts? Unlike Kant and in company with the common-sensism of Thomas Reid, Harris does not think so. "In sense-perception man has knowledge of the external world. He has immediate perception of his own body and of bodies immediately affecting him through the senses. I assume this on the principles of Natural Realism. It is unnecessary to enter into any vindication of the reality of this knowledge against phenomenalists and idealists." (PBT 88) It is unnecessary because these latter views cannot, he believes, sustain themselves against the arguments of Hume; unnecessary also in that every attempt to demonstrate the being of the physical world must fail because "our knowledge of it is not by reasoning or any reflective thought, but is by intuition." (PBT 88) That it is so, Harris contends, the history of eplstemology bears witness. Many writers, ancient and modern, have maintained the impossibility of demonstrating the existence of the world exterior to the senses.

> Many writers designate rational intuition as faith or belief; these intuitions are frequently called primary beliefs. Others

give the name faith or belief to both rational and presentative intuition. Among these are Clement of Alexandria.
And in modern times F.H. Jacobi. J.G. Fichte and Rothe.
To these may be added Dr. Dorner, who says: "Jacobi rightly
says that even our certainty of the world of sense is a
faith."(PBT 761)

With the generality of the Transcendentalists before and Santayana after. Harris agrees that "the validity of demonstration is accordingly a matter of faith
only, depending on the assumption of matters of fact incapable of demonstration."[7]

Having thus, to his own satisfaction, absolved himself of the obligation
to preface his theism with a theory of knowledge, Harris readily exposes the
assumption which, in his opinion, justifies this appeal to faith. Locke had
presupposed the passivity of mind in perception; this presupposition Harris
vigourously repudiates. "The mind is active in knowing, not passive. The object known does not imprint itself on the mind in a state of passivity as tracks
are imprinted in mud. Knowledge is an action of the mind. All knowledge
consists in knowing." (PBT 44) In other words, the subject perceiving, the
act of perception, and the object perceived are not, as Locke and his followers
would have it, three separate somethings. Rather is it that the subject perceiving
and the act of perception are one. "The perception is the act of the mind;
it is its primitive intelligence." (PBT 44) But lest we should be tempted to forget
that we have here to do with a realism, Harris immediately adds, "it is the
intellectual equivalent of the object known in the act of perceiving." That
this still leaves us with two separate somethings does not particularly disturb
him. "As to the mystery how material things can be apprehended by the mind
in an intellectual equivalent, we may," he reassures us, "say at least that the
universe is itself the expression of thought and therefore can be translated
back into thought....We may reasonably suppose that if the universe were not
originally the expression of thought, science and all other apprehension of
it in thought would be impossible." (PBT 90-91) And so we might, if the
universe is originally—thought.

Two types of intuition have been mentioned above; these now require to be defended. When the intuition is of some particular reality in some particular mode of existence present to consciousness, Harris calls it presentative or perceptive intuition. As thus understood, intuition includes sense-perception and self-consciousness. In these, he claims, we come face to face with our environment and our self. Such an intuition is, of course, *immediate;* it is also, Harris insists, *self-evident;* "it needs no proof; it cannot be proved, because nothing can be adduced in proof more evident than the intuition itself;' (PBT 45) It is something that has to be and is a matter of faith, for as Lord Bacon says, unless a man please to go mad he dare not deny it. When due regard is paid to these universal truths and principles which make perceptive intuition intelligible, Harris calls the intuition rational.' As by perceptive intuition we know phenomena, so by rational intuition we apprehend its noumenal antecedent, "for it is a rational intuition that every change must have a cause.' (PBT 89) To every act of knowing, then, we know at once the particular and its principle of organization; we experience at once the sensation and its source. And we know in knowing this "that the mind is not divided; the act is one act in which the mind, constituted both perceptive and rational, knows by intuition at once perceptive and rational.' (PBT 89) The authority of Hume and Kant denies that it is so, but Hume and Kant, says Harris,[8] are wrong; wrong because both proceed on the phenomenalist assumption that what is given to the senses is a manifold of impressions. Consequently, neither is able to affirm that we have any" certain knowledge of external objects, other persons, or even ourselves. The thoroughgoing phenomenalism of Hume culminates in a skepticism relieved only by its author's exhortation to us not to take him seriously. The phenomenalism of Kant, for all that it is qualified by the introduction of a mind competent to its task of transforming a chaos of sensations into an orderly realm of things, is, Harris finds, no less agnostic in its implications. It makes no difference that Kant also recognizes the existence of a noumenal "in-itself.' The Kantina system is not thus to be redeemed. "The reason is not here recognized as revealing the rational ground, the rational principles, laws, ideals and ends of objects known in sense-perception, self-consciousness and reflective thought, and thus in harmony with and supplementing these faculties. The line of demarcation separates all that is known by the human faculties on the one hand, as phenomenal, from the thing-in-itself out of all relation to our faculties, on the other, as *noumenon*. The two spheres are antithetic and reciprocally exclusive. Reason, therefore, in giving only these noumena, effects nothing towards lifting the phenomenalism of this theory into real knowledge," (PBT 102) For that purpose we require a theory which recognizes that every perception of phenomena is at once a conception of their noumenal ground, and this, Harris insists, is precisely what the intuitional view provides.

Just so, but what, it may be asked, has Harris demonstrated? That phenomenalism does not give us certain knowledge? Hume would admit it. That it is agnostic as regards theology? Kant would agree. If these concessions add up to an admission that phenomenalism is an "error," it is because both relativism and agnosticism as such are epistemologically indefensible. Does Harris mean to say then that any theory of knowledge which forbids the possibility of our knowing God, is false? Just so.

"If man cannot know God, he cannot know anything." (PBT 5) "If the true and ultimate reality is unknowable, all reality is unknowable." (PB 35) There is no middle ground. For where, asks Harris, will you draw the line between the knowable and the unknown? If with Kant you draw it just this side of the thing-in-itself, you are subject to the Hegelian objection of having misused the category of cause and effect, which as one of the structures of the pure reason is properly applicable only to phenomena, to describe the relation between the phenomenal and the noumenal. Will you then say with Spencer that every phenomenon is a manifestation of some omnipresent Power, of itself unknowable? Then, replies Harris, you contradict yourself in so far as you claim to *know* that this unknowable is a Power manifest and omnipresent. For either you know the unknowable, in which case it is hardly proper to refer to it as unknowable, or you do not, in which case you pretend to knowledge you do not really have when you characterize the unknowable as a Power. Nor, he adds, is this dilemma to be avoided by maintaining a posture of resolute agnosticism

> If the agnostic says that he does not dogmatically deny the existence or reality of everything or anything, but only affirms his ignorance, he at least avows knowledge of his own

ignorance and of himself as ignorant....If he says he does
not affirm even his own ignorance, but that his mind is in
a state of continuous skepticism, doubting, questioning, in
a continuous equipoise, neither believing or disbelieving, still
he affirms his knowledge of his own skepticism; also, some
knowledge is prerequisite to the possibility of skepticism,
questioning or doubt. (PBT 19)

In any agnosticism some small remnant of reason is operative. In the very
act of doubting the most thoroughgoing agnostic admits to an awareness of
himself as—agnostic. His act confesses what his cognomen belies and renders
his agnosticism a something self-annulling.

That man knows *some*thing is, therefore, established by the indefensibility
of an absolute agnosticism; that this *some*thing which he knows is that Other
of which he is immediately aware is confirmed in his recognition of the act
of knowing as an intuition at once perceptive and rational. But does it follow
from this that he *knows* God? Only, it would seem if *some* implies *all* which
surely it does not. For to say that one knows someone is manifestly not to
claim that one knows everybody. That person would certainly make himself
a laughingstock who asserted that he knew all science because he knew some
physics. And so he would, if the knowledge here in question was, as the objection persupposes, a matter of *quantity*. On the other hand, if it is, as Harris assumes, a question of *quality* with which we have to do, then the case
is entirely altered; the issue then being whether or not *some* knowledge and
all knowledge are the same in *kind*. But of that, says Harris, there can be
no doubt.

Reason in man must be essentially the same in kind with
the Reason that is supreme....The truths which regulate all
thought and are law to all action must be universally true
or they are never true; they must be eternal in Reason that
is absolute and supreme, otherwise thought can never attain
to truth nor action to righteousness. (PBT 145)

As before, there is no middle ground. Either the Real embodies Reason or it totally excludes it. To say, as some do, that the Real is partly rational and partially surd is to say what cannot without contradiction be said, for it is to say either that one knows what he can not *know* (that the Real is partially surd), or it is to say than one cannot *know* what he knows (that the Real is partially surd).

Moreover, if the truths and laws and ideals of Reason so far as known are not the same for all rational beings, then science is delusion and knowledge as such is non-existent. For, writes Harris,

> if there is no supreme and eternal reason essentially the same with human reason, knowledge is disintegrated into the sub-jective impressions of individuals, of which each individual necessarily believes his own, but which have no common standard of truth and, in different individuals, may be con-tradictory to one another. Therefore what are fundamental realities and ideas of reason to man, are fundamental ideas and realities to God; these at least are so, whatever, not con-tradicting them, God may know which we are yet do not know. (PBT 145-146)

It remains, then, that the Real is rational and that what is known in part be-ing all of a piece with the whole, the whole itself is, in principle, knowable once the separation of phenomena and noumena is overcome in rational in-tuition. "For we have seen that Reason, it if is Reason at all, must be the same everywhere and always; and so must be the same in man and in God." (PBT 145)

Should it be objected that knowing Reason to be the same in man and God is not equivalent to knowing God, since God is a Person, whereas Reason is a process, and that hence it still remains to be shown that a man who knows anything knows God, Harris would reply that the conclusion is invalid because based upon a premise misconceived. For the fact is that it is not Reason but reasoning that is a process, not the noun but the participle which denotes that power of reasoning by which the finite mind passes via inference from the known to knowledge of the unknown. Conversely, it is not the participle but the noun which is another name for God, not reasoning but Reason which is a synonym for Person.[9]

That reason may and does in finite minds imply the power and necessity of reasoning, Harris does not deny. In any case, that is not the point in question. What we want to know is whether Reason conducts us to God, and the answer is "that all the components of the idea (of God) are known in intuition....and are in thought legitimately combined into the idea of God, the absolute Spirit." (SRG 38) It will be said that the idea of God thus derived cannot be that Person previously mentioned, since knowing someone as a person and knowing something as a combination of components are two entirely different matters. The objection, Harris admits, is to the point. If God is known as Person, it is, he would agree, only by virtue of his having communicated himself to man, and been responded to by man.

> The idea of God constructed by combining elements of thought known in experience is a legitimate basis of thought and argument, but not of religion. After it all, God remains apart from us; he does not come into communion with us, does not reveal himself to us by direct action or influence; we have no conscious experience of his presence with us....God known thus and not otherwise could not be the object of religious trust and service. Religion in its essence implies communication with God; it implies the action of God on us, the conscious experience of his influence, the conscious yielding to or resisting his drawing, conscious trust and service. For religion he is essentially the God "with whom we have to do..".....If then religion is not a delusion, if its object is real, if its belief and service are demanded by reason, then we have real knowledge of God in the conscious experience of his presence and influence in the soul. (SRG 39-40)

Is it reasonable to believe this? Entirely reasonable, answers Harris:

> If God is the absolute Reason in whom the universe is grounded, by whom it is ordered and pervaded, if he is immanent in it and in him we live and move and have our being, if he is Love subordinating and directing all things to the highest spiritual ends, then it is reasonable to believe that God may act on man, may throw rays from the light of the universal reason into his mind, may quicken his spiritual susceptibilities, and so present himself in his consciousness and be known in experience. (SRG 38)

The posterity of Locke, seizing upon this metaphor of the raythrower, will wonder why savages and infants do not testify to this activity of God. The reason is, says Harris, that we do not have here to do, as they suppose, with a doctrine of innate ideas, but rather with rational intuitions, "constitutional norms," as Harris sometimes terms them, native to every consciousnes, albeit particular to none. "The doctrine is that men think and act under the regulation of these principles even when they have never consciously formulated them. The objection, therefore, is founded upon a misapprehension of the doctrine." (PBT 126) It pre-supposes an adventitious acquisition of the idea of God, where actually the doctrine assumes a common participation of all in him in whom we (figuratively)[10] live and move and have our being.

This assumption it is which, when all is said, guarantees our knowing God. "Like this," our author concludes, "was the position of Descartes.

> He recognizes, at the basis of all reflective intelligence, primitive beliefs on which the force of all proofs depends and without which man is condemned to irremediable doubt; he sees that these fundamental principles thus necessarily believed must have their reality in God, and that if God does not exist, our reason has no guaranty; and he proclaims God, as the first and the most certain of all truths. Thus the existence of God, the absolute Reason, is the ultimate ground of the possibility of scientific knowledge....Without this neither induction nor the Newtonian method can conclude

in real knowledge....In other words, Induction rests on the
assumption, as it demands for its ground, that a personal
Deity exists. (PBT 82-83)

So too does Reason rest on this assumption, as it demands for its ground,
our recognition of its identity with God.

III

The doctrine of the Trinity presents to the intellect the
clearest, most comprehensive, and reasonable idea of God
and of his relations to the universe. (GCL I. 341)

"God is rational Spirit," this much, Harris believes, our intuition allows
us to assume. "At this point in our investigations we are not atheists nor
disbelievers, but Christian theists." (GCL I. 3) That God is, we need not doubt.
"The idea of God as Spirit and the belief in his existence as such precede
the intellectual process of verification and definition." (GCL I. 47) What God
is, and we are in relation to him, is understood in our realization that "Man
is in the likeness of God as rational spirit and is capable of knowing him
so far as he has revealed himself." (GCL I. 44) That he has revealed himself
is presupposed. "In our theological investigation," writes Harris, "religion
with its spontaneous beliefs is presupposed. In the investigations of theological
doctrine to ascertain what we know of God as revealed, we presuppose
also....the existence of God and the reality of his revelation of himself in the
various lines of divine action already mentioned, and pre-eminently in the
reality of his revelation of himself in his action in human history developing
his kingdom and culminating in Christ and the Holy Spirit, the God in Christ
reconciling the world unto himself as recorded in the Bible; and continued
through all generations in the Holy Spirit." (GCL I. 2, 3) What demands to
be shown is that this revealed God is not, as orthodoxy tends to teach, in
essence simple, but rather complex; is not in Being monopolar, but bipolar.
For if God is "rational Spirit," he is also and at once "in the form of the
absolute," which is to say that he is at once transcendent, insofar as he is

"the Absolute Being, unconditioned and unlimited by any power or condition independent of himself," (GCL I. 44) and immanent, inasmuch as he is "rational Spirit energizing in the universe." (Ibid.) Qua transcendent he exhibits the traditional catalogue of attributes. Thus he is, *omnipotent,* able to interrupt any physical sequence, frustrate any plan of finite free agents, annihilate any creature if reason demands it in the interest of his glory; *omniscient,* knowing all that which is limited in space, time, and quantity, but not confined within these limits, *omnipresent,* equally and integrally in every place; *impassible,* it being involved in the idea of God that he cannot suffer; and *immutable,* inasmuch as it is the world rather than God that changes. Conversely, he is, qua immanent, "active in the universe, sustaining, evolving and directing its energies." (PBT 510)

It will be said that this conception of God is nothing novel, that it is, in fact, the common view of Christian theism. And so it is. But Harris takes it very seriously, and therein lies the difference between his position and that of uncritical orthodoxy. For where the orthodox are generally content to beg the question of reconciling God's transcendent attributes with his immanent activity by calling it a mystery of faith, Harris seeks a reasonable solution. And he will not allow that a reasonable solution is one which emphasizes one pole or aspect of the divine to the logical, if not the actual, exclusion of the other. To his way of thinking, those scholastics and idealists who reverently insist that God is One exclusive of the manifold are no less in error than those pantheists and naturalists who aver that God is the manifold conceived as One. The truth being rather, as he believes, that God is both One and manifold, the reasonable solution is, therefore, that which the defenders of the faith once given to the saints have always espoused, i.e., the doctrine of the Trinity.

In it alone are the transcendent and the immanent aspects of God comprehended in complete harmony and unity. To it alone can he appeal who seeks a worthy philosophical conception of God.

> Aside from the revelation of God as the Trinity, the human mind has never the conception of the universe in its relations to him, in its comprehensiveness, completeness and uni-

ty, but has stuck in one-sided or fragmentary apprehensions. No doctrine of God has so satisfactorily resolved into unity the dualisms and the seeming antinomies arising in every attempt to construct a theory of the universe and to grasp the idea of the absolute,—none has ever so completely comprehended the bipolar and complemental truths in the vast idea of the absolute Being and his relation to the finite, as the doctrine of the Trinity. (GCL I, 356)

Have we then here to do with but another in that long series of fruitless efforts to define the internal constitution of God? by no means. For all that Harris, like his predecessors in the quest for a consistent Calvinism, is unable to resist the temptation to answer those objections brought against the orthodox doctrine of the Trinity by its Arian and Unitarian opponents, he knows better than to rest his case on a mere theory. "The truth of the doctrines of the God in Christ, and of the one God, Father, Son, and Holy Spirit, is," he insists, "independent of the philosophical and speculative questions respecting them which have been discussed within the church, and of the failure to attain agreement in answering these questions." (GCL I. 397) The trinitarian revelation inwrought into the very fabric of historic Christianity finds its ultimate justification in his eyes not in theological logomachy but in the revelation of God in Christ as recorded in the Bible.

It is, Harris argues, no disproof of the Trinity that the name and doctrine are not explicitly formulated in scripture. He will not allow that Channing's objection is valid. "The fact that a truth of God is revealed in its practical relations rather than in a scientific formula does not make it any less a truth. If the elements of a great reality are separately revealed, and a theological doctrine takes them up and expresses them, the doctrine is as true as if it had been formulated in the revelation." (GCL I. 339) And certainly the elements of the doctrine are there. John ascribes the names and titles of God to Jesus. Paul explicitly identifies the one as the other. Jesus himself, at various times and in various places, asserts as much. As against the Unitarian interpretation, the scriptural evidence, as Harris reads it, is overwhelming. "With equal clearness, God is revealed in the Bible in a third mode of being, in the Holy Spirit....the same passages of Scripture which declare the distinction of the Son from the Father in repeated instances refer also to the Holy Spirit and reveal a similar distinction between the Spirit and the Father and the Son." (GCL I. 321) Confronting these facts of the Christian revelation and combining them into a unity of thought necessarily gives us the idea of God as triune. Indeed, says Harris, if we look to the history of the doctrine of the Trinity we find that what is denied is not that the doctrine is unscriptural but that it is unreasonable!

Is it unreasonable? Harris will not admit that it is. And if "true rationalism"[11] is, as he claims, that "which recognizes its own dependence on and affinity with God, the absolute Reason,—which recognizes the fact that God reveals himself, and accepts all that he has revealed wherever it finds it,—which seeks the guidance of the ever-present Spirit of God, and willingly trusts and follows his gracious illumination, quickening, and drawing," (GCL I. 386) then the doctrine of the Trinity is truly rational. Is the Trinity then no more than the mystery which the mass of theologians from Augustine onwards have declared it to be? It is, Harris answers, a mystery still, but not in the sense that it is utterly inconceivable. "Agnosticism fancies that because God is a mystery he cannot be known; anthropomorphism fancies that because God is known he cannot be a mystery;" (GCL I. 282) both err by confounding the inconceivable with the unknowable. That God as absolute Being is always transcendent of merely human knowledge is obvious, but this, Harris thinks, is not at all to concede that God is inconceivable. To realize that our thought of him must always fall short of what he is in himself is not to deny that we have a thought of him. Rather is it to affirm that our thought, limited by our finitude, is essentially mysterious. "A mystery, therefore, is always an object known, but with the consciousness of limits which, with our present opportunities, resources, and powers, we cannot transcend." (GCL I. 281) So too, then, with the Trinity; it is at once a mystery and that concept which alone makes the bipolarity of God intelligible.

Augustine and Calvin alike declare that it is so. "God is known more truly in our thought than in our words," says the saint, and adds, "he is more in reality than in our thought."[12] "The words Father, Son, and Spirit," the Genevan tells us, "certainly intimate a real distinction....but it is a distinction not a division....when this is honestly confessed, we have," he concludes, "no further concern about words."[13] Besides, Harris continues,

> the scriptures, as we have seen, present this distinction as eternal in God. They teach that the Father, Son, and Holy Spirit is each eternal, and ascribe to each the names, attributes and works of God. Thus it is evident that the doctrine of the one God, Father, Son, and Holy Spirit, involves no contradiction. God is not three in the same sense in which he is one. He is not three beings in one being, nor three gods in one God, nor three persons in one person. He is one God in three eternal modes of being. (GCL I . 327)

To Levi Leonard Paine this smells of Sabellianism, and that it is such is, he thinks confirmed by the Christology of Harris.

> The Sabellian strain that runs through it is seen in the statement that "Christ as mediator is not a third person between God and man," (GC 1. 433)—a statement that is based on the monistic modal theory that there are not three real persons in the Godhead, but that "one God exists in three eternal modes of being." Of course, then, Christ could not be "a third person between God and man." One may well ask what element of mediatorship is left. Has not the mediatorial office of Christ become a docetic farce?

Harris, of course, will not admit it. To begin with, Sabellianism, as he understands the term, does not denote modes of *being* eternal in God, but rather modes of *manifestation* in time, differing ways of action wherein God reveals himself to man. "The criticism of the form of expression which I have used, that it involves Sabellianism, is entirely unjustifiable. Calvin himself was at one time charged with teaching Arianism, and not long after with teaching Sabellianism." (GCL 1. 328) Harris forbears to compare his own situation with that of his spiritual peer, perhaps because he realizes that his critic will recognize how close to Calvin's view his own view is. As for the corollary suggestion that his view cannot in good conscience name the members of the Trinity persons, it is, he feels, a criticism that need not concern the Christian believer.

> At different times, when in the course of the ages this subject has been prominent in theological discussion, the suggestion has been made that the word "person" no longer be used in this application to the distinctions in the Godhead...But it has been so often and so earnestly explained that the word is used in a technical and qualified sense, that this ought to be generally understood by all who controvert the doctrine. And the word "person" is so fixed and universal in the creeds and theology of the western churches that it would be impossible without causing misunderstanding and division, and unsettling faith. It is to be noticed, however, that in the doxologies, the benedictions, the sacraments, the hymns and worship of the church, the biblical names, Father, Son, and Holy Spirit are commonly used, and the name "person" is rarely applied to them....It is evident, therefore, that if they are necessary to theology, they are not necessary to religion and worship. (GCL I 329-330)

Which being so, we had best be, like Calvin, "not so austerely precise as to keep up a strife about naked words."[15]

Having thus, to his own satisfaction, disarmed all possible internal criticism of the doctrine of the Trinity, Harris proceeds to outline the operation of the Trinity in creation.

> Before the creation and before all time God is eternal Father, Son and Holy Spirit. In the creation God, in the Son or Logos, is expressing the archetypal thought of perfect Reason, moulding it, as it were, into types in the forms of space and time...At first is the homogeneous nebulous mat-

ter,—then motion, and the inorganic universe with its mechanical and its higher chemical forces. But motion can begin only from a power transcending the motionless homogeneous matter...Then comes a time when organic vegetable life appears. But life can be produced only from previous life....Then again comes a time when an organism appears that is sensitive. Again the physical confronts the spiritual, and from the latter comes the power that lifts the inanimate organism into sensitive life....Then, after many ages of preparation, as soon as, in the progress of the evolution, a vital physical organism is developed, through which it is possible for a rational personal being to act, man appears....In man the physical evolution is transcended and becomes a moral and spiritual evolution under moral and spiritual influences; and moral law and government, discipline and education, redemption by the grace of God begin. (GCL 1. 408-410)

Excepting the accommodation to the fact of evolution, there is nothing in this interpretation which need trouble the biblically oriented Christian. The doctrine of creation here envisaged is the same in spirit as that described in **Genesis**, it is, Harris insists, compatible with any subsequent process of evolution. Professor Haeckel and others have claimed, with on air of triumph, that evolution disproves creation. But it is not so. Evolution gives no explanation of the origin of the homogeneous stuff itself, nor of the beginning of motion in it. It leaves the necessity of a creation as imperative as it was before." (GCL I. 465) Evolution is, he concedes, incompatible with that theory of creation which maintains that the universe is the product of divine fiat, completed at a stroke and then left for all eternity to run on by itself, but this, Harris is sure, is not the theory that theism implies. For theism would have it that God is immanent as well as transcendent, and immanence, he thinks, implies an evolution of some sort always going on. Conversely, the fact of evolution confirms the Christian belief in the continuing operation of the Holy Spirit, for "without God immanent in it the evolution cannot account for its own continuance and for the higher orders of being which at successive epochs appear in the universe." (GCL I.465)

This teleological aspect of things it is which, according to Harris, justifies the conclusion that the primary reality of the universe is spiritual or supernatural. "Instead of the common impression that the fundamental and substantial reality is matter and its forces, the things we see and feel and handle, and that spirit is ghostly, phantasmic and unreal, we must," he feels, "accept as true the very contrary,—that the spiritual and the supernatural is the fundamental reality, that the material is a medium in and through which spirit reveals itself." (GCL I.176) This being so, it cannot be, as some theologians have maintained, that the distinction between the natural and the supernatural is between God, the angelic hosts and immortal humanity on the one side and man in his material home on the other. Rather is it, says Harris, that the true line of demarcation is that between God and all finite rational or spiritual persons on the one side and the physical universe including irrational and impersonal beings on the other. "The real distinction (is) that between the spiritual, rational and personal, and the physical, irrational and impersonal." (GCL 1.71) Given that it is such, and Scripture, Harris finds, declares that it is such, that which has been said before concerning the capacity of man to know God as absolute Spirit and enter into communion with God as Holy Spirit is now confirmed. Now man appears to be what in truth he is, "a supernatural being, on the same side of the line with God and in the likeness of God as rational Spirit." (GCL 1. 71) In man material evolution attains its highest order of being;[16] with man moral evolution begins.

IV

> That God was in Christ reconciling the world unto himself
> is the only adequate explanation of his relation to human
> history before and after his coming. (GCL I. 318)

Levi Paine would have it that the weakest point of Harris's system is its christology. "Here," writes Paine, "he is obliged to enter directly the field of history, and his ignorance of recent historical and critical investigations is surprisingly revealed....There seems to be a fatal incapacity....to comprehend the revolutionary character of the new history and criticism. Dr. Harris writes church history just as it was written a hundred years ago. He still accepts the Nicene creed and the Chalcedon definition, with all their unhistorical assumptions....As we should expect, his trinitarianism and christology are wholly traditional."[17] That they are as such, therefore, in error is, of course, a conclusion that neither Harris nor more recent orthodoxy would concede, and perhaps rightly so since Paine does somewhat less than justice to our author when he charges him with ignorance of the findings of nineteenth century biblical scholarship. For the fact of the matter is not that Harris is ignorant of these findings; on the contrary, he discusses divers of them in each of his books. Rather is it that having considered the spirit, or, more accurately, the lack of spirit animating such criticism, he rejects the assumption on which all of its conclusions rest.

This assumption, whose falsity, Harris feels, should be evident to anyone who pauses to consider its consequences, is that the miraculous in scripture is mythical. The critic assumes, and, so too, presumably, does Professor Paine, that it is possible to isolate the historical and rational elements of the Christian religion from each other and from the supernatural experience of those to whom and through whom the revelation of God as recorded in the Bible has been made. He assumes this because it is convenient for him to do so, for thereby he rids himself of the incubus of miracle while yet retaining the element of the historical, and afterwards, as the historical is called in question, the assumption enables him to discard as much of the history as his rationalism may dictate. Should anyone object to his disregard of the experiential element in this proceeding, he has a ready answer: the religious experience, he would maintain, is the province of the mystic, and the truth or falsity of mysticism is no part of the critical concern. If he is right, and his assumption is justified, then, as Harris sees it, the case for Christianity is lost. "Nothing then remains but an ancient literature and history, and the only interest in the study of it is critical, archaeological and historical. Then the living water has dried away. Instead of a springing fountain we have only a well-curb and a bucket; instead of the river of life only the dry bed of a once running stream; and critical thought busies itself in laboriously tracing its dry and stony course." (SRG 129-130)

Faced with a disaster of such magnitude the thinking Christian has no choice but to believe that the critic errs who separates the experiential from the other elements in the knowledge of God. For in truth they belong together. "The true and largest knowledge of God is possible only in the synthesis of the experiential, the historical, and the ideal or rational. These must test, correct and restrain, and at the same time clarify, verify and supplement each other, and thus bring their several results into unity." (SRG 133) Hence the assertion that some have experienced God and subsequently borne witness to their revelation is not to be brushed aside as a matter for mysticism but is rather to be considered in terms of its consistency with the deliverances of reason and the pattern of history. It implies, therefore, no disparagement of the new history and criticism to suggest that it need not ignore religious experience. To grant the possibility that truth has been revealed to and through the authors of scripture were no sin of scholarship. No more, Harris believes, is it unscholarly to feel moved by the Holy Spirit as one studies scripture. "Devout scholarship may be as scholarly as the undevout." (SRG 130) For there is, he is sure, something in the Bible which mere scholarship misses. "If the student feels his spiritual needs, if his spiritual possibilities are awakened and his spiritual powers active, God will find him and he will find God in the Bible. If it is only critical and archaeological interest which moves him, criticism and archaeology will be all which he will find." (SRG 130) The argument is reminiscent of Calvin's notion that only the elect, illuminated by the Holy Spirit, have eyes to see in scripture that which ought to be seen by all. Nor does Harris deny that it is so. For who are these who see the truth of synthesis if not the elect? And who are saved if they are not saved who recognize in scripture the Word of God?

Is this to say, as Calvin does, that the original of scripture is inerrant? By no means. For Harris the Bible is the inspired record of God's action centering in Christ and establishing his kingdom in perpetuity in the Holy Spirit. "It is not itself the revelation, but it is the inspired record of the revelation and hence preserves its contents." (SRG 457) The distinction is important, for, as Harris notes, it gives a certain independence of historical criticism. "If the Bible is a collection of propositions given directly by God, then one error throws suspicion on all. But if the revelation is made in God's historical action in Israel preparatory to Christ's coming and then in Christ himself, then a single error of fact does not invalidate the history as a whole." (SRG 461) The credibility of the history of Israel is not destroyed because some scholar has his doubts about the date and authorship of Deuteronomy. "And if one is convinced on scientific grounds that Joshua did not cause the sun to stand still, or on critical grounds that an angel did not trouble the water in the pool of Bethesda, these conclusions do not make it necessary to disbelieve that God was in Christ reconciling the world to himself." (SRG 462) For nothing, he believes, can unsettle our belief which does not at once deny the role of reason in history. "If the ideal Christ is true the historical Christ is real. For the essence of Christianity is not speculative nor ethical philosophy, but the redemption of man from sin in the person of Jesus Christ." (SRG 472)

That the ideal Christ is true, Harris takes to be established by the doctrine of the Trinity, the truth of which latter is assumed by him to have been shown in the argument rehearsed above. As for the historical Jesus, the evidence of the Bible and of tradition suffices. On this point, Paine's judgement is correct. Harris is a traditionalist. The problems raised in Strauss's **Life of Jesus** and its successors do not disturb him; in his opinion they are settled in Neander's **Life of Jesus Christ.** He reads Renan as a defender of theism and finds his own view of Jesus to be substantially that of Endersheim. He takes no notice in his books of the discrepancies in the lives as chronicled in **Matthew, Mark, and Luke,** nor does the issue of their relation to **John** anywhere arise. No more than it did Calvin, does it trouble him that the evidences conflict. "If our faith rests on the letter of the Bible, it stands unstable, like an inverted pyramid on its apex, and the disturbance of a letter by criticism overturns our faith. But if our faith rests on God as the redeemer of men revealed by his gracious action in the history recorded in the Bible nothing can unsettle our faith which does not unsettle the whole course of the history." (SRG 462)

God was in Christ. That, as far as Harris is concerned, is settled truth, and the controversies which have arisen within the church concerning the construction of the person of Christ in thought do not, in his opinion, disturb that truth, for in none of these controversies has it been disputed that God was in Christ reconciling the world unto himself. "The common doctrine of the church has been, that Christ is one person possessing two natures, the divine and the human. The question is, What person is it that presents himself in Christ? Is it God or man?" (GCL 1. 399) Neither, answers Harris, if both be taken in exclusion. This person cannot be a particular man named Jesus, since such a one, however richly endowed, is incompetent to perform the work of God in Christ redeeming man from sin. Nor, on the other hand, can it be supposed that the person in Christ is God in that eternal mode of his being as the logos, for in this case the human in Christ is either displaced by or lost in the divine. What person is it then that presents himself in Christ? It is, Harris teaches, that person who is, in one aspect of his personality, divine, and, in another aspect of his personality, human. "For it must be remembered that personality is not the person, but is only the name of the abstracted qualities or nature which constitute a being personal, and that absoluteness and finiteness are not of the essence of personality, but only different forms in which personality may exist." (GCL I. 401) Therefore, the co-existence in one *incarnate* person of divine and human attributes of personality is nothing contradictory, for contradiction, Harris feels, only begins with the assertion that Jesus Christ exists as a human person antecedent to the incarnation. Thus we have only to deny that Christ, *before and apart from the incarnation,* is an individual man, is that human person which through the union of the divine and the human *in* the incarnation he becomes, and the primary problem of Christology is solved.

The thought will, then, be as follows: God, in the son, creates the universe and thus brings into being reality other than himself. He energizes in the creation, preservation, and evolution of the universe, and is thus continually and progressively expressing his thought therein in the finite, in the forms of space and time. He reveals himself in the physical system. He makes a higher revelation of himself in the spiritual system, every person in which is, as personal, in the likeness of God. In the fulness of time, when the world is prepared for it, he reveals himself in Christ. The Word or Son of God creates a germinal human being that would have developed into a man rational and personal. But, instead, the divine Son or Word takes possession of the germinal organization thus created, and from the beginning acts in and through it under the limitations and conditions of a human nature. But the personal nature or essence of God is the same in kind with that of man. And acting in Christ through a human organization and under human limitations and conditions, it is also the same in the form of its manifestation. Thus it is at once divine and human. And the two are the same in essence and in form. (GCL 1. 402)

Since the doctrines here expressed, the doctrines that is of anhypostasia and enhypostasia,[8] have been held by some to be heretic, Harris is at pains to point out the identity of his position with "that doctrine of anhypostasia commonly hold by the Reformed churches, "and maintained, in substance, if not by name, in the writings of Turretin, Hooker, and Samuel Hopkins.[9] "Trinitarians who reject it (anhypostasia) show," he thinks, "that they have not apprehended its real significance. It is commonly spoken of as the doctrine of the impersonality of Christ's human nature; and this is misunderstood as denying that he is human. But, in fact, the doctrine does not deny that Christ is human, but strenuously affirms that the one person, Jesus Christ, is both divine and human; in one aspect this one person is divine, having all the attributes essential to personality in God; in another he is human, having all the attributes essential to human personality." (GCL I. 401) What he is *after* his resurrection Harris does not say. Presumably the risen Christ reverts to his pre-incarnational status. Presumably, but by no means certainly, for there remains the problem of the preservation of his human personality in his heavenly being.

Of more immediate importance, however, is the problem of the relation of the person to its personalities. The problem, it must be admitted at the outset, finds no real solution in the christology of Harris. The distinction of the person from its human personality, assumed for the purpose of rendering intelligible the doctrine of anhypostasia, is irrelevant to the doctrine of enhypostasia. In this latter, the problem reappears in all its difficulty; nor does it avail to speak, as Harris does, of a difference of aspects since the Christian claim is that both aspects simultaneously qualify the one person, making him to be at once human and divine.

According to the doctrine of anhypostasia there was a time when Christ, possessed a personality purely divine. His human personality did not then exist, and hence is not essential to his being. Is his divine personality essential to his being? The essence of any person, human and/or divine, is, Harris teaches, a consciousness of self as persisting unchanged through all changes. "Persistence in unity and identity through all changes is central to the idea of an absolute Being." (SRG 213) From this we might infer that the divine personality is peripheral, hence not of the essence. The inference finds reinforcement in the dictum, previously noted, that personality is not the person, but is only the name of the abstracted qualities which constitute a being personal. It seems to be confirmed by the fact that the divine is not native to the "germinal organization" which was Jesus in embryo, for that which "takes possession" of such an organization can hardly be said to be of its essence. Consistency, therefore, would appear to require of Harris that he admit that the divine personality of the historical Jesus is not essential to his being as the Christ. Of course, Harris admits no such thing. Nowhere in his writings does he even imply the non-essentiality of the divine personality in relation to the divine person. On the contrary, he everywhere refers to these in conjunction, and he not infrequently confuses the one with the other as, for instance, in the following definition:

> A person is a rational free being conscious of self as persisting, one and the same, through all changes. Personality thus defined is not incompatible with the true absolute. (SRG 213)

It is as if he recognized that rationality is not only a quality, and hence *of* the personality, but that it is that one quality which, as he frequently implies, alone constitutes a being personal. It is, in sum, the essence of the personality *and* of the person. Through reason the union of the two is accomplished. Were this particular quality to be abstracted not only the person but that whole speculative scheme of which the person is the keystone must dissolve in chaos. Therefore, remembering the role of reason, we have no choice but to conclude that personality *is* the person, and thus we end, as Harris does, in contradiction!

May we assert, then, that his christology stands discredited? He would not concede it. "The truth of the doctrines of the God in Christ, and of the one God, Father, Son, and Holy Spirit, is," he insists, "independent of the philosophical and speculative questions respecting them which have been discussed." (GCL I. 397) It suffices that we have penetrated a little way into the mystery; being finite we cannot hope to do more, and indeed it is not necessary that we try. "The words with which Calvin closed his discussion of the Trinity in "The Institutes" are always pertinent. "Finally I trust that the entire sum of this doctrine has been unfolded, if indeed the readers impose some limit of moderation on their curiosity and do not call up troublesome and perplexing questions more eagerly than is fit. I do not in the least expect to satisfy those who are carried away in intemperance of speculation. I certainly have not craftily passed by anything which I might suppose opposed to me; but, while I study the edification of the church, I have purposely left untouched many points which are of little practical importance and would only cause useless perplexity to the readers." "[20]

V

> Scientific evolution, if true, demands the existence of the personal God, the absolute Reason energizing in all that is; but may modify some common opinions respecting Him and His relation to the universe. (PBT 502)

Three influences, pervasive and inescapable, dominate the philosophical and religious thought of Nineteenth Century America. In the earlier decades Calvinists, Unitarians, and Transcendentalists alike are captive to the German philosophy popularized by Coleridge, Carlyle, and Cousin. The theories of geological and biological evolution command the consideration of every serious thinker during the middle years, and condition them to accept, in the latter part of the century, the revolutionary developments in physics and mathematics foreshadowing the developing of the modern scientific world-view. Thus Samuel Harris, whose ministerial and professional career spans two-thirds of the century, finds it necessary to frame his epistemology in the light of the speculations of Kant, Schleiermacher, Hegel, and Lotze, and conform his cosmology to the theoretical requirements of Lyell, Darwin, Clerk-Maxwell, and DuBois Reymond. Most particularly is this the case as respects his account of the creation and the coming of man.

Hopkins and Emmons, taking the Bible at its word, could readily conclude that the event of creation had happened somewhat less than six thousand years before the settlement of New England, but for Harris, with the evidences of Lyell and Darwin requiring to be explained, this conclusion is false comfort. Nor can he rest easily in the classical notion a creation *ex nihilo.* Evolution is, he maintains, perfectly compatible with the idea of creation, but it is with a creation understood as an eternally continuous progression from potentiality to actuality. "Thus the universe which from eternity had existed potentially in God, is perpetually becoming actual in space and time by the individuating action of God, and is thus progressively revealing what God is....Creation, therefore, is not originating something out of nothing. On the contrary, in creating the Absolute Being calls into action power eternally potential in his infinite plentitude: and this power, energizing under the limits of space and time thus individuating and revealing itself, becomes cognizable as a finite reality or being." (PBT 515) Just how this happens, however, is and must ever remain, a mystery: "How God creates and sustains the universe, how the infinite reveals itself in the finite, are unanswerable questions."[21] (PBT 510) It is enough that we may say at every point of time, "In the beginning God."

Harris has read Herbert Spencer, and, agreeing with him, postulates an ultimate Power, specifically the power of Energizing Reason "realizing in finite creations the archetypes of all truth, right, perfection and good which it sees internal in itself." (PBT 192) Since power thus realized is, to Harris, unthinkable save as the action of a Person,[22] we are justified in equating this power of energizing reason with the God of theism, and supposing "that from him energy is continuously flowing into the physical system, sustaining it in being, and directing its evolution according to its constitution and laws and in the progressive realization of his archetypal ideal of all perfection and well-being possible in a finite universe." (GCL I. 83) Which is to say that evolution, as Harris conceives it, is in no way incompatible with the doctrine of creation as here understood since evolution embraces only the ongoing of the finite universe and does not reach to a concern for the ultimate beginning or infinite ground of things. That concern remains, as before, outside the province of physical science. Conversely, the assumption of materialism that evolution of itself suffices to account for everything is equally invalid since the theory always assumes a beginning.

> There must then be a cause antecedent to this beginning....
> But matter cannot have been the cause....for the evolution
> itself includes the entire activity of matter. If matter by its
> own action arranged itself and started the evolution, then
> evolution, even as a theory merely of the ongoing of nature,
> breaks down; since the most important action of matter was
> antecedent to the evolution and originated it. Also, since mat-
> ter is unintelligent and void of freedom, it could not have
> passed from previous inaction....to active energy, nor could
> it have been aware of any reason for so doing. Only a Reason
> energizing in freedom could do this. But if Energizing Reason
> is the ultimate ground of the existence of matter and all its
> forces, then the beginning of the evolution can be accounted
> for. Evolution, therefore, demands a doctrine of creation in
> the sense explained. (PBT 508)

Yet even as this infusion of divine energy is passing into the finite universe, God remains in principle for Harris what he was for Calvin and his early American expositors. The "archetypal ideal" is still conceived as the foreknowledge of a creator Spirit, "in which all of the powers revealed in the evolution of the Universe exist eternal, unlimited and unconditioned." (PBT 507)

The difference is that whereas the Hopkinsian conception of God envisaged an instantaneous actualization of the divine decrees, the notion now is one of continuous progressive creation, "a growth evolving higher and higher powers and revealing more and more the thought, the wisdom, the love and power of the Creator." (PBT 510) If creation is an instantaneous act in which the universe in all its detail is brought into being, then to assert that God is unconditioned would be indeed an inconsistency. But if the universe is not a finished product but a process in which God is ever active, then, Harris is sure, evolution is consistent with creation. "Then the essential significance of the doctrine of creation is simply this: The universe at every point of time is distinct from God but dependent on him for its existence. At whatever point the universe is thought of, it must be thought of as dependent for its being, as well as for its potential powers and its laws, on the absolute Being distinct from itself. At every point of time God is the *prius* of the universe, and is its cause. The doctrine of creation, therefore, is compatible with evolution, as it is with any other law of the ongoing of nature." (PBT 510)

The notion that the powers potential in God become progressively actual in space, conjoined with the recognition that the universe at any point in time is incomplete, suggests that God himself evolves or grows with his creation. But Harris will not have it so. His commitment to the God of consistent Calvinism, however attenuated by his awareness of the need to adapt that conception of God to the fact of evolution, inhibits any great leap forward to the conception of a God in the making as that is envisaged in contemporary process theology. To his way of thinking that would be pantheism, and with pantheism in any form Harris, as an orthodox Christian, will have nothing to do since that, as he defines it,[23] denies the conception of God as Person and as cause. His case against pantheism, however, as argued vigourously and at length in PBT and again in SRG rests not so much on any pantheistic denial of divine personality as it does on the conviction of common sense "that real knowledge begins in the knowledge of particular beings determinate both by their individuality as beings and by their peculiar modes of existence." (SRG 173) This, he thinks, excludes not only Spinozism and Hegelianism, but any and every variety of scientific materialism. In short, "God is not the sum total of finite things; he is not the largest general notion of logic; he is not the universal abstract idea of pure being; he is not the sum of all attributes; he is the living God, distinct in his divine oneness of being from all finite beings." (PBT 177)

The chief among these finite beings, man, is, for Harris, the culmination of the evolutionary process. "In the production of man the process of the physical evolution on the earth reaches its consummation. The zoological process is consummated and the psychological and spiritual process begins. There is not to be the genesis of a higher species but the educating, civilizing and perfecting of man." (SRG 489) The reason offered for this conclusion is that with the advent of man we reach the line of demarcation between the personal and impersonal, the supernatural and the natural, the line that is between matter and spirit. We know from scripture that man is made in the image of God, "that the essential elements of personality are the same in man and in God." (GCL I, 477) Knowing this, we know further that the future evolution of man is the spiritual development of his personality and infer therefrom that "the physical system as a whole exists not for itself, but as subservient to the bringing in of the spiritual system and of man as belonging to it." (SRG 286)

Withal, it would be incorrect to infer from this declared subservience of the physical system to its spiritual counterpart that Harris envisages a progressive idealisation of the universe. His sensitivity to the implications of Hegelian idealism, conjoined with his commitment to Christian realism, precludes his development of the doctrine of the two systems in the manner adopted by his younger contemporary, Josiah Royce. In Harris the emphasis throughout is epistemological rather than ontological. Thus to say, as he does, that man "as a personal or spiritual being is supernatural," is not to say that man is transmundane. Rather is it to say that, "as such man knows what the supernatural is." (SRG 85) "Are we," Harris asks himself, "rational, free, personal beings? If so, we are supernatural in the true meaning of the word," (SRG 86) supernatural, that is, understood as hypernatural or personal, known as such by intuition. As supernatural in this latter sense, we may, reasoning from the effect, man as personal, to the cause, God as personal Spirit, reconfirm our conviction of the existence of God (for the cause, notes Harris (SRG 342) must be adequate to the effect) and, what is perhaps of greater importance as respects the spiritual evolution of man, establish the freedom of the human will.

> The evidence of the existence of God already found in man's rational constitution reappears in his constitution as free will. Man is constituted free by his rationality. By virtue of this he is able, in the light of reason and under the influence of rational motives, to determine the ends to which he will direct his energies....Will is reason energizing, and reason is will potential. If, then, human reason and rational knowledge presuppose the existence of God, the absolute Reason, so also the will, which is free only as it is rational, must presuppose the same. (SRG 375)

That the argument involves a certain circularity does not seem to trouble Harris. What really matters for him is that this conception of the freedom of the will as consisting in the relation of will to reason offers an escape from the "ambiguities and perplexities" in which Edwards and those who have subscribed to his teaching on the freedom of the will have enmeshed the New England theology.

"According to his (Edward's) conception freedom is discussed from the point of view of efficient causation, and must be defined in terms of power only, as the power of contrary choice. Also the distinction of natural and moral ability which, in accordance with the universal use of language, is legitimately applied to outward acts, is illegitimately applied to the will itself as an explanation of its freedom; with the result, again, that freedom must be defined in terms of power only, overlooking all in which the freedom actually consists." (PBT 363) However, if freedom of the will is defined not in terms of power only, but with reference to reason, then we have "a conception of freedom which stands clear, unambiguous, self-consistent and reasonable, and is adequate to explain the nature and ground of moral responsibility." (PBT 364) Possibly so, but to establish this beyond cavil would require an exposition and analysis of an argument which in PBT runs to sixty pages, and that, I submit, may be safely left to those compulsively concerned.

Granting for the moment that Harris has freed us from the strictures of the Edwardsian conception of the freedom of the will, it remains to determine whether, in light of his conviction that the perfecting of man as person is the goal of the evolutionary process, he will allow that we are similarly freed from the onus of the New Divinity notion of original sin. Prima facie it would seem that such must be the case given the incongruity of spiritual evolution and total depravity, and the fact of the matter is that nowhere in his writings does Harris employ the terminology of Hopkins and Emmons. On the other hand, he does allow that sin is the essential, indeed, the only essential evil, evil in itself and in its outcome, and he concedes that this evil is actually in the universe forcing its reality on our notice every day through all the history of mankind. But he will not go so far as to maintain with Emmons that God is the author of this evil, in the sense that he does nothing to prevent it. "It (evil) came into the world by the action of finite free-agents transgressing the law of love. It is continued in the world in the same manner.... They (the free-agents) alone are the responsible authors of sin. God is not its author." (PBT 532) Harris will not have it that sin is by God's decree: "the separation of the wicked from the righteous is not first by the command of God, "Depart," but is first by their own choice departing from God and refusing and resisting all redeeming influences and agencies by which he seeks to draw them back. God's word, "Depart," is last and not first; it announces the continuance of that departure from him which they themselves have chosen." (PBT 533) That it is so, follows, according to Harris, from the assumption, implicit in the notion of a spiritual evolution, that the future is always to be better than the past. And that not as Hopkins would have it, in some glorious millenium, but in the progress of the material universe. "Evolution under the theistic conception is to be, with whatever rhythmic movements, a perpetual progress to the higher and better." (PBT 534)

Offhand, this would appear to contradict our previous denial that Harris envisages a progressive idealisation of the universe, but such is not his intention. His position is not idealism but meliorism, not an ontological passage to an Hegelian heaven but an epistemological realization of an exalted earth. In this realization of an exalted or transfigured earth, man finds at once his hope of heaven and his prospect of immortality, for, Harris thinks, it is reasonable to believe that "when the body dies the spirit lives, forming for itself it may be by its own plastic power a more ethereal medium through which it may act." (PBT 522) The fact that our minds appear to function by means of a physical organism does not, to Harris' way of thinking, invalidate this conclusion, for behind the perceptible world of organisms is an imperceptible universe. "Behind the world perceptible to sense is a world of molecules and ethers entirely imperceptible....Evolution assumes that the imperceptible universe existed before the perceptible, and that the latter evolved from the former. But behind this imperceptible world, and beyond and above it, we find mind revealing itself. If now it is admitted that mind in man is a causative energy, in the consciousness of which man knows himself as a personal being, and in this consciousness his knowledge of being in its deepest reality originates, it is entirely supposable that this personal spirit may have in itself energy to survive the catastrophe of death, taking with it or finding for itself in the extra-sensible sphere a finer medium through which to act in consciousness." (SRG 512) In the mission of the Christ touching sinful souls with his saving grace we discover that the universe is in truth the temple of God and the physical in it but the veil hiding the Holy of holies. "At death the veil of sense drops off, and with open spiritual vision man sees his spiritual environment." (GCL I, 419)

That this spiritual environment is not very far removed from that descried by Edwards and his disciple Hopkins is made clear by Harris in his account of God's chief end in creation. With these and their companions in the New Divinity he proclaims the biblical message that God does all things for his own glory,[24] but not, as they have been understood to hold, simply because it is the duty of the creature to glorify his creator forever. The glory of God, properly understood, is, Harris holds, his perfections and his actions expressing them. "The glory of God is that which makes him glorious." (GCL I, 494), that is, "the realization of all ideals of perfection and good which it is possible to realize....and which are the archetypes of the universe eternal in his all comprehending intelligence....In brief....God's end in creating the universe and in his immanent energizing in it is to realize in it the thought of his perfect wisdom by his action in perfect love."[25] (GCL I, 497)

VI

We have, then, here the Sir William Hamilton of the New England theology. Sir William was a loyal member of the Scotch school, but he enriched it with a learning which none of his predecessors had had....Such was Harris' relation to the New England school. And as Sir William was more than a member of his school, being in fact the thinker who formed the transition to later and different modes of thought, so Harris formed the transition from the New England to later theologies.[26]

The consensus of those few who have studied Harris is that he is indeed a transitional figure, and so he is, but not in the sense suggested by Foster. That he looked back to Locke and forward to Darwin is a fact. In point of time his thinking spans the pre- and post- evolutionary eras. But his relation to the New England theology was not, I submit, that of a thinker transitional to later modes of thought. Foster himself confesses as much when he tells us at the beginning of his exposition of Harris that he,

stood squarely on the ground of New England theology, and may be regarded in this respect a member of the school. He teaches the Trinity, the deity of Christ (but not as meagerly as Stuart and Park had), defines original sin as native corruption, thus making all 'sin to consist of sinning,' thoroughly adopts Edwards' doctrine of the nature of virtue as benevolence, teaches a true freedom with even more clearness than Taylor did, emphasizes the moral government of God, and accordingly affirms the governmental theory of the atonement, rejects imputation, and teaches regeneration by the use of means.[27]

Foster then proceeds to document these claims by reference to passages on the Trinity (GCL I, 322-353), Sin (GCL II, 193), Benevolence (PBT 209), and the Atonement (GCL 11, 486). This, he says, referring to the passages cited, "is New England theology, but it is that theology from a new point of approach. The materials are brought from new regions, but the starting point is new, and the methods, and the principles, in very many respects."[28]

Leaving aside the strong probability that the statement as printed is not what Foster meant to say, since he surely meant 'old' when he wrote (or the printer set) "new regions," and judging the issue solely on the basis of the passages cited by Foster and by ourselves earlier in this chapter, his conclusion hardly follows. The starting point is not new but old, is in fact that idea of God as absolute sovereign proclaimed in the Westminster Catechism[29] and subsequently subscribed to by each and all of Harris's predecessors in consistent Calvinism. True, this sovereignty is not for Harris *arbitrary* in the sense contended for by Hopkins and Emmons, but it is no less *absolute* for being characterized as rational. The fundamental truth of the Calvinistic system is still, for Harris,

> the doctrine of God's absolute and universal sovereignty. It is said, "there are theologians who accept this fundamental fact of Calvin's theology and then repudiate its legitimate and inevitable consequences." But usually this repudiation is not of legitimate inferences from the true doctrine of God's sovereignty, but only of inferences from the medieval conception of the naked sovereignty of absolute and almighty will or from some other erroneous representation. We do not deny God's absolute and universal sovereignty, nor any legitimate inference from it, when we affirm that its exercise is regulated by the eternal truths and laws of reason and directed to the progressive realization in the infnite of the archetypal ideals of perfection and well-being eternal in the absolute Reason. (GCL 1. 549)

Foster's "new point of approach," then, amounts to nothing more than the unsupported claim that this consistently Calvinist conception of God has in mysterious unspecified ways undergone a metamorphosis into an energizing reason subsequently identified as the divine ingredient in the process of evolution. But as far as Harris himself is concerned, the theological standpoint remains throughout resolutely New England new divinity.

Withal, it is new divinity with a difference, for if Harris remains squarely on the ground of the New England theology, he realizes, as Hopkins, Emmons, and Park had not, that it is not enough to define being-in-general as God and his intelligent creatures. The balance of nature does require to be accounted for, and Harris would claim that he has done just that. That this accommodation of consistent Calvinism to evolution is effected by the limitation of the province of the latter to the phenomena of growth reduces, but does not negate, his insight. His vision did not extend to the awareness that a theistic interpretation of evolution entails a conception of a creator *with* rather than prior to and independent[30] of, his creation. Nor does it ever occur to him that **Acts** 17:28, which he so frequently quotes, may, indeed must if evolution is taken seriously, mean what it says. But if the panentheistic implications of evolutionary theism completely escaped him, the importance of the theory of evolution did not, and after Harris there was for consistent Calvinism no going back to pre-evolutionary modes of doctrine.

Bibliographical Essay

The trio of works for which Samuel Harris is deservedly remembered are all the products of his old age. The first of these, **The Philosophical Basis of Theism** (New York: Charles Scribner's Sons, 1883), begun when he was already in his upper sixties, is for the secular reader the most important of the three. By the time he came to write it, Harris had resolved to his own complete satisfaction the issues raised by the theory of evolution, and his brief on behalf of Christian theism against its pantheist and materialist competitors reveals a large familiarity with the relevant scientific and philosophical literature. The case for evolutionary Christianity is continued with respect to the justification of the several faces of revelation in **The Self-Revelation of God** (Edinbrugh: T. & T. Clark, 1887), and reworked to conform to the rubrics of systematic theology in **God the Creator and Lord of All**, 2 volumes (New York: Charles Scribner's Sons, 1896). A third volume of this last, subtitled 'God our Saviour', was substantially complete in first draft when death overtook the author at age eighty-five. The 697 page manuscript, never published, remains in the Harris Collection at Sterling Memorial Library, Yale University.

Previous to the issuance of these major works, Harris had published during the course of his ministerial and academic careers some thirty-odd addresses, essays, articles, reviews, pamphlets and sermons on a variety of subjects mostly religious. None of this material is palpably significant for the appreciation, or even the understanding, of his theistic interpretation of evolution, although students of his doctrine of man should consult the slim volume entitled, **The Kingdom of Christ on Earth** (Andover, Massachusetts: Warren F. Draper, 1874), being twelve lectures delivered to the students at Andover Seminary in December, 1870. A rehearsal of the contents of each of these lectures, together with a chapter of biography and an exposition of the early writings, is given in Frederick William Whittaker, **Samuel Harris, American Theologian,** Ph.D. dissertation, Yale University, 1949. A comprehensive bibliography of all published and unpublished materials by and about, or remotely pertinent to, Harris is appended.

There is little of interest in the secondary literature to anyone other than the specialist in the period or the man. However, readers of PBT will profit from a reading of Newman Smyth's, 'Professor Harris's Contribution to Theism' **Andover Review** I (February, 1884), 132-148. Smyth Lauds Harris for his emphasis on the theistic function of intuition and the religious role of feeling (both were admirers of Schleiermacher) and sees him as a precursor of the new 'dynamic theism', which, incidentally, just happens to be Smyth's term for his own theology. As an antidote, I recommend consultation of Levi Leonard Paine, **A Critical History of the Evolution of Trinitarianism** (Boston: Houghton, Mifflin, 1900), 236-246. This is a brief, but trenchant and destructive criticism of the metaphysical and theological assumptions underlying Harris's version of theism. Offsetting Paine's judgement is the rather more favorable assessment of Frank Hugh Foster, **A Genetic History of the New England Theology** (Chicago: University of Chicago Press, 1907), 423-429. Foster sees Harris as the Sir William Hamilton of the New England theology: "as Sir William was more than a member of his school, being in fact that thinker who formed the transition (of the Scottish philosophy) to later and different modes of thought, so Harris formed the transition from the New England to later theologies...." (428). For the rest, there is a review of **God, Creator, and Lord of All** by N.S. Burton, **The American Journal of Theology**, II, 1 (January, 1898), 191-196; and a eulogy by George Harris, 'Samuel Harris, Theologian, Author, Preacher, Teacher,' **The Congregationalist** (13 July 1899), 46.

[1]Samuel Harris, **The Philosophical Basic of Theism,** revised edition (Edinburgh T. & T. Clark, 1883), 318. Hereafter cited in the text in parentheses as PBT with page reference.

[2]Frank Hugh Foster, **Genetic History,** 425-426

[3]Harris was born in June 14th, 1814 at East Machias, Maine, and spent his boyhood in that town. In 1829 he entered Bowdoin College, and following his graduation in 1833 taught school for a year. The following three years were spent studying for the ministry at Andover Theological Seminary. He was married in 1839 to the companion of his childhood, Deborah Robbins Dickerson. In 1876 his wife died, and a year later he married Mrs. Mary Sherman Fitch, the widow of a clerical colleague.

[4]Samuel Harris, **The Kingdom of Christ on Earth,** twelve lectures (Andover: Warren F. Draper, 1874).

[5]A third volume, subtitled **God our Saviour,** remained incomplete and unedited at his death.

[6]**God, the Creator and Lord of All,** 2 vols. (New York: Charles Scribner's Sons, 1896), I. 10. Hereafter cited in the text as GCL with volume and page reference.

[7]George Santayana, **Scepticism and Animal Faith** (New York: Dover, 1955), 118. Harris would, of course, emphatically disagree with Santayana's relegation of the data and doctrines of religion to a realm of essence. For him these are related rather to what Santayana calls the realm of matter, although just how they are related Harris does not tell us. See PBT 413, also PBT 77, 412, and 502.

[8]In this opinion Harris again approximates and anticipates the position of Santayana who tells us that "Hume and Kant never touched bottom, and nothing could be more gratuitous than their residual dogmas." Ibid., 293.

[9]"I commonly use the word reason," writes Harris, "not to denote merely the power of reasoning by which the finite mind by virtue of its rationality passes by inference from the known to the knowledge of what had been unknown, but to denote the mind or spirit itself considered as capable of the rational intuition of primitive and universal principles. This implies in a finite mind the power, as its finiteness involved the necessity, of reasoning. In God, the absolute Reason, all knowledge is archetypal and eternal." (SRG 7n) See also PBT 47 and GCL I. 129.

[10]'Figuratively' rather than literally because, as the sequel will show, Harris is no panentheist for all that he occasionally pens a passage lending itself to a panentheistic interpretation.

[11]False rationalism, as defined by Harris, is that view which either "fails to give due prominence to revelation as an essential factor in all human knowledge, or even overlooks it altogether". (GCL I. 383) Alternatively, it is the failure to "adequately estimate man's dependence on God for light and for guidance, his capacity to receive the illuminating and quickening influence of the divine spirit, and God's readiness to impart these influences to all who willingly receive and follow them". (GCL I. 385.)

[12]**De Trinitate,** Lib. vii, cap. iv, 9, 7. Cited by Harris (GCL I. 331).

[13]**Institutes,** Book I, Chapter XIII, 17, 5. See Harris (GCL I. 331).

[14]Levi Leonard Paine, **A Critical History of the Evolution of Trinitarianism and its outcome in the New Christology** (Boston: Houghton, Mifflin, 1900), 245.

[15]Calvin, **Institutes,** Book I, Chapter XIII, 5.

[16]"It may be added," Harris writes, "that man is, so far as this earth concerned, the highest end to which nature has attained and toward which it has always been striving. He (man) seems to be endowed with all the forces of nature as well as with the powers of spirit. They are all

taken up and represented in him....All this plainly indicates that man is at the head of all creatures on the earth, and to him all nature is and always has been tributary." (PBT 386)

[17]Paine, **Critical History,** 224-245.

[18]As Harris defines it, 'anhypostasia' is the denial of Christ's human personality antecedent to, and apart from, the incarnation of the logos; 'enhypostasia' is the assertion of his human personality in the incarnation of the logos.

[19]For the relevant supporting quotations from these authorities and from the Athanasian creed, see GCL I 402n-403n.

[20]**Institutes,** Book I, Chapter XIII 29. As quoted by Harris, GCL I. 404-405.

[21]"Hence," says Harris, "any attempt of the human imagination to picture the creative act of God must always be inadequate. The creative action of God may be known as a fact, but it can never be fully comprehended by the finite mind." (GCL I 464-465)

[22]Here, of course, Harris parts company with Spencer, who will not presume to equate Power with Person.

[23]"Pantheism is the theory that the absolute is the one and only substance, never as transitive cause creating or causing any effect, but within itself evolving and evolved, and that without consciousness or personality." (SRG 182) Harris had never heard of panentheism, but it is most probable that he would have rejected it also, and for the same reasons.

[24]Citing **Isaiah** 43:7, **Psalms** 19:1, **Philippians** 1:11 and 2:11.

[25]This, according to Harris, "distinguishes the true doctrine from both the supralapsarian and the sublapsarian or infralapsarian forms of it....In distinction from both of these, the truth is that God purposes primarily the system of things in which he is progressively realizing his archetypal world idea, and the character and destiny of individuals as they actually come to pass in the system." (GCL II, 5566)

[26]Frank Hugh Foster, **Genetic History,** 428.

[27]Ibid., 423.

[28]Foster, **Genetic History,** 427.

[29]The first passage cited by Foster in support of his contention defines God as numerically one in his substance or essential being and adds: "This is the common doctrine of our evangelical Protestant creeds; as the Westminster Catechism declares that the Father, Son, and Holy Spirit "are one true, eternal God, the same in substance, equal in power and glory." The same has been the teaching of the great Protestant theologians." (GCL I. 322)

[30]"According to theism," says Harris, "the Absolute is not that which exists out of all relations and therefore cannot be in relation to anything; but it is that which exists out of all necessary relations. It is capable of existing out of relation to anything; it contains all potencies it itself; if other beings come into existence it is only as dependent on it. It is independent of them." (PBT 513) It simply never occurs to Harris that there is, or even might be, any problem involved in rendering such a doctrine of relations consistent with evolutionary theism. Despite his scorn for 'the medieval conception of the naked sovereignty" his conception is one with that of high scholasticism.

EPILOGUE

Calvinism has a message, if it could be heard in our time, not only for the distressed but also for the prosperous. It reminds every man who will hearken to reflect that always in good or evil circumstances, he has to do with God!

In concluding his synoptic study of the history and character of Calvinism, John McNeill asks: "Is it still possible to speak of Calvinism in the present tense?" And answers—yes, with qualifications. We must distinguish, he thinks, between the body and the spirit, between institutional Calvinism and Calvinism as a faithful response to the Scripture revelation of a sovereign and redeeming God. Narrowing the question to the case of Consistent Calvinism, I too would say—yes, but enter a caveat that McNeill would reject. It is possible to speak of Consistent Calvinism in the present tense, but only if one is willing to accept the entire system of doctrine derivative from the assumption of God as sovereign. McNeill sees this as neither necessary nor desirable. Any contemporary recovery of the spirit of Calvinism is, he feels, "bound to be selective with respect to specific doctrines and practices."[2] With practices— perhaps. We need not stand upon a point of liturgy. But *selective* doctrine?

If Consistent Calvinism establishes anything at all, it is that the conception of God as absolute sovereign and redeemer entails commitment to decrees, election, reprobation, atonement, and regeneration, as these are authorized in Scripture revelation. Leeway in interpretation is permitted; choice among doctrines is not. The fair price of selectivity among doctrines is the abandonment of the Calvinist notion of God in favour of one consistent with the particular doctrines selected. McNeill would abandon the largest part of that which the heirs of Edwards have deemed essential corollaries of their conception of God. The true spirit of Calvinism today, he believes, can no longer "be reasonably held to be tied to the doctrine of reprobation, or to any specific treatment of the divine decrees, or to any assumption of the inerrancy of Scripture."[3] What, then, is left? Spirit as "faithful response." "Piety," but not a piety identified with "peculiar words and rules of worship." "God-consciousness with an urgent sense of mission" and an acceptance of guilt

414

as real but "submerged under grace." McNeill concedes that the Calvinist imbued with this "true spirit" may be "a very simple-minded theologian," but, he adds, "he is conscious that God commands his will and deed as well as his thought and prayer."⁴

The critic of this contemporary Calvinism may devoutly wish that it were so, even as he wonders what is left of Calvinism to proclaim to the modern world? The great strength of traditional Calvinism is its ruggedly honest refusal to ameliorate or diffuse the Scripture-conception of God to suit the tastes of those who prefer a less demanding deity. There is absolutely nothing wrong with seeking to make protestantism palatable. The error arises when the seeker deludes his- or her-self into thinking that such an amelioration is compatible with retention of the classical notion of God. "From this secret delusion (of their intellectual superiority) and prejudice they have almost all their advantages: 'tis the strength of their bulwarks and the edge of their weapons. And this is the main ground of all the right they have to treat their neighbors in so assuming a manner, and to insult others, perhaps as wise and good as themselves, as weak bigots, men that dwell in the dark caves of superstition, perversely set, obstinately shutting their eyes against the noonday light." So says Edwards, and so say all consistent Calvinists. The palliators, adds Emmons, cannot have it both ways. Those who now understandingly embrace genuine Calvinism....cannot consistently amalgamate with Arminians, Methodists, Antinomians, Sabellians, Arians, Socinians, or any species of Universalists and Enthusiasts." Either God is sovereign, with all that sovereignty implies, or He is not. If He is not *absolutely* sovereign, then it is incumbent upon those who maintain a modified conception to reformulate received doctrine in a manner consistent with the reformed notion of God. From the perspective of consistent Calvinism, this challenge remains, at the close of the twentieth century, unacceptable and unmet.

¹John T. McNeill, **The History and Character of Calvinism** (New York: Oxford University Press, 1954), 439.
²Ibid., 433.
³Ibid.
⁴ibid., 436.

APPENDIX I

The Westminister Confession of Faith
A.D. 1647

The Humble Advice of the Assembly of Divines, Now by Authority of Parliament Sitting at Westminister, Concerning a Confession of Faith, to give it its full title, was the doctrinal standard of New England Congregationalism to the end of the Eighteenth Century, and remains today the doctrinal standard of most Presbyterian Churches. What follows are those passages from the Confession most frequently referred to by Old Calvinists and New Divinity men alike in support of their respective positions. The text is that of the London edition reprinted at Edinburgh by Evan Tyler, Printer to the Kings most Excellent Majestie, 1647.

Chapter I: Of the Holy Scriptures

VI. "The whole counsel of God, concerning all things necessary for his own glory, man's salvation, faith, and life, is either expressly set down in Scripture, or by good and necessary consequence may be deduced from Scripture: unto which nothing at any time is to be added, whether by new revelations of the Spirit, or traditions of men. Nevertheless we acknowledge the inward illumination of the Spirit of God to be necessary for the saving understanding of such things as are revealed in the Word...."

IX. "The infallible rule of interpretation of Scripture is the Scripture itself: and therefore, when there is a question about the true and full sense of any Scripture (which is not manifold, but one) it must be searched and known by other places that speak more clearly."

Chapter II: Of God, and of the Holy Trinity

1. "There is but one only living and true God, who is infinite in being and perfection, a most pure spirit, invisible, without body, parts, or passions, im-

mutable, immense, eternal, incomprehensible, almighty, most wise, most holy most free, most absolute, working all things according to the counsel of his own immutable and most righteous will, for his own glory; most loving, gracious, merciful, long-suffering, abundant in goodness and truth, forgiving iniquity, transgression, and sin; the rewarder of them that diligently seek him; and withal most just and terrible in his judgements."

II. "God hath all life, glory, goodness, blessedness, in and of himself; and is alone in and unto himself all-sufficient, not standing in need of any creatures which he hath made, nor deriving any glory from them, but only manifesting his own glory in, by, unto, and upon them: he is the alone foundation of all being, of whom, through whom, and to whom are all things; and hath most sovereign dominion over them, to do by them, for them, or upon them whatsoever himself pleaseth. In his sight all things are open and manifest; his knowledge is infinite, infallible, and independent upon the creature; so as nothing is to him contingent or uncertain...."

III. "In the unity of the Godhead there be three persons, of one substance, power, and eternity: God the Father, God the Son, and God the Holy Ghost. The Father is of none, neither begotten nor proceeding; the Son is eternally begotten of the Father; the Holy Ghost eternally proceeding from the Father and the Son."

Chapter III: Of God's Eternal Decree

I. "God from all eternity did, by the most wise and holy counsel of his own will, freely and unchangeably ordain whatsoever comes to pass; yet so as thereby neither is God the author of sin, nor is violence offered to the will of the creatures, nor is the liberty or contingency of second causes taken away, but rather established."

II. "Although God knows whatsoever may or can come to pass upon all supposed conditions, yet hath he not decreed anything because he foresaw it as future, or as that which would come to pass upon such conditions."

III. "By the decree of God, for the manifestation of his glory, some men and angels are predestinated unto everlasting life, and others foreordained to everlasting death."

IV. "These angels and men, thus predestinated and foreordained, are particularly and unchangeably designed; and their number is so certain and definite that it can not be either increased or diminished."

V. "Those of mankind that are predestinated unto life, God, before the foundation of the world was laid, according to his eternal and immutable purpose, and the secret counsel and good pleasure of his will, hath chosen in Christ, unto everlasting glory, out of his mere free grace and love, without any foresight of faith or good works, or perseverance in either of them, or any other thing in the creature, as conditions, or causes moving him thereunto; and all to the praise of his glorious grace."

VI. "As God hath appointed the elect unto glory, so hath he, by the eternal and most free purpose of his will, foreordained all the means thereunto. Wherefore they who are elected, being fallen in Adam, are redeemed by Christ.

VII. "The rest of mankind God was pleased, according to the unsearchable counsel of his own will, whereby he extendeth or withholdeth mercy as he pleaseth, for the glory, of his sovereign power over his creatures, to pass by, and to ordain them to dishonor and wrath for their sin, to the praise of his glorious justice."

Chapter V: Of Providence

II. "Although in relation to the foreknowledge and decree of God, the first cause, all things come to pass immutably and infallibly, yet by the same providence he ordereth them to fall out, according to the nature of second causes, either necessarily, freely, or contingently."

III. "God in his ordinary providence, maketh use of means, yet is free to

418

work without, above, and against them, at his pleasure."

VI. "As for those wicked and ungodly men whom God, as a righteous judge, for former sins, doth blind and harden, from them he not only withholdeth his grace, whereby they might have been enlightened in their understandings and wrought upon in their hearts, but sometimes also withdraweth the gifts which they had, and exposeth them to such objects as their corruption makes occasion of sin; and withal, gives them over to their own lusts, the temptations of the world, and the power of Satan; whereby it comes to pass that they harden themselves, even under those means which God useth for the softening of others."

Chapter VI: Of the Fall of Man, of Sin, and of the Punishment thereof

I. "Our first parents, being seduced by the subtilty and temptation of Satan, sinned in eating the forbidden fruit. This their sin God was pleased, according to his wise and holy counsel, to permit, having purposed to order it to his own glory."

II. "By this sin they fell from their original righteousness and communion with God, and so became dead in sin, and wholly defiled in all the faculties and parts of soul and body."

III. "They being the root of all mankind, the guilt of this sin was imputed, and the same death in sin and corrupted nature conveyed to all their posterity descending from them by ordinary generation."

IV. "From this original corruption, whereby we are utterly indisposed, disabled, and made opposite to all good, and wholly inclined to all evil, do proceed all actual transgressions."

V. "This corruption of nature, during this life, doth remain in those that are regenerated; and although it be through Christ pardoned and mortified, yet both itself and all the motions thereof are truly and properly sin."

VI. "Every sin, both original and actual, being a transgression of the righteous law of God, and contrary thereunto, doth, in its own nature, bring guilt upon the sinner, whereby he is bound over to the wrath of God and curse of the law, and so made subject to death, with all miseries spiritual, temporal, and eternal."

Chapter VIII: Of Christ the Mediator

I. "It pleased God, in his eternal purpose, to choose and ordain the Lord Jesus, his only-begotten Son, to be the Mediator between God and man, the Prophet, Priest, and King; the Head and Saviour of his Church, the Heir of all things, and Judge of the world; unto whom he did, from all eternity, give a people to be his seed, and to be by him in time redeemed, called, justified, sanctified, and glorified."

VI. "Although the work of redemption was not actually wrought by Christ till after his incarnation, yet the virtue, efficacy, and benefits thereof were communicated unto the elect, in all ages successively from the beginning of the world...."

Chapter IX: Of Free-will

I. "God hath endued the will of man with the natural liberty, that is neither forced nor by any absolute necessity of nature determined to good or evil."

II. "Man, in his state of innocency, had freedom and power to will and to do that which is good and well-pleasing to God, but yet mutably, so that he might fall from it."

III. "Man, by his fall into a state of sin, hath wholly lost all ability of will to any spiritual good accompanying salvation; so as a natural man, being altogether averse from that good, and dead in sin, is not able, by his own strength, to convert himself, or to prepare himself thereunto."

420

Chapter X: Of Effectual Calling

III. "Elect infants, dying in infancy, are regenerated and saved by Christ through the Spirit, who worketh when, and where, and how he pleaseth. So also are all other elect persons, who are incapable of being outwardly called by the ministry of the Word."

IV. "Others, not elected, although they may be called by the ministry of the Word, and may have some common operations of the Spirit, yet they never truly come unto Christ, and therefore cannot be saved: much less can men, not professing the Christian religion, be saved in any other way whatsoever, be they never so diligent to frame their lives according to the light of nature and the law of that religion they do profess; and to assert and maintain that they may is very pernicious and to be detested."

Chapter XI: Of Justification

IV. "God did, from all eternity, decree to justify all the elect, and Christ did, in the fullness of time, die for their sins, and rise again for their justification: nevertheless, they are not justified until the Holy Spirit doth, in due time, actually apply Christ unto them."

Chapter XV: of Repentance unto Life

IV. "As there is no sin so small but it deserves damnation, so there is no sin so great that it can bring damnation upon those who truly repent."

Chapter XVI: Of Good Works

VII. "Works done by unregenerate men, altogether for the matter of them they may be things which God commands, and of good use both to themselves and others; yet because they proceed not from a heart purified by faith, nor are done in a right manner, according to the Word, nor to a right end, the glory of God: they are therefore sinful, and can not please God, nor make a man meet to receive grace from God. And yet their neglect of them is more sinful and displeasing unto God."

Chapter XXV: Of the Church

1. "the catholic or universal church, which is invisible, consists of the whole number of the elect, that have been, are, or shall be gathered into one, under Christ the head thereof; and is the spouse, the body, the fullness of him that filleth all in all."

II. "The visible Church, which is also catholic or universal under the gospel (not confined to one nation as before under the law) consists of all those, throughout the world, that profess the true religion, and of their children; and is the kingdom of the Lord Jesus Christ, the house and family of God, out of which there is no ordinary possibility of salvation."

Chapter XXXIII: Of the Last Judgement

II. "The end of God's appointing this day, is for the manifestation of the glory of his mercy in the eternal salvation of the elect; and of his justice in the damnation of the reprobate, who are wicked and disobedient. For then shall the righteous go under everlasting life, and receive that fullness of joy, and refreshing which shall come from the presence of the Lord; but the wicked, who know not God, and obey not the gospel of Jesus Christ, shall be cast into eternal torments, and be punished with everlasting destruction from the presence of the Lord, and from the glory of his power."

APPENDIX II

The Three Covenants*

I **The Covenant of Redemption**

parties: God the Father and God the Holy Ghost (parties of the first part), and God the Son (party of the second part).

made: in heaven before all the worlds.

conditions: 1. God will have some of fallen men to be monuments of His Grace in their Salvation.

2. The Son of God is looked upon as the next person to procure this Salvation for man.

3. That the Son of God may do this to good effect several things are requisite, viz.

   i. that he (the Son) become man's surety, and undertake for him to do all that is requisite to purchase his Salvation.

   ii. he must engage to take our nature upon himself.

   iii. he must engage in this nature to subject himself to God's holy law.

*As expounded by Samuel Willard in **A Compleat Body of Divinity,** Sermons XLIX, LXXVII, and LXXXIV.

iv. he must engage to fullfill the whole righteousness of the law in our stead.

v. this suretyship must be accepted of God.

vi. he must have an assurance given him that his obedience shall obtain the discharge of those for whom he under-takes from the law condemnation that is upon them.

    a. that they shall be atoned to him

    b. that hereupon they have all spiritual and eternal blessings bestowed on them for his sake.

    c. that all these things may be secured, they do mutually engage themselves one to another by firm promise.

articles:

1. God the Father offers to the Son that if he will do this work, he shall be sure of all the above.

2. God the Son accepts the offer, and upon the motion complies with it.

3. God the Holy Ghost undertakes and promises that he will see to the application of all the Grace appointed by the Father, and purchased by the Son to those for whom it is designed, and so to bring them to Salvation.

424

4. In and by this Compact the Salvation of God's Elect is made sure.

II. The Covenant of Works

parties: God the Father (party of the first part), and Adam (party of the second part).

made: in the first day of God's creation of man.

conditions: as recorded in **Genesis 2**. As the conditions were two, viz. Obedience and Disobedience, so were the consequences, viz. Life and Death. The condition of Life was Obedience. In this rule of Obedience man was required

1. to acknowledge God's supremacy.

2. not to have given ear to any temptation of Satan.

3. to have made an absolute choice of God for his portion.

4. from this principle he was practically to have attended to the faithful performance of the whole law or command.

articles: the reward promised to this Obedience was Life.

i. an immutable state of blessedness.

              ii. a full fruition of God to be his
                  (man's) portion.

     2. the condition of death was Disobedience.

              i. the punishment threatened for Disobe-
                 dience was Death.

     3. now these terms were fixed, ratified,
        unalterable; and that on God's part as well
        as man's. For the seal of which man was to
        faithfully observe the sacrament, which
        sacrament was the Tree of Life and the Tree
        of Knowledge, wherefore man was forbidden
        to eat. But he did eat, and by his apostasy
        his posterity are one and all under sentence
        of death.

III   The Covenant of Grace

parties: God the Father (party of the first part), and every
man (party of the second part) through the
mediatorship of Jesus Christ.

made: eternally and contemporaneously. "For this the
Son of God made that long journey from heaven
to earth, and back again that he might transact this
business. Deals with his Father immediately, and
with man by this means."

preamble: he proposeth articles of agreement, and those as
are most suitable for a good accommodation bet-
ween them. The design of the treaty is to bring
them (men) into a covenant of peace and love.

But no covenant is made without articles or terms on which it is to stand: and these must be such as will give content to both parties. For Christ is bound both for God's honor and man's happiness; such then he makes offer of in the transaction.

articles:

1. That God's righteous dealings with man in proceeding to condemn him for the breach of the first convenant (Works) be acknowledged and justified.

2. That the sinner shall freely and humbly confess all the indignities that he hath offered to God's glory.

3. That due recompense and full satisfaction shall be made to God's justice, for all the injury and wrong done to his name by the sinner.

4. That satisfaction being made, God shall forgive and forget all the offences the sinner hath given him.

5. That God shall of an enemy become a father to the sinner, and put on the bowels of a father to him.

6. That his (God's) people shall serve him as obedient children all their days.

7. That for the confirmation of all these Articles, there shall be a new and everlasting

Covenant plighted between them. "These things shall be signed, sealed, delivered, entered, and enrolled, for a perpetual Covenant never to be broken."

INDEX OF NAMES

INDEX OF SUBJECTS

436

Fall 20
False rationalism 410
False religion 105
Free will 5, 67-68, 403
Freedom 191, 402

God 14, 53, 54, 95-99, 157, 179,
219, 220, 223
  absolute sovereignty of 66,
  67, 118, 190, 243
  as all in all 53-97
  as the Abstract 14, 16, 38, 41
  as the author of sin 70, 101
  as Being-in-general 16, 50, 149
  as creator 15-17, 55, 77, 97, 186
  as efficient cause 157
  as Pure Act (*actus purus*) 75-76
  attributes of 14, 16, 96, 157
  Calvinist conception of 37, 108,
  193
  distributive justice of 274, 287
  glorification of 13, 17, 48, 61,
  80, 97, 108, 120-122, 226, 241
  glory of 154, 162, 167, 173, 224,
  404
  his decrees 1, 15, 21, 97, 98-99,
  103, 175, 182-185, 199
  his foreknowledge 182-185, 199,
  221
  incomprehensibility of 187
  man as enemy to 119, 155
  moral government of 102, 118,
  224, 248, 272, 274
  moral image of 98, 190
  perfection of 96-97
  proofs of 221-295
  space of 50-52, 61
  will of 154, 185
Grace 105-106

common 191, 199
  efficacious 71, 80, 89
  regenerating 144
  special 191, 199
  true 49-50, 106

Harvard College 20-32
Higher criticism 38
Hopkinsianism 3, 139, 158, 162,
167, 173, 174, 178
Holy Spirit 1, 104-105, 159, 189,
244
Hodge-Park controversy 300-315
Human soul 190, 239

Idealism 55, 158
Impenitence 159
Imputation 175
Indian Mayavada 64
Infant damnation 109-110, 114,
222, 252
Infidelity 203, 209, 211
Intuition 376-378

Justification 124-136, 174

Knowledge
  a priori 338-339, 375, 376
  theory of 338-339, 375, 376

Means 150, 247, 281
Meliorism 403
Mere speculation 95
Moral evil 174
Moral inability 68, 100, 104
Moral necessity 68, 70

Natural inability 68, 100-101
Natural necessity 68, 70

Gladys J. Willis

THE PENALTY OF EVE
John Milton and Divorce

American University Studies, Series IV (English Language and Literature), Vol. 6
ISBN 0-8204-0094-7   164 pages   hardcover   US $ 21.55
Recommended prices - alterations reserved

This book establishes the hypothesis that there are profound links between John Milton's «rule of charity» as described in *The Doctrine and Discipline of Divorce* and St. Augustine's exegesis in *De Doctrina Christiana* – as it pertains to the Christian man and the primary factor that should determine his earthly actions. The author stresses the point that Milton characterizes the Christian-wife-prototype as a «thing to be used» by her husband, which is founded in the Augustinian exegesis, *Paradise Lost* and *Samson Agonistes* are discussed as exempla of Milton's theory.

Contents: Commentary on Hermeneutics Theories – St. Augustine's Definition of *Caritas* – The Rule of Charity in Milton's Divorce Tracts – Marriage, Divorce, and Reconciliation in *Paradise Lost* – Divorce in *Samson Agonistes*.

 PETER LANG PUBLISHING, INC.
62 West 45th Street
USA – New York, NY 10036